China from the 1911 Revolution
to Liberation

The Pantheon Asia Library

New Approaches to the New Asia

China from the 1911 Revolution to Liberation

*by Jean Chesneaux, Françoise Le Barbier,
and Marie-Claire Bergère*

*Translated from the French
by Paul Auster and Lydia Davis*

Chapters 1 to 3 translated by Anne Destenay

PANTHEON BOOKS, NEW YORK

China from the 1911 Revolution to Liberation combines *De la guerre franco-chinoise à la fondation du parti communiste chinois* (chapters 4–6) and *La Chine: La Marche de la révolution, 1921–1949*.

Library of Congress Cataloging in Publication Data

Main entry under title:

China from the 1911 Revolution to Liberation.

   (The Pantheon Asia Library)
   Translation of chapters 4–6 of De la guerre franco-chinoise à la fondation du parti communiste chinois, 1885–1921, by J. Chesneaux, M. Bastid, and M.-C. Bergère, v. 2 of Histoire de la Chine; and La Chine: La Marche de la révolution, 1921–1949, by Chesneaux and F. Le Barbier, v. 3 of the Histoire.
   Includes bibliographies and index.
   1.   China—History—Republic, 1912–1949.
I.   Chesneaux, Jean.   II.   Le Barbier, Françoise.
III.   Bergère, Marie-Claire.
DS774.H47213   1977   951.04   77-76494
ISBN 0-394-41193-5
ISBN 0-394-73332-0 pbk.

Manufactured in the United States of America

98765432

Since this copyright page cannot accommodate all the acknowledgments, they are to be found on the facing page.

Grateful acknowledgment is made to the following for permission to reprint the following previously published material:

Cambridge University Press: A letter from W. R. Giles to G. E. Morrison from *The Correspondence of G. E. Morrison*, edited by Lo Hui-min (Cambridge, Cambridge University Press, 1978), vol. 2, letter no. 935.

Da Capo Press: Selections from *Report from Red China*, by Harrison Forman. Reprinted by permission.

Harvard University Press: Excerpts from *China's Response to the West: A Documentary Survey 1839–1923*, translated by John K. Fairbank and Teng Ssu-yu, and excerpts from *The May Fourth Movement*, by Chow Tse-tsung. Copyright © 1954/1960 by the President and Fellows of Harvard College. Reprinted by permission of the publisher.

Monthly Review Press: Selections from *China Shakes the World*, by Jack Belden. Copyright 1949 by Jack Belden. Introduction copyright © 1970 by Monthly Review Press. Selections from *Fanshen: A Documentary of Revolution in a Chinese Village*, by William Hinton. Copyright © 1966 by William Hinton. Selections from *The Great Road: The Life of Chu Teh*, by Agnes Smedley. Copyright © 1956 by the Estate of Agnes Smedley. All reprinted by the permission of Monthly Review Press.

G. P. Putnam's Sons and Jonathan Cape, Ltd.: Selections from *Birdless Summer* and *A Mortal Flower*, by Han Su-yin. Copyright © 1968/1966 by Han Su-yin. Reprinted by permission.

Robert P. Mills, Ltd.: Selections from *Red Star over China*, by Edgar Snow. Reprinted by permission.

William Morrow & Company, Inc.: Brief excerpt from *The Stilwell Papers*, by Joseph W. Stilwell. Copyright 1948 by Winifred A. Stilwell. Brief excerpt from *Thunder Out of China*, by Theodore H. White and Annalee Jacoby. Copyright 1946 by William Sloan Associates, Inc. Copyright renewed 1974 by Theodore H. White and Annalee Jacoby. Both reprinted by permission of William Morrow & Company, Inc.

Contents

Maps

China from the 1911 Revolution
to Liberation

China from the 1911 Revolution to Liberation is the second volume in this major new history of modern China. Volume 1, *China from the Opium Wars to the 1911 Revolution*, was published in 1976. The final volume, *The People's Republic of China, 1949–1976*, will be published in 1978. Written under the direction of Professor Jean Chesneaux of the Sorbonne, they are translated from the French edition.

The first three volumes of the French edition have been combined into the first two volumes of the Pantheon edition. The publishers have left the conclusion of the second French volume and the introduction to the third volume together in *China from the 1911 Revolution to Liberation*, despite some of their overlap, because of the fine overview they provide. The final volume will correspond to the fourth volume of the French edition.

Chapter One

From Republic to Dictatorship: *1912–1916*

Although hailed as a victory for the revolution, the elimination of the dynasty was not in itself a revolutionary event. It fit well the traditional Chinese cyclic conception of history: the sovereign's loss of the Mandate of Heaven was recognized, and, after a period of troubles, the way was prepared for a strong man who would found a new imperial line. Yuan Shi-kai's grasp for power and attempt to make himself emperor after the 1911 rebellion fell within this traditional pattern. However, the failure of his attempted restoration suggested that more than a break in the continuity of a dynasty had occurred. The revolutionary aspect of the events between 1911 and 1913 should be seen in the light of the impossibility of a restoration.

The Beginnings of the Republic:
January 1912–March 1913

At the beginning of 1912, China was in a state of utter confusion. The political framework of the nation had been destroyed by the revolution. The provinces which had seceded and proclaimed their autonomy tried to organize a government to meet their own needs. The old administrative structure was still intact in the North; new

3

governors, given the title of *dudu*,[1] were appointed in the Yangzi region and the southern provinces. The provincial structure, however, was beginning to disappear. Canton no longer controlled east Guangdong, for example. Sichuan had two governors, one in Chengdu and the other in Chongqing. Towns and districts declared themselves "independent states" and "autonomous communes."

The decline of political institutions was accompanied by generalized opposition to the established order. This manifested itself in a spontaneous outbreak of banditry. Fleeing peasants and unpaid soldiers operated in groups for their own benefit. This insecure situation was particularly marked in Guangdong, which a Western journalist nicknamed "The Pirate Republic." In spite of their traditions, the secret societies did not manage to arrive at a much more organized opposition than this. The regions over which they gained control, like northeast Sichuan, split into numerous fiefdoms, each maintained only by increased taxation and extortion. Even the earliest working class demonstrations retained the mark of traditional behavior, kept alive among the Shanghai workers, in particular, by the Green Band (Qingbang) or the Red Band (Hongbang). Strikes organized at the Chengdu and Hanyang arsenals, the Anhui coal mines, and the Shanghai silk-spinning mills did give promise of new forms of protest. At the time of the 1911 revolution, however, they were neither numerous nor widespread enough to threaten the social order.

The real danger confronting the gentry was not the rise of popular forces, but the rise of chaos and anarchy. The chief problem for them was the maintenance of order (*baoan*). Although particularly serious after the events of 1911, it was a problem which had always existed for Chinese administrators. However, the past experience of the local gentry enabled them to find a partial solution to it without any help from the government. Provincial assemblies, chambers of commerce, and professional guilds assured the payment of wages and salaries, guaranteed issues of bank notes, and paid for the departure of troublemakers, or else raised militia to drive them away. At a local level, some principles of administrative stability and continuity, as well as the foundations of the traditional social order, were maintained.

[1] As in Volume 1, *China from the Opium Wars to the 1911 Revolution,* the transcription of Chinese used in this book is Pinyin, adopted in the People's Republic of China in 1958 and gradually coming into favor among Western scholars. The only exceptions made here are a few proper names such as Peking, Nanking, Sun Yat-sen, and Mao Tsetung.

Economic difficulties, arising in the autumn of 1912, due to the interruption of traffic between the interior and the treaty ports, and to the lack of liquid assets resulting from the vast payments made by merchant communities (who paid the price both for revolution and for social order), were rapidly brought under control. The gentry's management of local affairs managed to effect a social and economic cohesion, in stark contrast with the crumbling of political authority. This process had its limits. However rich the gentry were, they could not (and would not) long provide for public needs. Moreover, the lack of coordination among local authorities hindered the maintenance of order. (Bandit gangs were paid to leave one place, only to continue their misdeeds elsewhere.) Such failures made the gentry call for the restoration of a central government to facilitate the maintenance of economic and social structures.

In the end, who was responsible for the reunification of China, and who gained from it? Was it Yuan Shi-kai, supported by the Beiyang army and strengthened by the legitimacy conferred on him by the throne, which delegated power to him via the edict of February 3, 1912? Or was it Sun Yat-sen, who, with the support of the Shanghai bourgeoisie, tried to adapt a Western political ideology and Western practices to China?

The Nanking government

The government of the Chinese Republic, established January 1, 1912, with Sun Yat-sen as president, was, theoretically at least, a national government. Its authority was ratified by the vote of the provincial delegates, who, on January 28, constituted a provisional parliament. Although not all its members belonged to Sun's revolutionary party, the new government did emerge from the United League. Huang Xing remained at the side of Sun Yat-sen and, as war minister and chief of staff, he was still the brilliant second-in-command whom he had been when the party was organized. Behind the scenes, the financial and political help of the Shanghai bourgeoisie facilitated the creation of the republican government. It is reckoned that during the revolution the business community contributed over 7 million Chinese dollars[2] to the United League. Merchants and compradors exerted pressure on foreign chambers of commerce to get them to oppose the Manchu government and

2 The Chinese dollar was a silver dollar worth roughly three quarters of the old tael.

threatened to boycott any power which granted loans to the imperial party. In return for its help, the bourgeoisie expected Sun to enact a program in line with its aspirations. The program formulated in the January 5 Manifesto reproduced the gist of the proposals of the United League: the departure of the Manchu dynasty, the reunification of China under a republican regime, and economic expansion.[3] No further allusion was made to the plan for agrarian reform put forward a few years earlier by Sun Yat-sen. It had never won the approval of the bourgeoisie.

During the few weeks of its short existence, the government worked to obtain the formal abdication of the dynasty (edict of February 12, 1912), to stimulate industrial development by creating new institutions like the Provincial Department of Industry, and to encourage overseas capital to finance the opening of a Chinese Industrial Bank, at the head of which would be Sun himself. But the efforts of the republican government came up against the obstacle of reunification. The government was national in title alone. It actually had full authority only over the lower Yangzi provinces. In the North, it ran into the power of Yuan. In the central provinces, Hunan and Hubei, the influence of Li Yuan-hong prevailed and he inclined toward an alliance with Yuan. Elsewhere, provincial particularism and the collapse of administrative structures paralyzed all initiatives coming from a central power.

The failure of the central government to reunify the country cannot be explained only by the inherent difficulties of the task. The weakness of Sun Yat-sen's authority was an additional reason. The Shanghai bourgeoisie was dynamic, but it formed an extremely limited social base for the republican government. The powerlessness of the Nanking regime reflected the marginal character of a modern bourgeoisie which was both small in numbers and unevenly distributed geographically. In addition, Sun could not look for support to the efficacity of a party apparatus. The United League had always been loosely organized. Under the pressure of revolutionary events, factions and dissent were rife. On February 21, Wang Jing-wei called a meeting in Tientsin in a vain attempt to reunite the party. The United League showed a growing tendency to include only those nearest to the president.

On January 1, 1912, the day he assumed office, Sun had declared that he was ready to surrender his post to Yuan Shi-kai, if Yuan

---

[3] See document 1 at the end of the chapter.

came over to the republic. Whether he thought that the revolution had achieved its goal with the abdication of the dynasty or he was more drawn to the technical problems of economic development, Sun made little effort to impose his government on the rest of the country. Or did he possibly withdraw to facilitate China's reunification, feeling, justifiably, that he could not achieve it himself? That kind of modesty was not one of his chief characteristics, but, in this context, it would bear witness to the deep desire for Chinese unity, which never left him.

Although short-lived, the Nanking government brought the ideological heritage of the United League into the political life of China. Too weak to impose a truly democratic regime, it did impose its likeness. To seize power, Yuan Shi-kai had to respect at least the vocabulary and the outward forms, if not the principle, of democracy.

Yuan Shi-kai's coming to power

In mid-January, after Sun's invitation, Yuan began to pressure the court to obtain the voluntary abdication of the emperor. At the January 7 Imperial Conference, however, this plan came up against opposition from Liang-bi, an influential general and a determined foe of Yuan. A few days later a bomb thrown by a revolutionary rid Yuan of his enemy and no one else at court could prevent his rise. On January 27, the generals and officers of the Beiyang army sent a telegram to the government and the Manchu princes demanding that the emperor abdicate immediately. This was agreed upon in principle. The terms and conditions were fixed by imperial edicts on February 12, 1912. The emperor lost all political power but retained his titles and property; an annual pension of 4 million taels was to be paid him by the republic; and the members of his immediate family also received special treatment. The same edicts empowered Yuan to organize a provisional republican government.

True to his promise, Sun Yat-sen handed in his resignation, though it was a conditional one. It was inconceivable to Sun that the Chinese republic should base its legitimacy on the imperial abdication in favor of Yuan. The future president, he felt, should be invested by the people and their representatives, gathered in a provisional parliament. It was imperative that Yuan leave Peking for Nanking. In Sun's eyes, Yuan's departure would have the added advantage of cutting him off from the Beiyang clique and the senior officials of the imperial administration who had remained in office. Yuan had no intention, however, of forgoing the support on which he relied for his real power. On the pretext of possible disturbances in the North and Peking, he stayed put. On February 27, a delegation of southerners led by Song Jiao-ren, Wang Jing-wei, and Cai Yuan-pei arrived in the capital. At this opportune moment a mutiny occurred in a garrison, showing that the danger was a real one. In their alarm, Sun's envoys abandoned their plan to take Yuan to Nanking, and asked that the demands concerning the choice of a capital give way before the need for the rapid establishment of a unified government. On March 6, the Nanking parliament passed a motion allowing Yuan Shi-kai to become president without leaving Peking. He was inaugurated on March 10 and entrusted Tang Shao-yi with the formation of a government. At the beginning of April, Sun Yat-sen sent in his formal resignation and it was decided that the provisional parliament should be transferred to Peking.

In Yuan's tests of strength first against the court, then the Nanking government, the intervention of the Beiyang army twice decided the issue. This was a symptom of the fact that militarism underlay the republic. Given this, the surprising thing was not that the attempt at parliamentary government (which Yuan developed the following year) was a false test from the start, but that this semblance of a parliamentary system should have seemed indispensable in providing Yuan with the foundation for his authority.

The experiment of parliamentary government

The leaders of the revolutionary party were firmly based in the lower Yangzi and southern provinces. In his capacity as war minister under the Sun government, and then from March 1912 onward as Nanking's resident general (*liushou*),[4] Huang Xing had an army of 50,000 soldiers. If Yuan Shi-kai wanted to control the whole country, it seemed obvious that he had to make some concessions. Yet, trapped by its principles or its illusions, the revolutionary party decided to abandon the use of force (Huang Xing disbanded his troops voluntarily in the spring of 1912), demanding instead the adoption of a democratic government. All efforts were

[4] This ancient title, used by the official left in charge of day-to-day affairs during the absence of an emperor, was brought back by Yuan Shi-kai in March 1912 and conferred on Huang Xing, to whom Yuan had just refused the post of minister of war in the Peking government.

directed at setting up an institutional and legal barrier against the ambitions of Yuan.

The provisional constitution, drawn up by the Nanking parliament in February and March 1912 and agreed to by Yuan when he became president, demonstrates this concern. Whereas the revolutionaries set up a presidential government in January 1912 with the aim of consolidating the authority of Sun Yat-sen, a few weeks later, worried at seeing the office of president falling to Yuan, they came around to a parliamentary system. The main aspects of executive power were to be entrusted to a cabinet. The application of new laws, the appointment of ministers and ambassadors, and declarations of war and signing of treaties were to be submitted to parliament for approval. Official documents were to be signed by the president and countersigned by the prime minister.

For a party system like this to work smoothly, a significant change had to take place in the Chinese political tradition, dominated as it was by the existence of secret societies. Even the United League, which had borrowed its program of political organization and economic development from the West, retained many features of a traditional secret society, such as secrecy, an oath of allegiance, and the predominance of personal ties. Consequently the new parties created in 1912 and 1913 cannot be compared to their European counterparts. The custom was to belong to several of them, because people in the public eye, either for propriety's sake or for personal benefit, rarely refused invitations from different sides. Their programs lacked clarity and definition. Personal affinities were more important than principles in bringing together these men from the money classes. The organizers, in short, had no roots among the people.

Nonetheless, the emergence of new parties during the early months of the republic constituted a new and important contribution to Chinese political practice. Among countless groups, two main currents may be observed, one originating in the United League and the other in the constitutionalist movement. Between 1905 and 1911, the fragile unity of the United League was constantly threatened by internal rivalry and disagreements. The success of the anti-Manchu revolution gave rise to further rifts. The southern leaders, Hu Han-min, Liao Zhong-kai, and Zhu Zhi-xin, who made up the left wing of the party, wanted to avoid a compromise with Yuan. They favored continuing the armed struggle by creating a revolutionary base in Guangdong. Their views were not shared by

Sun Yat-sen. Sun went over to the position of Song Jiao-ren and the Shanghai group, who were for cooperating with Yuan Shi-kai if he could be brought under parliamentary control.

The congress of the League in March 1912 confirmed the victory of the right wing and Song Jiao-ren, whose political activities tended to eclipse those of Sun Yat-sen during the following months. While these struggles were going on, the very existence of the League was threatened by the defection of militants who left it to set up their own organizations: the People's Society (Min she), founded in Hubei under the influence of Li Yuan-hong; the Union of the Chinese Republic (Zhongguo minguo lianhehui), led by Zhang Bing-lin, whose members, natives of Zhejiang, originally belonged to the Restoration Society (Guangfuhui); and the Society for the Promotion of Morality (Jindehui), formed by Wu Zhi-hui, Wang Jing-wei, and Zhang Ji (without their leaving the United League), all of whom had anarchist sympathies.

The constitutionalist movement, as it developed, showed even more pronounced centrifugal tendencies, giving birth to the United Republic Party (*Gonghe tongyidang*) and the Society for Discussing the Rebuilding of the Republic (*Gonghe jianshe taolun hui*), among many others. This profusion of groups worried the public and after a vigorous campaign led by Zhang Xin-yan on the theme of the two-party system, a new alignment of political forces emerged. It centered round the Guomindang,[5] founded in August 1912 on the left, and the Progressive Party (Jinbudang), founded on the right in April 1913 out of the fusion of three groups: the Republican Party (Gonghedang), the Democratic Party (Minzhudang), and the Unification Party (Tongyidang). The Guomindang, heir to the United League and dominated by Song Jiao-ren, abandoned its social platform. It was particularly committed to ensuring the proper working of the parliamentary institutions. The rival parties gave unconditional support to Yuan Shi-kai.

The first clashes between Yuan Shi-kai and the revolutionaries occurred over questions of parliament and government. In March 1912, Yuan chose Tang Shao-yi, who had negotiated a peaceful settlement after the southern rebellion, as his prime minister. Tang was linked to Yuan by long years of cooperation. The revolutionaries were reassured by the fact that Tang had recently joined the United League. Educated in the United States, he was both com-

[5] The first Guomindang Party was banned by Yuan in 1913 and should not be confused with the Guomindang of the 1920s.

petent and a man of character. In his main cabinet posts (the interior, the army, and the navy), he put men from the Beiyang clique, while members of the United League were put in charge of the technical ministries (finance, agriculture, industry and trade, justice, and education).

By August the cabinet was in disagreement with the president. In line with the procedure laid down in the provisional constitution, the Guomindang got the Zhili assembly to elect Wang Zhe-xiang provincial governor (*dudu*), in the hope that he would be able to exert some control over Peking. Yuan sensed the danger and refused to recognize the election, which had already been approved by Tang. The officers of the Beiyang army declared their opposition to Tang and he had to resign. A nonparty diplomat, Lu Zheng-xiang, was entrusted with the formation of a new cabinet. It was a difficult task, and one which set Yuan at loggerheads with the provisional parliament, which refused to ratify several of his ministerial choices. Once more the army and the police intervened to settle the dispute in Yuan's favor. As a result, the cabinet became simply a secretariat attached to the office of president.

In September 1912, however, when Zhao Bing-jun took over the post of prime minister from Lu Zheng-xiang, the conflict between Yuan and the Guomindang died down. Sun Yat-sen and Huang Xing went to Peking on an official visit and had honors heaped upon them. During his many conversations with the president, Sun Yat-sen put forward his plans for economic development, and on September 9 an order was issued, putting him in charge of a full-scale plan for the development of the railways. The Guomindang took advantage of this truce to prepare for the parliamentary elections scheduled for December 1912 and January 1913. It obtained the majority of seats in the new parliament and, by its victory, designated Song Jiao-ren as the new prime minister. But on March 20, 1913, when he was waiting at the station in Shanghai for the train to Peking, Song was assassinated. Although it was virtually certain that Yuan was responsible, the Guomindang had to accept the crime with resignation.[6]

Police provocation, military intervention, and political murder triumphed over constitutional opposition. The death of Song marked the end of the parliamentary experiment and opened the era of dictatorship.

[6] See document 2.

The Dictatorship of Yuan Shi-kai:
March 1913–June 1916

Yuan and the powers

When he started on the road to personal power, Yuan had one enormous advantage over his adversaries. He was seen as the strong man, and recognized and supported by the foreign powers. For a long time, he had had the sympathy of the diplomatic circles in Peking and was extremely careful of his reputation there. He surrounded himself with British and American journalists, one of whom, Morrison, the *Times* correspondent, became Yuan's personal adviser in July 1912. When he became President of the Republic, the powers were ready to help him. That help was precious, in enabling Yuan to strengthen his regime; but it was also costly in terms of independence and national sovereignty.

At the beginning of 1912, the resources at the disposal of the Peking government were extremely limited. The Manchus left an empty treasury behind them. To pay their own troops and meet local needs, the provincial governors kept the income from taxation. The revenues from the maritime customs were pledged to the foreigners as security for their loans. The salt-tax administration was completely disorganized. Government income amounted to barely 8 million taels a month, whereas the upkeep of troops in the North alone cost 3½ million taels, and repayment of foreign loans another 5 million. After the proposal for a domestically raised loan had fallen through in 1912, Yuan had no choice but to turn to the foreigners. Twice they gave him most timely help, lending him 2 million taels in February 1912, just before the "mutiny" of the Peking garrison, and another million at the time of his official investiture in March. This was merely first aid, however, and Yuan, who recruited thirty new military units under the pretext of maintaining order in the North, needed far more. Prime Minister Tang Shao-yi calculated that 1 million pounds sterling were necessary.

To meet these needs, the chief foreign banks formed an international consortium. To put a stop to the violent rivalries which arose among the powers at the time of the first railway loans, four financial groups—one British, one German, one French, and one

American, each with its government's support—decided in 1910 to carry out joint negotiations with Peking. In April 1911, a loan to finance the building of the railways in Central China was concluded.

The revolution offered new prospects to these financiers, whose aim was to gain control of the national revenues and government expenditures in return for their help. Agreements for the consortium were completed at the Paris Conference during June to July 1912, making room for Russian and Japanese interests. Yuan was then offered a large loan with strings attached. The loaning banks were to control the way in which the funds were used; and the salt-tax revenues, which were to guarantee the operation, were transferred to foreign management. The Yuan government tried several times to escape the monopoly which the foreign consortium thus established over the foreign financial market. But, one after another, loans from the Banque Sino-Belge (March 1912) and then from the Charles Birch Crisp Corporation of London (December 1912) fell through.

The defection of the American bankers, who withdrew from the consortium after being disowned by Woodrow Wilson, the new Democratic president, came too late to prevent the conclusion of the Reorganization Loan, signed on April 27, 1913. The sum involved was a large one: 25 million pounds. The contract stipulated how the funds should be used: about 10 million pounds were to assure the servicing of the foreign debt; 2 million pounds were to go into reorganizing the salt tax; and 5½ million pounds were to cover the government's current expenses from April to September 1913. The security was the maritime customs surplus, the income from provincial taxes directly controlled by the central government, and the salt tax. In addition, the Chinese government had to agree to the appointment of foreign technical advisers; Richard Dane was put at the head of the salt-tax administration, and Konavaloff and Padoux were in charge of the budget. The money deposited in foreign banks in Peking was to be paid out gradually, while justifications had to be produced, an onerous and extremely humiliating procedure for the Chinese government.

The concessions made by Yuan to obtain the Reorganization Loan struck a blow at government independence, but those he made to obtain diplomatic recognition threatened Chinese national sovereignty and territorial integrity. During negotiations on the subject in 1912 and 1913, Russia and Britain made China's acknowledgment of the autonomy of Tibet and Outer Mongolia a condition for any diplomatic agreement. Both these border areas had declared their independence in November 1911. The Russians had already set up a garrison at Urga and sent advisers to the Mongolian government, while Great Britain returned once more to its policy of expansion in Central Asia. The day Yuan agreed to sign away control over these two areas, on October 7, 1913, his regime was recognized by Great Britain and Russia, which were quickly followed by the rest of the powers.

Yuan's policy of concessions encouraged further foreign penetration. Through this policy of compromise and capitulation a dictatorial regime was built up within the country.

The "second revolution" and its failure

Yuan's ambitions fed on the weakness of his enemies and the power of his allies. Lassitude and betrayal undermined the opposition in parliament and in the provinces. The parliament elected in December 1912 met on April 8, 1913. Despite its Guomindang majority, it abandoned the idea of demanding that the enquiry into the murder of Song Jiao-ren be carried out. When the president violated the constitution by signing the Reorganization Loan without first submitting it for parliamentary approval, the members merely offered a motion of censure, of which nobody took any notice. Yuan, it is true, tried to allay the indignation with threats and rewards. Guomindang members of parliament who left their party were rewarded with the sum of 1000 pounds—drawn from the Reorganization Loan funds. Those who held to their position were threatened by the police. In this way the parliamentary opposition, on which the revolutionaries had based all, or almost all, their hopes, disintegrated.

Supporters of Yuan already controlled the Northern part of the country, and he extended his influence in South and Central China by means of alliances, but six provinces still eluded him—those stretching from Hunan to Shanghai and Canton, the traditional stronghold of the revolutionaries. The military governors there belonged to the Guomindang. However, most of them, either through caution or because they lacked the military means, were loath to come into open conflict with Yuan. They received little encouragement to do so from the Guomindang leaders, uncertain about what policies to adopt and inclined to follow the moderate advice of Huang Xing. Li Lie-jun, the governor of Jiangxi, was the only one who appeared willing and able to undertake armed resistance.

Yet the first move toward the break came from Yuan. On June 9, Li Lie-jun was dismissed from office by order of the president. During the bitter ensuing struggle, seven provinces again declared their independence, but Jiangxi and Jiangsu were the only ones to offer real resistance to the troops sent by Yuan Shi-kai. The fall of Nanking on September 2, 1913, marked the end of the rebellion. Contemporary observers, and particularly foreigners, saw the movement as "a rebellion of jealous and greedy politicians" and a last convulsion of the civil war. Present-day Chinese historians, however, lay great stress on this "second revolution," as they call it. Once the obstruction of the Manchus was removed, it became clear that the real choice behind a decision to support or oppose Yuan was between democracy and dictatorship, nationalism or colonization.

In 1913, the political aspects of the struggle were more clearly defined than in 1911. But public opinion, wearied by two years of troubles and changes, turned away from revolution. For example, in the spring of 1913 the merchants expressed discontent at Yuan's abuse of power. The Reorganization Loan aroused their economic nationalism, and, after the assassination of Song, prices on the Shanghai market underwent a violent upheaval. Yet, in the summer of 1913, the bourgeoisie did not rally to the support of the rebellion as it had in 1911. At a time when public freedom was seriously threatened, the bourgeoisie was chiefly disturbed by the inconvenience of another political crisis. This longing for peace and order played into Yuan's hands. Although he still lacked their support, he was aided by the merchants' apolitical attitude.

Perhaps the revolutionaries could have mustered support among the peasants. In the northwestern provinces an uprising known as the White Wolf (bai lang) Rebellion broke out in the summer of 1913 and threatened to take Yuan's forces from the rear. In fact, the rebels kept 30,000 men of the Beiyang army at bay for over a year. These White Wolf troops were recruited from among the Society of Brothers and Elders. Led by an officer from the South, a survivor of the second revolution, they moved from Henan to Shenxi and Gansu, living off the countryside and laying ambushes. Although the history of the movement is not yet well known, it seems that its political aspiration—the overthrow of Yuan—largely gave way to traditional pursuits, such as plundering and violence, and that its social aspirations went no further than the program common to all secret societies which are out to "strike the rich and help the poor."

The lack of liaison between the peasant rebellion in the Northwest and the rising in the Yangzi valley can be explained by the weakening of the revolutionary party as much as by the archaic nature of the White Wolf revolt. Sun's prestige had been exhausted by the Nanking government experience. The creation of the Guomindang had not renewed the ideology of the United League, and no common ideal emerged to replace the anti-Manchu slogans, which were now pointless.

The revolution, which lacked both a popular foundation and support from the main strata of society, and had no ideological structure, could hardly escape militarism when it resorted to arms. In 1913, individual and provincial loyalties blurred and sometimes effaced the idea of the revolutionary struggle. The conflict with Yuan became a rivalry between unequally prepared factions, the weakest of which was quickly crushed.

The failure of 1913 and its consequences

The failure of 1913 weighed as heavily on the evolution of modern China as did the success of 1911. Proving that a real revolution was not yet possible, it managed to postpone that revolution even further into the future.

In August 1913, Sun Yat-sen fled to Japan, where he was joined by Huang Xing and hundreds of militant members of the Guomindang. He was in exile once more. The failure of the Guomindang and of Western-type parties encouraged Sun to return to a traditional organization patterned on the secret societies of the past. In July 1914, the Chinese Revolutionary Party (Zhonghua gemingdang) was born. It was a party of brothers bound by an oath of loyalty to their leader. Sun saw this as a way of strengthening the cohesion, the discipline, and the efficacy of the party; but it met with opposition from many militant members like Huang Xing and Li Lie-jun, who preferred to break with Sun rather than comply with procedures which they considered humiliating (such as the taking of fingerprints upon joining). In the years that followed, this revolutionary party, in exile and divided against itself, lost most of its former influence. Ideological work was sacrificed in the pursuit of funds from overseas Chinese communities. The Pan-Asianism of Sun, and his admiration and friendship for Japan, cut the Chinese Revolutionary Party off from the great post-1915 Chinese Nationalist movement which took shape in reaction to Japanese expansion on the continent. Sun and his friends had begun their sojourn in the wilderness.

Yuan Shi-kai meanwhile took advantage of his victories. He tightened his control over the central and southern provinces by sending his generals there (Ni Si-chong in Anhui, for example) or by obtaining the submission of governors already in office—in particular, Zhu Rui, *dudu* of Zhejiang. He managed to depose Li Yuan-hong, who had become too independent in his Hubei base, and invited him to Peking, where he showered him with honors and wealth. The provincial power of Yuan was based chiefly on the military governors' loyalty, but that of the *dudu* in the Southwest (Guangdong, Guangxi, Sichuan, Guizhou, and Yunnan) was still extremely uncertain. China had nevertheless attained a fragile unity centered around the Peking government.

However, China was weakened by internal struggles and its sovereignty continued to decline under further international assault. Japan had entered the world war alongside the Allies. Seizing on the pretext of military operations against the German possessions in Shandong, it took advantage of the European preoccupations of the Western powers to impose on China a plan for political and economic control which was tantamount to making it a protectorate. The Twenty-one Demands, presented to the Peking government in January 1915, called for recognition of Japanese predominance in Shandong, Inner Mongolia, Manchuria, the southeastern coastal provinces (opposite the Japanese island of Taiwan), and the Yangzi valley. Article 5 of the document made provision for Japanese "advisers" to be appointed to the key posts in the civil administration, the government, the army, and the police. It also gave Japan the sole right to supply China with most of its armaments. As soon as these diplomatic proceedings were made known, they provoked an outcry from the Chinese public. A great feeling of national humiliation aroused Chinese intellectuals, and the national bourgeoisie organized a vast movement to boycott Japanese goods. Even so, Yuan Shi-kai agreed to submit to these demands in the treaty of May 25, 1915. He was probably unable to offer any resistance to them. And he was quite willing to comply, anxious as he was above all to strengthen his own power.

Yuan Shi-kai and personal power

After his victory over the rebels in 1913, Yuan created an office for himself commensurate with his new power. On October 6, he had his election to the presidency confirmed by the new parliament, sitting under the threat of a body of citizens gathered at the doors. On October 25, amendments to the provisional constitution gave Yuan the rights to appoint ministers and senior officials, declare war or sign peace, and make and unmake laws. On November 4, the Guomindang was declared illegal, and shortly afterward parliament was adjourned indefinitely. From then on Yuan governed with the help of a Consultative State Council. In March 1914, he ordered the dissolution of provincial assemblies, and in December an amendment to the constitution extended the presidential term of office to ten years, after which it was renewable without elections. Lastly, the president was given the right to designate the three candidates who were to stand for election as his successor. These new dispositions ensured that Yuan would have tenure for life and paved the way for hereditary transmission of power.

The man who rose to power in this way was fifty-five years old;[7] physically, he had a massive frame and a powerful neck. His whole body was animated by great liveliness of gesture and expression. His piercing eyes would follow his interlocutor, while he was mentally already far ahead of what was being said. His thick, drooping mustache added to his slight physical resemblance to the French premier, Clémenceau, which was often noted by his contemporaries. Yuan's energy and intelligence compelled respect from his entourage. However, his evident contempt for his fellow men was denounced by Liang Qi-chao: "Yuan draws no distinction between an animal and a man. All that he knows about men is that they fear the dagger and love gold . . ." He naturally attached no importance whatsoever to the ideological impact of the 1911 revolution. This judgment, supported by his own political success, encouraged him to crown his rise by founding a new imperial dynasty.

The attempt to restore the monarchy

The restoration campaign began at the end of 1914 with a return to Confucianism. Yuan assumed the title of Protector of the Faith

---

[7] See document 3.

and at the winter solstice he went to the Temple of Heaven in imperial pomp to celebrate the traditional rites. His plan became clear when a memorandum by Dr. F. J. Goodnow appeared in August 1915. Goodnow was a constitutional law specialist who had recently given up his post at Columbia University to become an adviser to the Chinese government. He favored a restoration of the monarchy in China and supported his case with all the authority granted him by his background and the fact that he belonged to a republican nation. His arguments were taken up by the Peace Plan Association (Chouanhui), led by Yang Du, Yan Fu, and Hu Ying. It had cost Yuan over 2 million Chinese dollars to set up the organization. Liang Shi-yi created a National Petitioners' Association, which sent countless letters and telegrams to Yuan calling for a transformation of the regime. Thus "solicited" by public opinion, Yuan convened a National Congress of Representatives, which on November 21, 1915, voted unanimously in favor of a restoration of the imperial regime. The weeks which followed were devoted to preparing the enthronement ceremonies. Not one detail was overlooked. Even the omens which traditionally accompanied the arrival of a new dynasty were not forgotten: the skeleton of a dragon was discovered at Yichang.

Yuan's imperial designs, once uncovered, aroused growing opposition. At first, the resistance came from the moderates and the Progressive Party (Jinbudang); they were joined by a few former Guomindang members who had stayed in China. Liang Qi-chao abandoned his official post and led a violent press campaign. At the center of these activities were some generals from the Southwest, the most enthusiastic of whom was Cai E, the former governor of Yunnan, who was recalled to Peking by Yuan after the rebellion of 1913. Cai E went back to his provincial base, gave Yuan an ultimatum, and on October 25, 1915, proclaimed the independence of Yunnan. The aims of the antimonarchical movement launched by the southwestern junta were to protect the constitution, drive Yuan out of the office of president, reorganize the central government, and restore provincial liberties. It was supported by its National Protection Army, which, in January 1916, went on the offensive in Sichuan. Despite Sun Yat-sen's return to Shanghai, the Chinese Revolutionary Party played a very minor role in this antimonarchical movement. It was victories and the winning over of new members that spread the movement to Guizhou, and in March 1916 it reached Guangxi and Guangdong. Chinese unity was threatened once more. As in 1911–1913, the political crisis caused a split in the nation. Only this time, Yuan no longer had the means to patch it up.

He had much less control over the Beiyang army. Busy with political tasks, he had left others—Duan Qi-rui and Feng Guo-zhang—in charge of his military units. New loyalties had formed within the ranks; new ambitions had taken shape among its leaders. The Beiyang army, instead of being Yuan's instrument, became that of his former lieutenants. In addition, hostility from the powers, who had been warned by Japan, deprived Yuan of the financial and diplomatic aid which had been so useful to him in 1913. Finally, the restoration movement and the campaign against the Southwest were financed by inflation. The Bank of China and the Bank of Communications directed by Liang Shi-yi issued notes which no longer had any gold and silver to guarantee them, and repayment of them in silver was refused in April 1916.

So Yuan was isolated in the diplomatic and political fields, had no further financial resources, and had lost the support of his former henchmen. He had to make concessions. On March 22, he decreed the abolition of the empire, before it was officially established, and offered ministerial posts to the republicans. However, Cai E and Liang Qi-chao continued to denounce his betrayal and call for his resignation.

Yuan died suddenly, from natural causes, on June 6, 1916, thus solving the situation. In accordance with the desires of the opposition, and with the terms of the constitution, he was succeeded by Li Yuan-hong, the acting vice-president. The new president's very weakness made him acceptable to Feng Guo-zhang and Duan Qi-rui, the rival generals in whose hands real power lay. Their hour had not yet come. Li's presidential term of office was a moment of calm, a temporary return to republican legality and national unity, before the widespread chaos of the warlords' campaigns.

The Revolution of 1911 and the Evolution of Modern China

Failure or success of the revolution

The death of Yuan Shi-kai marked the end of a revolutionary cycle which had lasted about ten years. Any assessment of the significance of the 1911 revolution must come to grips with this decade-long period, since a judgment on the revolution's success or failure involves a comparison between its aims and the results it achieved. This process is less simple than it seems, since the relationship between the pre-revolutionary movement and the revolution itself must be taken into account. It is difficult, in fact, to see the revolution as the outcome of the actions of the United League and Sun Yat-sen, and as the work of a liberal, democratic, national bourgeoisie, as the Chinese Communists today would have it. If the revolution of 1911 is seen simply as growing out of the ideological movement which preceded it, then the events of 1911 to 1916 are made virtually incomprehensible. For the contradictions between the supposedly dominant role of the United League and the rapid withdrawal of Sun, and between the strength of the revolutionary forces and the general takeover of power by the gentry, express quite clear differences between two distinct, successive phases of Chinese evolution: the pre-revolution, characterized by the rise of the United League, and the revolution. In many ways the revolution was a victory for the local elite, though a short-lived one. By overthrowing the imperial regime, the gentry deprived themselves of the ideological and political support on which their power was based, preparing the way for the rise of a new group of leaders, the warlords.

All the ambiguity of the anti-Manchu policy was inherent in the 1911 revolution. This policy did not always embody the hopes of the revolutionaries, and it rapidly disappointed those of the conservatives. The issue of the foreign dynasty was decidedly a secondary problem. And if the fall of the Manchus could not provide the revolution with enough of a foundation, the failure of Yuan's monarchical restoration suggests its broader impact.

Unfortunately, there is still little known about the years from 1912 to 1916. Historians have searched the pre-revolutionary movement for an explanation of what occurred, although the study of later events, particularly the antimonarchical movement of 1915–1916, would probably provide more plentiful and better material. In June 1915, Yuan Shi-kai, feeling that the time had not come to reveal his plan for the monarchy, wanted to reassure his entourage. He declared that he had no reason to transform the political regime because his presidential powers were unlimited. The difference between the hereditary dictatorship which he had managed to establish and the empire to which he aspired was in fact very slight. Nevertheless, public opinion accepted one and rejected the other.

The nature of the obstacle confronting Yuan was ideological, or at least psychological. The republic, whose destiny was in his hands, was no more than a meaningless word for him and for many of those around him. But the fact that Sun Yat-sen and the United League had managed to introduce republican vocabulary, even in the absence of republican practice, was significant. It is, of course, difficult to assess the role of words outside the reality they are meant to represent, but Yuan's failure sealed the decline of Confucian political philosophy. As a result, the ideological influence of the United League appears much stronger in retrospect than the relatively secondary role played by its militant members suggested at the time. But above all, it was a negative influence.

After the disappearance of the empire, the flickering myth of the republic never corresponded to any existing reality. In fact, the 1911 revolution did not produce any new political values; it only created an ideological vacuum. Although, in the long run, the vacuum created called forth entirely new solutions, on a short-term basis it led to regression. Power, no longer based on a guiding principle, was exercised in the light of immediate interests and by virtue of the strength of those who held it. Consequently, the warlord era often appears darker than that of the empire in the days of reform.

Actually, the new warlord era—with its main characteristics of militarism and regionalism—began with the rise to power of Yuan Shi-kai. He was in fact the first warlord, although he was more intelligent and more energetic and worked under better circumstances than his successors. However, his power was subject to similar hazards: rebellion by unpaid troops, treachery by corrupt officers, outbursts of hostility among the elites, and the indifference of the people.

The question of what kind of political regime should govern China, which the 1911 revolution raised without providing an answer, was only one aspect of a more fundamental crisis, that of China's integration into the modern world. The way in which the 1911 revolution acted upon the modernization process constitutes, finally, the essential standard for judging its importance.

The 1911 revolution and the modernization of China

The economic development which was a feature of the first years of the republic suggests a liberation or at least a stimulation of productive forces. Yuan Shi-kai wanted to win over the bourgeoisie, so he took the requests of the merchants into consideration and tried to satisfy them. He gathered round him heads of enterprises like Zhang Jian, whom he put in charge of the Ministry of Industry and Commerce. In a long speech to the provisional parliament in April 1912, he outlined his program: the suppression of internal dues (*lijin*), reduction of the export tax, standardization of the currency, and industrial development.

The most important promise to be carried out was the monetary reform of February 1914. About forty specialists in finance, among them several foreigners (Morrison, Goodnow, and Wissering), attended a meeting in Peking presided over by Liang Shi-yi. After refusing to adopt the gold standard or bimetallism, the experts agreed on the maintenance of silver currency, and recommended the minting of a national dollar intended to replace foreign coinage and the "dragon dollars" from provincial mints. The Yuan Shi-kai dollar, whose weight remained fixed, quickly obtained recognition on the market. Once defined and minted, it proved the first stage in the standardization of China's currency, though this was hindered for another twenty years or so by the uncontrolled issue of notes.

The Chinese economy, which had stood up quite well to the autumn 1911 disturbances, went through a sharp depression during 1912. In February, business in Shanghai amounted to only 7 percent of the normal figure. The situation improved in the summer. The economy then began a phase of relative expansion which continued, with a few fluctuations, until the end of the First World War. The most important factor contributing to this improvement was probably the abundant harvests throughout the country. Plentiful agricultural products supplied the export channels (silk, cotton), and encouraged revived import activity, whose value in 1912 reached a record 473 million taels.

The same energy was transmitted to industry. In the mines, in heavy and light industry, and in transport, countless projects were proposed and some were carried out. New tin mines were opened in Fujian, financed by overseas capital. The Hanyang iron foundries, which had been abandoned during the disturbances, were put into working order again by exclusively Chinese work teams. In the lower Yangzi valley, mechanized rice and cotton mills[8] and also industrial flour mills were created.

---

[8] Factories combining the spinning and weaving of cotton in a single plant.

Towns were modernized. Many of the old town walls, which hindered activity and growth, were demolished. In the Chinese city of Shanghai (Nandao), a streetcar was built within the space of a few months without any foreign help. Every sector gained from the enthusiasm which seemed to pervade business circles. In spite of political difficulties, this impetus was maintained in 1913 and the economy of the treaty ports, which was highly sensitive to fluctuations in the international situation, escaped the crisis experienced by Europe and the United States.

The world war opened new prospects for the Chinese. They hoped that "as long as the most cruel war of all lasted, China would be able to bring off an important victory in the commercial field." But during the early months of the war, the spread of military operations to Shandong,[9] the decline in imports of manufactured goods, the falling demand for such luxury goods as silk, and the transfer home of much foreign capital upset the commercial and financial market in China. Substituted industrial or handicraft production like flour mills, cotton-spinning mills, and sugar refineries did not even take root until 1915. The same was true for the development of mines to meet the growing demands of the warring nations for tin and antimony, and for the organization of commercial channels which funneled to Europe increasing quantities of foodstuffs (eggs, flour) and raw materials (leather, oil).

Industries and foreign trade went through a golden age, which began just after the 1911 revolution and lasted about ten years. This relative prosperity was a reflection of the world situation and the withdrawal of foreign competition during the war rather than a true liberation of productive forces due to the revolution. It was consequently of a frail and ephemeral nature. Without the special circumstances created by the world war, the expansion which began in 1912 would probably have been rapidly paralyzed both by the archaic structures still in existence and by the anarchy which developed under the reign of the warlords. Yet, at a more abstract level, a major development had come about in Chinese economic thinking. The subject for debate was no longer whether or not production had to be modernized, nor how far modernization should go, but how most suitably to ensure the most rapid development possible.

The social transformations which the revolution brought about

[9] Attacks by Japanese troops on German possessions.

are still harder to assess. Nothing is known about the cooperation or the rivalry which grew up between the local elite and the new power-holders, the generals and local potentates. Nothing, or virtually nothing, is known about the aftereffects of the peasant rebellions, or about the progress or retreat of the secret societies. Simply put, the revolution seems to have encouraged the development of urban classes like the intelligentsia and the business bourgeoisie. A regime of liberty succeeded the police terror which had reigned in liberal or revolutionary intellectual circles under the imperial government. In 1912 and 1913 countless journals and newspapers were published, and discussion groups were formed. Of course, the more Yuan strengthened his power, the more censorship was re-established, and prosecution began again, though this did not completely paralyze intellectual activities. For once, the great ideological debates took place inside China rather than abroad amid groups of exiles. Out of all this, a new revolutionary intelligentsia was created, of greater numbers than in the preceding generation, and more in tune with Chinese realities.

The economic expansion which began just after the revolution paved the way for the development and the transformation of the business bourgeoisie. Merchants and heads of enterprises formed increasing numbers of chambers of commerce. According to the statistics of the minister of commerce, 794 chambers of commerce existed in 1915, representing 208,436 enterprises. The National Federation of Chambers of Commerce, organized in 1913, studied general economic problems during its annual sessions and became the official voice of the new bourgeoisie. Such official organizations were always dominated by the powerful compradors.

However, young businessmen who were educated abroad and had returned to China after 1912 to take advantage of the new possibilities for development created by the revolution turned willingly to industry and banking. Mu Ou-chu, who became one of the foremost leaders of the Chinese textile industry after 1920, abandoned his technical studies in Texas in 1914 and founded his first big spinning mills in China. Sun Yuan-fang also returned from the United States, in 1912, to lay the foundations for a modern flour industry and pursue his banking activities in Shanghai. The essential factor in their success was clearly the withdrawal of foreign competition, but their initial enthusiasm sprang from their hopes for a China renewed by the revolution. At first they were absorbed by the management and development of their enterprises, but in the 1920s they began to play an important political and social role. The social upheavals brought on by the revolution, of which almost nothing is yet known, seem to have been enough to enable new forces to be developed and prepared for participation in the Chinese political scene.

China's integration in the modern world raised the question of her relations with the powers. Had the imperialist threat which had been denounced with such vigor just before 1911 been turned aside by the revolution? On the surface the contrary would appear to be true. The weakening of central power after 1911 made it more difficult to defend national interests. China lost control of territories like Tibet and Outer Mongolia. Encouraged by various foreign countries, the movement toward provincial autonomy on the borders of the Chinese empire became a real secessionist movement.

The powers took advantage of the absence or the weakness of central power to obtain new privileges, to the detriment of Chinese sovereign rights. Customs revenues, which until then had been paid directly to the Chinese authorities, were now paid into foreign banks, which then transferred the money to the Peking government. This was one of the country's main sources of taxation revenue, because it represented a large and regular income; so the powers had at their disposal an excellent means of exerting pressure to obtain the appointment or keeping in office of statesmen of their choice. Yuan Shi-kai was the first of a long line of men who benefitted from this. In 1913, the negotiation of the Reorganization Loan was a new step in the process of the colonization of China.

Although it was the start of a further decline in Chinese sovereignty, the 1911 revolution nevertheless helped to strengthen nationalism. The disappearance of the Manchu dynasty made it possible to pose the problem of the Chinese nation in terms of Western and Japanese domination. In this way, too, the 1911 revolution prepared the ground for future struggles.

1911 and the Chinese revolutionary movement

The importance of the 1911 revolution lies both in its actual achievements, in the hopes that it raised, and in the new consciousness that it provoked. The changes it produced in administrative practices, class structure, and economic activities were not fundamental. Nevertheless, it is difficult to understand the scope and success of the revolutionary movement from 1919 onward if the contribution of 1911 is ignored. This Double-ten Revolution, as the Chinese historians call it, is a stage in a struggle rather than its culminating point (which is no doubt the reason why these historians prefer to consider 1919 as the starting point for the contemporary period). But it was a stage of particular importance. On the one hand, it sanctioned the success of traditional forms of opposition: the peasant disturbances; the part played by the secret societies; the intervention of the gentry; and the antidynastic nature of the conflict. On the other hand, it revealed the limitations of tradition and tried to replace it with new forms of action: the parliamentary system, patriotic zeal, and economic development. Although all these innovations did not become concrete reality, at least the principles behind them—democracy, nationalism, and material progress—were forced upon many people.

In reaction to the Western invaders and the Manchu usurpers, the Chinese found a new definition of themselves and tried to identify their own destiny with that of their country. After a maturing process lasting several decades, a modern conception of the nation emerged which was different from traditional xenophobia and racial hatred. This idea of a nation-state first gained a foothold during the revolution, making it an important turning point in Chinese political thought. For the Chinese, exacerbated by a succession of failures, this patriotism became one of the basic factors in all future revolutionary mobilization. The introduction of democratic principles created another current, initially closely tied to that of nationalism. It did not, however, benefit from equally favorable conditions of development, though the 1911 revolution finally did cause the need for economic development to be recognized.

Many other currents of action and revolutionary thought originated in the 1911 revolution, including socialism, anarchism, and federalism. Despite its many failures, the revolution undermined the old order just enough to make new solutions absolutely necessary. The Western patterns it proposed, though without always being able to apply them, were later taken up and adapted to China's needs. The court intrigues, the generals' military *coups*, the peasant rebellions, and the actions of the secret societies broadened the impact of the revolutionaries and helped spread their ideas. In spite of the numerous distortions involved in a process like this, the 1911 revolution was a direct prelude to the explosion of the first cultural revolution in 1919.

ADDITIONAL BIBLIOGRAPHY

Eyewitness accounts

Jean Rodès, *Scènes de la vie révolutionnaire en Chine* (Paris, Plon, 1917).
Fernand Farjenel, *A travers la révolution chinoise: Moeurs, partis, emprunts* (Paris, Plon, 1914).

A study of the period

Jerome Ch'en, *Yuan Shih-k'ai, 1859–1916* (London, Allen & Unwin, 1962).

DOCUMENTS

1. Manifesto from the Republic of China to all friendly nations (January 5, 1912; Promulgated January 9, 1912, at Nanking)

Source: Frederick McCormick, *The Flowery Republic* (London, John Murray, 1913), pp. 456–458.

GREETING—The hitherto irremediable suppression of the individual qualities and national aspirations of the people having arrested the intellectual, the moral, and the material development of China, the aid of revolution has been invoked to extirpate the primary cause, and we now proclaim the resultant overthrow of the despotic sway wielded by the Manchu Dynasty and the establishment of a Republic.

The substitution of a Republic for a monarchical form of government is not the fruit of a transient passion. It is the natural outcome of a long-cherished desire for broad-based freedom making for permanent contentment and uninterrupted advancement. It is the formal declaration of the will of the Chinese nation.

We, the Chinese people, are peaceful and law-abiding. We have waged no war except in self-defence. We have borne our grievances during 267 years of Manchu misrule with patience and forbearance. We have by peaceful means endeavoured to redress our wrongs, secure our liberty, and ensure our progress, but we have failed. Oppressed beyond human endurance, we deemed it our inalienable right and our sacred duty to appeal to arms to deliver ourselves and our posterity from the yoke to which we have so long been subject, and for the first time in our history inglorious bondage has been transformed to an inspiring freedom splendid with the lustrous light of opportunity.

The policy of the Manchu dynasty has been one of unequivocal seclusion and unyielding tyranny. Beneath it we have bitterly suffered, and we now submit to the free peoples of the world the reasons justifying the revolution and the inauguration of our present government.

From Light to Darkness

Prior to the usurpation of the Throne by the Manchus the land was open to foreign intercourse and religious tolerance existed, as is evi-

denced by the writings of Marco Polo and the inscription on the
Nestorian tablet of Sian.

Dominated by ignorance and selfishness, the Manchus closed the
land to the outer world and plunged the Chinese people into a state of
benighted mentality calculated to operate inversely their natural talents
and capabilities, thus committing a crime against humanity and the
civilized nations almost impossible of expiation.

Actuated by a desire for the perpetual subjugation of the Chinese,
by a vicious craving for aggrandizement and wealth, the Manchus
governed the country to the lasting injury and detriment of our people,
creating privileges and monopolies and erecting about themselves
barriers of exclusion in national custom and personal conduct which
have been rigorously maintained throughout the centuries.

They have levied irregular and unwholesome taxes upon us without
our consent, have restricted foreign trade to Treaty ports, placed
lijin embargoes upon merchandise in transit, and obstructed internal
commerce.

They have retarded the creation of industrial enterprise, rendered
impossible the development of natural resources, and wilfully neglected
to safeguard vested interests.

They have denied us a regular system and imperial administration
of justice; inflicted unusual and cruel punishments upon all persons
charged with offences, whether innocent or guilty; and frequently en-
croached upon sacred rights without due process of law.

They have connived at official corruption; sold offices to the highest
bidder, and subordinated merit to influence.

They have repeatedly rejected our most reasonable demands for
better government, and have reluctantly conceded pseudo-reforms
under most urgent pressure, making promises without intention of
fulfilling them; and obstructing efforts towards national elevation.

They have failed to appreciate the anguishing lessons taught by the
foreign Powers in the process of years, and have brought themselves
and our people beneath the contempt of the world.

New Pledges

To remedy these evils and render possible the entrance of China to
the family of nations, we have fought and formed our government,
and lest our good intentions should be misunderstood we now publicly
and unreservedly declare the following to be our promises:

All treaties entered into by the Manchu Government before the date
of the Revolution will be continually effective up to the time of their
termination; but any and all entered into after the commencement of
the Revolution will be repudiated.

All foreign loans or indemnities incurred by the Manchu Government before the Revolution will be acknowledged without any altera-
tion of terms; but all payments made to, and loans incurred by, the
Manchu Government after the commencement of the Revolution will
be repudiated.

All concessions granted to foreign nations or their nationals by the Manchu Government before the Revolution will be respected; but any and all granted after the commencement of the Revolution will be repudiated.

All persons and property of any foreign nation within the jurisdiction of the Republic of China will be respected and protected.

It will be our constant aim and firm endeavour to build upon a stable and enduring foundation a national structure compatible with the potentialities of our long-neglected country.

We will strive to elevate our people, secure them in peace, and legislate for their prosperity.

To those Manchus who abide peacefully within the limits of our jurisdiction we will accord equality and give protection.

We will remodel our laws; revise our civil, criminal, commercial and mining codes; reform our finances; abolish restrictions to trade and commerce, and ensure religious toleration.

The cultivation of better relations with foreign peoples and governments will ever be before us. It is our earnest hope that the foreign nations who have been steadfast in sympathy will bind more firmly the bonds of friendship, that they will bear in patience with us the period of trial confronting us in our reconstructive work, and that they will aid us in the consummation of the far-reaching plans which we are now about to undertake, and which they have so long and so vainly been urging upon the people of this our country.

With this message of peace and goodwill the Republic of China cherishes the hope of being admitted into the family of nations, not merely to share their rights and privileges, but also to co-operate with them in the great and noble task called for in the upbuilding of the civilization of the world.

(Signed) Sun Yat-sen, President.

Dated at Nanking, fifth day of the first month of the first year of the Republic of China (January 5, 1912).

2. A POLITICAL ASSASSINATION

SOURCE: Jean Rodès, *Scènes de la vie révolutionnaire en Chine* (Paris, Plon, 1917), p. 151. Jean Rodès, who for a long time was the correspondent for *Le Temps* in China, describes how Yuan Shi-kai had two officers from Wuchang —Zhang Zhen-wu and Fang Wei—assassinated in 1912, thus revealing his real intentions regarding the revolutionary party.

In the middle of the summer of 1912, the new regime seemed to have reached a period of calm and stability . . . Countless Chinese banquets took place, doubtless to celebrate this restoration of peace and harmony. For several years it had been the fashion to hold them in the foreign hotel in the legations quarter . . . One of the biggest of all was given in honor of a Hubei general . . .

The reconciliation feast took place on a Saturday evening. The facade of the cosmopolitan caravansary glittered with lights. One after another, European-style carriages with rubber-tired wheels drew up to the central entrance and strange figures got out. Some, wearing Japanese-style uniforms, walked up, rattling their sabers at each step; others, dressed in rich silk brocades and thick-soled sandals made of white-lacquered felt, carried fans and on their heads, instead of pig-tails, wore bowler hats, pulled down almost over their ears, thus producing startling caricatures of the monstrous union between China and the West . . .

The host was one of the most important officials in the president's entourage . . . The Houpe general . . . though growing stout, was thoroughly at ease in his Japanese uniform . . . He rattled his spurs and carried himself with the German stiffness fashionable among officers in the modern army. The dinner began straight away. The host, his good-natured face wreathed in smiles, throughout the meal ad-dressed flattering compliments to the general from Houpe, sitting on his right. The latter replied as best he could. They called one another "elder brother" and made such a display of courtesy that one would have thought them irresistibly drawn to each other . . .

The Chinese banquet ended. One by one, the guests bowed cere-moniously to their host and withdrew. Only the general from Houpe and his secretary were left, kept back by the special favors shown them. They all went out together. Once outside, the official asked his most honored guests to get into his victoria, so that he might enjoy their company a little longer . . . When they arrived at the appointed place, he (the general from Hubei) and his secretary were seized and dragged to the ground. Not a shot was heard, but the bayonets flashed as they stabbed repeatedly at the gasping human form huddled in a heap on the ground. Nearby, another group fell on the boy.

Two days later parliament, then three months old, made a violent protest against the double murder. The president smoothed over the situation by conferring the posthumous honors usually awarded to heroes killed in action on the man whom he had just had executed in this way.

3. A PORTRAIT OF YUAN SHI-KAI

SOURCE: Fernand Farjenel, *A travers la révolution chinoise* (Paris, Plon, 1914), pp. 293–294. A French observer of Chinese political life, F. Farjenel, gives a portrait of Yuan Shi-kai, after meeting him in person.

When seen close up, the effect he produced was not that which might have been expected judging by what his enemies said of him. The impression he gives when seen in the flesh is not at all in keeping with his reputation for double-dealing, deceit, and treachery. His looks, which to a European observer are pleasing rather than otherwise, work in his favor.

Compared with his entourage, he gives an impression of loyalty. And yet the story of his life is there to tell us exactly what has happened.

Must we therefore believe in an unparalleled capacity for dissimulation? I do not think so.

Yuan Shi-kai seems to me to be an atavistic product of an ancient society, come too late into a new world.

His acts of duplicity and cruelty, which in the eyes of the new Chinese appear as so many inexpiable crimes, are not so to him; he can understand neither how untimely they are, nor how truly immoral . . . Absolute sovereigns reasoned in the same way.

His misfortune, and that of his country, was that he stood for a bygone age.

His views on government, on the administration of finance, and on centralization, were a statesman's views, but of the sort of statesman he was capable of being, an old-time despot. He would perhaps have made a good tyrant . . .

Chapter Two

The Republic
of the Warlords:
1916–1919

Except in name, the republic barely survived Yuan Shi-kai's presidency; but the apparatus and authority of the state remained intact, at least until the attempt to restore the monarchy and the secession of the Southwest. Under Yuan's successors, the instability of the central authority became chronic. Real power belonged to rival military cliques, hiding behind a fragile facade of republican institutions no one took very seriously. Each province tended to live its own life; the South again seceded. China remained in a state of crisis, provoking vigorous reactions from the intelligentsia, which paved the way for the May Fourth Movement in 1919.

Central Power
in China

The succession to Yuan

In 1916, as soon as Yuan was dead, the dissident provinces in the Southwest annulled their declarations of independence. The northern military leaders (the Beiyang group) agreed to allow Li Yuan-hong, a brigade commander of uncertain convictions, to become president, in accordance with the constitution. He had been elected vice-president to Yuan in 1913, but had not had any role whatsoever to play during the latter's term in office. With the support of the southerners and the liberals, Li called the "old parliament," elected in 1913 and dissolved by Yuan, back to Peking. However, he had to make some concessions to the Beiyang military leaders, who preferred to maintain the more authoritarian 1914 constitution imposed by Yuan. He gave them two key posts; chairmanship of the council to Duan Qi-rui and vice-presidency to Feng Guo-zhang. Duan formed a compromise ministry consisting of army supporters, moderates belonging to Liang Qi-chao's group, and members of the right wing of the Guomindang.

The constitutional facade

Republican legality was thus re-established. To all appearances, Chinese politics hinged on the same rules and machinery—the parliament, the cabinet, and the office of the President of the Republic—as in Western democracies. But the constitutional parliament of 1913 was in fact deeply divided and totally discredited. Split into countless cliques, clubs, and parties, it had been unable to resist Yuan Shi-kai. Now many of its members were ready to go over to any civilian or military politician who approached them, money in hand. Caricaturists compared parliament members to the voracious, docile vagabond herds of swine wandering about the Chinese countryside.

The ministries were brittle coalitions of cliques. There were frequent crises and ministry reshuffles. The office of chairman of the council was an important one, however, and fought over by influential military leaders. The office of President of the Republic was characterized by the same instability, being the competed-for prize among the military factions. Three different men held it in the period between Yuan's death and the May Fourth Movement.

Military power

The real power was wielded by military figures, the provincial governors (officially *dujun*, although Westerners called them "warlords"). They were the actual heirs to Yuan Shi-kai, who had given them power (many of them having been of humble origin) and to whom they had given unconditional support during the 1911–

1912 crisis. They were also called the Beiyang group (from the name of the modern military academy where many of them were trained). They had a strong foothold in the provinces, where they constituted a cruel, rapacious neofeudal force. At the same time, they tried to maintain their control over what remained of the central apparatus of the state.

The following were the most influential of the *dujun*. Zhang Xun (1854–1923 was a soldier of fortune who escorted the Empress Dowager to Sian in 1900. A former protégé of Yuan, he was so intensely conservative that he forced his solders to wear their hair in a pigtail. Feng Guo-zhang (1859–1919), a poor peasant's son and an opium addict, was appointed governor of Nanking by Yuan, and created an autonomous zone of influence there. Ni Si-chong (1871–1919) was appointed governor of Anhui in 1913. Duan Qi-rui (1865–1936) was Yuan's right-hand man in military matters and became head of the Beiyang group when Yuan died. He was prime minister three times between 1916 and 1919. Xu Shu-zheng (1880–1925), the son of a village scholar and a close associate of Duan, was the real political leader of the Beiyang group. In his capacity as principal private secretary to the chairman of the council, he preserved military control over civil power and attended all ministerial meetings. This group dwindled rapidly, nearly all the Beiyang leaders disappearing from the political scene after 1920, leaving the way open for a second, and finally a third, generation of warlords.

Initially, the *dujun* tried to maintain a sort of corporate spirit among themselves, holding official interprovincial meetings; three of these took place between the Peking and the Yangzi groups at Xuzhou, which was considered a neutral town. In 1917, this de facto military authority, the *dujuntuan* (*dujun* association), spoke out on the entry of China into the European war even before the government did so. The militarists were antiparliamentarian, and in January 1917 the third Xuzhou meeting called for the abolition of parliament. A conservative Confucianist ideology seemed to them a palliative for the disappearance of the imperial order and loyalty to the dynasty; so several times they pressed for the restoration of Confucianism as a state religion.

But the tendency to form into rival groups was stronger than any agreement among the *dujun*. In 1917, the group led by Feng Guo-zhang opposed that of Duan and Ni. This was the beginning of the rivalry between what were later known as the Zhili group (despite the fact that it was originally based in the lower Yangzi valley) and the Anfu group.

Civilian political cliques

The two main political currents which confronted each other from 1911 to 1913 still dominated parliament when it was reconstituted in 1916; the progressive group of moderate constitutionalists and friends of Liang Qi-chao, and the radical republicans of the Guomindang gathered round Sun Yat-sen. Each current itself had split several times. The progressives were grouped into several cliques concerned with "research" into the constitution. The chief one (the Research Clique) was made up of the most loyal supporters of Liang Qi-chao, still active enough himself to become minister of finance in 1918 in the cabinet of the militarist Duan Qi-rui. The Guomindang members of parliament were divided into four factions; the 1916 Political Club and the Political Studies Group were two of these. Their leaders—Zhang Ji, Wang Zheng-ting, and Lin Sen—were former supporters of Sun Yat-sen who had become politicians in their own right. Sun himself, whose remaining supporters in 1914 formed a sort of secret society, the Zhonghua gemingdang (Chinese Revolutionary Party), stayed aloof from these rivalries.

Other civilian political groups existed in the administrative apparatus and not in parliament. The Communications Clique was led by a group of bankers and senior officials in the railways, which became their private domain. The Anfu Club, founded in 1918 by Beiyang leaders like Duan, Ni, and Xu, also included civilian members who were politicians or senior civil servants.

The rivalry between cliques embroiled only a tiny section of society; the majority of the population remained outside the sterile jousting that went on between politicians who were also taking advantage of their influential and lucrative positions at the top of the political structure. This new class of politicians included scholars and officials of the old regime like Xu Shi-chang (1855–1939), who was President of the Republic in 1918; Tang Shao-yi and Wu Ting-fang, both of whom were diplomats under the empire and went over to the republic in 1912; semimodern intellectuals like Liang Qi-chao (1873–1929), the reformer of 1898; bankers like Liang Shi-yi (1869–1933), the leader of the Communications Clique; graduates from American universities like Wellington Koo

(Gu Wei-jun, born in 1887) and Alfred Sze (Shi Zhao-ji, 1877–1958), both young diplomats who set great store by their Western names; and Protestants like Wang Zheng-ting (1882–1961), who was one of the leaders of the moderate branch of the Guomindang.

The crisis arising from China's entry into the war

For a variety of reasons, the powers wanted China to enter the war against Germany. Britain wanted to liquidate German positions in China; Japan hoped to gain control over the Peking government; and the United States, which had declared war in April 1917, hoped it could thereby extend its influence in China.

Chinese political circles were in profound disagreement over the matter. The Beiyang militarists wanted to declare war because it would strengthen the position of the army in the country; their political allies, the Research Clique of Liang Qi-chao, supported them. But the president, Li Yuan-hong, and most members of parliament were against it. The movement for neutrality, supported by the chambers of commerce and other unofficial organizations, also had the backing of Sun Yat-sen. In a famous letter to Lloyd George, Sun explained that quarrels among whites did not concern the Chinese.

In March 1917, the prime minister, Duan Qi-rui, at the urging of the *dujun* association, got parliament to break off diplomatic relations with Germany. But in May, President Li counterattacked and had him deprived of office. With nine provinces behind him, Duan formed a schism, and Li had to call on another military clan, led by the diehard conservative Zhang Xun, for help. The latter occupied Peking and, in exchange, got Li to dissolve parliament, an act the Beiyang group had been pressing for since 1916.

The failure at restoration

Zhang Xun was a convinced monarchist. On July 1, 1917, he had the child emperor, deposed in 1912, restored to the throne; Kang You-wei, the old 1898 reformer, who was still a monarchist, drew up proclamations in the ancient style. But the 20,000 soldiers of Zhang Xun, who still wore their hair in a pigtail, could not stand up to the combined forces of Duan and the other northern *dujun*. Zhang Xun gave in after a few days. Li Yuan-hong resigned from the presidency. A compromise between the two main Beiyang military factions resulted in Duan becoming prime minister once more, while Feng Guo-zhang, the lower Yangzi valley leader, became President of the Republic.

The Anfu Club in power (1917–1919)

In August 1917, China declared war on the Germans and Austrians. No military effort was involved. German property and ships in China were seized. The territories and concessions previously controlled by Germany or Austria (Qingdao, Tientsin, Hankou) were occupied, and 200,000 Chinese coolies were sent to the West, though not to fight. In return, the powers agreed to exempt China from payment of the Boxer indemnity for five years.

In China, it was said jokingly that Duan Qi-rui, the new strong man in Peking, was content to declare war abroad without waging war, whereas his home policy was to wage war without declaring it. In the summer of 1917 Duan had to fight against further dissent in the South, but, by 1918, the political-military group led by Duan had gradually strengthened its hold over Chinese politics. This group was commonly known as the Anfu Club or the Anhui group. The Anfu Club had strong support from Liang Qi-chao, who entered the government in 1918. For a time they had to reckon with another military clan, led by the President of the Republic, Feng Guo-zhang. Feng, whose power was firmly based in the lower Yangzi region, was against war with the South. In November 1917, he managed to get Duan to resign from his post as chairman of the council. Duan returned to that post in March 1918, however, and forced Feng to retire. Duan then had the control of the army, although in September 1918 he pretended to resign from his post of prime minister again. He controlled the new parliament set up in August 1918, in which members of the Anfu Club were in the majority. The new President of the Republic, Xu Shi-chang, elected in September 1918, was a veteran of the imperial administration and former secretary to Yuan Shi-kai. He was also a member of the Anfu clique. It is significant to note that the *dujun* association proposed him for the office of president.

The Peking government's dependence on the powers

Basically, the independence of the Chinese central government was still curtailed by the complicated structure of unequal treaties and foreign privilege which gradually grew up in the nineteenth and early twentieth centuries. Territorial privileges took shape as concessions in the big trading ports and leased territories. Legal privileges meant extraterritoriality and consular courts. The military privileges consisted of the right to send squadrons into inland waters, and to station troops in the concessions, in Peking, and along the road between Peking and the sea. Most important of all were the financial privileges—the customs and salt-tax revenues which were paid directly to the powers, the surplus going to the government once the yearly payments on the various Chinese debts and indemnities had been subtracted. A slight breach in the edifice of unequal treaties was created in 1917 when Germany and Austria lost their concessions, which were, however, placed under a provisional regime. In order not to create a precedent, the Allies forced China to agree that, at a later date, they should be transformed into international concessions and not given back to China (despite China's declaration of war on Germany).

The indirect control of China by the West increased instead of lessening as the situation of the central government became more critical. The big public administrations which the Westerners dominated (the customs, the salt tax, the post office) became in fact powerful autonomous bodies. All the men in leading posts were foreigners, and those foreigners who directed them were all-powerful: the Englishmen Aglen (customs) and Dane and Gamble (salt tax), and the Frenchmen Piry and Picard-Destelan (the post office). To this must be added the influence of foreign advisers assigned to various government departments, where, on the Chinese payroll, they were entrusted with unofficial powers: the Australian Morrison and the American Willoughby (advisers to the president), the Frenchman Brissaud-Desmaillets (army), and the Japanese Aoki (army), Sakatani (finance), and Ariga (politics). During this period, when the authority of the Chinese state was considerably weakened, the diplomatic corps in Peking played an important role. It either granted or refused diplomatic recognition in the case of dissent or a *coup d'état*. In reality, this was a disguised right of political investiture and of interference in Chinese internal affairs since recognition, of course, brought with it payment from surplus customs and salt revenues, essential for the financial survival of any government. These surpluses were almost always refused to the dissenting southern governments.

The debt, or the total financial obligations, incurred by China toward the powers was the key to this system of indirect control. It provided justification for intervention by the diplomatic corps or by the foreign management of the customs or the salt tax. According to the *China Year Book 1919*, an unofficial publication produced by British business interests in China, the foreign debt amounted to a yearly total of 10,800,000 pounds. This was payment for loans dating from the "breakup" period: the Boxer indemnity; the railway loans (thirty-one between 1899 and 1918); general loans (including fourteen main ones, like the Reorganization Loan of 1913); and short-term loans to various ministries. These obligations formed an inextricable web, largely sufficient in itself to secure for foreign financiers the control of Chinese finance and the Chinese financial market.

The special position of Japan

Until 1914, in spite of various crises, some of which (like the Russo-Japanese War of 1904–1905) were serious, foreign ascendancy in China retained a certain spirit of collegiate fellowship. ("There is room in China for all of us," Lord Salisbury said at the time of the breakup.) With the First World War, things changed. France and Great Britain were absorbed by the fighting in Europe, Germany was eliminated, the tsar overthrown. Only Japan and the United States were left with a free hand.

The financial and political penetration of China by the United States, which was so striking during the Second World War, began between 1915 and 1920. Big American bankers like Lamont, the associate of Pierpoint Morgan, began to take an active interest in China. In 1917, the American *Milliards Review of the Far East* (later to become *China Weekly Review*) was founded in Shanghai. It had both strong links with American business circles and a great influence on the Chinese bourgeoisie. Chinese students in the United States were numerous and active, and Chinese intellectuals were already looking toward the United States. Wu Ting-fang, who was a minister first under Duan Qi-rui and then under the dissident southern government, declared in July 1917: "I hope to see the day when the Stars and Stripes and the five-colored flag of China will be intertwined in an everlasting friendship."[1] At the time, however,

---

[1] Hu Sheng, *Imperialism and Chinese Politics, 1840–1925* (Peking, Foreign Languages Press, 1955), p. 237.

the United States, unable to contest the pre-eminence of Japan, recognized the latter's "special interests" in China, as in the Lansing-Ishii agreements of November 1917.

Japan's financial, diplomatic, and military control of China increased in 1917 and 1918. China's participation in World War I served as a pretext for the signing of several agreements and loans. Thirteen loans had already been concluded between the Chinese republic and Japanese financial groups between 1912 and 1916. Eight more were undertaken in 1917 and eleven in 1918, according to lists in the *China Year Book*. The largest of them was officially called a "loan for China's participation in the European war." It financed the equipping of Duan Qi-rui's troops, while other loans assured them direct supplies of arms and munitions. As a guarantee for several contracts, the Japanese banking group (Bank of Korea, Bank of Taiwan, Industrial Bank of Japan) gained control of the mines, forests, and railways in the Northeast, the Grand Canal revenues, the stamp duty, and the telegraph. At the beginning of 1918, the Nishihara loans authorized the Japanese government to "cooperate" in the control of the Chinese army and navy.

One consequence of the setting up of this Japanese semiprotectorate was the sending of Chinese troops to share in the foreign intervention against the new Soviet government. Xu Shu-zheng, an active Anfu leader who dreamt of vast plans for Mongolia, sent a Chinese army to fight alongside the Japanese troops who invaded Soviet Siberia in 1918–1919. The idea that Japan would be a sort of gendarme of the Far East, capable of bringing communism to heel, accounted largely for the freedom of action which the Westerners allowed it in China. In fact, the Westerners went so far as to sign secret treaties acknowledging Japan's "special rights" in the Far East, at the expense of their ally, China. In this situation originated the diplomatic crisis which precipitated the May Fourth Movement in 1919.

Legal versus real China

In spite of the brutality of the Anfu regime, Duan Qi-rui and his civilian and military allies found their power reduced to a mere facade. The machinery of state was just spinning its wheels, and getting further away from the realities of Chinese life in the process. The central government no longer received financial resources, or even information, at regular intervals. The public felt nothing but contempt for the rivalries between the cliques in Peking. This led to the discrediting of the last remnants of the republican regime which had aroused so many hopes in 1911 to 1912.

The army leaders were vaguely conscious of this state of affairs. To avoid losing all contact with public opinion, they resorted to the curious custom of sending "circular telegrams" to voice their opinions and further their plans in times of crisis. This was tantamount to admitting that the official political apparatus was cut off from the people. On February 14, 1918, Feng Yu-xiang, a virtually unknown general in command of a brigade in Henan, sent a circular telegram setting out a program for civil peace between North and South. It was the starting point of his spectacular political rise during the next decade.

In the absence of other political machinery, the press had considerable influence. On May 18, 1918, the journalist Eugene Chen, editor of the Peking *Gazette*, an influential Peking daily paper, published an article entitled "Selling out China" which caused such a great stir that he was arrested. According to an incomplete list compiled by the postal service, in 1918 there were 49 Chinese newspapers in Peking, 35 in Tientsin, 16 in Hankou, 73 in Shanghai, 39 in Canton, and 118 in fifteen smaller towns.

The sensitivity of the national movement

The public did not remain passive. Several times it made its views known as clearly as during the great movement of protest against the Twenty-one Demands of 1915; these occasions heralded the explosion of May 4.

The October 1916 Laoxikai affair, for instance, caused a great local uproar. When the authorities of the French concession in Tientsin decided to annex the Chinese quarter of Laoxikai and occupied it by force, feelings ran high throughout the town. Motions were passed in street meetings; a boycott was called by the chamber of commerce; mass meetings were held; the schools and the university staged a strike; petitions were sent to the Peking government; and everyone employed in the French concession went on strike. The movement was so sudden that the French were forced to pull back.

This incident was characteristic of the latent state of Chinese political life. One event was enough to awaken it; and, once awakened, it expressed itself spontaneously, directly, and collectively, without the mediation of official institutions and organized groups.

The conclusion of the Nishihara agreements in 1918 provoked a similar reaction. This time it spread to the whole country. In May 1918, 2,000 Peking students demonstrated outside the residence of the President of the Republic. Chinese students in Japan left the country in protest and formed a Students' Assembly for the National Welfare (later one of the slogans of the May Fourth Movement). The Peking press joined the movement with, for example, articles like the one resulting in the arrest of journalist Chen. Other demonstrations were held in Shanghai, Tientsin, and Fuzhou. The National Federation of Chinese Chambers of Commerce, representing the moderate bourgeoisie, also protested against the Sino-Japanese military agreements.

When in 1919 the Chinese government was invited to send a delegate to the Versailles Peace Conference, the national movement exerted pressure once more. The delegation included nonpolitical figures whose prestige was greater than that of the professional politicians. In addition, its program was a fairly daring one, calling for the suppression of zones of influence, the evacuation of foreign troops and police from China, the abolition of extraterritoriality, control of customs, and the return to China of concessions and leased territories. The press, chambers of commerce, university associations, and student groups all supported the demands. The widespread disappointment lent vigor to the May Fourth Movement.

Provincial and Regional Dissent

Provincialism

The tendency toward regional particularism was not new in China. At the time of the suppression of the Taiping, and increasingly during the modernization movement between 1860 and 1880 (*yangwu*), real politico-military provincial powers emerged. The 1911 republican revolution had a strong provincial coloring, and the break with the monarchy took the form of declarations of independence by various provinces. The same thing happened during the antimonarchical movement in 1915.

The Chinese provinces were in fact vigorous and coherent units. Merchants traveling in distant towns, students sent abroad, and coolies emigrating to new industrial centers often formed provincial organizations as refuges against isolation in a hostile environment. The layout of most of the provinces, with the rice-growing central part controlled by the local gentry and surrounded by under-developed and underadministered mountains—traditional hotbeds of rebellion—provided solid geographical and political foundations for provincial particularism.

The province was the normal setting for the activities of the conservative gentry, who were Confucian scholars and landowners. Among them, only a thin upper layer came to think in pan-Chinese terms, or undertook the responsibilities of senior official posts. The provincial congresses, created by the Manchus just before their fall, and dissolved by Yuan Shi-kai in 1914, were quickly reconstituted in 1916 and provided the gentry with the platform and the scope they needed for their activities.

Provincial power of the military

Under the empire, the duties of provincial military and civil governor were performed by a single man. In 1912, however, the new constitution divided the office in two. But Yuan Shi-kai looked to the army for his chief support; so, as time went on, the military governor (called *dujun* since 1916, that is, army inspector) came to hold all real power in the province, the civil governor only being appointed with his agreement.

Some *dujun* looked on their provincial base as a stepping-stone to the control of the central plain, or, in other words, the Peking government. The lower Yangzi provinces were intended to serve this purpose in Feng Guo-zhang's plans. Ni Si-chong, leader of the Anfu group and governor of Anhui, also thought of his province in this way. For others, control of a province was an end in itself, a means of securing material gains and power. The most extreme case of this was Yan Xi-shan, lord of Shanxi from 1911 until the fall of the Guomindang in 1949.

In both cases, the provincial power of the *dujun* was firmly rooted in their control of the local armed forces and the local finances. The latter became intermingled with the private fortunes of the *dujun*, usually based on opium smuggling, smuggling of arms, or other exactions. The *dujun* could count, for a time at least, on the semifeudal allegiance and personal loyalty of their subordinates and soldiers. They practiced intrigue and dissuasion as much as the resorting to force. So China experienced for a second time the confused, cunning exploits of the medieval *Three Kingdoms*.

These provincial potentates could nevertheless be differentiated along subtle political lines. Some were ultra-conservative. Some had progressive leanings, like Feng Yu-xiang in Henan, who called his troops a model army of worker-soldiers, or Chen Jiong-ming in the Southeast, who had anarchist intellectuals as his advisers. Some *dujun* in the central regions described by Zhu De in his autobiography[2] still thought that they were fighting to defend the republican revolution, although they were no more than unscrupulous condottieri.

The power of the *dujun* was also based on their alliance with the local gentry, who wanted to consolidate their own power within a province without paying much attention to politics in general. The gentry's slogan *bao jing an min* ("protect the district by maintaining order among the people") meant exactly that. This withdrawal of the provinces into themselves was apparent in the economic sphere (provincial offices controlling mines or industry), and even in the diplomatic and financial spheres. *Dujun* sometimes negotiated loans from a foreign banking group, with some of the province's resources as a guarantee.

The provinces were the stage on which political-military struggles took place and political decisions were made without reference to the rest of the country. In each province, different coalitions and different personal interests confronted one another. The political history of China from the death of Yuan Shi-kai almost to 1949 often disintegrates into accounts of a series of obscure local conflicts. A few examples for the 1916–1919 period provide ample illustration.

Sichuan

This province went over to the republic in October 1911, giving active support to the antimonarchical movement in 1915. Particularist feelings were extremely strong. Because of its geographical position, Sichuan was the key to the whole of Western China, so in 1916 the Anfu group leaders tried hard to get it back under their control. But the *dujun* whom they appointed was eliminated in 1918 by a former republican officer turned warlord, Xiong Ke-wu,[3] who had the support of the local gentry.

[2] See document 1 at the end of the chapter.
[3] Xiong Ke-wu, born in 1881, went over to the People's Republic of China in 1949. In 1970, his name was still on the list of leaders of the "Revolutionary Guomindang," the ally of the Communist Party.

Yunnan

The strong man of Yunnan was Tang Ji-yao (1881–1927), who took part in the 1911 revolution in the Southwest. His active role in the 1915 antimonarchical movement led him to conceive ambitious plans for a "great Yunnan" embracing part of Guizhou and Sichuan. In 1917, he invaded Sichuan and got as far as Chengdu. At the same time, he went over to the Canton dissident movement. It seems likely that he was also in contact with the Hanoi colonial authorities, who were pleased at the prospect of a more or less independent buffer state on the borders of French Indochina.

Fengtian (also known as Moukden)

The situation of Fengtian was similar to that of Yunnan in that it was an outlying province open to foreign influence (in this case, Japanese). Zhang Zuo-lin (1873–1928), a former bandit chief who joined the army, was appointed governor of Moukden by Yuan Shi-kai in exchange for services rendered. Using political intrigue and military pressure, he got Heilongjiang (1917) and Jilin (1919) under his control, thus becoming master of the three provinces of Manchuria. He was an ally of the Anfu group and had direct contacts with Japan. In 1917 and 1918 he signed two financial agreements with the Bank of Korea, and in July 1918 he obtained a loan of 30 million yuan (or Chinese dollars) from Japan, mortgaging the rich forests of Jilin for it.

Hunan

Politics in Hunan were complicated, because the province was the meeting point of the northern and southern zones of influence. Tan Yan-kai (1879–1930), a descendant of a great Hunanese family of scholars, went over in a timely fashion to the 1911 revolution and was appointed governor of his native province. He had the support of the local gentry. Between 1916 and 1918 the political and military situation in Hunan was extremely unstable. Tan returned to power after the death of Yuan Shi-kai, but clashed with the Anfu group when it attempted to gain control of the province in September 1916, and again in 1917 and 1918. The military clique of the neighboring Guangxi province also had its eyes on rich Hunan. In 1918, Hunan became a battlefield for the armies of Peking and the

Canton dissident government. Changsha, the provincial capital, changed hands several times and the southerners finally brought Tan Yan-kai back to power. But a warlord of the Anfu party, Zhang Jing-yao, recaptured control of Hunan in 1919.

The dissident government in Canton (1917–1918)

When Duan dissolved the "old parliament" in 1917, Sun Yat-sen thought that the time had come to leave his retreat. With his own party, the Zhonghua gemingdang, backing him, he negotiated with the southern military leaders who were hostile to the Anfu party, and in particular with Tang Ji-yao in Yunnan and Lu Yong-ting in Guangxi. The coalition they formed took in several groups of conservative politicians. It also included the navy, which at that time acted as a sort of independent political force in China and had been in contact with Sun Yat-sen for several years.

In July 1917, the navy brought Sun back to Canton. Two hundred and fifty members of parliament joined him there. They elected a military government led by Sun, who was granted the title of Grand Marshal, and Tang and Lu, who were both made marshals. Its theoretical aim was to restore republican liberties, in accordance with the 1912 constitution. However, quarrels soon arose among the different factions in the parliament in Canton, just as they had in Peking. In addition, Sun Yat-sen quickly realized that he was merely an instrument in the hands of the militarists and that the slogan "Protect the constitution" (*hu fa*) was meaningless. He resigned in May 1918 and withdrew to Shanghai. The Canton government was reorganized, the Guangxi military clique, led by Lu Yong-ting, taking it over, with the cooperation of various moderate politicians.

Relations between North and South

Peking and the Anfu group never accepted the secession of the South. In vain, they tried to crush the movement by military force in 1917 and 1918. But there were also those in favor of a compromise, including Feng Yu-xiang; the delegates from the provincial congresses, who held a national conference in Peking in June 1918; and the chambers of commerce. Among them too were some of the northern militarists. In 1918, the group led by President Feng Guo-zhang was dislodged by the Anfu group for this reason.

A peace conference between North and South opened in Shanghai in February 1919. However, it was rapidly suspended, since Peking refused to comply with the requests of the southerners that it annul its military agreements with Japan.

The powers had refused to recognize the dissident Canton government in 1917. In practical terms this meant refusing to hand over its share of the customs surplus. It was not until January 1919 that the diplomatic corps decided to allocate 13 percent of the Chinese customs revenues to Canton (a figure commensurate with the traffic in the ports controlled by the South). This belated motion did not change the basic nature of the discriminatory policy the foreigners practiced against Sun Yat-sen in 1917 and 1918. Funds for his supporters were cut off by the Westerners just as they had been in 1912 when he first became president.

The crisis in public life

The pressure from centrifugal provincial and regional forces increasingly deprived the state machinery of all cohesion and efficacy. Each province drew into itself, even going so far as to negotiate financial agreements directly with foreign countries. The ensuing disorganization in China's administrative life is illustrated by the provincial postal service reports written each year. They are full of instances of military mutinies, plundering by bandits, civil war operations, extortion of funds by the *dujun*, interruptions in road and railway traffic, requisitioning of coolies, and destruction of every kind.[4] The development of banditry was an indication both of the political-military crisis, which was causing the disintegration of the state, and of the agrarian crisis, which was driving the poorest peasants out of the villages.

The situation of the peasants deteriorated throughout this period. Land became concentrated in the hands of fewer and fewer landlords as peasant landowners were reduced to the status of tenants. Moneylending was rife. Land rents rose and payments were claimed more often now in money than in kind. To the traditional effects of the semifeudal landowning system (which themselves were becoming steadily worse) was added the impact on the peasants of the savage domination by the *dujun*. They claimed increasingly heavy taxes and surtaxes, collected them in advance, and sometimes sev-

[4] See document 2.

eral times a year. They allowed their soldiers to plunder and kill at will. They requisitioned the peasants' animals and vehicles, if not the peasants themselves, without ceremony or compensation. China sank into chaos and poverty.

Economic Expansion

The contrast between the sad state of the Chinese countryside and the progress of the capitalist economy in the towns seems almost paradoxical, but only on the surface. In fact, profits from the exploitation of the peasantry by a bourgeoisie which had retained powerful landed interests contributed significantly to the expansion of the modern economic sector.

The rise of industrial production

The period of World War I, which extended through to 1920–1921, was known in Chinese business circles as the "golden age of the Chinese bourgeoisie." The economic situation was propitious for Chinese national capitalism. The Westerners, engrossed in the war, exerted less pressure on the Chinese market. Chinese industry benefitted both from the rise in the price of silver (on which the Chinese currency was based) and from the opening of new markets. Chinese flour exports, for example, were forty times higher in 1920 than in 1914; and the number of Chinese mills increased from 75 to 117 during the same period. This was also true for tobacco; 2 factories existed in Shanghai in 1914, 9 in 1918. It was during this period that the Chinese carpet industry came into being in Peking and Tientsin and took advantage of the fact that the war had closed off the Middle East. The silk industry also made substantial progress and the cotton industry even more. Between 1914 and 1918, the number of Chinese cotton mills in Shanghai rose from 7 to 11, and the number of their spindles from 160,900 to 216,236. In China as a whole, the number of cotton spindles owned by Chinese national capitalists rose from 484,192 in 1914 to 658,748 in 1918 and to 1,218,282 in 1921.

It should be pointed out, however, that it was above all a golden age for processing industries. Chinese heavy industry was still either nonexistent, dependent on foreigners, or backward.

The progress of the capitalist economy

The entire modern sector of the economy gained from this propitious situation. For the year 1919, the banking investments of Chinese national capitalism were estimated at 204 million yuan,[5] and industrial investments at 108 million yuan. In 1918, a survey covering 956 industrial enterprises revealed a considerable number of enterprises with large capital:

Yuan	Enterprises
100,000–500,000	157
500,000–1,000,000	27
Over 1,000,000	33

Large dividends were paid out: 34 percent in 1919 at the Shanghai Commercial Press, which was China's largest publishing house.

Foreign trade also improved:

	Taels in 1914	Taels in 1919
Exports	356 million	630 million
Imports	569 million	646 million

The very noticeable rise in prices during the war and the years immediately following it exacerbated the poverty of the lower classes but strengthened the tendency toward economic expansion. In Shanghai, given a price index of 100 in 1915, prices were at the 230.7 mark in 1919.

This economic expansion sometimes even reached the villages, particularly those surrounding large cities like Canton, Hangzhou, Ningbo, and Shanghai. Contractors installed looms in peasant households or distributed other types of work assignments (straw hats, match boxes). This infiltration of modern industry into the countryside only occurred in economically and geographically limited areas.

Organization of the bourgeoisie

Chambers of commerce, which had begun to develop in China in 1902, grew more numerous, totaling 794 by 1915. They en-

---

[5] After 1914, when the first Chinese silver dollars were minted by Yuan Shi-kai, Chinese statistics sometimes used the tael (unit of weight) and sometimes the yuan (or silver dollar).

compassed 208,436 traditional and modern enterprises of all kinds. In addition to serving an economic and technical function, they often fulfilled an unofficial social and political role. Their moral authority grew as the official state machinery weakened.

Other, more restricted groups were just as active. Chinese bankers' associations were formed in 1917 in Shanghai and Peking, then in other cities. In 1920 they joined together to form a national association. Similarly, the Chinese Cotton Spinners' Association was founded in 1919, led by a Protestant industrialist, Nie Qi-jie (C. C. Nieh). Large numbers of returned students populated the organizations of modern businessmen. The American philosopher John Dewey, who visited China in 1920, said that the country was "full of Columbia men," a phrase no doubt applicable to the modern business circles in which he moved, but not to the country as a whole.

A utopian capitalism

In 1918, when a disappointed Sun Yat-sen withdrew to Shanghai, leaving Canton to the southern militarists, he meditated on Chinese prospects for economic development. In 1921, he actually published a plan for the "international development of China." His grandiose program reflected the confused aspirations of the Chinese bourgeoisie. Among other things, he proposed:

building 200,000 kilometers of railway lines

building wide canals between the Xijiang and the Yangzi, and repairing the Grand Canal

development projects for the large rivers

creating three ports "the size of New York" in the North, the Center, and the South

founding large modern towns at all railway junctions

irrigating Mongolia and Xinjiang

settling Mongolia and Manchuria

He hoped to finance the program with international aid, that is, Western resources made available by the ending of World War I.

Not all circles of the bourgeoisie shared his illusions regarding the West, however. When World War I was over, Chinese economic expansion once more came up against foreign competition and the prohibitions of unequal treaties. At the end of 1918, a Chinese campaign began to regain control of the Chinese customs service, implying the right to fix high duties on imports. The Society for Equality and Reciprocity in Customs Matters was formed in Shanghai. In January 1919, forty-six chambers of commerce sent a telegram on the subject to the Versailles Peace Conference. Later, the May Fourth Movement expressed the economic aspirations of the bourgeoisie, as well as the desire for political and ideological renewal on the part of the radical intelligentsia.

The industrial proletariat

Industrial growth went hand in hand with the numerical growth of the industrial proletariat. This trend was more pronounced in Chinese capitalist enterprises, but was still important in some sectors controlled by foreign capital (textiles, mines, heavy industry).

Statistics are very imprecise. They often make no distinction between workers in truly modern factories and those working in still archaic workshops. With this reservation, the number of workers in industry may be reckoned at a million and a half, including transportation workers who participated in the cycle of large-scale modern production. The main groups of workers were:

Workers around 1919 (approximate estimate)	Overall total	Chinese enterprises	Foreign enterprises
Cotton	100,000	62,000	38,000
Silk	200,000	180,000	20,000
Tobacco	50,000	20,000	30,000
Metallurgy	45,000	40,000	5,000
Shipyards and arsenals	45,000	20,000	25,000
Coal mines	180,000	60,000	120,000
Railway workers	120,000	74,000	46,000
Sailors	115,000	30,000	85,000
Laborers and coolies	200,000	50,000	150,000

In the largest sectors, particularly mines and transport, the number of workers working for foreign employers equalled or surpassed that working for Chinese employers. Countrywide, the distribution of the industrial proletariat was by no means even. It constituted up to 20 percent of the population of Shanghai, which was surrounded by large workers' suburbs like Hongkou, Yangshupu, and Pudong. It was also an important element in centers like Wuhan,

Qingdao, and Canton, but of no consequence in the immense rural interior of China.

Living and working conditions

Most workers came from among the common people in the towns, or from the peasantry. Second-generation workers were extremely rare. Peasants were often recruited by middlemen, with whom they signed work contracts (the *baogong* system). For a term of years, these middlemen collected the workers' wages, imposing a sort of servitude on them, assuring them only of minimal food and lodging.

This system existed particularly among young female workers in the Shanghai textile industry. Generally speaking, the Chinese industrial proletariat included a high proportion of women and children. The qualifications required for employment were extremely low. Wages were miserable, allowing for only the poorest living conditions. Even for children, the working day lasted twelve or thirteen hours and included night work. The hard working conditions were aggravated by tyrannical foremen (especially in British and Japanese enterprises) and by a total lack of sanitary and safety measures. Accidents occurred very frequently.

The working class, poor and inexperienced as it was, still managed to make itself felt as an independent unit in the social and political life of the country. It was looking for new forms of organization. The old corporate guilds could not fill the role any more than could the coolies' associations (*bang*).

The strikes in 1917–1919

During the war period the workers were badly hit by rising prices and this rise was further aggravated by the devaluation of copper coins (used for wages) vis-à-vis the silver currency on which prices were based. Twenty-five large strikes took place in 1918. The workers in the Japanese Rihua cotton mill in Shanghai stopped work four times. The strikes had only the most elementary economic character but were not defeats. At the beginning of 1919, for example, the big foreign Shanghai cotton mills were forced to increase wages by 12 to 15 percent. These economic protests prepared the ground for the outbreak of the political strikes which were one of the main features of the May Fourth Movement.

The Beginnings of Intellectual Radicalism

The new intelligentsia

The rise of the intelligentsia was linked with the rise of modern educational establishments. The Confucian examinations were abolished in 1905 and increasing numbers of new schools and colleges with modern curricula were founded. The official statistics, although somewhat unreliable, show a clear general tendency. The following figures apply to education as a whole, from primary school to university:

	1905	1916–1917
Number of establishments	4,222	121,119
Number of pupils	102,767	3,974,454

Peking University had 818 students in 1912, 1,333 in 1915, and 2,228 in 1919.

In December 1916, a well-known reformer and former anarchist, Cai Yuan-pei (1876–1940), became chancellor of Peking University. He proclaimed a reorganization program stressing freedom of expression and research, and said that the university ought not to act as a recruiting ground for mandarins.

The new intelligentsia also included doctors, who were often trained in British and American mission hospitals; lawyers, who formed a Chinese lawyers' association in 1912; journalists, who were extremely active because the press played an important role in what otherwise was a period of political stagnation; and engineers and technologists like the geologist Ding Wen-jiang (1887–1936), educated in Edinburgh, who founded the Chinese Geological Service in 1914. (The Chinese bourgeoisie hoped that his prospecting for mines would open new fields of activity to them.) The opinions of members of the liberal professions and those close to them were reflected in a modern cultural journal, the *Dongfang zazhi* (*Eastern Miscellany*), published in Shanghai from the beginning of the century. Its political views were moderate, but it gave modern education and pure and applied science a great deal of attention.

The majority of intellectuals and students came from among the rural gentry or families of Confucian scholars, less often from the new bourgeoisie. However, they were beginning to break away from their class backgrounds. Although their views remained timid and vague, they were acutely aware of China's need for internal modernization and for amelioration of its situation in relation to the outside world.

The disappointment of 1911

It left its mark on an entire generation of intellectuals: for the first time in the history of China a dynasty had collapsed without being replaced by a new holder of the Mandate of Heaven. And yet the country had never been in such a state of disorder, its prestige abroad so low, nor its government so despised and incompetent.

Disappointment led the most thoughtful among the intellectuals to a more detailed analysis of events. They came to feel that the failure of 1911 was due to a revolution which restricted itself to politics, leaving China's traditional social apparatus intact. This analysis naturally led them to more radical ideologies (anarchism, Marxism). But this disappointment also brought the realization that properly so-called political struggles, conducted only through political institutions and led by a centralized political machine, were not effective. One original aspect of the May Fourth Movement would be a renewal of mass political struggle but without the mediation of parties and other organized political forces.

The Chinese anarchists

From the early years of the twentieth century on, anarchism played an influential role in China. In 1907 a group of young Chinese students founded the anarchist review *Xin Shiji* (*The New Century*) in Paris, while others in Tokyo founded the *Tianyi bao* (*Natural Law Review*). Influenced by Reclus, Bakunin, and Kropotkin, they also appealed to the Chinese dissident tradition (Taoist scholars).

Anarchism made further inroads after the 1911 revolution. Its chief advocate was Liu Si-fu (1884–1915), who in 1913 founded a Consciousness Society (Xin she) in Canton. Its "twelve prohibitions" were famous throughout China; it forbade meat, wine, tobacco, servants, marriage, surnames, official posts, the use of rickshaws, running for parliament or belonging to a party, military service, and religion. Liu and his followers also formed a Chinese Esperantist group.

When Liu Si-fu died of tuberculosis in 1915, his group faded away. The founders of pre-war anarchism—men like Wu Zhi-hui and Li Shi-zeng—had become respectable politicians, whose views placed them near the right wing of the Guomindang. Anarchist ideas were still popular among young intellectuals in Peking and Shanghai, however, and had spread to a few workers' circles in Canton and Hunan. At this time Mao Tsetung, a young man attracted by anarchism, was wandering about the countryside, a ragged, free beggar.

Foreign influence on the intellectual left

The oldest and most far-reaching foreign influence was that of the Japanese left wing, which relayed Western anarchist and socialist ideas to China. Of all the Chinese students abroad, the largest and poorest group was in Japan, a Westernized country close at hand, where they could live in Chinese style. The Chinese words for communism and socialism were borrowed from Japanese. Lu Xun and Li Da-zhao (a later leader of the Chinese Communist Party) were educated in Japan.

French influence was more limited, but strong. The first Chinese pre-war anarchists lived in Paris in the circle formed by the Reclus brothers. For a large group of Chinese intellectuals like Cai Yuan-pei or Chen Du-xiu, France was the country of philosophers and the Revolution rather than the power which controlled Vietnam and half of Shanghai. The Work and Study Movement founded in 1912 by Cai Yuan-pei strengthened these links with France still further. During the war, dozens of students went to Paris and Lyons, working part-time to keep themselves alive.

Others, mainly technicians and engineers, turned toward the United States for their education. They were attracted by the pragmatism of John Dewey and by American society as a whole. They published a journal in New York, the *Chinese Student Monthly*, which contained some of the ideas of the May Fourth Movement before 1919. Students of literature, on the other hand, were drawn in great numbers to France and students of medicine to Japan (among them Lu Xun and Li Da-zhao).

Chen Du-xiu and *New Youth*

The leftist journal *Xin Qingnian* (*New Youth*), which had a French subtitle, *La Jeunesse*, was founded in Shanghai in September 1915 by Chen Du-xiu, an intellectual who had taken part in the 1911 and the 1913 revolutions. It was backed by the Chinese students who had just returned from Japan as a protest against the Twenty-one Demands. The "Call to Youth"[6] was deliberate, signifying the determination to make a total break with the old China, which the 1911 revolution had only shaken on the surface.

The review had considerable influence among students, particularly once Chen Du-xiu was appointed dean of the arts faculty in Peking by Cai Yuan-pei. Although it discussed the condition of women and the family, the review's main subjects were culture and education. Politics in the strict sense figured little in it, proof of the continuing bitterness over the failure of 1911, and of the contempt felt for the republican regime. In Chen Du-xiu's view, China was gravely ill and should take the advice of the two gentlemen from the distant West, Mr. Sai (Science) and Mr. De (Democracy). The review also devoted much space to philosophy and literature. Hu Shi, a student returned from the United States, denounced the use of the antiquated classical language (*wenyan*) and called for a literature in the language spoken by the people (*baihua*).

The movement for cultural renewal politicized (1918–1919)

At the end of World War I, the influence of the new journals continued to spread. New periodicals appeared and were as successful as *Xin Qingnian; Xin chao* (*New Tide*) was founded in January 1919 and *Meizhou pinglun* (*The Weekly Critic*) in December 1918. Even the moderate press and periodicals published articles by radicals, as, for example, the Shanghai review *Taipingyang* (*The Pacific Ocean*). The Peking daily paper *Chen bao*, which belonged to the progressive current (Liang Qi-chao), created a weekly supplement in February 1919 and entrusted it to Li Da-zhao, a member of the group in charge of *New Youth*.

Debates on new ideas from the pages of *New Youth* grew and set Chinese intellectual life afire. Students and other readers of leftist publications engaged in passionate discussions of internationalism as it related to China's unique character, of historical relations between East and West, and of the structure of Chinese society. They devoured every available piece of information on Western literature, ideas, and history.

The October 1917 Soviet revolution aroused more interest than

[6] See document 3.

anything else. A telegram from Sun Yat-sen to Lenin in 1918 showed that the echoes of October reached beyond advanced intellectual circles. Li Da-zhao, who had recently been appointed head librarian of Peking University, and who had considerable prestige in the students' eyes, published an article in October 1918 on "the victory of bolshevism" which was a proclamation of allegiance to the Soviet regime. This movement of political interest in Russia led the intellectuals toward Marxism as an ideology, rather than the other way round. *Xin Qingnian* devoted a special issue to Marxism which appeared just as the May Fourth Movement was coming to a head. In it, Li Da-zhao wrote a study, "My Marxist Views," affirming his adoption of Marxism. At the end of 1918, a Society for the Study of Marxism was founded by students in Peking, with the support of Li.

Thus, the radical intelligentsia found itself face to face with immediate political problems. Leaders like Chen Du-xiu and Li Da-zhao, the student groups, and the periodicals with advanced views took an active part in the protest movement against the Nishihara loans in spring 1918. In the early months of 1919, they also took part in the campaign to prevent the Chinese delegation to Versailles from giving in to the West on all the problems which it had come to put before the conference.

This politicizing movement could be seen in the founding of associations of a political nature, at least in the most general sense of the word. In April 1918, Mao Tsetung and some other Hunanese students formed the New People's Study Society (Xinmin xuehui) in Changsha. The Canton students formed a Students' Union for the Salvation of the Country. In June 1918, a Young China Society was founded in Peking, with the aim of continuing the struggle against Japanese domination and "saving the country." All these groups combined regard for study, denunciation of the old society and culture, and at least a confused search for some sort of political action.

Nevertheless, this sudden rise of radicalism was restricted to a very small section of society, the modern intelligentsia, and to limited areas (Peking, Shanghai, Canton, and a few important inland towns). The mass of the people did not impinge on the lives of the advanced intellectuals, although those intellectuals sincerely wanted to go to the people, an attitude which may be compared to that of the Russian populists between 1870–1880. In November 1918, Cai Yuan-pei launched the famous slogan "Work is sacred"

(*Laodong shensheng*). Some of Li Da-zhao's students, among whom were several future Communist leaders, formed "groups of lecturers to educate the people" in March 1919. Li Da-zhao himself was much more aware than was Chen Du-xiu, who was influenced by the West, of the need to maintain contact with aspects of traditional China, especially the peasant. In February 1919, he published an article, "Youth and the Villages," in which he recommended to students that they maintain an invigorating contact with the natural world and the countryside.

The May Fourth Movement did not break out by accident. It was the result of years of intellectual, political, social, and economic ferment. The artificial struttings of the politicians and militarists who, in the republic of the warlords (1916–1919), commandeered the forefront of the stage should not allow us to lose sight of this deeper and, in the long run, far more productive turmoil.

ADDITIONAL BIBLIOGRAPHY

Chow Tse-tsung, *The May Fourth Movement: Intellectual Revolution in Modern China* (Stanford, Calif., Stanford University Press, 1960).

Mao Ze-dong [Mao Tsetung], *Une étude de l'éducation physique*, translated and annotated by Stuart Schram (Paris, Mouton, 1962).

James E. Sheridan, *Chinese Warlord: The Career of Feng Yu-hsiang* (Stanford, Calif., Stanford University Press, 1966).

Siao Yu, *Mao Tse-tung and I Were Beggars* (Syracuse, N.Y., Syracuse University Press, 1959).

DOCUMENTS

1. How REPUBLICAN OFFICERS DEGENERATED INTO WARLORDS OF MARSHAL ZHU DE

SOURCE: Agnes Smedley, *The Great Road: The Life and Times of Chu Teh* (London, John Calder, 1958), pp. 121, 125–126.

This account was written by the American journalist Agnes Smedley after her conversations with Zhu De during the Sino-Japanese War, nearly a quarter of a century after the events described. The time lag does not detract from its freshness and historical interest. It illustrates how critical Zhu De the Communist was of Zhu De the militarist.

Before 1916 was out the local Sichuan militarists attacked Chengdu, and Zhu De was ordered to lead two brigades to relieve it. He had gone halfway when the city fell and the governor general, Luo Pei-jin, was in flight. Zhu De drew back to his Luzhou base while the Protection Army,* as the Yunnan army still called itself, established a truce with the Chengdu victors, after which both sides, while pretending to be friendly, settled down to recruiting and training new troops for the final contest of power. From that moment onward Zhu De was caught in the net of warlordism without recognizing it as such. For, he argued, was not the Yunnan army the one armed force in West China for the protection of the Constitution, the one army loyal to Sun Yat-sen and the Republic? It was, indeed, yet here and there some of its commanders were lending an ear to the jangle of silver in the hands of Premier Duan's agents. They had not yet deserted, but the temptation was great.

Cai† was hardly cold in his grave when the local Sichuan militarists paid by Duan seized Chengdu from the Yunnan "Protection Army." During the brief truce that followed, the new Chengdu rulers imposed new taxes, sold offices to the highest bidders, and seized and imprisoned rich men until they paid the bribes demanded. Peasants who could not pay the land taxes, collected for years in advance, were dispossessed and their land taken by the new rulers. The great landed estates of Sichuan which the generals built up at that time were taken from dispossessed peasants, yet this process of founding estates had continued down to the time General Zhu was talking. Some of these estates were thousands of acres in extent.

After seizing power in Chengdu in 1917 and establishing a truce with the Yunnan Protection Army, the victorious warlords sent an emissary to the Protection Army to propose a military alliance against the neighbouring provinces of Guizhou and Yunnan. At the same time the Chengdu warlords sent other emissaries to Guizhou and Yunnan to propose a military alliance against the Protection Army. This kind of double-dealing and double-crossing was typical of warlordism, General Zhu explained. Principle played no role whatsoever. The emissary sent by them to the Protection Army was a young man named Liu Bo-cheng, who thirty years later became known to the Western world as the communist "one-eyed general" and one of the most brilliant revolutionary strategists China had ever produced.

"Men travelled different roads," General Zhu remarked in connection with Liu Bo-cheng. "Some became and remained warlords, some floundered in the swamp of militarism until they found a new revolutionary road, while some who clearly saw the new road were so poisoned by the past that they still remained warlords. Many *Guomindang* military men became new warlords. Both Liu Bo-cheng and I found and followed the new revolutionary road."

---

* The republican army, which had opposed the monarchist plans of Yuan Shi-kai in the Southwest.
† Cai E (1882–1916). One of the leaders of the antimonarchical movement in 1915. He was governor of Sichuan when he died.

2. DISORDER IN THE PROVINCES AT THE TIME OF THE WARLORDS: THE POST OFFICE REPORT FOR THE YEAR 1917

SOURCE: *China Year Book, 1917*, pp. 267–269.

Shanxi. The year opened with improved conditions in Shanxi proper, but these were not maintained. Revolting troops and roving brigands combined, by their lawlessness and depredations, to hamper postal operations. Besides pillaging and burning villages and hamlets, they twice looted Wanquanxian, took Yunghexian, and besieged Linjinxian and Zixian. Couriers were attacked and mails lost, but postage stamps and official funds were in all cases saved. In one case the courier managed successfully to arrest his attacker and bring him to the magistrate. Mail services were seriously affected by the floods in Zhili, mails from other districts being on one occasion delayed for twenty days. Toward the end of the year preventive measures had to be enforced to meet the outbreak of pneumonic plague; the parcel service from the infected area was suspended and the fumigation of mails undertaken at various points. Beginning from June, martial law was declared in the provincial capital, and censorship of mail matter enforced throughout the province. The smuggling of morphia pills under the disguise of anti-opium pills was detected, and twenty-two seizures were made.

Shenxi. The year has been a very bad one from the point of view of postal operations. Bands of *tufei** roamed through the province, plundering and looting, and rendering frequent suspension of the mail services necessary. Towards the end of the year revolting troops added to the chaos by capturing a convoy of 250 camels, with guns and ammunition for Sichuan, which they proceeded to use for an attack on Sian. An attempt on the *dujun*'s life failed, and after two days' fighting the rebel *tufei* combination was driven from the city. Most of the fighting during these two days, however, was in the neighborhood of the Sian head office, making the position of the staff, most of whom were unable to return to their homes, a dangerous one. After leaving Sian, the rebels fled west, looting towns and villages en route. Eight agencies lost practically all their postal funds and private effects. Offices and agencies looted during the year numbered nineteen. Trade is in many parts non-existent, the wealthier traders having removed elsewhere, while the remainder fear to resume business. On almost any of the main roads can be found the walls of what used to be thriving cities, but which are now merely walled enclosures of vacant ground.

3. CHEN DU-XIU: "CALL TO YOUTH"

SOURCE: Published in *Xin Qingnian* (*La Jeunesse*). English translation by Teng Ssu-yu and John K. Fairbank in *China's Response to the West: A*

---

* "Local bandits."

Documentary Survey 1839–1923 (Cambridge, Mass., Harvard University Press, 1954), pp. 240–245.

The Chinese compliment others by saying, "He acts like an old man although still young." Englishmen and Americans encourage one another by saying, "Keep young while growing old." Such is one respect in which the different ways of thought of the East and West are manifested. Youth is like early spring, like the rising sun, like trees and grass in bud, like a newly sharpened blade. It is the most valuable period of life. The function of youth in society is the same as that of a fresh and vital cell in a human body. In the processes of metabolism, the old and the rotten are incessantly eliminated to be replaced by the fresh and the living. . . . If metabolism functions properly in a human body, the person will be healthy; if the old and rotten cells accumulate and fill the body, the person will die. If metabolism functions properly in a society, it will flourish; if old and rotten elements fill the society, then it will cease to exist. . . .

1. Be independent, not servile

All men are equal. Each has his right to be independent, but absolutely no right to enslave others nor any obligation to make himself servile. By slavery we mean that in ancient times the ignorant and weak lost their right of freedom, which was savagely usurped by tyrants. Since the rise of the theories of the rights of man and of equality, no red-blooded person can endure the name of slave. . . .

Emancipation means freeing oneself from the bondage of slavery and achieving a completely independent and free personality. I have hands and feet, and I can earn my own living. I have a mouth and a tongue, and I can voice my own likes and dislikes. I have a mind, and I can determine my own beliefs. I will absolutely not let others do these things on my behalf, nor should I assume an overlordship and enslave others. For once the independent personality is recognized, all matters of conduct, all rights and privileges, and all belief should be left to the natural ability of each person; there is definitely no reason why one should blindly follow others. On the other hand, loyalty, filial piety, chastity and righteousness are a slavish morality. . . .

2. Be progressive, not conservative

"Without progress there will be retrogression" is an old Chinese saying. Considering the fundamental laws of the universe, all things or phenomena are daily progressing in evolution, and the maintenance of the *status quo* is definitely out of the question; only the limitation of man's ordinary view has rendered possible the differentiation between the two states of things. This is why the theory of creative evolution, "L'Evolution créatrice," of the contemporary French philosopher Henri Bergson, has become immensely popular throughout a whole generation. . . . All our traditional ethics, law, scholarship, rites and customs are survivals of feudalism. When compared with the achievement of the white race, there is a difference of a thousand years in thought, although we live in the same period. Revering only the history of the twenty-four dynasties and making no plans for progress and improvement, our people will be turned out of this twentieth-century world, and be lodged in the dark ditches fit only for slaves, cattle and horses. . . . The progress of the world is like that of a fleet horse, galloping and galloping onward. Whatever cannot skilfully change itself and progress along with the world will find itself eliminated by natural selection because of failure to adapt to the environment. Then what can be said to defend conservatism!

3. Be aggressive, not retiring

While the tide of evil is now rushing onward, would it not be rare virtue for one or two self-respecting scholars to retire from the world, to keep themselves clean? But if your aim is to influence the people and establish a new tradition, I suggest that you make further progress from your present high position. It is impossible to avoid the struggle for survival, and so long as one draws one's breath there can be no place where one can retire for a tranquil hermit's life. It is our natural obligation in life to advance in spite of numerous difficulties. Stated in kindly terms, retirement is an action of the superior man in order to get away from the vulgar world. Stated in hostile terms, it is a phenomenon of the weak who are unable to struggle for survival. . . .

4. Be cosmopolitan, not isolationist

Any change in the economic or political life of one nation will usually have repercussions over the whole world, just as the whole body is affected when one hair is pulled. The prosperity or decline, rise or fall of a nation of today depends half on domestic administration, and half on influences from outside the country. Take the recent events of our country as evidence: Japan suddenly rose in power, and stimulated our revolutionary and reform movements; the European War broke out, and then Japan presented her demands to us; is this not clear proof? When a nation is thrown into the currents of the world, traditionalists will certainly hasten the day of its fall, but those capable of change will take this opportunity to compete and progress. . . . A proverb says, "He who builds his cart behind closed gates will find it not suited to the tracks outside the gates." The cart-builders of today not only close their gates, but even want to use the methods contained in the chapter on technology in the *Rites of Chou* for use on the highways of Europe and America. The trouble will be more than not fitting the tracks.

5. Be utilitarian, not formalistic

The social system and the thought of Europe have undergone a change since J. S. Mill's advocacy of utilitarianism in England and Comte's advocacy of positivism in France. . . .

Though a thing is of gold or of jade, if it is of no practical use, then it is of less value than coarse cloth, grain, manure or dirt. That which brings no benefit to the practical life of an individual or of society is all empty formalism and the stuff of cheats. And even though it were bequeathed to us by our ancestors, taught by the sages, advocated by the government and worshiped by society, the stuff of cheats is still not worth one cent.

6. Be scientific, not imaginative

What is science? It is our general concept of matter which, being the sum of objective phenomena as analyzed by subjective reason, contains no contradiction within itself. What is imagination? It first oversteps the realm of objective phenomena, and then discards reason itself; it is something constructed out of thin air, consisting of hypotheses without proof, and all the existing wisdom of mankind cannot be made to find reason in it or explain its laws and principles. There was only imagination and no science in the unenlightened days of old, as well as among the uncivilized peoples of today. Religion, art, and literature were the products of the period of imagination. The contribution of the growth of science to the supremacy of modern Europe over other races is not less than that of the theory of the rights of man. . . . Our physicians know no science; not only are they not acquainted with human anatomy, but also they do not analyze the properties of medicines; as for bacteria and contagious diseases, they have never heard of them. They can only parrot the talk about the five elements, their mutual promotions and preventions, cold and heat, *yin* and *yang*, and prescribe medicine according to ancient formulae. Their technique is practically the same as that of an archer! The height of their marvelous imaginations is the theory of *qi* [primal force], which even extends to the technique of professional strong men and Taoist priests. But though you seek high and low in the universe, you will never know what "primal force" exactly is. All these nonsensical ideas and unreasonable beliefs can be cured at the root only by science. For to explain truth by science means proving everything with fact. Youth, take up the task!

Chapter Three

The May Fourth Movement: *1919–1921*

In 1919 and 1920, many Chinese politicians and observers of Chinese affairs were unaware of the radical changes taking place just beyond their view. The political-military cliques went on blindly fighting for the control of the central government, a ludicrous fiction of a republic increasingly subject to the intrigues and desires of the great powers. So the outbreak of anger among the students on May 4, 1919, and the movement of solidarity which followed (workers' strikes, anti-Japanese boycotts, denunciations of the old culture and the old society), caught them totally off guard. This was a sign of the deep cleavage which set in from then on between the two levels of political life—the new social forces on the one hand and the de facto and *de jure* authorities on the other. May 4 was the climax of the intellectual ferment which had begun in 1915 or even earlier. It was also the start of a movement of growing political awareness which affected mainly young intellectuals but also workers, resulting in the founding of the Communist Party in 1921. For Chinese contemporary historians 1919 is an important date; they regard it as the turning point between the modern (*jindai*) and contemporary (*xiandai*) history of their country.

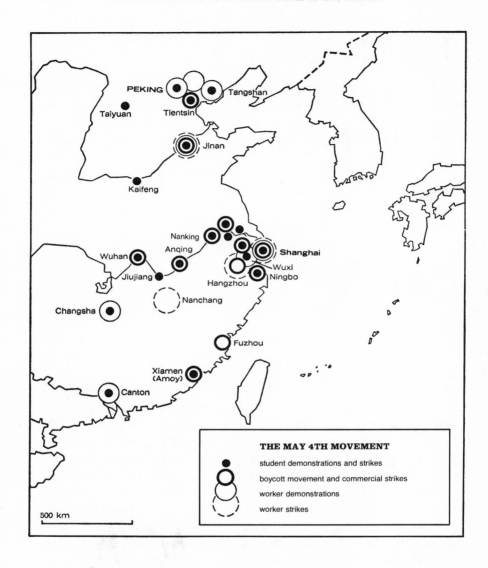

May 1919 and Its Significance

Student demonstrations on May 4

At the beginning of May 1919, the telegraph, which was already operative in all large towns in China, spread the news that the peace treaty just signed in Versailles, bringing World War I to an end, had not taken Chinese claims into account. Germany's rights and privileges in Shandong (its zone of influence, mines and railways, military base at Qingdao) had been transferred to Japan instead of being given back to China. The Westerners had preferred giving Japan satisfaction, thinking they might need an ally willing to bar the way to communism in Asia. They also refused to run the risk of creating a breach in the unequal treaties system by returning to China even a small part of the advantages the powers had won since the Opium Wars.

For months China had been keenly aware of the Shandong question. After the Versailles decision, the Peking students decided to organize a large protest demonstration against Japan and against the members of the government who supported Japan. Several thousand took part on May 4. They marched through the town and vented their anger on three notoriously pro-Japanese politicians, setting fire to the house of one of them, and beating up another. The next day, the Peking Students' Union was officially founded, to organize and spread the movement. The press supported the students, as did the moderate sections of the bourgeoisie (the chambers of commerce, the liberal professions, groups of teachers).

During the next few weeks, student demonstrations spread throughout China; students' unions were founded in the main centers; and the students launched a general boycott of Japanese goods. Cai Yuan-pei, the chancellor of the university, who supported the students, was forced by the authorities to resign; large numbers of people were arrested; and the police put down the student movement with great severity. On May 19, the Peking students went on strike and their example was followed in all the large towns in China.[1]

The spread of the movement in May and June

The repression became harsher at the beginning of June. Martial law was proclaimed in Peking. The Japanese government made official representations to the Chinese government, asking it to put an end to the agitation, and sent marines into the large ports as a show of force. In Peking 1,150 people were arrested between June 3 and 6. In response, the Shanghai merchants, urged on by the local

[1] See document 1, at the end of the chapter.

students, called for a general trade strike. The workers in the large concerns in Shanghai (textiles, transport, tobacco) spontaneously decided to strike to symbolize their solidarity. Over 60,000 workers joined in. In many towns, particularly in South China, merchants and workers went on strike, organized demonstrations and marches, and held meetings. On June 12, the government had to agree to free the students and intellectuals under arrest, dismiss the three ministers originally attacked by the students, and refuse to sign the Treaty of Versailles.

The May Fourth Movement really consisted of two phases; each had a different geographical center of gravity because the political context for each was different, and different sections of society were involved. The first phase took place in Peking, the main Chinese intellectual center; the second, from the beginning of May onward, developed in Shanghai, the main commercial and working class center of the country.

The student agitation and the merchants' and workers' strikes immediately came to an end. The boycott continued throughout the summer, however. "Groups of ten" formed by the students kept a watch on the ports and did not hesitate to search shops. Japanese trade in China was seriously affected.[2]

Political characteristics of the May Fourth Movement

The most popular slogan of the time was "save the country" (*jiu guo*). It was a matter of patriotic protest against the humiliating situation imposed on China, and the powers' encouragement of Japanese ambitions through the peace treaty. But the most original aspect of this national upheaval was that its targets—perhaps for the first time in modern Chinese history—concerned both home and foreign affairs. The demonstrators in Peking stated that their aims were: "externally, struggle for sovereignty" (*wai, zheng guo quan*) and "internally, throw out the traitors" (*nei, chu guo zei*). In other words, the May Fourth political struggle focused simultaneously on denouncing the powers' policy in China and the unequal treaties system, and on criticizing the conservative sections of society which had given in to foreign greed. This conjunction, which twenty years later led Mao Tsetung to define the Chinese revolution as "anti-imperialist" and "antifeudal," was entirely new. The movements for

2 See document 2.

The Central-Government Crisis Worsens

Repression of the May Fourth Movement

The Anfu government acted harshly during the spring and summer of 1919. Thousands of students were arrested. The police scattered demonstrators, and martial law was proclaimed several times. On June 11, 1919, when the movement was virtually over, Chen Du-xiu himself was arrested while distributing a manifesto calling for the dismissal of the Anfu government, the dissolution of the Peking police, and guaranteed freedom of speech and the right to hold meetings. He was not freed until September.

Several government decrees prohibiting the anti-Japanese boycott had only a limited effect, particularly in South China. In November 1919, groups of Japanese civilians and soldiers attacked students organizing the boycott in Fuzhou (capital of Fujian, the province lying opposite the Japanese colony of Taiwan and consequently a de facto Japanese zone of influence). Large numbers were killed and wounded. The Peking government put up no resistance.

In 1920, the anti-Japanese movement flared up again. Japan had proposed opening direct negotiations with Peking on the subject of Shandong. Groups of shopkeepers, businessmen, and students responded by convening an unofficial National Assembly in Peking to get the anti-Japanese campaign under way once more. The police broke up the meeting. The National Association of Chinese Students, heir to the May Fourth Movement, was banned by the police from the French concession of Shanghai, where its headquarters were located. In Fuzhou, as in Shanghai, the weakness of the Peking government was revealed by its acquiescence in acts of repression carried out directly by foreign authorities on Chinese soil.

The fall of the Anfu party

The Anfu party was intensely unpopular. Its representatives in the provinces, including Ni Si-chong in Anhui, Wang Zhan-yuan in Hubei, and Zhang Jing-yao in Hunan, symbolized all the cruelty and greed of the warlords' regime. Two other military cliques wanted to eliminate the Anfu. One was the circle of supporters of the late President Feng Guo-zhang, who died in 1919. They were known as the Zhili clique, for the province surrounding Peking, although their principal base was in the lower Yangzi region. The leaders were General Cao Kun and General Wu Pei-fu. The other was the Fengtian clique (Fengtian was one of the names for the province of Moukden), whose leader, Zhang Zuo-lin, had gradually made himself master of the whole of Manchuria.

The two groups connived to launch an attack in the spring. Xu Shuzheng, one of the most active members of the Anfu clique, commanded the troops in the Northwest and had vast ambitions in Mongolia; his plans worried his neighbor Zhang Zuo-lin. Threatened by a coalition of the Fengtian and Zhili cliques, the President of the Republic agreed to dismiss Xu from office in July. However, when Duan, the head of the Anfu clique, decided to counterattack, war broke out. The troops of the two camps fought several brief battles (July 14 to 18, 1920). Duan was beaten. He withdrew and the power of the Anfu party collapsed, in Peking as well as in most of the provinces.

The Anfu clique succumbed, belatedly, to the popular upsurge of the May Fourth Movement, but the movement did not manage to get Chinese politics to follow a new course. The immediate result of this upsurge of popular forces was merely to facilitate the ambitions of other equally conservative military cliques.

The ambiguities of the new government

The coalition between the two cliques did not last long. Fengtian and Zhili stood for different geographical and political interests: the former controlled the northeastern regions, the latter, the communications between Peking and the middle and lower Yangzi regions. But their ambitions reached beyond this regional framework. They hoped to get their hands on the central government, an additional source of power and profit. This interplay of rival factions in Peking was further complicated by the presence of a civilian clique in the government, the Communications Clique. The head of this group was the banker Liang Shi-yi, Yuan Shi-kai's former secretary.

The new government, whose coming to power was facilitated by the unpopularity of the Anfu clique, made a few tries at winning over public opinion. In October 1920, for example, Wu Pei-fu said a few words of comfort to the miners in the big British coal mines at Tangshan in North China who had been victims in a mining accident. He addressed the miners again in May 1921 when they went on strike. Repressive measures against the left-wing intellectuals and the students who had led the boycott were abandoned.

Nevertheless, the republican government was incapable of carrying out a policy fundamentally different from that of the Anfu clique. It too was merely a coalition of cliques looking for riches and influence, unable to deal with the critical social and political situation into which the country was sinking under the heel of the warlords. It was powerless, for example, in the face of such evils as opium and famine.

Opium and famine

During the years after the war, enforced cultivation of opium and opium traffic did take on disastrous proportions. The international agreement of 1911 which made it illegal from December 31, 1917, on either to trade in foreign opium or to grow opium on Chinese soil was totally disregarded.

A report for the summer of 1921 by the international anti-opium committee gives a detailed account of how the military authorities forced the peasants to give up rice growing and to plant opium instead. That opium was then heavily taxed, eventually sold by the warlord, and finally distributed by peddlers who were often military deserters. This was the case in Guangdong; Fujian; Henan; Anhui; in Guizhou, "which was nothing but a vast poppy field"; in Shenxi, "the worst province of them all"; and in Sichuan, where "the poppy flourished as the troops arrived." The interlopers who swept into the big Chinese ports after the end of World War I, making money in countless different ways (smuggling arms and other surplus equipment abandoned by the armies in Europe, prostitution, and various rackets), also took advantage of the Chinese authorities' weakness and the passivity of the powers; they controlled incoming Persian or Indochinese opium. (For the French colonial government sold opium officially, in spite of the condemnation from the League of Nations; it was one of the three state-owned enterprises on which the financial balance of the colony depended.) Customs seizures of foreign opium, although not very efficiently carried out, showed a steady increase:

Year	Pounds
1917	20,468
1918	26,676
1919	48,375
1920	96,627

The 1920–1921 famine in North China also underlined the total incompetence of the authorities. In 1920, the five provinces of Zhili, Shandong, Henan, Shanxi, and Shenxi (those affected by the terrible famine of 1876–1878) suffered severe drought. The summer and autumn harvests were extremely poor. In 1921, the scanty food reserves in the villages were exhausted. On the basis of incomplete statistics, a Protestant rescue committee estimated that, in 317 *xian* (districts) of the five provinces, 19 million out of 48 million peasants had lost everything. Hundreds of thousands of the more vigorous among them fled to the towns. Leaves and tree bark were used for food. Draft animals were eaten, agricultural tools pawned, and children sold in town, either for work or pleasure. It was estimated that hundreds of thousands died.

The governing warlords were incapable of carrying out a coherent policy to fight the famine. The government did try to impose a customs surtax, for which it had to get permission from the diplomatic corps. To add to the humiliation, the diplomats insisted that six foreigners be added to the six Chinese appointed to administer this special source of aid. But the incompetence of the local administrative structures often prevented the aid from reaching those for whom it was meant.

The gravity of the famine was not just due to the rigors of the climate, the inadequate waterworks, or the crumbling state of the Confucian reserve granaries, but above all to the feudal state of Chinese agriculture. The vast majority of the peasants, living always on the verge of ruin, were at the mercy of any natural disaster that might occur. The warlord government was totally incapable of seeing these problems, let alone resolving them.

Renewal of diplomatic rivalries in China

After their joint victory over Germany, Britain and the United States found themselves confronting Japan in the Pacific. Japan had taken advantage of the war to strengthen its position in China and had penetrated deep into East Siberia as part of its "intervention" in the Soviet revolution. This Japanese advance worried Great Britain and especially the United States, which was going through a period of economic growth.

In spring 1919, the powers made another effort at concerted action. A second international consortium was formed (the first, dating from 1913, had been dissolved by the war). The initiative came from the big American banks, with the collaboration of

British, French, and Japanese financial groups. In the same year a plan was put forward by an American named Baker to establish international control over the Chinese railways. Japan refused to cooperate.

The second consortium existed only on paper. British and American interests conflicted with Japanese interests to such an extent that it was impossible to imagine renewing the 1902 Anglo-Japanese alliance, which had just expired. This conflict with Japan came to a head at the 1922 Washington Conference, which called for a "halt to Japanese expansion."

This was the background against which the Zhili-Fengtian coalition ousted the Anfu clique. The Zhili group belonged to the British clientele in the Far East, and its geographical and political zone of action corresponded to the British zone of influence, stretching from the Yangzi basin to the Tangshan coal mines. The Zhili clique's attack on the Anfu clique in spring 1920 coincided with the return, in full force, of the United States and Britain to the Far East. Because the May Fourth Movement had attacked Japan rather than the principle of domination by the powers, a political-military group connected with the rivals of Japan was more easily accepted.

In 1920, however, Japan would not agree to be excluded. Aware of the unpopularity of the Anfu group, the Japanese disowned it publicly in 1920 and maintained contact with the new government through the Fengtian clique, over whose northeastern domain they had economic control, and through the members of the civilian Communications Clique.

Chinese internal politics were still dominated by the interplay of the economic and diplomatic rivalries of the great powers, as at the time of the struggle between Yuan Shi-kai and Sun Yat-sen. To this state of political dependence was added, as in the past, financial dependence. In 1919, the total official revenue amounted to 231 million dollars; the Chinese government drew 75 million from the salt-tax revenues and 34 million from the customs. In 1920, customs revenues amounted to a total of 49½ million customs taels; the amount paid to the Chinese government was only 20 million Shanghai taels, or less than half. In each case this was the surplus, or what was left over from the revenue of this Chinese public service once the West had claimed the sums due in payment of vast Chinese debts and indemnities. Nearly half the state revenues depended on the good will of the Peking foreign diplomatic corps, because it had to give its assent to unfreeze the customs and salt-tax revenues surplus.

Pressure from Centrifugal Forces

The critical situation of the southern military government

Southern provincial dissent was originally of a political nature. The southern provinces invoked the republican tradition of 1911 and protested against the ludicrous caricature which the Peking regime made of it. However, in 1918, after Sun Yat-sen left, the Canton military government became merely another military faction, under the control of the Guangxi clique (so-called from the poor, mountainous province of the same name). Its leader, Lu Yong-ting, was a former bandit chief affiliated with the Black Flags whose sole aim was to grow rich by fleecing the fertile plains of the neighboring Guangdong.

In June 1919, the Cantonese bourgeoisie had tried to stand up to him by launching the slogan "Canton for the Cantonese" and proposing to have a member of the provincial gentry, Wu Ting-fang, elected provincial governor. The Guangxi clique vetoed it. The authority of the Canton government had also been weakened by the failure of the peace negotiations with the North; the Shanghai talks dragged on throughout the year 1919 and eventually the conference was adjourned, having achieved nothing. The last semblance of authority retained by the military government evaporated when the members of parliament, whom Sun Yat-sen had called to Canton in 1917, left in March 1920 to go to Yunnan, whose *dujun* offered to welcome them for purely demagogic reasons.

In Canton, the Guangxi militarists were thoroughly detested. The time was ripe for a counterattack by Sun Yat-sen and his supporters.

Canton for the Cantonese: Sun Yat-sen returns to Canton

In October 1920, the troops of General Chen Jiong-ming, a Cantonese militant who had joined in the republican revolution and had been fighting on the Fujian border for several years, returned to Canton and called Sun Yat-sen back.

Chen's slogan was the provincial "Canton for the Cantonese" (*Yue ren zhi Yue*), echoing the federalist movement which was extremely strong in China in 1920. He had the support of all the Guangdong gentry, who were weary of the Guangxi clique's exactions.

This new Cantonese government, however, was based on another political force as well: Sun Yat-sen's Nationalists, who had reorganized their party in 1919 and once again called it Guomindang, as they had in 1912. Abandoning the narrow scope of the Zhonghua gemingdang of 1914, which was inspired by the secret societies, the Nationalists restated their determination to make China a modern, democratic country on the basis of the "three people's principles." Their political authority had also been strengthened by the founding of the periodical *Jianshe* (*Reconstruction*) in the summer of 1919. The May Fourth Movement had caught Sun Yat-sen's supporters unprepared, but had shown them the political strength of the left-wing journals. They had learned from their mistaken lack of interest in ideological struggles, and, from then on, the participation of the foremost intellectuals in the party—Hu Han-min, Liao Zhong-kai, and Zhu Zhi-xin—gained them a real audience for *Jianshe* among young intellectuals.

Only a fragile political connection existed between the national progressivism of the Guomindang, for which Canton was a base for broader actions, and the regionalism of Chen Jiong-ming, who merely wanted to re-establish order in his province. Yet both sides agreed in April 1921 to elect Sun Yat-sen President of the Republic in accordance with the 1912 constitution, which was brought back again (thanks to the votes of the itinerant parliament members who had returned to Canton). The new Canton government set out to be progressive; Chen Du-xiu, who was already openly Marxist, was appointed education commissioner. The mayor of Canton, Sun Fo, who was Sun Yat-sen's son, launched a vast town-planning program. But the latent disagreement between the allies would burst out in the open in 1922.

The federalist movement

What Chen Jiong-ming was doing in Canton was part of a much broader movement. Many Chinese, tired of interprovincial warfare and disappointed by the unfit centralized government in Peking, longed to transform their country into a federation of independent provinces (*liansheng zizhi*). In 1920 and 1921 many periodicals campaigned for this program, which, paradoxically, was also supported by intellectuals of the extreme left, moderates like Liang Qi-chao and his group, and even some warlords. Although the federalist movement was only a flash in the pan, its complexity lends it interest.

The complicated ideological foundations of federalism

For left-wing intellectuals, federalism was above all a tactical withdrawal. They hoped that in a more modest provincial setting the radical ideas they had not managed to impose on China as a whole might triumph. "Don't criticize us for being concerned only with Shandong . . ." ran an editorial in *Xin Shandong* (*New Shandong*); "on the one hand we will build a new Shandong and on the other we will unite with our compatriots to build a new China."

As Kang You-wei and Liang Qi-chao had done in 1898, the republicans in 1911, and some of the leading members of the May Fourth Movement (like Hu Shi) in 1921, the moderates again looked to the West for a federalist example. They studied American constitutional theories on the respective rights of states and the federal authority, and analyzed the examples of Switzerland and Brazil. Finally, the federalist movements probably had the support of the anarchists, who still exerted considerable influence in China in 1920 to 1921; the emphasis on local power was right in the tradition of Bakunin's polemicizing in 1860 against Marx's centralist approach.

Social and political bases of federalism

The idea of federalism was popular with intellectuals, the radicals as much as the moderates. Its chief support within Chinese society, though, came from the rural gentry and provincial merchants. As the country gradually sank into chaos, they restricted their ambitions more than ever to their native regions. Slogans like "Canton for the Cantonese" were taken up in many other provinces: "Hunan for the Hunanese," "Sichuan for the Sichuanese," "Hubei for the people of Hubei," for example. This gentry particularism was strongest in South China, where the provinces were most clearly defined, the regional economy more lively (due especially to the importance of water routes), and there was a long-standing tradition of political independence.

Politically, the Guomindang around 1920 and 1921 seems to have been deeply involved in several attempts at independence, particularly in Hunan, Hubei, and Shenxi. Sun Yat-sen's return to Canton and his espousal of provincialism was part of a more far-reaching plan. His goal was to strengthen the Nationalist position in various provinces, before envisaging a return to power in the country as a whole. The intellectuals of the Guomindang took an active part in this campaign for federalist ideas. One of them, Wang Zheng-ting, the author of the 1912 republican constitution, made drafts for independent constitutions at the request of several provinces.

However, the federalist movement came to a sudden halt because the civilians behind it, whatever their political allegiance or their social origins, were powerless in the face of the de facto military power established in the provinces.

Provincialism and military power

After Yuan Shi-kai's death the scourge of militarism grew steadily worse. There were exactions and depredations of all sorts. Trains were requisitioned, and coolies were levied by force. Traffic in arms and opium was rife. Actual military operations were carried out and whole towns were sacked. The paradox of the federalist movement was that it voiced the general protest at this scourge but in the end nevertheless helped the warlords, who wanted to strengthen their power in the provinces.

An examination of the situation in several representative provinces shows clearly how the attempts at independence backed by the politically active people failed, and how the provincialist slogans were seized on by the *dujun*, whose intrigues still dominated the Chinese political scene.

Hunan

When the provincial governor appointed by the Anfu clique was driven out in the summer of 1920, his adversary Tan Yan-kai, a politician who had been extremely active in the province since 1911, immediately took up the slogan of independence for Hunan. After a few months, personal rivalries led to his making way for the warlord Zhao Heng-ti (born in 1880), who continued the same policy. Zhao proclaimed the independence of the province of Hunan. He even got experts to draw up a provincial constitution, the text of which was submitted to the gentry in each district for discussion and was eventually promulgated in January 1922.

Zhao was skillful enough to obtain support from the Hunanese gentry (through the provincial assembly) as well as from left-wing intellectuals, and he even reached into the realm of the workers. The radical Hunan Students' Association started the slogan "A Monroe doctrine for Hunan," suggesting that the province should remain outside the struggle between North and South just as Monroe's United States remained outside the conflict between the absolutist and the liberal blocks in Europe. Mao Tsetung afterward told Edgar Snow how much the idea had attracted him. The Hunan Workers' Association, which was aligned with the anarchists, also backed Hunanese provincialism. In March 1921, it went so far as to organize a protest strike against the possible transfer of Changsha's main factory, declared to be the "property of thirty million Hunanese," to merchants from Hubei. The break between the warlord and left-wing groups came in 1922, when the warlord used force to put down the student movement and the workers' movement.

Sichuan

In this province the federalist movement also had some initial support from radical intellectuals of the May Fourth Movement. In April 1921, under the leadership of Wu Yu-zhang, a veteran of the Sichuan republican movement who later became one of the early members of the Communist Party, these intellectuals founded a Union for the Independence of Sichuan. Its modernist program called for democratic rights, the equality of the sexes, and the development of industrial cooperatives. However, the movement for independence in Sichuan became merely an instrument of propaganda for the two leading militarists in the province, Liu Xiang and Xiong Ke-wu. In the summer of 1920 they drove out the Yunnan troops led by Tang Ji-yao and ruined his plans for a "Greater Yunnan." When the left-wing intellectuals realized that their situation was highly ambiguous, they decided to dissolve the Union for Independence.

The theme of Sichuan provincialism from then on only served the ambitions and intrigues of the *dujun*. Liu Xiang ousted Xiong Ke-wu in spring 1921 in the name of provincial independence, only to find himself confronted with several small cliques of condottieri with footholds in different parts of Sichuan.

Hubei

In spring 1921, a rebellion broke out against the domination of the Anfu governor, Wang Zhan-yuan. The rebels claimed to be federal-ists (*Chu ren zhi Chu*, "Natives of Hubei should govern Hubei") and were led by the Guomindang militants, who were known and esteemed in the province for their role in the 1911 revolution. A provisional provincial government was established. Its leaders were in contact with the group supporting Hunanese independence and also with the Sichuanese militarist Liu Xiang, another upholder of independence for the provinces. The Zhili clique, which came to power in Peking in 1920, did not want to run the risk of losing control of the region, the heart of Central China's network of railways and waterways. So General Wu Pei-fu's northern troops easily stamped out the federalist troops in the 1921 "war to rescue Hubei."

Zhejiang

The special position of this coastal province—away from any main economic axis or great political upheavals—explains why, after the war between the Anfu and Zhili cliques, it was the only one still to have a governor from the Anfu faction. The governor, Lu Yong-xiang, was aware of the precariousness of his position and tried to strengthen it by championing Zhejiang's independence. He announced the creation of a constitutional committee, which was to draw up a constitution based on that of Hunan. The text, with its complicated clauses, bore the stamp of lawyers who knew more about Western law than the real social situation in China. Though formally adopted in September 1921, it hardly changed the real structure of military power in Zhejiang.

Shenxi

This still more outlying province had a special place in the Chinese geopolitical system; it was a zone for withdrawal and observation, a possible base for launching attacks on North China as a whole. It was no mere coincidence that it provided the Chinese Communists with their chief bastion (Yanan) after 1934.

In the summer of 1921, a militant nationalist from the province, Yu You-ren, launched a movement for the independence of Shenxi, supported by a "Citizens' Assembly." For the Guomindang, the operation had strategic as well as political interest. Shenxi, where Sun Yat-sen had looked for support in 1911 and again in 1916, offered the Canton dissidents a possible base for diversionary operations in the North, as well as for taking their enemy in the rear.

Toward the Founding of the Communist Party

The progress of Marxism

Initially, Marxism was only one of the many ideologies which aroused passionate interest among the young radical intellectuals of the May Fourth Movement. However, its influence was strengthened by the prestige of the Soviet Union, a growing interest in the workers' movement, and the development of the idea of a revolutionary party. In 1919 and 1920, Marxist ideas spread across China. The *Communist Manifesto* was translated, as was *Utopian Socialism and Scientific Socialism* by Engels, and *The Class Struggle* by Kautsky. Study groups were formed, which already tried to link a deeper study of Marxist theory with everyday political activity; the Society for the Study of Socialism was formed in Peking followed by the Society for the Study of Marxist Theory, while the Awakening Society appeared in Tientsin, the New Study Society in Canton, and the Literary Study Society in Hunan.

On the other hand, some intellectuals were interested in Marxism only at a purely intellectual level. They thought it preferable to go through a long period of propagating the ideology and engaging in the theoretical study before using Marxism and communism as political forces capable of transforming Chinese society. This tendency to "legal Marxism" slowed down activity in the Communist Party during the first stage of its existence.

The prestige of Soviet Russia and its actions in China

The October Revolution broke the common front of the powers profiting from the unequal treaties. On July 25, 1919, Georgy Chicherin, the minister of foreign affairs of the Moscow government, publicly renounced the privileges held by Tsarist Russia in China: the Russian concessions in Hankou and Tientsin, extraterritoriality, Russian participation in the running of the customs and the salt tax, and the Russian share in the Boxer indemnity. The Russian railway in East China was promptly transferred to "international" (Western) control, one more operation in the powers' armed intervention in Siberia during 1918 to 1919. The Karakhan Declaration produced a lively response in China, not only among the left-wing

intellectuals but also in bourgeois circles. Sun Yat-sen and his supporters were particularly impressed. Russia already appeared as a
potential ally.

The new Soviet government, in turn, was aware of China's importance in the face of Western and Japanese encirclement. The
Asian "semi-colonies," countries under Western economic control
whose nominal independence assured them some measure of political freedom, provided the Russians with a possibility of dealing with
some countries that were not as totally hostile as the capitalist
West. Turkey under Mustapha Kemal, Persia under Rezah Chah,
and the China of the warlords all fell into this category.

Consequently, representatives of the Soviet government, with
orders to gain at least the opening of trade relations, and delegates
from the Comintern, who came to look into the possibility of im-
planting sections of the Communist International in China, visited
the country in 1920. The chief Comintern delegate, Voitinsky,
probably met Li Da-zhao in Peking and Chen Du-xiu in Shanghai
in spring 1920. As a result of these first contacts, a Chinese Comintern office was opened in Irkutsk in April 1921, to which Li Da-zhao
sent young Chinese associates, and which maintained contact with
the first Communist groups in China.

The first Communist groups

The decisive passage from Marxist study groups to militant political organization may be said to have taken place in the summer
of 1920. This new stage grew out of both an internal process (the
radicalization of one of the currents of May Fourth) and an external
process (stimulation by the Soviet revolution). The two processes,
however, cannot be compared, nor even less the influence each had
be fully gauged. What counts rather for the historian is the close
connection between them. Even so, contemporary Soviet historians
naturally tend to stress the role of the first Comintern delegates,
particularly since the Sino-Soviet break in 1960. Chinese historians,
on the other hand, emphasize the maturation of Marxism inside the
country from May 4 onward.

The Communist group in Shanghai apparently first called itself
a party in the summer of 1920 and, what is more, formed a central
committee. Probably because such groups' numbers were very small,
and their political orientation still uncertain, writers of the official
Chinese Communist history later preferred to call them "cells"

(*xiao zu*) and to set the official founding of the Chinese Communist Party at July 1921. The Shanghai group was led by Chen Du-xiu, and *New Youth* became its official organ. One of its initiatives, apart from approaching workers, was to create a Socialist Youth Corps, which organized Russian lessons and from whose ranks came Liu Shao-qi, one of its first militants.

Other small groups which also called themselves Communist were formed in autumn 1920 in Peking under the leadership of Li Da-zhao; in Canton when Chen Du-xiu went there as education commissioner in the new constitutionalist government; in Changsha (Mao was one of its first members); and in Jinan, Tientsin, and Wuhan.

Left-wing eclecticism, which was a feature of the May Fourth Movement, was still to some extent a characteristic of the ideology of the early Communist groups. Among their members were to be found Marxists, who were still very inexperienced; anarchists (particularly in Hunan, Canton, and Peking); Guomindang left-wing intellectuals (particularly in Shanghai); and Socialist guild members who were supporters of Liang Qi-chao (also in Shanghai). At the end of 1920, the Shanghai Communist group ("party") began to publish a theoretical journal, *Gongchangdang* (*The Communist Party*), probably to start the process of ideological clarification. The first issue appeared on November 7, 1920, as a symbolic gesture of affiliation with the Soviet revolution. The journal concerned itself mainly with ideological problems, which to a large extent took the form of a long and lively controversy with the anarchists. It also translated numerous articles on theory or current affairs coming from Moscow, as well as from the American Communist Party. On the other hand, it didn't emphasize the link between this effort toward an education in theory and international affairs and the concrete social and political struggles then going on in China.

Another Communist group was formed by Chinese students in Tokyo in 1920, and another in Paris, led by Zhou En-lai and Li Li-san.

Contacts between the workers and the Communist groups

The principle that the industrial proletariat takes the leading role in the revolutionary struggle is an essential part of Marxist doctrine, so the young Communist intellectuals naturally sought to make contact with the workers' movement. In addition to such ideologically inspired motives, there was the fact that the years following the May Fourth Movement in China were years marked by outbreaks of protest strikes and even union action. A partial estimate shows 66 strikes in 1919, 46 in 1920, and 50 in 1921. The most important of these were staged by workers in the Shanghai cotton mills and silk-spinning mills, by dockers, by Canton machinists, by miners in the coal mines of the British firm KMA at Tangshan in the North, and by railway workers on several railway lines. Most of the strikes were spontaneous, but some may have been due to trade union organizations of moderate political persuasion. This was certainly true in the case of the machinists' strike in Canton.

From the beginning, the Communist groups made great efforts to reach workers through the press. They issued several short publications addressed to the workers, described how they were being exploited, published their letters, and opened political prospects to them. The most important of these publications was *Laodong jie* (*Labor World*), nineteen issues of which appeared in Shanghai in the latter half of 1920.[4]

Several times, Communist intellectuals attempted to make direct contact with the workers and help them get organized. Those in Peking started an evening school for the railway workers of Changxindian, the main depot on the Peking-Hankou line. Those in Shanghai created a workers' club in the suburb of Xiaoshadu for cotton mill workers. Those in Hankou helped the rickshaw coolies start a trade union, which led an important strike at the beginning of 1921. Those in Changsha, including Mao Tsetung, cooperated with an anarchist-oriented trade union, the Hunan Workers' Association.

The celebration of May 1, for the first time in China, was a symbol of this awakening of the working world. In 1920, May Day was celebrated by only seven workers' organizations of moderate views, while *New Youth* devoted a special issue to the problems of industrial work. In 1921, May Day was observed in Shanghai by the Communists and the moderate trade unionists jointly.

The first congress of the Chinese Communist Party

The congress for the founding of the Chinese Communist Party was held in Shanghai sometime in July 1921 (the sources do not

---

[4] See document 4.

agree on the exact date). It was attended by twelve delegates representing seven of the little Communist groups created in 1920, which are traditionally held to have had fifty-seven members. The Paris group was the only one not represented. The twelve did not include either Li Da-zhao, who was unable to leave Peking, or Chen Du-xiu, who was then in Canton. Those who were later to become most famous were Zhang Guo-tao, the Peking delegate, Mao Tsetung, the delegate from Hunan, and Dong Bi-wu, the delegate from Hankou. A delegate from the Communist International was also present—Maring (alias H. Sneevliet), a Dutchman who was very familiar with the Far East and had witnessed the birth of the Indonesian Communist Party the year before at Batavia.

The first sessions were held in a house in Shanghai's French concession. Disturbed by the police, the delegates moved from there to Zhejiang, near the tourist center of Hangzhou; there they completed their work on board a pleasure boat. Lively discussions took place, in spite of the fact that the delegates were both few in number and not very representative. Neither the group advocating "legal Marxism" (main efforts to be concentrated on the propagation of Marxist ideology) nor the left-wing group (advocating an immediate struggle for the dictatorship of the proletariat and refusing to cooperate with other intellectuals in nonclandestine work) managed to prevail. Other discussions referred to cooperation with Sun Yat-sen and the Guomindang. The congress was frankly opposed to this, although Maring, in line with the Theses on the National and Colonial Questions adopted in 1920 at the Second Congress of the Comintern, advocated a more flexible position.

The congress decided to found the Communist Party as a clandestine revolutionary organization, with Chen Du-xiu as secretary-general. To make its special mission with regard to the workers more concrete and effective, the congress decided simultaneously to set up under its control a legal organization, the Trade Union Secretariat, which was to stir up the workers' struggles and help organize trade unions. Its headquarters were at Shanghai, and Zhang Guo-tao was placed in charge. The Secretariat also had help from provincial offices. Mao Tsetung, for example, was in charge of the Hunan office.

The Chinese Communist Party introduced a totally new element into Chinese political life. Whereas other political parties (the Guomindang, small groups of 1912) looked to the West for an example (both in ideology and forms of organization), the Chinese Communist Party drew its inspiration from the October Revolution,

Marxist ideology, and from the Leninist conception of the party as the vanguard of the revolution.

This party, which assigned the chief role in the revolution to the proletariat, was nevertheless founded by twelve young intellectuals. They were determined to direct their work mainly toward the workers in the large towns, with whom they had already established contacts before July 1921. This was why the congress was held in Shanghai, the main Chinese industrial center. The peasants, on the other hand, hardly mattered to them at that time, even though several of them had come from the countryside.

The Chinese Communist Party was heir to the May Fourth Movement and therefore associated from the start with the whole Chinese national movement. However, it was free of any social-democratic influence. Unlike the Western Communist parties, it was not born of a difficult scission from the Socialist movement, for the latter scarcely existed in China before the First World War. Its great problem would be to define itself in relation to the national non-Communist current, and not, as in the West, in relation to the Socialist parties and trade unions.

ADDITIONAL BIBLIOGRAPHY

Jean Chesneaux, *The Chinese Labor Movement, 1919–1927* (Stanford, Calif., Stanford University Press, 1968).

Jean Chesneaux, "Le Mouvement fédéraliste en Chine," *Revue Historique*, October 1966.

Chow Tse-tsung, *The May Fourth Movement: Intellectual Revolution in Modern China* (Cambridge, Mass., Harvard University Press, 1960).

Maurice Meisner, *Li Ta-chao and the Origins of Chinese Marxism* (Cambridge, Mass., Harvard University Press, 1967).

Benjamin I. Schwartz, *Chinese Communism and the Rise of Mao* (Cambridge, Mass., Harvard University Press, 1951).

DOCUMENTS

1. "MANIFESTO FOR A GENERAL STRIKE," ADOPTED BY THE STUDENT UNION IN PEKING AT A MEETING ON MAY 18, 1919

SOURCE: Chow Tse-tsung, *The May Fourth Movement* (Cambridge, Mass., Harvard University Press, 1960), pp. 139–140.

"Externally preserve our sovereignty and internally eliminate the traitors!" This is the repeated demand we students make of the government and the incessant call to our fellow citizens since the May Fourth Incident. There has been no response, only some added mis-

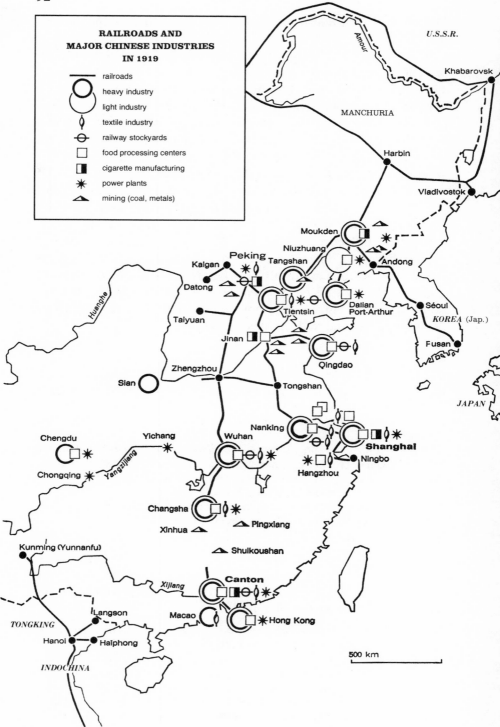

RAILROADS AND MAJOR CHINESE INDUSTRIES IN 1919

- railroads
- heavy industry
- light industry
- textile industry
- railway stockyards
- food processing centers
- cigarette manufacturing
- power plants
- mining (coal, metals)

U.S.S.R.

Khabarovsk

MANCHURIA

Harbin

Vladivostok

Moukden

Niuzhuang

Andong

Kalgan   Peking   Tangshan

Datong

Tientsin   Dalian
Port-Arthur   Séoul

Talyuan   KOREA (Jap.)

Jinan   Fusan

Zhengzhou

Sian   Tongshan   Qingdao

JAPAN

Nanking

Chengdu   Yichang   Wuhan   Shanghai

Chongqing   Ningbo

Hangzhou

Changsha

Xinhua   Pingxiang

Shuikoushan

Kunming (Yunnanfu)

Xijiang   Canton

TONGKING   Langson   Macao   Hong Kong

Hanoi   Haiphong

INDOCHINA

500 km

chief. We have focussed our appeal on the Shandong question. Yet the government at this critical moment fails to take a firm stand against signing the peace treaty which summarily rejects the Chinese request. Instead, it breaks off the internal peace conference in Shanghai, a move that will help the enemy. We are deeply distressed at this situation. Secondly, we are disappointed to observe that the government, ignoring public opinion, refuses the blackmail resignations of Cao Ru-lin, Zhang Zong-xiang and Lu Zong-yu, whose execution has been demanded by the whole nation, and instead publicly praises them while dismissing Minister Fu.* It is also predicted that educational circles will undergo thorough and severe discipline. If this is true, what an inconceivable disaster to the nation it will be! Thirdly, we are dumbfounded that the government in its two orders of May 14th prohibits by threat of armed force public meetings and student intervention in government policies and suppresses all expression of patriotic conscience, whereas it turns a deaf ear to the news of the arrests of Chinese students by the Japanese police in Tokyo. We students have to have clear minds in order to pursue our studies; now our minds are confused by these grave disappointments. We resolve to start a general strike on May 19th to continue until we are satisfied with the settlement of the above-mentioned matters. During the period of the strike, we shall abide by the resolutions set forth in our telegram of May 14th: first, to organize a Peking Student Volunteer Corps for the Defense of Shandong to concern itself with the potential national emergency; second, to establish units in schools to spread popular education by public speeches and awaken the people to the importance of nationhood; third, to organize in schools Groups of Ten for the maintenance of order to lessen the danger to our country; fourth, to make more extensive study of the economy in order to benefit our country. We students have been educated and self-cultivated for so long that we will advisedly follow our national traits of wisdom, virtue, and courage and will not by exceeding accepted rules of action shame our national history. We shall behave according to our own natural ability and innate knowledge, and do not care whether you understand or censure us at the present but wait for the judgement of posterity.

2. THE PEKING STUDENTS ORGANIZE THE ANTI-JAPANESE BOYCOTT IN MAY 1919

SOURCE: A letter from W. R. Giles, an American correspondent in China, to G. E. Morrison, dated July 1, 1919. From Lo Hui-min, ed., *The Correspondence of G. E. Morrison* (Cambridge, Cambridge University Press, 1975–1976), vol. II, letter no. 935.

When I got back to Peking, I found things in their usual state of chaos and uncertainty. The cabinet was again on the verge of being

---

* Minister of education, accused by his colleagues of tolerance toward the students.

wrecked on account of the activities of the pro-Japanese organization, the Anfu Club, the latter being supported by the military clique. A few days before my return it became known that the Peace Conference had determined to hand over Germany's Shandong concessions to Japan. This was the cause of the present boycott against the Japanese. All the educational institutions struck, formed processions and marched around the city. They intended to hold a mass meeting in the Central Park, but the police and military drove them back and made numerous arrests. This was the greatest mistake the government could have made, for if the students had been allowed to hold the meeting they would not have had the opportunity of making themselves martyrs. A large crowd of the students then went to the residence of Tsao Ju-lin,* Lu Chung-yu† and another pro-Jap official and began hunting for the owners. Tsao managed to escape unhurt, and Lu was wounded as he was escaping.

During the next few days excited students could be seen in small parties in every street of Peking, working themselves into a state of delirium by telling the passers by of the indignities being thrust upon them through the fault of the pro-Japanese members of the Cabinet, whom they rightly stated were nothing more than the paid agents of Japan. The Government tried to get them to go back to their schools but with no success. They eventually camped outside of the Presidential Palace until he saw fit to see their representatives, which finally he was forced to do. These men demanded the dismissal of Tsao Ju-lin and Lu Chung-yu, and further that the Government should not sign the Peace Treaty without reservations concerning Shandong. So strong had their movement become, the Chambers of Commerce and merchants suporting them, that the President finally accepted the resignation of Tsao Ju-lin and Lu, who had tendered their resignation . . .

But to come back to the boycott. This movement is the strongest move of its kind that the Chinese have made. The *Tatsu Maru* and the 1915 boycotts sink into insignificance beside it. Not only has it spread all over China, but in Australia, Singapore, Hongkong, Vladivostok, and even as far as America. Already it has caused great alarm in Japan. This boycott is different to all others. On previous occasions it has been the Chinese merchants who have been the mainstay of such attempts, but this time it is the *consumer* who is carrying it on. The students not only shamed the people into a refusal to purchase Japanese goods, but each one of them took a certain part of a street and explained why they should not. Another thing the students did was to show the people and merchants that there were articles made in China equal to those of the Japanese, if not better, and that they would be encouraging their own industrial expansion by purchasing them. Lectures are being given all over the country encouraging manufacturers and merchants to open up new industries, with the

* Cao Ru-lin.
† Lu Zong-yu.

result that millions of dollars have been collected to start making articles which have heretofore been purchased from Japan. It will not surprise me if this boycott within the next eighteen months does not cost the Japanese four hundred million dollars. A member of the Japanese Legation told me that the *Tatsu Maru* boycott cost them over two hundred million dollars. Basing my estimate on that I think you will agree with me that I am not overstating the case.

3. LI DA-ZHAO FORESEES A RADICAL REORGANIZATION OF SOCIETY FROM A VERTICAL ORGANIZATION TO A HORIZONTAL ONE

SOURCE: Huang Sung-Kang, *Li Da-zhao and the Impact of Marxism on Modern Chinese Thinking* (The Hague, Mouton, 1965), pp. 60–61.

Formerly society was organized vertically, while we now require society to be organized horizontally. Vertical organized society was one in which the upper class and the lower class stood in opposition to each other, while the society we now require is one of equal partners which does away with class inequality. The former society was one in which force dominated, while the society we now demand is one in which love will be the cementing force.

Take politics as an example. In former times, subjects were subordinated to the king, people were ruled over by officials, local districts were governed by the central authority; it was a vertical organization. Now the people have united to form a horizontal organization and to overthrow the power of kings and officials, and all the local areas have united to resist the concentration of power in the central authority.

As for economics. In former times, the rich hired the poor, capital robbed labour, and the landlords enslaved the tenants; it was a vertical organization. Nowadays, the working class, the proletariat unite to form a horizontal organization to resist the rich and powerful class and the capitalist class.

As for society. In former times, those who worked with their intellect were honoured and those who worked with their hands were despised; the gentry, the nobility and men were exalted whereas the country-folk, the ordinary people and women were debased—it was a vertical organization. Now the class of manual workers are united to resist the class of mental workers, the class of country-folk against the gentry class, the class of women against the class of men.

As for the family. In former days, the patriarch governed the family, father and elders ruled sons and the younger ones, husbands lorded it over their wives—it was a vertical organization. Nowadays, sons and youngsters want to shake off the power of the patriarchs, wives want to shake off the power of their husbands, they walk out from their families to join youth and women's organizations which are of the horizontal type.

The primary cause of this change is the economic change. The old economic organization was vertical; accordingly all social organizations are following this trend and moving towards horizontal structures.

The tendency of today's world is that the vertical organizations decline all the time while the horizontal organizations are increasing and expanding every day. Even in China, all kinds of people's autonomous groupings begin to take shape. In the future, students, teachers, merchants, workers, peasants, women and every kind of occupation will have their own organizations, these organizations will eventually transcend national boundaries and join great world associations, and all these will be united into a great horizontal world confederation. In this confederation, every person will be free and all will be equal; love and mutual aid will prevail: such will be the prospect of the Great Unity.

In a vertical organization, the personality of the oppressed lower class is restricted, trodden upon, humiliated and ill-treated by those who set themselves in the position of the upper class, so that the personality of the lower class people is entirely sacrificed for the sake of the upper class. But when there is a horizontal organization, the persons of the lower class can unite and become a great force against the powerful class of the vertical organization and restore the dignity of their personalities. Thus we can see our liberation movement is a movement aiming at the overthrow of vertically organized society, and our reconstruction movement is a movement aiming at the establishment of a horizontally organized society.

The basis of a vertical organization is force, while the basis of a horizontal organization is love. Our supreme ideal consists in freeing all human relations from force and basing them purely on love, so that the totality of human life will not be based on strife but purely on love.

4. A SHANGHAI METALWORKER BECOMES AWARE OF THE STRENGTH OF THE WORKERS' MOVEMENT

SOURCE: *Laodong jie* (*Labor World*) (Shanghai, September 26, 1920). Translated from the French version in Jean Chesneaux, *Les Syndicats chinois* (Paris, Mouton, 1965), pp. 108–111.

We, the workers' minority, must unite with the great majority of workers who speak and live like us, to form a large group. Our group must then unite with other groups to form a great group for the whole of China! This great group for the whole of China must unite with great groups from other countries, to form a great group for the whole world! Whatever it may be, a world group, a Chinese group, or a workers' group, our workers' minority must take the first step. But three points are important for our workers' minority.

The first is to be thoroughly familiar with our own situation. Dear brother workers! When this moment comes, all the mists and heavy clouds will vanish, all the hells and prisons will be abolished, all the chains of class will be broken. This wave will be more terrible and rapid than the waters of the Huanghe which come down from the sky;

no man, no matter who he is, will be able to hold this water back, or keep it in place so as to make it rise back up from the earth to the sky. The workers' movement is a swifter and more terrible wave than the waters of the Huanghe. The society of the future must be made into a workers' society. The world of the future must be made into a workers' world. Those who are not workers will not be able to live in a society, a China, a world of workers. We will send them away from the earth, have them go look for their means of subsistence in Heaven. Dear brother workers! Russia is already a workers' Russia. Italy will soon be a workers' Italy, and England a workers' England too. The wave will reach China soon. We are the masters of the wave, and as masters of the wave we must create a workers' China. But are we going to understand this point properly?

Secondly, we must carry on the work of uniting. If we want to create a workers' China, the workers must first be united. This unity can exist amid a minority, in a group, in a village, in a town, in our country, in the world, in a profession, in an industry. Let us occupy the houses we build! Let us eat the rice we grow! Let us wear the silk we spin and the clothes we sew! They must not be handed over to the good-for-nothings who live in them, eat and wear them without work-ing! Let us take charge of the railways we build! Let us sail the ships we build! Let us take up the arms we cast! Let us occupy the fac-tories we build! They must not be handed over to the robber-governments, to the robber-capitalists who run them by force, sail them by force, take them by force, and occupy them by force! It is not only that they earn money with little outlay, the worst of it is that they maltreat us, we at whose expense they earn their money cheaply. To think we work nine, twelve, or fifteen hours a day! To think we receive one *jiao* and a few cents, or two or three *jiao* a day, and that we are reduced to clothing ourselves, eating and living in a loathsome manner. From every point of view, our suffering could not be worse. In this situation I am overcome and shed tears. Mustn't we unite on a large scale to settle the issues of working hours and wages first of all, and then to settle all these issues: "live there ourselves," "eat it ourselves," "sail them ourselves," "take them into our own hands," "occupy them ourselves"? But if we do not achieve unity, we will not have the strength to do it.

Thirdly, we must show our enthusiasm. The best thing we workers can do is to work on the one hand, and unite on the other. To work is every man's destiny, to unite is the instrument of success. It is the unchangeable principle for our whole lives, thanks to which we will be able to act in a positive way.

Signed: Li Zhong, worker in the Shanghai arsenal

Conclusion:
1885—1921

From the first Opium War to the mid-1880s, China was embroiled in conflicts with the great powers and slowly penetrated by Western capitalism. Yet China's traditional culture and society remained basically intact. During the next half century, from the 1880s to the founding of the Chinese Communist Party, however, Chinese society was shaken to its very foundations, both from within and without. The historical conditions which prepared the way for the Chinese revolution in the twentieth century, and for the victory of the Chinese Communists after 1949, were gradually emerging: the growing weight of imperialism and the development of the national movement, superficial modernization, and the continuation of the ago-old opposition between peasants and landlords.

The pressure exerted on China by the great powers and the big foreign interests grew steadily stronger after 1885: the Sino-Japanese War, the 1896–1898 scramble for the concessions involving the "breakup" of China, the Boxer crisis, the first consortium, the Twenty-one Demands, the crisis of World War I, and the second consortium. New privileges were added to the political advantages acquired by the powers at the time of the Opium Wars (extraterritoriality, concessions, control of the customs): permanent military bases on Chinese soil ("leased territories"), the right to station troops in certain areas, and the extension of foreign control over a certain number of state services (customs, salt tax, post office). To this partial dismemberment of Chinese sovereignty was added economic control: zones of influence, financial subordination, foreign control over important sections of the railways, mines, and industry. Foreign domination translated itself into exploitation, profit (hard to evaluate, especially since those concerned took precautions), but also into a deeply engraved humiliation in the Chinese collective consciousness.

For these reasons, the national movement gained strength throughout this period and finally caused the Westerners serious worry. At first it took the form of a series of unconnected, episodic, and specific demonstrations with no consequences: the Boxer Uprising and the other antimissionary movements; the primitive Luddism of peasants, who destroyed the machinery in their factories; the 1905 anti-American boycott (when the prohibition against Chinese immigration to the United States was renewed); the 1908 anti-Japanese boycott (the *Tatsu-Maru* affair); and the movement for the protection of the railways in the summer of 1911. But from the First World War on, the national movement became more coherent in its political analyses, more firmly rooted in the various levels of society, and more capable of fighting bigger battles. The movement against the Twenty-one Demands in 1915, and that against the Nishihara loans and the Japanese semiprotectorate in China in 1918, heralded the May Fourth Movement and had the same characteristics: energetic voicing of popular emotion, the combination of struggles in domestic politics with protest against foreign dangers, and the beginnings of a united front among the different levels of urban society for the sake of "saving the country." At least in the towns, the national movement became a real mass movement.

Of all these characteristics, the most important for the future was the tendency to link internal struggles with resistance to threats from abroad. The Boxers were loyal to the Manchu dynasty and only struck at the Western missionaries. The leaders of the boycotts of 1905 and 1908 began to link the struggle against the foreigner with the republican movement, which was then in full progress. The same was true of the movement to protect the railways in 1911. The imperial government came under attack, but out of implicitly nationalist motives, since its adversaries suspected it of being ready to hand over to the foreigners the local railways it wanted to nationalize. The movement in 1915 against the Twenty-one Demands and the anti-Anfu movement in 1918 were still clearer.

The protest against a foreign policy of national failure developed ipso facto into a political struggle against governments whose conservatism was such that they could only continue to exist through foreign support. It was a gradual progression toward the May Fourth slogan: "Externally, let's struggle for sovereignty; internally, throw out the traitors."

However, the linking of the internal and the external struggles did not yet have about it a revolutionary aspect. It went no further than criticism of the central authority (the regent in 1911, Yuan Shi-kai, the Anfu clique), and the social structure as a whole was not questioned. The 1911 revolution had been very timid in the international field. The leaders of the republic of Nanking devoted their efforts to calming the Westerners' anxiety rather than attacking head-on the entire apparatus of the unequal treaties.

The Chinese bourgeoisie, which provided the chief support for the national movement, was a prey to those feelings of doubt and hesitation resulting from the situation in 1911. The archaic proto-nationalism of the secret societies still had a strong hold on the lower classes, but the failure of the Boxers revealed its limitations and showed that it could not fit into a modern China. Workers in the towns (factory workers and coolies) became active (the boycotts of 1905 and 1908, the movements of 1918 and, above all, 1919). But they were still only a force in themselves, not yet a force *for* themselves. They supported movements which they neither initiated nor led.

The bourgeoisie and the sections of society connected with it (intellectuals, students, tradesmen) were the most active and conscious elements of the national movement at that time. They were deeply committed to "national salvation"; yet they still entertained many illusions about the West, about the priority to be given to a modernization of the country modeled on the West. Others entertained similar illusions about Japan. Among these were Sun Yat-sen and his followers; their hatred for Yuan was so intense that it led them to open secret negotiations with the Tokyo financiers in 1915. This accounted for the hesitation of the Guomindang when the anti-Anfu and anti-Japanese movements broke out in May 1918 and in May 1919.

Even so, in spite of its discontinuous and heterogeneous aspects, in spite of uncertainty and inadequate organization, the Chinese national movement did manage to keep the West at a respectful distance during the quarter of a century between the Boxers and the May Fourth Movement. "The sick man of the Far East" eventually inspired fear, which was sometimes exaggerated until it produced the frenzied image of the "yellow peril." The plans for dividing up China, which were rife in some business circles and embassies at the beginning of the century, were finally put into mothballs.

The bourgeoisie was enmeshed in the contradiction resulting, on the one hand, from its determination to rise politically in the name of national interests (partly by means of struggles against the threat from abroad), and, on the other, from its concern with achieving modernization on the Western model. This contradiction was illustrated by Sun Yat-sen's whole political career and all his political writings.

The modernization of China was still very limited. It only affected small coastal areas; numerically tiny groups of society (the bourgeoisie and the intelligentsia); minority sections of the economy, albeit very active ones; and very partial aspects of everyday culture (the press, the calendar, educational curricula, for example). Yet it should not be thought, as the "dual sector" theory would have it, that any sort of rigid division existed between the modern and the traditional in China—either in the economy or the society, in intellectual life or the political machinery. Chinese society was distended, disjointed, and distorted, but it was not cut into two separate parts. The capitalist economy lived mainly off old-style agricultural production. This provided a large proportion of the resources available to factory owners, who at the same time remained landowners. The modern political parties and the modern movements (in particular the republican movement in 1911) had not broken with the practices of the old secret societies, nor with the mass of the people whom the latter influenced. In everyday life, even in the towns, the solar calendar adopted in 1912 by the republican government coexisted with the festivals of the ancient lunar calendar.

It is tempting, but somewhat misleading, to conclude that between 1885 and 1921 traditional China gradually disappeared. The Confucian examinations were abolished in 1905 and the thousand-year-old body of scholar-officials thus doomed to extinction. The Manchu dynasty was overthrown in 1911 without giving way, as in the past, to a new dynasty. This new reality was confirmed by the two vain attempts at restoring the monarchy in 1915 and 1917. On May 4 ("the day Confucius died"), the old culture as a whole was brought up for trial. However, the basic mold of society—the exploitation which had hundreds of millions of peasants under the domination of landlords and rural gentry—was not broken by the republican revolution, and still less so by the May Fourth Movement, which was confined to the towns. These feudal agrarian relations ultimately determined the balance of the political forces (to the advantage of the conservatives), the dynamics of the economy (by thwarting capitalist inclinations in business circles), and the family structure (founded on the submission of the wife and children to the father).

Until now, China had been regarded as a single entity ("pan-Chinese," *quanguo*). But particularism in the different regions and provinces became very pronounced throughout the half-century under consideration. The fact that around 1890 the West moved from trading activities in the strict sense to financial penetration and heavy investments (railways, mines) tipped the balance in favor of the North. Up till then, the North had been less developed economically than the South, which had benefitted from early Western attempts at penetration between 1830 and 1840 (silk, tea). The Boxer movement, coming in the wake of the breakup, was a northern movement. On the other hand, the republican movement was stronger in the South, which was the home of the old merchant bourgeoisie, the old emigration overseas, the old resistance to the Manchus (the Triad), and the old radical intelligentsia. The conflict between Yuan and Sun early in 1912 was largely a conflict between North and South. Southern particularism asserted itself again in 1915 (the antimonarchical movement designed to "protect the country," *huguo*) and in 1917 (*hufa*, the movement to "protect the constitution").

The provinces frequently demonstrated their vitality throughout the period, particularly in 1911. Then the withdrawal of allegiance from the Manchus took the form in some provinces of declarations of independence. The failure of the federalist movement in 1920 to 1922 did not mean that the provinces had ceased to be independent as far as political decisions were concerned. They simply fell within the sphere of activity of the warlords, who took over federalism and led it to failure.

These regional and provincial differences only emphasize all the more the profound originality of the May Fourth Movement, a deeply unitarian movement in the pan-Chinese sense, which swept along with it all the regions in the country in a common protest.

Between 1885 and 1921, China's privileged relation with its tributary neighbors gradually broke down. With Vietnam and Burma in 1885, Laos in 1893, Korea in 1896, and with Nepal and the Ryukyu Islands. Although for a long time Japan had developed by modeling itself on China, it crushed and humiliated its former suzerain in 1894 and 1895. China was no longer the Middle Empire. Instead it was part of the collective progressive movement of the Asian peoples. The founding of the Tongmenghui and the 1911 revolution fall into the same general movement which sparked off the radicalization of the Congress Party in India in 1905, the beginnings of revolutionary nationalism in Vietnam (the departure of Phan Boi-chau for Tokyo in 1905), and the young Turkish and Persian revolutions in 1907 and 1908. China did not develop in a vacuum. But neither was it the passive toy of movements whose main stimulus came from outside the country. The pressure of imperialism, World War I, and the rivalry which set the United States and Britain against Japan were external phenomena which undoubtedly weighed heavily upon Chinese affairs. But these phenomena were equaled by transformations within society, the development of capitalism and the bourgeoisie, popular movements, and the national movement.

During the half-century between the Sino-French War and the founding of the Chinese Communist Party, the Chinese people were often mute and almost passive spectators of the political joustings which took place well above their collective heads, within a small elite: the Confucian mandarins of the former monarchy; the warlords who followed the failure of the 1911 revolution; and, to a certain extent, the republican intellectuals. On several occasions, however, the ordinary people became a collective force with a determinative role in the evolution of Chinese history: The Boxer Uprising, the fall of the Manchu dynasty, and the May Fourth Movement saw hundreds of thousands and sometimes millions of people enter into action and prove their ability, albeit temporary, to profoundly influence their destiny.

Chapter Four

China
in 1921

Between 1921 and 1949 the balance of social and political forces in China was completely upset. Minuscule at its inception, the Chinese Communist Party took power over the largest country in the world in the space of twenty-eight years. This rapid advance of the Chinese revolution was possible only because its leaders were able to fuse two fundamental struggles which both preceded the Communist movement: the national struggle against foreign domination and the peasant struggle against the old "feudal regime" (a term that will be kept for the sake of its simplicity, but which will require certain qualifications). This fusion, however, was itself made possible only after a series of experiments in other directions, particularly during the revolution of 1925–1927.

The picture of China in 1921 shows the acuity of these two major problems: national dependence and peasant dependence. But the development of communism after 1921 also stemmed from the failure of earlier experiments, particularly during the republican and Western-influenced revolution of 1911. The Western model was inadequate for China, as much on the economic as on the political level.

Finally, China in 1921 remained as intimately tied to the millennia of its traditional history as to the eventful years of the early twentieth century. It was massive, stable, aware of its coherence, of its uniqueness, and of the weight of its traditions; this was the case even though its immensity gave way to a certain number of regional differences and to an unequal development which had its roots in the distant past but which recent events had reinforced even more.

The Burden of the Unequal Treaties

The machinery of the unequal treaties, which dated from the time of the Opium Wars and which the powers had gradually perfected, was in full force following the First World War. But the war itself, in altering the balance of imperialist forces in the Far East, placed China in a different situation and opened up new possibilities for the Chinese national movement.

Territorial privileges

During the nineteenth century China gradually lost its sovereign rights over certain parts of its territory. England annexed Hong Kong, Russia took over the vast territories of the Northeast and Northwest. In the major ports, the concessions were merely disguised annexations; the powers there controlled the police, levied taxes, took care of public services, and in general collaborated with the municipal council, which was elected solely by the foreign residents but whose budget was nevertheless supplied by Chinese funds. There were approximately thirty areas controlled by the powers either singly or in concert. In Shanghai, for example, where there were 700,000 Chinese, there was an "international" concession as well as a smaller French concession.

The "leased territories" included another category of de facto annexation; these were the military bases held by France (Guangzhouwan), England (Weihaiwei), and Japan (Port Arthur). In addition, the zones of influence that had been established at the end of the nineteenth century were still in force, and the powers controlled large bases around their iron and mineral enterprises: the British coal mines at Tangshan (KMA, Kailan Mining Administration), the French Railway Company of Yunnan, and the Japanese "South Manchurian" wielded a partial de facto sovereignty, maintained their own armed forces, and managed public services.

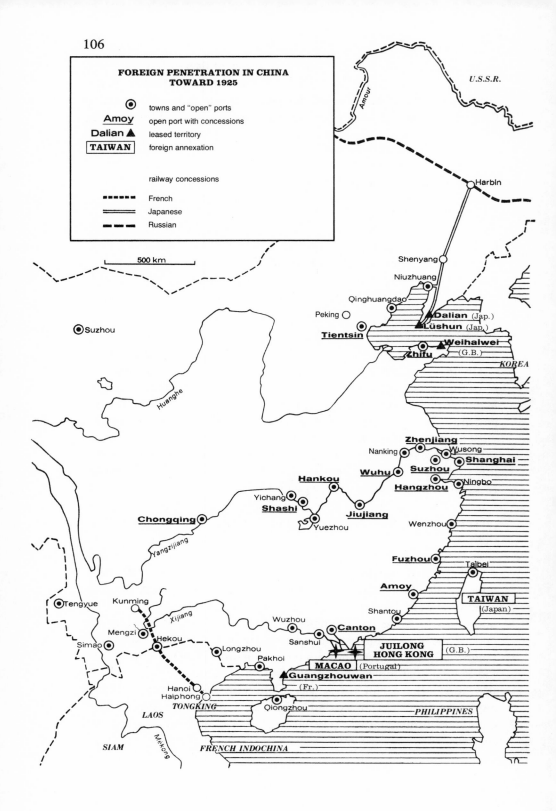

FOREIGN PENETRATION IN CHINA
TOWARD 1925

⊙ towns and "open" ports
Amoy open port with concessions
Dalian ▲ leased territory
TAIWAN foreign annexation

railway concessions
French
Japanese
Russian

500 km

U.S.S.R.

Amour

Harbin

Shenyang

Niuzhuang

Qinghuangdao

⊙Suzhou

Peking ◯

Dalian (Jap.)
Lüshun (Jap.)

Tientsin

Zhifu
Weihaiwei
(G.B.)

KOREA

Huanghe

Zhenjiang
Nanking
Wusong
Shanghai
Wuhu
Suzhou
Hankou
Hangzhou
Ningbo

Yichang
Shashi
Jiujiang

Chongqing
Yuezhou

Wenzhou

Yangzijiang

Fuzhou
Taibei

Tengyue
Kunming
Amoy
Shantou
TAIWAN
(Japan)

Xijiang
Wuzhou
Mengzi
Hekou
Canton
Sanshui
JUILONG
HONG KONG
(G.B.)
Simao
Longzhou
Pakhoi
MACAO (Portugal)
Guangzhouwan
(Fr.)

Hanoi
Haiphong
TONGKING
Qiongzhou
PHILIPPINES

LAOS

Mekong

SIAM
FRENCH INDOCHINA

Foreign control of public services

Foreign troops could be stationed in various parts of Chinese territory (around Peking, in the concessions), and the naval fleets of foreign military forces could enter interior waters. According to the arrangement of extraterritoriality, foreigners residing in China were exempt from the normal jurisdiction of Chinese courts. The Western nations also managed the Chinese postal service and, most important, controlled Chinese finances. The revenues from the Chinese customs service and the salt-tax administration were not only under the control of foreign functionaries but were deposited directly into the large foreign banks of China (Banque de l'Indochine, Hong Kong and Shanghai Banking Corporation) to guarantee the payment of the charges and indemnities that had been forced on China (the loans of 1896–1900, the indemnity from the Boxer rebellion, and the loan of 1913 to Yuan Shi-kai).

Only the surplus from these revenues was given back to China; and even this required a special decision of the diplomatic corps in Peking, which was invested with de facto control over Chinese finances. In 1920, Chinese customs took in 49½ million customs taels, of which China received only 23 million. The salt-tax administration took in 79 million silver dollars, of which China received 64 million.

Exemption from the *lijin*, a heavy internal tax, was another privilege that benefitted Western goods and assured them of a favorable position on the Chinese market.

Economic dependence on foreigners

China was heavily indebted to the West and Japan; its debts amounted to approximately a billion and a half Chinese dollars in 1921, the result of various loans contracted by China from the end of the nineteenth century on.

The Western countries and Japan had directly invested almost two billion American dollars in China over a period of about twenty-five years. They therefore controlled large areas of the Chinese economy: certain northeastern and southwestern railroads, the principal mines (Japanese coal mines in the Northeast, English coal mines at Tangshan near Peking) and heavy industry, a part of the textile industry (Japanese cotton mills in Shanghai, Western silk factories), the principal urban services (telephones, trolleys, water), and the major share of steam navigation. This control was all the more solid because foreign capitalism in China, unlike Chinese capitalism, was highly integrated. An English firm such as Jardine and Matheson or a Japanese firm such as Mitsui simultaneously managed a wide variety of businesses: import-export, textiles, insurance, steam navigation, and printing, for example. They were de facto powers in themselves, linked to the large foreign banks in China.

China's economic dependence could also be seen in the typically colonial imbalance of its foreign trade. Imports (906 million customs taels in 1921) consisted mainly of manufactured products and equipment; they far exceeded exports (601 million), which consisted mainly of minerals other than iron, vegetable products (plant oils, tea), and various animal products (powdered eggs, boar's bristles, silk). The West controlled both the export and import prices.

Even Chinese money, which was based on the silver standard, was subject to the fluctuations of the gold-silver relationship on the Western financial markets. The tael was worth seven francs in 1918, ten in 1919, seventeen in 1920, and ten again in 1921. In 1921, the customs surplus, measured in silver taels, increased by 5 million taels over the year before; but, owing to the devaluation of silver, the customs revenue was counted by the foreign banks only in terms of gold value (the Chinese debts having been measured in gold), which was 6 million sterling less than in 1920.

The very nature of the ties between China and the West, the complexity of the multiple obligations imposed by the powers on China and the privileges that were received, makes it very difficult to calculate the total profit that financial groups from abroad realized in China. But this profit was clearly quite considerable.

Cultural and religious influence

Foreign language newspapers proliferated. Some were read mainly by foreign residents in China, and others, such as the *China Weekly Review* of Shanghai, were very influential among the Chinese bourgeoisie. There were also approximately forty foreign universities and colleges, mostly run by Catholic and Protestant missionaries, where courses from curricula totally foreign to the Chinese system were given in French and English. These universities produced graduates familiar with Western life who usually agreed to collaborate with the Westerners in carrying out the "treaties." The foreign hospitals, also run by missionaries, were similar in character.

The Christian missions (there were 1,300 Catholic missionaries and 18,000 Protestant missionaries) had been established in the wake of the arrival of the powers; in the great majority of cases they remained loyal to them. Only a very small Catholic fringe (including, for example, Père Lebbe) and a group of liberal Protestants (for the most part American) tried to dissociate Christianity from the system of Western domination in China.

The division between the minuscule white minority in China and the huge mass of Chinese was sharpest in the years immediately following the war. The rich foreign residents of Shanghai and Peking belonged to deluxe private clubs, attended mass at a different time than the Chinese, and were also assured of never encountering any Chinese in the grandstands of their race tracks, on the greens of their golf courses, or in the groves of their parks (entrance being forbidden to the Chinese). They read their local newspapers in French or English, exchanged no more than a few words in bad "pidgin" (Shanghai slang) with their boy or amah, and paid almost no taxes on their profits and earnings, which were nevertheless proportionally much higher than in the West. Besides their economic, financial, military, administrative, and legal implications, the unequal treaties also signified humiliation for China.

Renewal of international rivalries

After the end of the First World War the balance among the various powers was significantly changed in the Far East. Russia had withdrawn after the Soviet revolution. Germany and Austria-Hungary, on whom China had belatedly declared war, were no longer in the picture; they had given up their concessions at Hankou and Tientsin and their share of the Boxer indemnity. But China was forced to accept the fact that Japan had succeeded Germany in Shandong; it took possession of the German mines, ironworks, and harbor installations, and set itself up in the Qingdao military base.

The Japanese advance into China disturbed the British, and all the more so because it was accompanied by a similar advance into Eastern Siberia. England therefore refused to renew the Anglo-Japanese alliance, which had been in force since 1902 and which had encouraged the rise of Japan to the rank of a great power. The second consortium of China, which was organized by the Americans and which was supposed to bring together the most important foreign banks and financial groups in the Far East in 1919, was paralyzed by this rivalry between the Japanese and the British; it never really got off the ground. In July 1921, the American government felt strong enough to propose to Japan (in fact impose on Japan) an international conference in Washington at the end of the year which would air the opposing points of view in order to attempt to reorganize the community of interests of the powers in the Far East on a new basis.

The necessity of solidarity among the powers

The very conditions of their presence in China made it imperative that the powers seek a compromise among themselves each time a crisis arose. For they remained profoundly interdependent.

The system of the unequal treaties, in fact, could function only through the joint action of the powers: the foreign consuls' joint control over the municipal council of Shanghai; the joint management of customs and the salt-tax administration (as well as the postal service) by foreign personnel; the cooperation among the large foreign banks in managing the funds from these two financial services; and the collective decision of the Peking diplomatic corps over releasing the surplus from customs and the salt tax.

Only Soviet Russia decided to break away from this unified stand. Chicherin, the minister of foreign affairs, declared in 1919 that all rights and privileges acquired in China by the tsarist government would be given up. The Russian government thereupon withdrew from the old Russian concessions, abandoned its share of the Boxer indemnity, and refused extraterritoriality to Russians residing in China. In 1920, a Soviet mission led by I. Yurin arrived in Peking. By the time it left in August 1921, it had persuaded Peking not to recognize the old tsarist ambassador any longer and therefore to refuse to turn over to him the Russian share of the Boxer funds. In spite of Soviet objections, however, the North Manchurian Railway (the Chinese Eastern Railway) remained in the hands of a White Russian bank and under the supervision of an international commission. Soviet Russia also protested the fact that it was not invited to the conference in Washington, but to no avail.

The national movement

The May Fourth Movement of 1919 had been a remarkable expression of the desire for change in China. But this popular protest, in spite of its size, obtained on a short-term basis only a few, meager results: the ousting of several pro-Japanese politicians and the refusal of the Peking government to sign the Treaty of Versailles. The results of the anti-Japanese boycott which began at the time of the May Fourth Movement and which lasted through 1919 and 1920 had more noticeable results, particularly in the Yangzi region. Japanese exports to China, which amounted to 656 million yen in 1919, fell to 598 million in 1920 and to 424 million in 1921.

More than anything else, the May Fourth Movement had dramatically revived Chinese hopes for restoring the "rights of the country" (*guoquan*). The call to promote "national goods" (*guohuo*) was popular not only among the bourgeoisie but also among the masses.

On the diplomatic level, the problem of revising the unequal treaties had become a public issue, and the surprising action of the Soviet Union in 1919 made the obstinacy of the powers even more apparent. In May 1921, China signed a treaty with the Weimar Republic that did not include an extraterritoriality clause for German nationals living in China. Public opinion began to make itself felt. In the summer of 1921, as soon as the news of the conference in Washington was announced, numerous petitions and letters were circulated, and members of intellectual groups, chambers of commerce, and student associations took action to support the Chinese delegation and to influence it to take a firm position.[1]

The Burden of the Old Agrarian Regime

Conditions unfavorable to agricultural production

In the nineteenth century, Chinese agriculture remained what it had been for many centuries: dependent on the climate, subject to terrible natural hazards, and based on exhausting human labor. The irregularity of the rains threatened the harvest on the average

---

[1] See document 1 at the end of the chapter.

of one year in three, either from drought or flood. To this were added the damages from typhoons, desert winds, and locusts.

The struggle against this difficult situation (in spite of the traditional fertility of China's "good earth") required arduous labor: scooping up marsh land for use as fertilizer; the use of human waste; hydraulic techniques; the scattering of plots of land to lessen the risk of total crop failure. There were few draft animals (since they were more expensive than human labor), and the animals used were of poor quality. The agricultural yield was thus rather low.

To all this was added the demographic problem, since the Chinese population had been growing steadily since the beginning of the nineteenth century. On the average, a family had no more than two to five acres at its disposal.

Feudal exploitation: peasants against *dizhu*

Natural calamities, technical backwardness, and overpopulation were relative problems, but within the context of the feudal regime they could not be overcome.

No matter how considerable the differences between the agrarian economy of the European Middle Ages and that of China, one basic fact is common to them both: the exploitation of the peasants by the landowners by means of extra-economic pressure. The system was based on force, not simply on the law of the labor market.

Rural society was dominated by the antagonism between the landowners, the "masters of the earth" (*dizhu*), and the small tenant farmers who worked their lands. The landowners charged high rents, which were always greater than half the harvest and, depending on the region, were paid in livestock, in produce, or in work. Often, there was a substantial guarantee deposit. The peasants also depended socially on the *dizhu*; they had to hold banquets in honor of their stewards, send them expensive presents on the birthdays of members of their families, and were often forced to send their own daughters off into slavery in the manors of the rich. All these restraints put the peasants in a state of fear, of ideological and psychological dependence, which became one of the major obstacles to the growth of the peasant revolution in the twentieth century. Their age-old experience taught the peasants that in the end the *dizhu* were stronger than they were. In fact, the *dizhu* often had at their command private militias that were an integral part of the system of agrarian exploitation.

Undoubtedly, in practice, the social structure of the countryside was more complex. There were many small landowners, but they were spread out unequally over the various regions: the greatest concentration was in the South and outside the cities. There was thus a distinction—and it would play an important part in the agrarian strategy of the Communists—among the poor peasants (who rented land and tools from the *dizhu* and even, when necessary, rented out their own labor), the middle peasants (who owned a part of their land), and the rich peasants (who for the most part were landowners able to hire laborers). But it was nevertheless the mass of peasants as a whole who were under the domination of the *dizhu*. The *dizhu* acted as usurers in case of poor harvests (at rates often as high as 100 percent); as wholesalers when a farmer wanted to sell a portion of his harvest; and especially as people of high standing with influence among public officials.

The political power of the *dizhu*, therefore, survived the fall of the empire. Of course, the *dizhu* no longer possessed the authority bestowed by Confucian rank. And since they now lived for the most part in the cities, they no longer fulfilled the traditional mediating functions of the gentry. Instead, they were represented in the villages by agents even more rapacious than they and class antagonism was considerably sharpened. The crisis of the central government following the death of Yuan Shi-kai further reinforced the de facto local political authority of the landowners, who remained in control of the situation.

State exactions

In effect, the landowners controlled the local power of the state—when they did not actually identify themselves with it—and this added further to the burden of the peasants. Taxes were very heavy, and there were also numerous surtaxes, which were often levied long in advance (up to thirty years in advance in Sichuan). The gentry, however, were all but exempt from them because of their connections and influence. When a peasant was called before the local state bureau (*yamen*), he had to pay bribes or remain in prison. The state also hurt the peasants through its monetary manipulations, for taxes were computed in silver money, while the copper sapeque, used for peasant accounts, was increasingly devalued. In Shanxi, the silver yuan was worth seventy cents in copper in 1912 and 170 in 1920. The peasants also had to put up with the exactions of the mercenary armies then fighting in China; forced labor, requisitions, and pillaging were common occurrences.

Peasant misery

The peasants were at the limit of physical misery, and often beyond it: their bodies covered with lice, barely warming themselves in winter with trash fires (the trees had been cut down long before), drinking hot water instead of tea, dressed in rags, selling their children or abandoning them in times of famine. For famines were a constant threat, claiming hundreds of thousands of victims at Hebei and Shandong, for example, in 1920 to 1921, as a result of drought. In 1921, in Zhili, 8,736,000 peasant homes out of 19,819,000 were considered to be in "total distress"; in Shandong, 3,827,000 out of 7,461,000; in Henan, 4,370,000 out of 11,461,-000.[2] In that same year, in the summer, catastrophic floods ravaged Central China, particularly in the Huai basin.

Rural craftsmanship, which had been a traditional complement of the peasants' resources and activities, declined because of competition from products made in the city, particularly paper, oilseeds, and weaving. This decline was not compensated for by the fact that around certain large cities merchants began giving out piecework (for making matches, straw hats, and the like) to the rural laborers, who charged less.

Worsening conditions

The nature of rural Chinese society during this period makes all exact measurement of conditions impossible. But there are certain indications that confirm the nature of the situation. The burdens on the peasants were increasing: rents, guarantee deposits for tenant farmers, taxes, debts. This led to the concentration of land ownership at the expense of the small peasant landholders, who were forced to sell their lands to the usurer-*dizhu* and become tenant farmers. From 1909 to 1924, in the district of Nantung (lower Yangzi), the average rent per mou of land went from 1.31 yuan to 3.14 yuan; the percentage of cases in which a guarantee was required for tenancy went from 72 percent to 88 percent; and the proportion of tenant farmers and semitenant farmers went from

[2] See document 2.

79 percent to 85 percent. The small landowners thus became tenant farmers; and in cases of bankruptcy the tenant farmers were evicted without due process and thrown into the ranks of the rural proletariat. This category, which had existed for centuries in China, swelled enormously during this period. It included day laborers, porters, vagabonds, and beggars.

The feudal regime had therefore come to a dead end. The path toward small and moderate agrarian capitalism was blocked, except in the outlying districts of large cities. It remained easier and more profitable to lend money at a usurious rate than to invest it in the production of goods whose sale was not assured.

Escape

Millions of peasants attempted to leave their villages, to leave behind their servitude and misery. They went to recently reclaimed regions in Manchuria (whose population increased tenfold during the first third of the twentieth century and which thus became Chinese land in spite of the arrival of the Russians and Japanese). They left for the "seas of the South" (Nanyang), that is, the European colonies of Southeast Asia, to become small merchants, longshoremen, and miners. They left for the cities, hoping to find in industry any work that was available, no matter how precarious. They left for the armies of the rival warlords—which numbered at this period more than a million men. They also left for the "green forests" (lülin)—to join the bands of thieves that were springing up all over China and whose raids were terrorizing rich Chinese merchants and foreign travelers.

The struggle

The struggle took many forms. Sometimes it was expressed in sudden outbursts of individual or collective anger, without plan or ultimate purpose. Tax collectors and stewards of the dizhu were beaten or murdered; yamen and manors were burned.

In some cases the peasants organized themselves at the village level, particularly against the militarist leaders and their mercenaries. They formed village militias for self-defense, as well as leagues. In still other cases, the peasant struggle erupted from within the traditional secret societies: White Lotus in the North, Triad in the South. Brothers and Elders in the Yangzi basin, and their many affiliates. These clandestine groups recruited their members particularly from among the peasants, although their original membership had consisted mainly of the marginal and mobile elements of rural society, which were more dynamic and liberal: peddlers, ferrymen, itinerant craftsmen, discharged soldiers, traveling actors, and drifters. They were united by their superstitious beliefs (amulets, initiation rites, nocturnal cults). Their ideology was a combination of primitive egalitarianism and nostalgia for a "good government." These societies remained solid and influential, capable of mobilizing the peasants and leading them into combat. In May 1921, bands of peasants from Sichuan attacked the city of Wanxian. They were led by Taoist priests under the glorious slogan of *taiping* ("great peace").

All these peasant struggles were provoked by famines and natural disasters, the outrageous demands of the *dizhu* and the tax collectors, and the injustices of the soldiery. That is to say, the peasants were against the *abuses* of the feudal system, not against the system itself. The political consciousness of the peasantry was not, by itself, capable of arriving at such principle-based social criticism. The transition from rebellion to revolution was accomplished only through an outside catalyst: communism.

The local character of peasant life

In 1921 the political horizon of the peasants was as limited as the area in which the products of their work were distributed. Local conditions varied enormously: forms of land rent, natural conditions, the exactions of the militarists. In their misery and confusion, the peasants clung to local superstitions. In times of drought they prayed to their local rain god, whose idol sat in the village pagoda. The forms that their spontaneous struggles took were equally local: riots, militias for self-defense, the actions of secret societies. Armed disputes between villages were not infrequent. For these disparate peasant rebellions to unite into a movement of national dimensions, the intervention (after 1925) of political forces from the cities—ideas, cadres, and political and military structures—was necessary.

The Failure of the Western Model

In China, following the Western model meant both the progress made by the capitalist economy and the bourgeoisie in China

and the attempts to direct China along a path defined by Western criteria. But this progress remained very limited and these
attempts failed, most notably with the 1911 republican revolution,
which left the social structure of the old regime intact. On the other
hand, this failed Westernization gave birth to new political and
social forces outside the old regime, forces which in 1921 had
already begun to lean in the direction of a real revolution: radical
intellectuals and the industrial proletariat.

The capitalist sector of the economy

There had been a Chinese national capitalism since the end of
the nineteenth century, in modern industry (particularly in textiles,
food, printing, and tobacco), banking (there were twenty-five large
banks in 1920 with a combined capital of 50 million Chinese dollars), modern transportation (particularly steam navigation), and
wholesale trade. In 1921, the boom period which had begun with
the First World War was still going on. The number of cotton
spindles doubled between 1913 and 1919 (from 484,000 to
842,000); and the profits on a bale of cotton went from 7.61
Chinese dollars in 1916 to 70.43 dollars in 1919.

But this Chinese capitalism remained dependent on the West
in many ways: banking and credit, equipment, technicians and
technology, changing stock market conditions and world markets,
and sometimes even for a market (for flour and silk, for example).
The conditions under which Chinese capitalism competed with
foreign capitalism were very unequal. Foreign companies were more
dynamic and experienced, and they also benefitted from the exemption from the *lijin*. And, most important, since the end of the nineteenth century they had been tied to the large foreign banks, while
the process of fusing industrial capital and bank capital into financial capital had only just begun in China. The first repercussions of
the world economic crisis had already been felt in the West immediately following the war. When it reached China in 1920 to 1921,
Chinese capitalism was less able to resist. Industrial development
went on, but the effects of the reversal of the international situation
were already beginning to take their toll in the falling prices of
Chinese products in the West, the instability of the gold-silver relationship, the tightening of credit, and the decrease in bank revenues.

The two capitalist structures (the foreign sector and the Chinese
national sector) were not absolute separate entities. For beyond this

duality there existed a coherent capitalist machinery, a total system of production: wage earners and the labor market, capital and credit, the law of expanding production. But for the Chinese this capitalist system was actually well established in only a few places, most of them peripheral: Shanghai and the lower Yangzi, Canton-Hong Kong, Hankou, Tientsin, Qingdao, and the southern part of Manchuria.

The weaknesses of the Chinese bourgeoisie

The capitalists on the one hand (industrialists, bankers, wholesalers) and the modern professionals on the other (doctors, engineers, lawyers, various degree holders) formed a relatively coherent bourgeois class. These groups led similar lives in Westernized centers such as Shanghai. They belonged to the same social and professional associations—chambers of commerce, groups of degree holders, groups from the same province—and they often held the same views on the issues of the moment. The chambers of commerce were particularly influential.

There were ambiguities in the relationship of this bourgeoisie with the old agrarian regime, however, as well as with the large Western interests. Many of the city bourgeois continued to receive money from old-style tenant farms and kept their income-producing lands. The old family and social relationships continued among the bourgeoisie, as formerly among the gentry; nepotism, patronage, private loyalties, and "face" were major factors.

The bourgeoisie was involved with the West, whose arrival in China in the nineteenth century had favored its growth. There was just as much dependence in the relationship as rivalry. Instead of identifying a national wing and a comprador wing within Chinese capitalism, it would be more accurate to say that the bourgeoisie oscillated constantly between comprador activities and national activities, depending on the economic circumstances.

On the political level, in spite of its failures in 1911, the bourgeoisie was a force. Separated more and more from the Peking government (which was economically oppressive, uncertain in its dealing with the Westerners, and confused in monetary matters), the Chinese bourgeoisie began to become conscious of all that the power of the warlords was costing it domestically and all that the unequal treaties were costing it on an international level. With participation in the May Fourth Movement, it had experienced a radical struggle whose economic results were positive; the anti-Japanese boycott, supported by left-wing militants, had been profitable.

The cities

In appearance, there was a deep contrast between the modern cities of the coast and the traditional cities of the interior. The former were rapidly expanding. Between 1910 and 1920, the Chinese population of Shanghai went from 488,000 to 759,000; huge office buildings stood next to miserable workers' districts; there were universities, large newspapers, publishing houses, a "Western style of life" (golf courses, race tracks).

The walled cities of the interior, such as Suzhou in the lower Yangzi and Chengdu in Sichuan, closed their gates at night in accord with the old cultural traditions. Social life continued to be organized within the guilds, clans, literary clubs, and Taoist pagodas. The city was no more than a maze of one-story gray brick buildings.

But the contrast between the two types of cities was mostly superficial. Even in the modern cities, the old social fabric remained intact: production by craftsmen, peddlers, religious and family relationships, and the excessive number of service jobs (domestics, coolies).

A caricature of a republic

Theoretically, China was a republic, ruled by the constitution of 1912. In 1919, the President of the Republic was the old mandarin conservative Xu Shi-chang. The prime minister was General Jin Yun-peng. The parliament, which had been re-elected in 1918, was dominated by the Anfu clique, one of the military and political groups that had been vying for power since the death of the dictator Yuan Shi-kai in 1916.

In effect, it was these rival factions which actually held power; the republican institutions were no more than a facade. The Anfu group had lost control of the Peking government in 1920 following a brief civil war. It had been ousted by a coalition of a group known as the Zhili, which was influential in North and Central China, with the Fengtian group, which had been established in the Northeast under the leadership of Marshal Zhang Zuo-lin. The militarists of the Fengtian and Zhili groups relied upon a civilian group known as the Communications Clique, which was led by the conservative bankers Liang Shi-yi and Ye Gong-chuo.

To separate the political and military struggles in Peking from the intrigues of the foreign powers in China is almost impossible. The ousting of the Anfu and the rise of the pro-English Zhili corresponded to the break between the British and the Japanese. But the Japanese remained present in Peking because of the Fengtian, whose area of control was actually a Japanese protectorate. The Zhili were not strong enough to seize power by themselves and had to form an alliance.

The political and military factions which came to power one after another in Peking were each recognized by the diplomatic corps, which meant that these factions would be assured of receiving the customs surplus. In this way, recognition by the foreign powers gave the ruling faction an important edge against their domestic rivals.

In the provinces as well, the real power belonged to the feudal militarists. Yan Xi-shan, a soldier of fortune, had controlled Shanxi since 1911. General Wu Pei-fu, one of the leaders of the Zhili, was in command of Hubei. After 1920, one of the members of the Anfu, Lu Yong-xiang, controlled Zhejiang. Lu called for "provincial autonomy," a catch phrase invoked to mask despotic domination not only by him but also by Liu Xiang in Sichuan and Zhao Heng-ti in Hunan.[3] These warlords, who were in fact independent, were constantly at war with one another. In 1921, there were practically 1½ million soldiers under arms.

The republic, which had been the object of so many hopes in 1911, was therefore no more than a meaningless caricature. Public opinion turned against it. The Western model proved to be inadequate.

The decline of the state

The power of the state declined considerably in all areas. The central ministries usually lost contact with the provincial agencies they were supposed to administer. The monetary system was thrown into disarray by the inflationary practices of Peking, by the instability of the relationship between copper and silver money, and by the appearance of provincial money (the warlords issued paper

---

[3] See document 3.

money and minted coins in order to have ready cash). The disintegration of the state apparatus was evidenced also by the frequency of military mutinies (the city of Yichang, for example, was sacked in June 1921) and by the increase in banditry. Soldiers and bandits were often interchangeable. Through his raids the head of a group of bandits would hope to gain enough of a following to be incorporated along with his men into a regular army. Discharged soldiers would often become brigands.

The authorities were equally powerless in the face of the famines, such as the one in North China in 1920 to 1921. But they grew rich from an opium trade that was tolerated and often supported by the warlords. The warlords themselves cultivated and engaged in the sale of poppies; they also profited from smuggling arms, a very active business in the Far East following the First World War. From this point of view, the proliferation in China of the warlords and their armies was a long-range effect of the arms market run by the Westerners before and during the war.

Canton and the Guomindang

The Guomindang, in spite of its defeats in 1913, maintained a national following and organization. It had been reorganized by Sun Yat-sen in 1919 in such a way that the authority of its leader was maintained while the rules governing the functioning of the party were loosened. Sun Yat-sen's ideas still formed the organization's body of doctrine: the three people's principles (the independence of the people, or nationalism; the power of the people, or democracy; and the well-being of the people, which tended to be associated with a vague socialism); the "five powers," whose balance would be essential to the future democratic constitution of China (legislative, executive, judiciary, supervisory, and investigatory); the "three stages" (seizure of power by a military government, tutelage by the party, democracy). The Guomindang remained influential not only among the bourgeoisie and the intellectuals but among the great mass of people, who remained loyal to Sun as the first President of the Republic in 1912.

However, as a real political force the Guomindang was reduced to Sun Yat-sen's immediate entourage: Hu Han-min, a Marxist theoretician; Liao Zhong-kai, the son of a rich bourgeois family from overseas; and Wang Jing-wei, an old anarchist who was very close to Sun. At the end of 1920 Sun Yat-sen and his team returned to Canton with the support of a local warlord, Chen Jiong-ming.

The members of the coalition, under the slogan "Canton for the Cantonese," had driven from the city a military clique that had come from the neighboring province of Guangxi in 1918.

The new Cantonese government claimed republican legitimacy. Sun Yat-sen had recalled to Canton the members of the old parliament of 1912, and they had elected him President Extraordinary of the Republic in April 1921. But this alliance with the militarists of the South was filled with problems. The militarists, in fact, limited their ambitions to the single province of Guangdong, while Sun Yat-sen and the Guomindang had much greater plans: to launch the Northern Expedition (Beifa) from the revolutionary base of Canton in order to unite the nation. The Guomindang no doubt controlled a certain number of positions in the Cantonese government and did its best to initiate a number of democratic reforms. Sun Fo, Sun Yat-sen's older son and the mayor of Canton, sponsored progressive municipal policies and had the walls of old Canton demolished. Liao Zhong-kai administered the finances of the South. Chen Du-xiu, the Marxist intellectual, had been called to Canton to be commissioner of education.

But Sun and his friends depended on the Southern militarists for the survival of their dissident government. In the summer of 1921, in order to expand their bases of action, they organized a military expedition against the province of Guangxi. Nanning was occupied on August 1. In Sun's mind this was the first step toward the "punitive expedition against the North," in which he wished to include the southern armies. But his allies were more than a little hesitant, and the political situation in Canton remained unstable.

The radical intelligentsia

Modern intellectuals came into being in China along with modern institutions of learning (there were 200,000 professors and instructors in 1919), the press (1,000 newspapers), publishing houses, medicine, and the modern courts.

They participated in huge numbers in the May Fourth Movement, which embodied their aspirations for both the national renewal of China and modern progress. The May Fourth Movement failed in the short run, but it was the starting point for an intellectual ferment which remained very intense in 1921 and which was expressed, for example, in the many serious and critical journals published at that time.

In 1920 to 1921 the eclecticism of the left which had marked the May Fourth Movement gave way to a clear polarization. One tendency, which looked especially to the United States and American empiricism, preferred intellectual debates: scientific and metaphysical reports, critical studies of Chinese antiquity, studies of relationships between Eastern and Western philosophers. The men in this group, mostly professors, leaned toward cautious reforms. On the other hand, the left-wing intellectuals of the May Fourth Movement, who were largely from the younger generation, were especially drawn to the Soviet Union, Marxism, and the revolutionary struggle. They sought contact with the working class and the workers' movement. By 1921 many of them had begun to participate in Communist actions.

The working class and the workers' movement

The industrial proletariat developed along with modern industry. In 1921 there were about 1½ million workers engaged in major capitalist production, of which about a third were employed by foreign companies: one third of the 100,000 cotton workers, one half of the 50,000 tobacco workers, one half of the 45,000 naval construction workers, two thirds of the 180,000 coal miners, one third of the 120,000 railwaymen, two thirds of the 120,000 seamen engaged in modern navigation, and three quarters of the 200,000 coolies in the large ports. The working class, therefore, largely found itself ipso facto involved in a double antagonism—one that was both social and national. Structurally, the workers' movement was called upon to play a very active role in the national movement.

These workers (excluding the railwaymen and miners) were concentrated in a small number of industrial centers spread out along the coast: Shanghai, Qingdao, Tientsin, Canton-Hong Kong, and Hankou. They were therefore in a position to influence local events actively, especially where political struggles were concerned. But on the national level they remained a minority, almost too isolated to affect the immense sea of peasants that surrounded the islands of industry.

The conditions for a merging of the workers' and peasant movements were nevertheless favorable. The great majority of workers were peasants who had recently come to the cities, recruited according to the quasi-feudal system of *baogong* (hiring agents). They were in effect under the personal control of the agent, who received their salary and guaranteed them no more than a miserable lodging and a tiny wage.

Women and children formed a large part of this unskilled proletariat. A work day of twelve or fourteen hours, brutal foremen, wages barely sufficient for subsistence, and unstable employment made up the almost unbearable working conditions. The Chinese proletariat was extremely militant. The absence of a workers' elite (and therefore reformist tendencies) outweighed the lack of a union tradition, inexperience, or the weak organization of the movement. Corporate tendencies were also very weak, since the proletariat had only rarely come from the old craft guilds (as had the printers, for example). The workers' movement was in a good position to have a strong impact on the course of Chinese politics.

May 1919 gave great impetus to the workers' struggles. The movement of political strikes in 1919 was extended to economic strikes provoked by the poor working conditions and the rising cost of living. There were forty-six strikes in 1920 and fifty in 1921. The beginnings of class consciousness could already be seen in the letters sent by workers to leftist periodicals. May 1, 1921, was celebrated in Shanghai as a way of consciously participating in the struggles of the international workers' movement. It was sponsored both by professional organizations of semi-unionist character and by a group of militant Communists.

The beginnings of Chinese communism

After 1920, the most advanced intellectuals from the May Fourth Movement gradually moved from the study of Marxism to political action. They made contact with the workers, helped set up workers' clubs, published newspapers aimed at the workers, and helped to organize and support strikes. This coalition between the left wing of the May Fourth Movement and the workers' movement did not take place in a vacuum, but under favorable international conditions. The Soviet Union was systematically attempting to help form Communist parties in the Asian countries in order to "take imperialism from behind" (according to Leninist strategy). The prestige it had acquired by unilaterally abandoning the unequal treaties in July 1919 eased the task of its first representatives in China. In 1920, these representatives had made contact with the leaders of the left-wing intelligentsia, the university professors Li Da-zhao and Chen Du-xiu, both of whom had already gone over to Marxism.

The contacts between the Soviets and the small groups of Chinese Communists which had sprung up here and there were furthered in 1921.

On the other hand, anarchism, which had been so popular among left-wing intellectuals during the May Fourth period and the preceding period as well, lost ground. By 1921 it was no longer a factor. The young radicals turned away from individual solutions in favor of the more collective and practical activities represented by Marxism, solidarity with the Soviet Union, and organized communism.

In 1921, the Chinese Communist Party was minuscule, with only about a hundred members. It was inexperienced and not very homogeneous. Most of its members were intellectuals, and its secretary-general, Chen Du-xiu, was a professor. But it had already been in contact with the workers, having set up a Trade Union Secretariat, which would play an important role in the developing workers' struggles of 1921 to 1923.

Unequal Development and National Cohesion

The coast and the interior

Imperialist penetration had been very unequal in the various regions. It was particularly concentrated along the coast, where almost all the elements of modern life were to be found: industrial centers, universities and newspapers, foreign concessions, concentrations of the modern bourgeoisie. These were the elements that characterized cities such as Canton, Amoy, Fuzhou, Hangzhou, Shanghai, Qingdao, Tientsin, and Dairen. The only apparent exception was Hankou, but it was an inland seaport owing to the waters of the Yangzi.

As opposed to these coastal areas, there were the immense zones of the interior, which were essentially rural and where the relationship between city and country continued to be defined in terms of the old feudal economy. The city, where the rich country people lived, existed at the expense of the peasants without giving them anything in return. A fundamental question for both the Guomindang and the Communists during this entire period was the place the modern coastal areas and the interior zones would have in the general political strategy.

RAILROADS AND MAJOR CHINESE INDUSTRIES IN 1935

railroads
heavy industry
light industry
textile industry
railway stockyards
food processing centers
cigarette manufacturing
power plants
mining (coal, metals)

U.S.S.R.

Khabarovsk

MANCHURIA

Amour

Tsitsihar

Harbin

Vladivostok

Shenyang

Niuzhuang

Andong

Séoul

KOREA (Jap.)

Fusan

Guisul

Kalgan   Peking   Tangshan

Baotou

Datong

Taiyuan

Tientsin

Dalian
Lüshun

Jinan

Qingdao

Donghai

Sian

Zhengzhou

Tongshan

JAPAN

Chengdu

Yichang

Nanking

Shanghai

Chongqing

Wuhan

Ningbo

Yangzijiang

Hangzhou

Changsha

Xinhua

Pingxiang

Shuikoushan

Kunming

Xijiang   Canton

Macao

Langson

Hong Kong

TONGKING

Hanoi   Haiphong

INDOCHINA

Huanghe

500 km

North and South

The contrast between the North and the South was another area of unequal development inherited from ancient China. Transportation by boat, which was much easier in the South, helped to create bases for a wider market, a more advanced urban development, and a more active merchant bourgeoisie. The contrast was accentuated from the end of the nineteenth century on, since the large mines and railways were almost all located in the North and Northeast.

Particularist traditions were more alive in the South and were emphasized again during the revolution of 1911, which was especially strong in the South. The South seceded in 1913 (the second revolution), in 1915 (the antimonarchist movement), and in 1920 to 1921 (the movement for the "protection of the constitution").

The provinces

Each province, especially in the South, maintained its own traditions and political system; the balance of social forces was different in each. The federalist movement (based on provincial autonomy) was very strong in 1921, particularly in Shenxi, Hunan, Sichuan, Zhejiang, Yunnan, and Guangdong. In all these provinces autonomist aspirations were expressed through various political forms such as provincial constitutions, declarations of independence, and resolutions by chambers of commerce. The provinces' regionalist slogans were used by the warlords, however, to consolidate their power.

Rice-growing plains and mountain regions

Within each province, unequal development also characterized the relationships between the rice-growing basins of the central regions and the mountain and forest areas. This ancient contrast led to a major geopolitical localization of traditional dissident movements—secret societies, banditry, peasant uprisings. The uprisings, for example, took place in the less accessible border regions of the provinces or where the primitive subsistence economy allowed for better resistance, while the fertile basins at the heart of each province were more easily controlled by the authorities. This geopolitical law would continue to play a role in the twentieth century, when the Chinese Communists would have to define the location of their bases for armed struggle.

Chinese cohesion

These factors of unequal development are very important for understanding the nuances of Chinese political history in the twentieth century. But they occurred *within* a remarkably coherent whole, a unity which no one in China wanted to challenge.

The daily life of the Chinese as it had developed through history was unique in all aspects: food, writing, the lunar calendar and traditional festivals, amusements, theater and music, the reference to commonly known literary works. Ancient Chinese philosophy continued, as in the past, to shape thinking and behavior: a sharp sense of contradiction (*yin* and *yang*),[4] the doctrine of *wu wei* (minimizing of action upon other things), unity of form and content (which resulted in issues of "saving face" so often ridiculed by the Westerners).

Of course, a certain number of traditions were increasingly seen to be negative or repressive, at least in radical circles;[5] this applied to the dependent situation of women (bound feet, forced marriages), the authority of old people, and gambling (which the peasant unions banned in 1926). Also, the Westernized groups of Shanghai no doubt preferred medical treatment in the Western manner and scorned acupuncture. But the great majority of national traditions (such as writing) were simply considered by the Chinese as part of the collective heritage of the people. The sense of their national cohesion and uniqueness was deeply felt among the Chinese, all the more so because the relationships contrasting them with those whose way of life was different (the Westerners) were relationships in which they were dominated and exploited. The national movement was a fundamental incentive in Chinese politics in the twentieth century. The attempts to destroy Chinese unity all ended in failure.

ADDITIONAL BIBLIOGRAPHY

Jean Chesneaux, *Le mouvement ouvrier chinois de 1919 à 1927* (Paris, 1962).

Hu Sheng, *Imperialism and Chinese Politics, 1840–1925* (Peking, Foreign Languages Press, 1955).

Maurice Meisner, *Li Ta-chao and the Origins of Chinese Marxism* (Cambridge, Mass., Harvard University Press, 1967).

---

[4] The female (*yin*) and male (*yang*) principles, whose duality characterized all situations.

[5] See document 4.

L. Wieger, *La Chine moderne*, vol. II, *Le flot montant* (Hien-hien, 1921), vol. III, *Remous et écumes* (1922).
The China Year Book (Peking, years 1921–1922).

DOCUMENTS

1. THE HOSTILITY OF THE CHINESE BOURGEOISIE TOWARD CHINA'S SITUATION OF ECONOMIC AND DIPLOMATIC DEPENDENCY: CHINESE BANKERS' MANIFESTO, OCTOBER 1921

SOURCE: *Bulletin Commercial d'Extrême-Orient* (Shanghai, October 1921). This text consists of excerpts from a manifesto drawn up by the Chinese bankers when they met in conference in Tientsin on the occasion of the Washington Conference.

Resolution 1

The principle of preservation of territorial integrity and respect for the sovereignty of China are to be placed above all other considerations and no infractions will be tolerated through concessions conferring preferential or exceptional rights to foreigners working for the Chinese government. Extraterritoriality will be abolished and replaced by the jurisdiction of Chinese courts of justice, which will be voluntarily reformed by China.

Resolution 3

(China) . . . will recognize the so-called "open-door" policy and will, of its own accord, join in close international cooperation, on condition that all nationals of foreign powers personally and forever renounce their so-called "spheres of influence" and their special rights and privileges.

Resolution 4

We are favorably disposed to financial cooperation with other nations, on condition that an open policy, opposed to secret agreements, be adopted for such cooperation, a policy which must in no way interfere in our national finances or impede our economic development. Any agreement or any other contract contrary to the preceding is to be exposed before this conference.

Memorandum B

1. The government is to prepare a map of the railway systems for the entire country and, on its own initiative, is to establish a system of unification for all existing railway lines,* but is not to accept the

---

* The railways, which had been built by various powers or foreign financial groups, were very different from one another (technically, financially, and in other ways).

proposition concerning the so-called "international control of the railways."*

2. All Chinese railway lines may borrow money from foreign and domestic sources. The lenders will have only the right of auditing the accounts and will not be able to obtain any right of control or of inspection.

3. The government will have the exclusive right to decide on the order in which the railroads will be built.

4. No foreigners, except technical experts, will be employed and no distinction will be made among those who are employed as such. With the exception of those who hold clearly defined special positions, all employees, whether Chinese or foreign, will be required to pass an examination before entering the Chinese railway service.

5. China reserves for itself the right to set rates for the transportation of merchandise, without consulting or negotiating with the foreign powers.

6. Police authorities will be responsible for protecting the railways in the areas where there are no troops.

7. A bank, or banks, appointed by the government, will take charge of the railways' expenses and receipts.

2. MAKESHIFT FOOD EATEN BY THE PEASANTS OF NORTH CHINA DURING THE 1920–1921 FAMINE

SOURCE: *Report by the Peking United International Famine Relief Committee* (Peking, 1921), p. 13.

chaff from grain, mixed with cereal grain sprouts killed by the drought
flour made from leaves
fuller's earth
flower seeds
poplar buds
corncobs
steamed balls of grass
sawdust
thistles
inedible wild berries
kaoliang chaff
cotton seeds
elm bark
peanut shells
soybean residue (after extraction of the oil)
sweet potato stems
roots
flat cakes made of powdered pumice stone.

* Proposal recently made by an American financial group.

3. YOUNG MAO CONFRONTS THE WARLORDS OF HUNAN (1919–1921)

SOURCE: Edgar Snow, *Red Star over China* (New York, 1938), pp. 153–155.

I went to Shanghai for the second time in 1919. There once more I saw Chen Du-xiu. I had first met him in Peking, when I was at Peking National University, and he had influenced me perhaps more than any one else. I also met Hu Shi at that time, having called on him to try to win his support for the Hunanese students' struggle. In Shanghai I discussed with Chen Du-xiu our plans for a League for Reconstruction of Hunan. Then I returned to Changsha, and began to organize it. I took a place as a teacher there, meanwhile continuing my activity in the Hsin Min Hsüeh Hui. The society had a programme then for the "independence" of Hunan, meaning, really, autonomy. Disgusted with the Northern Government, and believing that Hunan could modernize more rapidly if freed from connections with Peking, our group agitated for separation. I was then a strong supporter of America's Monroe Doctrine and the Open Door.

Tan Yan-kai was driven out of Hunan by a militarist called Zhao Heng-ti, who utilized the "Hunan independence" movement for his own ends. He pretended to support it, advocating the idea of a United Autonomous States of China, but as soon as he got power he suppressed the democratic movement with great energy. Our group had demanded equal rights for men and women, and representative government, and in general approval of a platform for a bourgeois democracy. We openly advocated these reforms in our paper, the *New Hunan*. We led an attack on the provincial parliament, the majority of whose members were landlords and gentry appointed by the militarists. This struggle ended in our pulling down the scrolls and banners, which were full of nonsensical and extravagant phrases.

The attack on the parliament was considered a big incident in Hunan, and frightened the rulers. However, when Zhao Heng-ti seized control he betrayed all the ideas he had supported, and especially he violently suppressed all demands for democracy. Our society therefore turned the struggle against him. I remember an episode in 1920, when the Hsin Min Hsüeh Hui organized a demonstration to celebrate the third anniversary of the Russian October Revolution. It was suppressed by the police. Some of the demonstrators had attempted to raise the Red Flag at that meeting, but were prohibited from doing so by the police. They then pointed out that, according to Article 12 of the (then) Constitution, the people had the right to assemble, organize, and speak, but the police were not impressed. They replied that they were not there to be taught the Constitution, but to carry out the orders of the governor, Zhao Heng-ti. From this time on I became more and more convinced that only mass political power, secured through mass action, could guarantee the realization of dynamic reforms.

4. Revolt of youth against family oppression: the denunciation of novelist Ba Jin

Source: Ba Jin, *The Family* (Peking, Foreign Language Press) p. 81. The novel was published in 1931 by Ba Jin, a left-wing writer with anarchist tendencies.

Qiue-hui continued hanging around the house reading the newspaper. The paper was full of items in which Qiue-hui had no interest. Its coverage of the student strike dwindled steadily until there was no news at all. By that time, Qiue-hui had stopped reading even the newspaper.

"You call this living! A prisoner in a narrow cage!" he would fume. Often he grew so exasperated he didn't want to see any member of his family. To add to his troubles, Ming-feng seemed to be avoiding him. He seldom had an opportunity to speak to her alone.

As usual, he went every morning and every evening to pay his formal respects to his grandfather. He could not avoid seeing the old man's exhausted dark face and Mistress Chen's crafty powdered one. In addition, he also frequently encountered a number of expressionless, enigmatic visages. Qiue-hui felt ready to burst. "Just wait," he would mutter. "The day is coming. . . ."

Exactly what would happen when the day finally came, he wasn't quite sure. All he knew was that everything would be overthrown, everything he hated would be destroyed. Again he looked through his *New Youth* and *New Tide* magazines. He read an article entitled "Impressions of an Old-Style Family," and its biting attack pleased him immensely; it was almost as if he had already gained his revenge.

But his joy was only momentary, for when he tossed the magazine aside and came out of his room, he was confronted with all the things he so disliked. Lonely and bored, he returned to his room.

It was mostly in this manner that he whiled away his days.

Chapter Five

From the Founding of the Communist Party to the Reorganization of the Guomindang: *July 1921–January 1924*

China Under the Warlords

The warlords, powerful in every province, were ravaging the country. The Peking government, which had no real power, was being fought over by the two military factions in North China while the great powers looked on, complacent and interested. The West gave the Chinese government diplomatic recognition, and yet, in the opinion of a tired and irritated public, the government's credibility and authority had sunk as low as possible. Sun Yat-sen's government in Canton, which claimed to be the lawful republic, had only a shaky authority over part of South China. The bourgeoisie, which had been sorely tried by the 1921–1923 crisis, was reaching the limits of its political capabilities. Once again, militarists drove Sun Yat-sen from his base in Canton. As for the Communist Party, its early successes on the labor front were short-lived. Both Nationalists and Communists were seeking an ally. With the active support of the Soviet Union, they were to come together.

China and the Washington Conference

The conference of the great powers, which lasted from November 1921 to February 1922, had not only established a new balance of power in the Pacific (putting a limitation on naval armament) but had also sanctioned the withdrawal of Japan, which had been forced by the English to return Shandong peninsula to China. But there had hardly been any response to China's national demands, apart from the decision to do away with the zones of influence created at the end of the nineteenth century. The possibilities that China might recover its autonomy where customs revenues were concerned and that extraterritoriality might be abolished were mentioned in only the vaguest terms and no specific measures were brought up. The Peking government (which had taken part in the discussions) refused to sign the treaty, but China remained under the control of the powers.

The power of the warlords in the North

The republican institutions were only a facade. The real power lay in the hands of the military men. At this time, there were four who were most influential nationally. Marshal Zhang Zuo-lin (1873–1928), a former bandit leader who had since taken control of Manchuria with the backing of Japan, was head of the so-called Fengtian group. General Wu Pei-fu (1874–1939), a former Confucian scholar who had made a military career for himself at the end of the empire and who was one of the leaders of the Zhili group, controlled the whole area north of the middle Yangzi. Marshal Cao Kun, who had once been an old clothes peddler and a soldier of fortune and whose career had been made for him by Yuan Shi-kai, was the nominal head of the Zhili, though he depended on Wu Pei-fu for military aid. And Feng Yu-xiang (1882–1948) was even odder. The son of poor peasants, he had joined the army as a common soldier at a very young age and had been converted to Protestantism. Feng tried to imbue his army with discipline and moral strength, first in his position as governor of Henan and then as commanding officer of the Peking region.

These military leaders were backed by civilian politicians belonging to various conservative groups, such as the members of the pro-Japanese Communications group, headed by the banker Liang Shi-yi (1869–1933) and the group of American-trained diplomats which included Gu Wei-jun—known as Wellington Koo (born in 1887)—and Shi Zhao-ji—known as Alfred Sze (1887–1958)—and Wang Chong-hui (1881–1958). They fought for the prestigious ministerial positions, which were a source of profit and which often opened the way to lucrative smuggling.

The break between the Zhili group and the Fengtian group

Since 1920, the central government had been controlled by a coalition of the Fengtian and Zhili parties. In December 1921, the head of the Communications Clique, Liang Shi-yi, became prime minister, which increased Japanese influence in Peking. But this influence could hardly survive for long given the new balance of power established by the Washington Conference. Japan lost ground, while the English gained. The Zhili group, protected by the latter, profited from their active support. Wu Pei-fu, at his headquarters in Luoyang, had at his command a fleet of American airplanes; what was more, he had received massive shipments of arms from the United States as well as loans from English banks.

In April 1922, Zhang Zuo-lin decided to make the first move. He attacked the Zhili troops near Peking, but was stopped and beaten by Feng Yu-xiang's forces. He was driven back beyond the Great Wall. Liang Shi-yi and his friends left the government and took refuge in Japan. The victorious Wu Pei-fu decided to have the members of the old parliament of 1913 and the former President of the Republic Li Yuan-hong brought back to Peking. The president then in office, Xu Shi-chang, yielded his position to Li Yuan-hong. At the same time, Wu asked Sun Yat-sen and his southern government to resign. Thus the new government claimed to be the legitimate republic; it urged demilitarization and the peaceful reunification of China. But it was nevertheless based on the power of its army.

The evils of militarism

Militarism was now at its height, dominating the political and social life in China both in the capital and in the provinces.

Among the warlords a certain hierarchy existed. Above the minor local potentates were the *dujun* who governed entire provinces; a small number of these, in turn, were "inspector generals"— familiarly referred to as "super-dujuns" by Western newspaper reporters—who were even more ambitious (Zhang Zuo-lin, Cao Kun, and Wu Pei-fu). But whether their power happened to be great or small, it was always the same kind of power.

They practiced every variety of extortion on the countryside: forced labor, the impressment of coolies, the requisitioning of transport and provisions, and pillaging.[1] Arbitrary taxes proliferated. In January 1924, in Amoy, a warlord collected seventy-one different taxes, seven levied on pigs alone (there was a standard tax, a slaughtering tax, a raising tax, a tax on pig inspection, a surtax on breeding, a tax on cooked pork, and a tax on the sale of pork), and there were taxes on every kind of commodity or transaction (such as tulip bulbs, fireworks, fishing, police, opium growing).

The militarists were particularly hard on the chambers of commerce, resorting to a form of blackmail that was effective and easy to carry out: the threat that their troops would mutiny if they did not receive help in paying their wages. In fact, the frequent mutinies which sometimes ended in the total destruction of towns induced the merchants to give in to these demands. Using this method, Wu Pei-fu extorted 300,000 yuan from the Hankou chamber of commerce in April 1922, and 100,000 from the city's association of bankers.

Thus, the power of the warlords was as oppressive to the bourgeoisie as to the people. It was a factor in the economic stagnation and contributed to the crisis in the national industry, primarily because of unsafe transport systems and the instability of the market. Because of the wars between rival cliques, the railroads were monopolized by the militarists and were therefore not available for civilian passengers and merchandise:

Soldiers transported by Chinese railways in 1921–1924

Line*	1921	1922	1923	1924
Peking-Suiyuan	54,922	17,931	34,824	13,672
Tientsin-Pukou	75,119	69,858	102,858	760,552
Peking-Moukden	191,116	1,425,348	57,608	2,665,405
Peking-Hankou	228,426	196,132	161,242	273,418

* These figures show how the 1922 and 1924 wars between the Zhili and Fengtian groups affected the traffic of the Peking-Moukden and Peking-Hankou lines and how the 1924 war between the Zhejiang and Jiangsu groups affected the traffic of the Tientsin-Pukou line.

All in all, the warlords were harshly repressive where the peoples' struggles were concerned, whether it was the national movement or the demands of labor. The *dujun* Zhao Heng-ti brutally stopped an anti-Japanese boycott movement which the students tried to start

---

[1] See document 1 at the end of the chapter.

after Japanese marines, attacking a demonstration (June 1, 1923) for the return of the Japanese port Dairen to China, killed four people in Hunan. Similarly, in February 1923, Wu Pei-fu brutally crushed the strike of the railwaymen on the Peking-Hankou line.

The Lincheng affair

If the militarists benefitted from Western backing (which included diplomatic support and the provision of military equipment, supplies, "advisers"), the disorder into which China had been plunged by militarism[2] also further whetted the powers' appetites. This was clearly shown by the Lincheng affair of May 1923 when the Tientsin-Pukou luxury train had been stopped by bandits in southern Shandong. These bandits had kidnapped twenty-six Westerners, among them several women, and were asking for a very large ransom. The diplomatic corps in Peking took advantage of this incident to demand that a system of inspection and supervision of the Chinese railways by foreigners be set up, a system that actually came much closer to financial exploitation of the railway lines than to a guarantee of the passengers' safety.

But the reaction of Chinese public opinion, as expressed by chambers of commerce, political and professional organizations, and student groups, was extremely violent. The Westerners withdrew their demand to supervise the railways, the victims were compensated by the Chinese authorities, and the bandits were incorporated into the regular army, as they had asked to be.

The 1923 political crisis: Cao Kun in power

Not long after the elimination of Zhang Zuo-lin, the Zhili faction split in two. Entrenched in his camp at Luoyang, Wu Pei-fu was losing influence by comparison with the immediate entourage of his superior, Marshal Cao Kun. The latter controlled Peking and was backed by the commander of the city's garrison, Feng Yu-xiang. Cao Kun coveted the post of President of the Republic, occupied by Li Yuan-hong, whom Wu Pei-fu had been supporting.

In 1923, a financial crisis allowed Cao Kun to take the initiative. The state was without resources. No one was being paid wages,

[2] See document 2.

from the ambassadors down to the musicians in the president's orchestra, and including the police. Li was attacked through his minister of finances, whom Cao had arrested. Wu Pei-fu did not dare intervene. Faked popular demonstrations demanded the removal of the President of the Republic, who resigned in June. Cao Kun, in an overtly corrupt act, bribed the least principled members of the parliament with 5,000 dollars apiece to elect him President of the Republic. In October, for the sake of appearances, the new president put through a new constitution.

This crisis further aggravated the degeneration of the Western parliamentary institutions established in 1911. Cao Kun had openly defied public opinion. But his government, though scorned by the public, was immediately recognized by the diplomatic corps of Peking, which had been so supercilious six months earlier over the Lincheng affair. And this implied that another slice of the customs surplus and excise surplus would be handed out. The combined appetites of the powers and the warlords seemed increasingly incompatible with China's national interest.

The provincial military cliques

The warlords, entrenched in their provincial governments, were in fact independent. Some of them paid allegiance to more powerful groups (as the governors of Hubei and Henan did to the Zhili clique, which took control over Shandong again in 1922, after the decision was made in Washington that the Japanese should leave). Others were solidly entrenched in single provinces and confined their ambitions to that province, like Yan Xi-shan in Shanxi. Still others shared the control of one particular province, like the small rival military feudal systems in Sichuan. Others, like Zhang Zuo-lin, formed a sort of regional empire (in Zhang's case, consisting of the three provinces in the Northeast). Tang Ji-yao unsuccessfully tried to do this with his "Greater Yunnan," but in 1922 he only managed to maintain himself in that one province. As for the Anfu party, which had been driven out of power in 1920, it remained influential in the provinces of the Southeast; it controlled the Zhejiang, the lower Yangzi zone, including Shanghai, and one of its principal leaders, Xu Shu-zheng, tried to regain some power in Fujian.

In short, the political geography of China under the warlords was extremely complex and unstable, with a proliferation of temporary coalitions and changes of allegiance that depended on the interests of the moment. If fighting was frequent and wars between provinces sometimes bloody, rivalries between the various *dujun* were often settled in other ways: through intrigue, corruption, the defection of units into the enemy's camp. One's adversary was customarily offered an honorable way out, including, and most importantly, a financial way.

The political and social bases of the warlords

Conflicts among warlords were limited by the system of power to which they all belonged and the specific political structure in which they were all deeply involved. Their power was territorial in nature. The ambition of each was to establish himself in a given area (usually a province) and draw the largest possible revenues from it through taxes, manipulation of the provincial currency, extortion, and various illegal trafficking. It would not be going too far, therefore, to speak in terms of a neofeudal system which resulted from particular circumstances (many of the *dujun* came from among the people), but which was fundamentally still the feudal exploitation of the peasant population of a given territory. The warlords worked closely with the gentry, the leading rural citizens and the landowners, and guaranteed orderly villages and docile peasants. In return, the gentry assured them of the services necessary for the (relatively) smooth functioning of the local administration.

This neofeudal system did not neglect the profits to be derived from the capitalist environment of the 1920s: the *dujun* bought factories and participated actively in the opium trade and the arms traffic. Herein lies the significance of the *dujun*'s struggle to gain control of the coastal provinces, for possession put one in an advantageous position as an intermediary in dealing with the militarists inland. Political and military instability was particularly marked in the provinces of Guangdong, Fujian, Zhejiang, and Jiangsu.

Ideological differences were quite notable among the *dujun*. Some were concerned only with brute force. Others, more cunningly, invoked the spirit of provincial autonomy: for instance, Liu Xiang (1890–1932) in Sichuan, Lu Yong-xiang in Zhejiang, and especially Zhao Heng-ti in Hunan. Zhang Zuo-lin, ousted from Peking in 1922, also tried to justify his power through public statements about the benefits of decentralization. In a China which was still marked by the hopes of 1911 and of the May Fourth Movement, the warlords were seeking to win over public opinion with a progressive form of demagogy. Xan Xi-shan wanted to make his Shanxi into a "model province"; the youth were organized and people urged to practice Confucian virtues. In Hunan, Zhao Heng-ti undertook to support "the people," and for some time he even cooperated with the students and the workers. Feng Yu-xiang preached a form of nationalism colored both by Protestant progressiveness and Confucian morality.

The Hesitant Experiments of the Bourgeoisie and the Communists

The economic crisis of 1921–1923

The industries of Chinese national capitalism, for which the First World War had created an unexpected boom, had not been able to withstand the flood of Western capital and products into China, nor the new pressure from Japan. Because they were inexperienced, handicapped by the obligation to pay the *lijin,* and without the backing of large banks as strong as the ones in London and Tokyo which were supporting their English and Japanese rivals, the Chinese manufacturers were at the mercy of the slightest fluctuation in the economic situation. As a result of a rise in the price of raw cotton and a slump in the price of thread, the Chinese cotton mills went through a crisis from 1922 to 1924. Their owners in Shanghai decided to cut production by 25 percent, creating 10,000 unemployed. Production also fell in the cotton factories of Tientsin, Changsha, and Wuhan,[3] and stopped completely in Wuhu and Ningbo. In 1924, a million cotton spindles were lying idle in China—one third of all the equipment.

The crisis was no less severe in other sectors of light industry, such as flour mills, oil mills, and silk factories. American wheat, freed from the demands of the international military market, came back into the Far East. Competition from Japanese silk became tougher. On top of this were the troubles caused by militarism in China and by the wars between the provinces, such as blocked convoys and the requisitions. Everywhere flour mills were partially

---

[3] The agglomeration of Wuhan included Hankou, Hanyang, and Wuchang.

closing down, as were oil mills, or they were taken over by the Japanese. Chinese oil mills in Dairen lowered their production by two thirds in 1924. There were 20,000 to 30,000 unemployed workers in the silk-producing district of Shunde, near Canton, in 1924. The crisis also affected the heavy metal industry of the middle Yangzi, one of the few sectors in which China had attempted to establish heavy industry. The steelworks of Hanyang and the iron-works of the Yangzi shut down altogether.

The manufacturers vainly tried to shift the burden of the crisis onto the workers by putting them on part-time work or letting them go, by cutting their wages, and by stepping up the work pace. Salaries fell in the silk-spinning factories of Shanghai and Shunde. Payment by piecework, which was less profitable, was often substituted for hourly wages. In other enterprises, the weight of the baskets of cotton, for which the workers were paid at a fixed rate, was increased.

There was also an acute monetary crisis. In Shanghai, a silver dollar (yuan) was worth 138 coppers in 1919 and 217 in 1925; in Peking, its value changed from 138 to 285 coppers during the same period. Prices rose. In Canton, on a base index of 100 in 1913, prices rose to 136.4 in 1919, and 175.5 in 1924.

This economic crisis led the Chinese bourgeoisie to a thorough re-evaluation of the political situation.[4] It lost confidence in the West and in the conservative forces with which it had joined during the time of Yuan Shi-kai. It was prepared to consider a complete change of alliances in the direction of the workers' movement, the Soviet Union, and the Communists. This change would later be officially supported by the Congress for Reorganizing the Guomindang in January 1924.

Sun Yat-sen loses Canton

The economic disappointments of the bourgeoisie went hand in hand with political disappointments. The crisis between Sun Yat-sen and the gentry of Canton, which had been brewing since 1920, broke out in May and June 1922. Chen Jiong-ming, head of the Cantonese armies, mutinied while Sun Yat-sen was at the northern front. Sun and his friends in the Guomindang, driven out of Canton once again, took refuge in Shanghai.

[4] See document 3.

This incident extended into the South the political conflict which had broken out at the same time in the North. What Sun Yat-sen had been trying to do was to consolidate his power by forming a triple alliance with the enemies of the Zhili group and the Peking government, namely Zhang Zuo-lin of Manchuria and the Anfu of Zhejiang. As for Chen Jiong-ming, his hostility toward Sun had drawn him to Wu Pei-fu, who had brought former President Li Yuan-hong back into power in July 1922, after having demanded the simultaneous ousting of the two rival presidents of the North and the South, Yu Shi-chang and Sun Yat-sen.

Sun, defeated once again, nevertheless still symbolized the hopes of the Chinese bourgeoisie. In January 1923, he headed the list (1,315 votes) in an opinion poll the Shanghai *China Weekly Review* conducted of its readers, many of whom were Chinese intellectuals and businessmen. Feng Yu-xiang, the "Christian marshal," was second with 1,217 votes.

Other unsuccessful efforts by the bourgeoisie

At the time the Washington Conference was announced, and as long as it continued, more and more professional organizations (of jurists and educators, for example) took stands on the issues. In October 1921, the National Federation of Chambers of Commerce had decided to send two delegates "from the people" to Washington with the government's delegates. It had also voted to abolish the *dujun* and to disband the provincial armies. It had called for a "Conference for the Good of the Nation" (Guoshi Huiyi), which met in March 1922. Taking part in this conference were the chambers of commerce, the provincial assemblies, the education committees, the associations of agronomists, industrialists, and bankers, and the jurists' and journalists' groups. But the resolutions passed by this veritable Estates-General of the Chinese bourgeoisie against militarism and the unequal treaties had no more effect than those of the October 1921 conference.

In March 1923, the question of the renewal of the lease of Dairen and Port Arthur (given for twenty-five years to Russia in 1898, but recently transferred to Japan) was the occasion for another national campaign. The chambers of commerce, backed by student associations, began another anti-Japanese boycott; the association of Tientsin cotton merchants and the guilds of Peking and Wuhan joined in. The movement was strong and continued until August, but with no results. The Peking government did not dare defy Japan and end the lease.

The vitality of public opinion

The May Fourth spirit remained very much alive, particularly among the intellectuals. The feminist movements was especially active; the magazine *Funü Zhoubao (Woman's Week)* was carrying on a very lively propaganda campaign. Each year a conference was held by the League for the Promotion of Woman's Rights, which was supported by a number of radical intellectuals.

When the international conference of the Protestant youth associations (the YMCA) met in Shanghai in 1922, the leftist intellectuals countered by organizing a National Anti-Christian Conference. The activity of the Protestant missions had always been resented as representing imperialist penetration.

It was partly in answer to this accusation that groups of liberal Chinese Protestants, with the support of certain missionaries, decided in that same year, 1922, to form the Chinese National Christian Council, which most of the Protestant sects joined and which was directed not by white missionaries but by the Chinese.

The beginnings of the Communist Party

The young intellectuals who had formed the Communist Party in July 1921 were moving in a completely different direction.

The party was created to be an instrument of revolutionary war. Its line was more exactly defined at the Second Congress (July 1922), which emphasized the importance of an overall revolutionary strategy opposed to that of the bourgeoisie, operating both within the country and on an international level. The party put out several publications, notably *Yiangdao (The Guide)*, its official weekly paper. In 1923, it took over the monthly *Xin Qingnian (New Youth)*, which had become very prestigious during the May Fourth Movement. The party helped form Socialist youth groups and took active part in the international Communist movement. Delegates were sent to the annual congresses of the Comintern and also, in January 1922, to the Far Eastern Workers' Congress, which was held in Petrograd and in which the Soviets intended to present the opposite point of view from that of the Washington Conference. Some party members lived in France, where there were many

Chinese students and workers, during the period from 1921 to 1923. Among them were Zhou En-lai, Li Fu-chun, Deng Xiao-ping, and other important future leaders.

However, the party was not growing very fast. At the time of the Second Congress there were 123 members, and 432 at the time of the Third Congress (June 1923).

The beginnings of the workers' movement: strikes and unions

During this early stage, most of the Communist cells' militant work was in the labor movement. As confirmed Marxists, the Communists believed that it was up to the proletariat, the revolutionary vanguard, to lead the people, even in a country like China that was hardly industrialized. The party's labor activity was under the control of the Trade Union Secretariat, which was run by the Communist militants Deng Zhong-xia and Zhang Guo-tao.

As was shown by the large strike of Hong Kong sailors in early 1922, the workers' movement was not an artificial creation of the Communist Party. The strike was run by a traditional corporate union; it lasted from January 12 to March 5, involved 40,000 sailors who were supported throughout South China by a large sympathy strike, and won wage increases of 15 to 30 percent for the strikers. Other independent strikes took place, and there were other corporate unions for printers, postal employees, and mechanics.

But the Communists were essentially responsible for the wave of workers' struggles from 1921 to 1923. They planned strikes and founded militant workers' organizations. Among the railwaymen of the northern and central railway lines, for example, they launched several large strikes and formed workers' "clubs" (*julebu*), a new term which made the establishment of these associations easier than the term "union." The Communists were also very active in Hubei and Hunan; they were involved in strikes in the Wuhan arsenal and steelworks and the strike of the Anyuan coal miners, and in the formation of workers' clubs and unions among miners, metalworkers, and textile workers. These workers' organizations were grouped together in provincial union federations of Hunan (with Mao Tsetung as secretary) and of Hubei.

On the other hand, the strike of 50,000 Tangshan coal miners in October 1922 was a failure, as was the August strike in the silk-spinning mills of Pudong, in the outlying districts of Shanghai. The latter was the first large strike by women in the history of China.

The development of workers' consciousness

There were fifty major strikes in 1921, and ninety-one in 1922. Workers' consciousness was evident in the very content of the demands made during the various strikes. The issues were no longer confined to low salaries and long hours, but included the workers' dignity in their relations with the foremen and the rejection of hiring agents, who in effect forced the workers to become their submissive instruments.

On May 1, 1922, a day whose international significance had only recently become important in China, the National Labor Congress held its first meeting in Canton, with the support of Sun Yat-sen's government. A hundred and sixty delegates from twelve cities attended, representing about 300,000 workers. They voted in favor of an eight-hour day and reaffirmed workers' solidarity during strikes. Militants from the Trade Union Secretariat were active in the congress, which also included more moderate elements.

During the summer of 1922, a new government came to power in Peking, providing the Trade Union Secretariat with an occasion for popularizing workers' problems. Wu Pei-fu in fact declared that he was in favor of a policy of "work protection." The militant Communists decided to take him at his word and to ask the old parliament, which had returned to Peking with President Li Yuan-hong, to vote in labor laws. A program of nineteen articles was drawn up, including the eight-hour day. The articles were distributed all over China, approved by the workers' assemblies, and sent to Peking. Undoubtedly the authorities were not in a position to adopt the program and they were even less prepared to apply it. But as propaganda it had a real effect.

The antiworker repression of 1923

Apart from the sailors' strike in the South and the meeting of the congress in Canton, the main thrust of the workers' movement was in the warlords' sphere of influence. At first, this neofeudal circle hardly paid any attention to the activities of the proletariat, a historic force completely foreign to its system of values and its experience. Some warlords, like Wu Pei-fu in the North and Zhao Heng-ti in Hunan, even tried to gain favor with the public by adopting a liberal policy toward the unions.

What changed the situation was the progress of trade unionism and strikes within the railway system. Here the *dujun* system and the workers' movement came into direct conflict (specifically, because of the transport of troops required by the rivalries between the *dujun*). In February 1923, Wu Pei-fu banned the Unified Syndicate of Railway Workers of the Peking-Hankou system—which was the backbone of his territorial power—from holding its founding congress; sixteen local clubs had been planning to merge. When the workers went on strike in protest, he attacked. His soldiers killed thirty-five and wounded many others.

The brutal massacre, which shocked people all over China, marked the beginning of a wave of antiworker repression. Warlords everywhere closed down unions and broke strikes, whose number dropped in 1923 to forty-eight (down by a half). This decrease was also due to the economic crisis, salary cuts, and to the closing of factories.

In spite of its strong beginnings, the workers' movement had not been able to brave the warlords alone. The workers needed allies, just as the bourgeoisie needed allies in its so far fruitless fight against the militarists and the unequal treaties.

A marginal peasant movement

After 1927, the Communists would seek their allies among the peasants. But this fundamental strategic turning point was still far in the future. At this early stage, the workers' movement was isolated in the cities, cut off from the immense peasant forces. The Communists were only concerned with the industrial proletariat, in line with their application of Marxist theory.

An exception to this was to be found in the work of Peng Pai (1896–1929), a Communist from Canton who began to organize peasant unions in the district of Haifeng (in east Guangdong) in 1922 and 1923. These unions supervised rural markets, established mutual aid and unofficial arbitration among the peasants, and supported those who refused to pay the farm rents. But in the rest of China, the discontent of the peasants was still expressed in the archaic forms of secret societies and spontaneous riots.

Contacts between the Guomindang and the Soviets

The Soviets had an important part in bringing together the Guomindang and the Communists, who agreed upon a formal

alliance in January 1924. In November 1921, while he was preparing for his Northern Expedition, Sun Yat-sen had been visited
at his Guilin headquarters by Maring, the Soviet agent who had
just taken part in the founding of the Chinese Communist Party.
Maring had told him about Soviet views on methods of political
struggle (which involved a party of the masses) and on economics
(this was during the period of the New Economic Policy). He had
suggested that the Guomindang work in cooperation with the USSR.

Sun Yat-sen, who was then at the height of his power in the
South, had turned down these offers. Yet the contacts continued.
The Guomindang participated in the Far Eastern Workers' Congress
in Petrograd, which publicly supported struggles for national liberation.

In 1922, after he had been driven out of Canton again by militarists and was in exile in Shanghai, Sun Yat-sen was more receptive.
In August, he met with Maring to discuss possible military and
political cooperation, and then received a visit from another Soviet
agent, A. A. Joffe. These negotiations resulted in the famous Sun-
Joffe Declaration (January 26, 1923): China was not ready for
communism; priority had to be given to the struggle for reunification of the nation and full independence; the Soviet Union would
support this struggle.

Contacts between the Guomindang and the Communists

It was natural that the Guomindang and the Communists should
come together, not only because of the close ties between the
Chinese Communist Party and Moscow, but also because Sun
Yat-sen had seen something of the dynamism of the workers' movement in 1922 (especially during the sailors' strike) and foresaw how
strong was the political support it could offer the Guomindang.

The Guomindang, which met in Shanghai in autumn 1922, discussed both an alliance with the Soviet Union and the admission of
Communists into the party. In January 1923, the Guomindang
approved a proclamation which formally announced the complete
renewal of the party and promulgated new statutes. These statutes,
which at one and the same time promoted the party's collective
course and the participation of its membership, enlarged a political
machine which had in fact included only one person—Sun Yat-sen
—up to then. The proclamation emphasized the need for a united
struggle against the militarists in the North and the powers who

were benefitting from the unequal treaties, and this gave a wider meaning to the traditional three people's principles, part of the Guomindang's charter since 1905.

As for the Communists, they had come just as far. It was true that as early as 1920, in its "Theses on the National and Colonial Questions," the Second Congress of the Comintern had confirmed the revolutionaries' support of struggles for national independence, even when they were led by a bourgeois party. But in 1922, the Second Congress of the Communist Party was still giving priority to the struggles of the proletariat and to its own political mission. Only at the time of the Third Congress of the CCP (Chinese Communist Party), in June 1923, were these priorities reversed in favor of supporting the Guomindang and the struggles for national liberation. This congress reaffirmed the central role of the Guomindang in the Chinese revolution and decided that Communists would join it (something the Guomindang had just agreed to as well). Apparently Maring had played an important personal role in these difficult discussions. Within the congress, there was leftist opposition which rejected the idea of alliance with a bourgeois party. The secretary-general, Chen Du-xiu, was in favor of a wait-and-see policy in which they would first let the Guomindang bring about its own bourgeois revolution.

The return of Sun Yat-sen to Canton and new progress with the United Front

Chen Jiong-ming's power in Canton was shaky, in spite of the help he received from the English in Hong Kong. In February 1923, Chen was driven out by troops which favored Sun Yat-sen, and Sun returned to Canton.

Sun's rapprochement with the Soviet Union and the Communists, which had been sketched out during his exile in Shanghai, could now be pursued on a concrete basis. In August, Sun sent a mission to Moscow led by Tchiang Kaï-chek, one of his military associates who was little known at the time. In return, a Soviet mission led by Michael Borodin arrived in Canton in September.

Borodin participated actively in the movement to reorganize the Guomindang, serving as political adviser. A temporary executive committee was formed in October which included the Communist Tan Ping-shan. The time was approaching for the Congress for

Reorganizing the Guomindang, which had been planned for January 1924.

On the other hand, the gap between Sun Yat-sen and the West continued to widen. In July, in an interview given to *The New York Times,* Sun declared that he had lost all faith in the Western powers and no longer trusted anyone but the USSR. As a matter of fact, claiming it wished to remain neutral, the diplomatic corps in Peking had refused to give Sun Yat-sen the comfortable customs surplus which it handed out so obligingly to the militarists of the North. In December 1923, Sun threatened to seize the revenues of the customs offices in the port of Canton, but backed down before a threat of Western military intervention.

ADDITIONAL BIBLIOGRAPHY

Jean Chesneaux, *Sun Yat-sen* (Paris, 1959).

Hu Sheng, *Imperialism and Chinese Politics* (Peking, Foreign Languages Press, 1955).

Lucian W. Pye, *Warlord Politics, Conflict and Coalition in the Modernization of Republican China* (New York, Praeger 1971).

James E. Sheridan, *Chinese Warlord: the Career of Feng Yu-hsiang* (Stanford, Calif., Stanford University Press, 1966).

L. Wieger, *La Chine moderne*, vol. IV, *L'outre d'école* (Hien-hien, 1923).

The China Year Book (Peking, years 1923–1924).

Sun Yat-sen, *Le Triple démisme ou San Min chuyi* (various French and English editions).

DOCUMENTS

1. THE DISTRESS OF THE PEOPLE OF SICHUAN UNDER THE WARLORDS

SOURCE: L. Wieger, *La Chine moderne*, vol. IV (Hien-hien, 1923), pp. 262–264. Copy of a letter which appeared in the *Da-gong-bao* of Tientsin (September 14, 1923).

Poor people of Sichuan, for ten years now we have suffered the scourge of militarism, more destructive than the floods, more destructive than savage beasts. Will it continue until not a single man, not a single hut remains in this wretched land? Ah! these military governors* and their officers! . . . We must have soldiers, people say, so that the country will be strong. We must have armies to protect

---

* The 1912 republican government had divided provincial power between the civilian governor and the military governor. But only the latter actually counted.

ourselves from foreigners. And the armies are continually recruiting men. And the people become poorer and poorer! Our old Lao-Tse said it so well: where an army has passed, nothing grows but brambles. This is the case with us, where armies pass through again and again. Our situation has become intolerable.

At present, all over the world, the people are calling for disarmament, and our entire country is calling for the removal of the military governors. Out of the 70 million men in our province, couldn't we find enough men to defend it? But no; the people remain unarmed; soldiers come and bandits follow them, then the bandits withdraw and the soldiers come back.— And what's more, it is the armies who maintain the scourge of banditry here. All discharged soldiers become bandits; and when the army needs one more soldier, it enlists a bandit. The army buys munitions, and it is the bandits who get them. Though the bandits pillage as much as they want, the officers pretend not to know and not one soldier makes a move. Let us not mince words, soldiers and bandits are two names for the same thing. . . .

2. THE DISINTEGRATION OF RURAL SOCIETY: THE FOUR BRIGANDS OF FUKIEN [FUJIAN]

SOURCE: An account by W. B. Cole in *The China Weekly Review* (Shanghai, October 10, 1925), vol. 34, pp. 137–138.

The other day one of the preachers of the Methodist Episcopal Church was returning to his parish in the country. As he passed out of the City gate he fell into the company of four brigands. His conversation with them illuminates the why of the bandit situation that exists in many parts of China to-day.

At first the preacher did not know that his fellow travellers were brigands. There were four ordinary-looking men in the road a step or two ahead. Catching up with them he addressed them with the customary politeness;

"Where are you going?"

"We are returning to our headquarters at——," was the astonishing response naming the retreat of a well-known brigand chieftain.

This unexpected information sent a bit of a shiver up the preacher's spine. It was strange to find himself in such company and he wondered at their boldness in entering the garrisoned city where they must pass under the scrutiny of armed guards who would arrest them immediately once their identity became known. But the preacher decided to make the most of the situation, so put on a friendly attitude and again addressed them.

"How is it that you dare to come into the City?"

"We carry no implements of war, we have on no uniforms, nor do we wear an announcement printed on our faces that we are brigands. Why should we fear to enter the City?"

"You are all young men of good appearance, why is it that you are not engaged in some respectable calling but rather prefer to be bandits bringing ruin and disorder upon the country?"

To this question one of the four speaking of his case made reply:

"I formerly was a farmer but I got involved in a quarrel with a group of men over the water supply for the irrigation of our fields. One of the group being a police inspector of course had special influence with the government. Taking advantage of it he had me seized and handed over to the yamen, making false representations about me. The judge listening to his words rendered a decision against me. I was thrown into prison. I got my freedom by paying the sum of $120. I rebelled at this unjust treatment and seeing the present opportunity of becoming a brigand and getting revenge I proceeded to join. I succeeded in my objective. One night I led a group of fellow brigands and captured my enemies. It cost the group over a thousand dollars to get their freedom. Now they have joined a rival group of bandits and we must be constantly on our guard against an attack. They mean to get even with me."

When he had finished speaking Brigand Number Two gave his reason.

"I was also a farmer. There were eight in my household. The typhoon last summer destroyed most of our crops. This alone reduced my family to serious straits. I had a relative who was an opium smoker. The suppression officer found this out. He sent a group of soldiers to arrest him. But when they found that he had no money to pay a fine they released him. Yet they did not like to return without something to show for the raid made. They seized me on the false charge that I had resisted the officers in arresting my relative. I was forced to pay two hundred dollars before securing release. Besides this the government has collected many and heavy taxes upon our land and upon our house deeds. They have forced us to buy large quantities of salt, levied a heavy poppy tax upon our village although we planted no poppy and forced us to carry heavy loads as transport for the army without pay and with little or no food. I was forced to become a brigand in order to escape further oppression."

The Third Brigand took up the story.

"I likewise was a farmer. Alas there was a feud that divided my village into two opposing clans. The other faction was stronger than my group. One of their leaders also belonged to a bandit group, bringing this added strength to their side. My group saw no other way than to have one of their number join a rival bandit group. I was selected as the one to do this."

"Have you not a wife and children?" interrupted the pastor.

"I have an old mother of sixty, a young wife and three small children. Not long ago my mother was taken ill. I asked my chief to let me go home for a few days. He refused. I then offered him a present of ten dollars if he would let me go. Still he refused me. I saw nothing else to do but to steal away by night and go home. He sent a squad and arrested me, brought me back and fined me for going home without his consent."

"Everyone loves a family; how is it that you brigands thus abandon old mothers of sixty and young wives and children?"

"I cannot go back now. Had I known this step would have involved me for life I would have preferred to remain at home with only two mouthfuls to eat rather than becoming a brigand."

"I was a respectable citizen," said Brigand Number Four in turn, "but I was seized in a bandit raid. The ransom fixed for my release was five hundred dollars. I could not pay it. Finally the chief said I could get off for sixty dollars if I would join his force, adding that this step would give me and my clan protection as no one would dare molest us for fear of the brigands who would stand back of their fellow brigand and his relatives. Thus I was persuaded."

"Has your chief kept his promise and given you the protection you had hoped to get?" inquired the preacher.

"There has been a continual fight between my group and rival groups of bandits. Recently government forces raided my village and my property was stolen and my house burned to the ground because I was known to be a bandit. My family fled to a neighboring village."

"Would it not be better for you to move away to the Straits Settlements and earn your living there until your locality becomes more peaceful?"

"I cannot go now. I would involve a friend who is my security with the Brigand Chief."

The preacher turned to Brigand Number One and asked him that since the other three could not withdraw from the brigand army at this time, what was there to prevent him from doing so.

"I wanted to return long ago but have not dared. I fear that the moment I return some enemy will report my presence to the government and I will be captured and beheaded."

"But are you not in danger while serving as a bandit?"

The pastor had probed a tender spot. They admitted, "Each day brings several big scares, and each night we move several times."

"There is only one way out of this," said the pastor. "If China will accept the teachings of Jesus, we Chinese will learn to love each other as brothers, and officials and soldiers will be led to administer justice."

They had come to the parting of their ways. The Four Brigands told the preacher that his doctrine was good but they bade him a respectful goodbye and turned to the road leading up into the mountain fastness to rejoin their Brigand Chief.

But the conversation gives a clear revelation of how many brigands are made and kept as such. It is a machine largely of the government's own making. The raw material it uses is dependable farmers and humble laborers who could be the foundation stones of the country. The power that runs this machine is greed and selfishness. Order and justice gives way and chaos takes its place.

Sept. 19, 1925

3. Economic troubles of the Chinese bourgeoisie: the cotton crisis as viewed by a Chinese manufacturer

Source: H. Y. Moh, "Causes for the High Cost of Cotton and Low Price of Yarn," *The China Weekly Review* (Shanghai, December 23, 1922), vol. 23.

Political unrest and troubles caused by the bandits play an important part in shutting up the cotton in the growing districts. At such a disturbing time the cotton growers in the interior find it difficult and even dangerous to ship cotton to the manufacturing cities and bring back home their silver dollars. They think it wiser to keep their cotton at home and wait for some better time. This causes a great curtailment in the amount of cotton coming to the market and accounts also for the constant rise in the price of Chinese cotton.

When cotton for which tax has already been paid, on its way to the market, comes within the district of any troops, it is apt to be held for further taxation. The imposition is sometimes regarded as insurance fee, but anyway it tends to increase the expenses of bringing cotton out and raises its price when it comes to the market.

The high price of Chinese cotton is also attributable to the increase of cotton export to Japan and the United States. The cotton mills in Japan usually get their raw material from the United States and India, but this year they find not only American, but Indian cotton also, too dear to use for the counts of yarn which they spin. For this reason they buy large quantities of Chinese cotton to substitute for American and Indian cotton. This is even true to some extent with the cotton mills in the United States. It is reported that a larger amount of high grade Chinese cotton has been exported to the United States this year for use in spinning than the previous years.

Recently the Japanese have done a great deal in extending their cotton manufacturing business in China. In Shanghai and Tsingtao they own altogether 1,500,000 spindles, of which 1,000,000 are already in operation. All of their cotton mills, like the Chinese mills, use chiefly Chinese cotton which is still cheaper than American. They take advantage of their enormous capital and familiarity with the Chinese market conditions in buying large quantities of Chinese cotton and thus cause it to remain at a very high price.

1. There are several reasons why the price of cotton yarn has dropped so much this year. The first is found in the dullness of the yarn market in Japan. Great Britain and Japan are alike in being great cotton manufacturing countries. It is, however, easier for Great Britain to remain a competitor in the future cotton industry in the world, since all her cotton mills spin yarn of fine counts for which there is always an unfailing demand. The Japanese cotton mills, on the other hand, turn out more coarse yarn, which has a rapid production but a slow consumption. The yarn made in Japan must have an outlet so most of it has been sold to China for a number of years. The situation of the "Sampin" yarn in Japan has for years determined the price

of cotton yarn on the Chinese market. The prospects of the yarn market in Japan now being so dull, there is very little hope for the yarn market in China to have any favorable change.

2. Amid lootings and political disturbances the yarn dealers in the interior have not the courage to place any new orders. On the other hand, large quantities of yarn are waiting for opportunity for disposal at the various shipping points, which have been kept long in stock, because the trains along the different railways are busily engaged by the troops and leave no space for the transportation of cotton yarn. There is very little business done in cotton yarn and that is a great cause of the difficulty for the price of yarn to go up.

3. As stated above, there is now little buying and selling in cotton yarn in China. Whenever there is a chance for doing any business, the yarn made in Japan pours in in any amount and the Japanese cotton mills in China also try to sell as much of their spot goods or goods for future delivery as they can, thus making the price considerably lower than it would otherwise be. This is also one of the reasons for the cheap price of cotton yarn at present.

Our cotton industry has now reached a very critical stage. It is to be recollected that in February, March and April of 1916, when Yuan Shih Kai made himself emperor, 16s yarn was sold at Tls. 84 only per bale, while raw materials alone cost Tls. 86 per bale and cost of production was wholly a loss to the cotton mills. Such a state of affairs again happens in the present year. The decline of our cotton industry is due partly to the pressure of external forces and partly to internal troubles. We should be aware that to remove the pressure of external forces we are in a position to ask for assistance from our government, but to remove internal troubles we cannot go to and get help from foreign nations. If our internal affairs keep on going off the track, it is not only destructive to cotton manufacturing business, but to all lines of business as well. The old idea that we held that businessmen should only care for business is no more useful today. It is the duty of our businessmen to get together and devise every way and means to force our government to improve our internal affairs. We believe that only by so doing can we find hope in the recovery of the business of our country and that our failure to take such steps will result in the complete failure of all business, the impossibility for our people to make livings and finally the destruction of our nation.

Shanghai, December 18, 1922.

Chapter Six

The Growth of the Revolution from 1924 to 1927 and Its Failure

The Congress for Reorganizing the Guomindang in 1924 established the alliance between the workers' movement and the bourgeoisie, between the Communists and the Nationalists. This United Front, which served the interests of both groups, favored the development of large popular movements in 1925 to 1926, the consolidation of the revolutionary base of Canton, and the offensive of the southern armies against the warlords in July 1926. But the great success of this revolutionary wave provoked a reaction from the right-wing forces, now wishing to eliminate these increasingly dangerous allies. The break became complete in Shanghai during spring 1927 on the initiative of the Guomindang right wing, and was facilitated by the wait-and-see policy of the Communists and their supporters in Moscow. The final blow came in July 1927 with the fall of the Wuhan government, a brief and belated coalition between the Communists and the left wing of the Guomindang.

Reorganization of the Guomindang and the Development of Popular Struggles

The congress of January 1924

The national congress of the Guomindang, which met in Canton, adopted a new general platform for the party. The manifesto of the

155

congress called for a joint struggle against the unequal treaties and the militarists. It proposed a reorganization of the state based on decentralization, universal suffrage, an army of conscripts which would be charged with nonmilitary tasks, aid to workers and peasants, and state control of the largest industries.

The three people's principles were reaffirmed, but in such a way as to make their content much clearer. The principle of nationalism was equated with anti-imperialist struggle; the principle of democracy moved away from Western parliamentarianism and underscored the power of the people; and the principle of the well-being of the people moved toward socialism. These three renewed principles were extended into three new policies: cooperation with the Soviet Union, alliance with the Chinese Communists, and support of the worker and peasant movements.

The members of the Soviet political and military mission who had arrived in Canton at the end of 1923 played an important role in the congress. Three Communist members were elected (including Li Da-zhao) to the Central Committee of the party and six others (including Mao Tsetung) were elected as alternates. The Communists became full-fledged members of the Guomindang, on an equal footing with the other members.

Consolidation of the Canton regime

With the aid of the Communists and the Soviet advisers, the Guomindang apparatus was reorganized. The brunt of the leadership was taken on by various departments, particularly the departments of organization and propaganda, in which there were many Communists. The military government (which became the nationalist government in June 1925) was also consolidated. Liao Zhong-kai, one of the men closest to Sun Yat-sen, put the finances in order; T. V. Soong, Sun's brother-in-law, became director of the National Bank.

Most of the effort was concentrated on the army. A military academy, founded in Whampoa in May 1924, formed solid political units. The head of the academy was Tchiang Kaï-chek, the adviser was the Soviet general Vasily Blücher (better know as Galen), and its political commissar was Zhou En-lai. The army itself was reorganized and given political commissars. The regime could now do without the small military feudalities which Sun Yat-sen had relied on as recently as 1923 to help him return to Canton. Some of the condottieri, who had taken control of the city, were defeated and chased out in June 1925. The gangs under the direction of Chen Jiong-ming were purged from eastern Guangdong in February and November 1925. The Nationalist government was in full control of the revolutionary base.

Canton actively supported the popular forces. With the enactment of a law in November 1924, the unions received many benefits. Liao Zhong-kai often settled arbitrations in favor of the workers and encouraged them to regroup themselves in a "conference of worker delegates." The union militias were very active during strikes. The government also helped to set up an institute for the creation of cadres in the peasant movement.

The masses became more and more active in the political life of Canton; there were street demonstrations, popular marches, and public meetings. Tens of thousands of people listened to the public lectures in which Sun Yat-sen developed the new meaning of the three people's principles. There were festivals on May 1 and for the anniversary of the October Revolution. Western journalists spoke of "red Canton." However, Soviet policy was more complex. While cooperating with Canton, the USSR had also signed a treaty with the Peking government in May 1924, normalizing diplomatic relations, recognizing the separation between China and Outer Mongolia (under Soviet influence), and placing under Soviet control the East China Railway (the Trans-Manchurian). This balancing game became even more pronounced when Moscow signed a special treaty with Zhang Zuo-lin, the leader of Manchuria, in November 1924.

Political overtures to the North and the death of Sun Yat-sen

Sun Yat-sen's objective had been to "punish the North" (Beifa) and to liquidate the *dujun* cliques by force. He had already prepared this project in 1921, but had to give it up because of Chen Jiong-ming's military offensive in Canton. In 1924, he put it off once again when the political situation in the North was suddenly thrown into upheaval.

The Zhili group had controlled North China since 1922; it coveted Shanghai, which remained under the influence of the Anfu and the Fengtian cliques. During the second Fengtian-Zhili war in September 1924, Wu Pei-fu at first seemed victorious. But he was suddenly attacked by his ally, Feng Yu-xiang, whose troops occupied Peking and ousted President Cao Kun. Wu Pei-fu retreated to the Yangzi with what remained of the Zhili forces. A new coalition brought to power the Anfu leader Duan Qi-rui (who had been ousted in 1920), Zhang Zuo-lin, and Feng Yu-xiang. Feng Yu-xiang, who had named his troops the "National People's Armies" (Kuominjun), who had chased the House of the Qing from the Forbidden City of Peking and had lived there since the abdication of 1912, seemed to a progressive military man. He asked Sun Yat-sen to come see him, and Sun agreed.

Sun left for Peking in November 1924. He proposed a national convention, which would bring together delegates from among the businessmen, industrialists, teachers, union workers, the peasant unions, and the universities. Feng supported this project. But Duan and Zhang were in favor of a more conservative approach and wanted to hold a reorganization conference limited to military leaders and the most prestigious civilians. In order to impose the national convention's more democratic approach, the Guomindang and the Communist Party launched a mass campaign of meetings and rallies throughout the country.[1] But Sun was unable to keep up the fight for very long. He was very ill when he arrived in Peking and died of cancer of the liver in March 1925. In his will, he called for the continued struggle for the three principles.

In the end, the crisis of 1924 did not affect the *dujun*'s system of power. Feng was disappointed and retired to the Northwest with his People's Armies. The complicated rivalries among the Anfu, the Zhili, and the Fengtian groups continued to hold center stage. In spring 1925 a new war pitted the Jiangsu (pro-Zhili) against the Zhejiang (pro-Anfu), who were defeated. A new "super-dujun," Sun Chuan-fang, the current rival of Wu Pei-fu, took control of the five provinces of the lower Yangzi.

These fruitless games played by the warlords became wearisome to the people. They looked more and more to the revolutionary base of the South and to the surviving prestige of Sun Yat-sen.

Reawakening of the workers' movement (1924–1925)

The political conditions favored this reawakening. The Zhili, who had been the principal initiators of the antiworker repression in 1923, had been defeated. The new Canton government, and par-

---

[1] See document 1 at the end of the chapter.

ticularly Liao Zhong-kai, officially supported the workers' struggles. The same was true of Feng in the North.

At the end of 1924 and the beginning of 1925, a campaign for the restoration of the unions had good results—among the railwaymen, for example. There were new strikes, particularly in the Japanese cotton mills of Shanghai (February 1925) and among the employees of the Western concessions at Canton, on Shamian Island (July 1924). These two strikes were essentially economic in their objectives, but they were aiming at the centers of foreign imperialism and thus were part of the Nationalist movement line sketched by the congress of January 1924.

In May 1925, the Second National Workers Congress met in Canton, with 281 delegates from 166 unions, representing 540,000 members. The congress affirmed its support of the struggles for national liberation, called for the strengthening of union organizations, and set up a national body, the General Pan-Chinese Union.

In February 1925, the Fourth Congress of the Communist Party also emphasized workers' struggles. But, in a somewhat restrictive manner, it called for the strengthening of purely working class organizations and the workers' own class struggle. However, the sudden explosion of large popular movements in June 1925, participated in by millions of people across China, owed its force to the militancy of the masses, to the ripening of the political situation, and to the unpopularity of the *dujun* and the unequal treaties. The existing organizations (the unions, the Communist Party, and the Guomindang) were caught somewhat off guard by this ferment from the base. But they immediately lent it their support and the experience of their militants. Without this support, these movements could not have become so widespread or have lasted for such a long time.

The May Thirtieth Movement in Shanghai

On May 30, 1925, the English police of the international concession at Shanghai fired on unarmed Chinese demonstrators, killing ten and seriously wounding fifty. These demonstrators were protesting the killing of a Chinese worker on May 15 by a Japanese foreman in a Japanese cotton mill that was on strike.

The protest movement against this shooting brought together very diverse forces: the General Union of Shanghai, which had been formed on May 31 at the call of the Communists and whose member unions were solidly entrenched in the big factories; the student associations, which had regained the patriotic spirit of May Fourth; the Shanghai Chamber of Commerce, which represented the capitalist bourgeoisie; and the associations of street merchants, which represented traditional small business. This gathering reflected the political progress of the United Front since the congress of 1924. But it was also the expression of the Shanghai bourgeoisie's willingness to engage in struggle after having submitted impatiently to the guardianship of the concession's foreign municipal council and futilely asking to have a place in it.

The Federation of Workers, Merchants, and Students (Gongshangxue lianhehui), which supported all these forces, led the movement. It demanded at one and the same time indemnities for the victims, certain improvements for the workers (better salaries and working conditions), and reform of the status of Shanghai according to the wishes of the bourgeoisie (legal status for the Chinese, the right to vote, for example). To support these demands, the merchants and students went on strike, closing their businesses and refusing to go to classes, and work ceased in the foreign enterprises of Shanghai. In June there were 160,000 people on strike, which cost the strike fund a million yuan per month. Collections were taken up throughout China, but most of the money came from the chamber of commerce, which backed the strikers politically and stood to profit from the work stoppage in the foreign factories, which were in competition with the factories of the Chinese bourgeoisie.

However, the Chinese bourgeoisie hesitated when faced with the risk of sympathy strikes being staged in their own factories. The diplomatic corps held out the prospect of an impending revision of the customs and legal status of China. The movement stopped when the General Union negotiated a relatively advantageous agreement with the Japanese in August and with the English in September.

These three months of general strike did more than simply affirm the strength of the workers' movement in Shanghai and the authority of its union organizations. With meetings, street marches, tracts, and the whole patriotic and anti-imperialist fervor of the May Thirtieth Movement, the vitality of the popular movement in Shanghai (and its strong worker representation) was clearly expressed in China's largest city, which had been silent since May to June 1919 because of the oppression of both the warlords and the Westerners.

The May Thirtieth Movement in
North and Central China

Throughout the areas of China controlled by the warlords, solidarity with the strikes in Shanghai was expressed in many and various forms: "Committees to wipe out the disgrace," attacks against Japanese companies, boycotts of foreign goods, collections, political agitation, and sympathy strikes. These strikes took place in the large foreign factories: the Japanese cotton mills in the North, the KMA English mines in Tangshan, the English powdered egg factory in Nanking. Everywhere the same spirit of understanding that had been established in Shanghai among workers, students, and small businessmen came into play, while the hesitant bourgeoisie slowed down the movement. In the beginning, the warlords changed their ways in the face of this wave of national emotion, sometimes even contributing money, but they soon returned to putting down popular agitation.

This movement of solidarity with the May Thirtieth Movement contributed to a vigorous renewal of the workers' movement and the unions. It was also the occasion of a political renewal, of a re-awakening of popular militancy which would be of enormous help to the revolutionary army of Canton when it arrived in the Yangzi region in 1926.

On the other hand, the peasantry did not take part in the May Thirtieth Movement. The emphasis had been placed on the struggle against the Japanese and English who had been responsible for the initial incidents, and more generally against imperialism, which was not significantly present in the villages. For the Communists, who took such an active role in the May Thirtieth Movement, the peasantry was no more than a minor force. "The political struggle will be decided in the cities," declared a resolution of the Second National Workers Congress in May 1925.

The strike-boycott of Canton–Hong Kong

On June 23, 1925, a procession of people demonstrating their solidarity with the Shanghai strikers passed near the French and English concessions of Canton and was fired upon by the French and English guards. Fifty-two were killed and more than a hundred were wounded. In retaliation, the workers' and people's organizations of Canton called for a general strike of the Chinese workers in the British colony of Hong Kong; the workers were asked to leave the island and a boycott of Hong Kong began. All commerce between Hong Kong and the territory held by the Nationalist government was declared illegal.

The strike and boycott, which were immediately put into effect, lasted until October 1926, making the strike one of the longest in workers' history. The movement was very well organized, with a strike committee at its head that was led by the Communists. The committee provided lodging for tens of thousands of strikers from Hong Kong, organized detachments of armed pickets to keep watch over the coast, had a budget of several million yuan (advanced by the Canton government), and exercised certain statelike functions (police, courts, the imprisonment of "scabs"): in Canton, it was familiarly called "Government Number Two" (*dier zhengfu*). The Nationalist government gave it financial and political support. The struggle against Hong Kong followed the anti-imperialist line of the congress of January 1924.

Also supported by the basic population of Canton, which sheltered the strikers, backed them, and participated in anti-English political agitation, the strike-boycott movement was very successful. It cost the English in Hong Kong millions of pounds sterling. The island was on the verge of suffocation and even had to have drinking water and vegetables shipped from the Philippines. Initially hurt by the boycott, the Cantonese bourgeoisie supported it after the strike committee allowed their "special permit" boats to operate, exempting them from the control of the pickets.

By the impetus it gave to the popular struggles in the South, the strike-boycott helped to reinforce the left wing of the Guomindang in the tense period that followed Sun Yat-sen's death. In particular, it favored the moving toward the left of the Cantonese unions, which were nevertheless strongly marked by the corporate tradition of the guilds. At the Third National Workers Congress held in Canton in May 1926, the Communist influence in the union movement was consolidated. The emphasis was put on the political struggle of the workers and on the necessity of organization in industrial rather than trade unions.

Theoretical and political problems of the United Front

For a brief while the United Front was founded on the cooperation of two political structures—the Communist Party and the

Guomindang. This cooperation itself reflected a fundamental con-
vergence between the interests of the proletariat and the workers'
movement, which was broadly represented by the CCP, and those
of the bourgeoisie, to which the Guomindang was closely tied. After
several failures, the proletariat and the bourgeoisie had gradually
come to give priority to the joint struggle against the unequal
treaties, imperialism, and the forces of social conservatism and
political repression, the warlords.

This fundamental polarity was not always clear-cut. Certain
groups of workers, for example the Cantonese mechanics, were still
attached to their corporate traditions and were anti-Communist.
Certain groups within the bourgeoisie were very unhappy with the
alliances made by the Guomindang in 1924, alliances which had
come about only through the personal prestige of Sun Yat-sen. The
major compradors from Shanghai had pushed for compromise during the summer of 1925 and had cut the May Thirtieth Movement
short. On the other hand, the social base of the Guomindang was
extended to groups other than the bourgeoisie per se: the middle
classes from the cities, the intelligentsia, and the army.

The Comintern, which had played such a large role in the formation of the United Front, particularly through such agents as
Borodin, defined the Guomindang in 1924 to 1925 as a "bloc of
four classes": the bourgeoisie, the working class, the petite bourgeoisie, and the peasants. In the China of 1924, however, these
classes were still rather vaguely defined and the degree of their
internal political cohesion very unequal. The new Guomindang
might be better defined in terms of a single category, the people, a
category which broadens the political field of the classes properly
so called and unifies their struggle. The militancy of the people, at
least the city people, had been present in the streets of Canton, in
the factories of Shanghai, in the demonstrations throughout the rest
of China during the May Thirtieth period, and in the strike-boycott
of Hong Kong.

In 1924 to 1925, the proletariat and the Communist Party
accepted the obligations entailed by participation in the United
Front and at the same time benefitted from the advantages it
afforded. On the other hand, hostile tendencies were expressed
several times from the Guomindang side. As early as April 1924,
several elder statesmen of the party resigned from the Control
Committee as a sign of protest. In the summer there was a more
serious crisis between Sun Yat-sen and the Cantonese bourgeoisie.
The bourgeois militia of "merchant volunteers," led by a pro-English

comprador who claimed to be an admirer of Mussolini, Tchem Li-pak, attempted an armed revolt that Liao Zhong-kai, the leader of the left, put down with the help of the union militias.

The political crisis in Canton after Sun Yat-sen's death had many repercussions. A triumvirate took control of the party and the government: Liao Zhong-kai; Wang Jing-wei, a former anarchist who continued to pose as an intellectual of the left; and Hu Han-min, a reformed Marxist who represented the right wing. In August, Liao was assassinated, and Hu Han-min, who was implicated in the plot, was forced to flee. But the right wing continued its offensive. The conservative leaders gathered in November 1925 at Sun Yat-sen's tomb in Peking (they were called "the Western Hills Group") and discussed the reorganization of the party without the Communists. In Shanghai, another anti-Communist group, led by the Nationalist intellectual Dai Ji-tao, continued to proclaim a militant anti-imperialism. In order to put an end to this splintering, the left, supported by the Communists, called an emergency meeting in Canton of the Second Congress of the Guomindang in January 1926. The left consolidated its positions: out of thirty-six members of the Central Committee, thirteen were from the left and seven from the center. But no major figure had stepped forth since the death of Liao Zhong-kai, and Tchiang Kaï-chek was already waiting in the wings.

The Nationalist Government's Offensive Against the North

The situation in 1926: the revolutionary camp

The Nationalist government controlled Guangdong and Guangxi, but the rifts that had opened after Sun Yat-sen's death continued to grow. The victory of the left wing at the congress of January 1926 was short-lived. Tchiang Kaï-chek, who skillfully avoided being precise about his political plans, organized an attack in March 1926 against the Soviet advisers and Communists. Apparently, this was only a test, because several days later he claimed that it had all been due to a misunderstanding. By May, the Communists were already ousted from the leadership of the departments of organization and propaganda, and measures were taken in Canton to restrain the activity of the unions. Tchiang officially took control of the government army in June. Wang Jing-wei, the major leader of the left, went into exile in Europe.

The Communist Party, which had grown from 1,000 to 30,000 members in 1925 to 1926, preferred to bide its time and not provoke a confrontation. The CCP hoped that the Northern Expedition, which was now imminent, would allow it to re-establish its influence by freeing the popular forces it would have to call upon in the struggle.

The National People's Armies of the Christian marshal Feng Yu-xiang were a useful strategical counterbalance for the Nationalists in the South. They had been in the Northwest since their departure from Peking in 1925 and were in a position to help take the northerners from behind. Allied to Canton, they had Soviet advisers and materiel. Feng followed a progressive policy, supporting the peasant unions and labor unions.

The situation in 1926: the northern camp

The complicated Chinese map of the warlords became increasingly simplified as the test of power with the revolutionary armies of Canton approached. Sun Chuan-fang, the new "super-dujun," controlled the five provinces of the lower Yangzi. Wu Pei-fu, who controlled Hubei and Henan, extended his influence to Sichuan. Zhang Zuo-lin, the leader of Manchuria, also took over Shandong, and once again, in April, 1926, had the Anfu leader Duan Qi-rui ousted from the Peking government. The armies of Sun, Wu, and Zhang had between 600,000 and 700,000 men, compared to 100,000 for the Nationalist army. But the political relations were poor among these three feudal groups, each hoping that its rivals would be worn down by the battle against the southerners to its own advantage.

Beifa, revolutionary war

As much as from the dissension among the northerners, the Canton armies benefitted from their own revolutionary dynamism and the popular support which they had. Solidly led by political commissars, these soldiers knew that they were fighting for a cause. Their political consciousness had been formed in 1924 to 1925 and had fed on the antifeudal and anti-imperialist ideology developed by the

Guomindang. As the soldiers advanced toward the North, the peasants fed them and furnished them with guides and carriers, while their adversaries saw all support from the population denied them and were subjected to worker sabotage, especially on the railways. The Beifa and the arrival of the armies from Canton in the large cities were greeted by great celebrations and demonstrations of enthusiasm. In addition, the left was influential in the army. A certain number of units and officers leaned toward communism, particularly in the Fourth Nationalist Army, which was led by General Zhang Fa-kui. The entire force of the workers' militias from the Canton-Hong Kong strike committee was brought into the Beifa army, which opened its ranks to include the miners, railwaymen, and the coolies from Hunan and Hubei as it advanced toward the North.

On the other hand, the Canton army was prematurely swelling with all the deserters and defectors streaming from the northern forces during the debacle of autumn 1926. Following an old Chinese tradition, these troops had changed sides with the victory. They worked under Tchiang Kaï-chek with a mercenary and feudal allegiance, and their revolutionary consciousness was nonexistent. This situation fit into Tchiang's plans and assured him of loyal troops regardless of the political situation.

The campaign of August–December 1926

Wu Pei-fu was the first to be defeated. The southerners entered Changsha, the capital of Hunan, in July, opened the passes that led to Hubei in August, took Hankou and Hanyang in September, then surrounded and took Wuchang after more difficult fighting. Wu, who was detained by the battles against the Guomindang armies in the Northwest, could not bring his forces together in time. He had to abandon the Yangzi and withdraw to Zhengzhou in the North.

Sun Chuan-fang had let his old adversary be defeated. But he himself was also attacked by the revolutionary troops, who entered Jiangxi in September, took the provincial capital, Nanchang, in November, and then the chief port of the Yangzi, Jiujiang. In the autumn, other southern armies occupied Fujian and its capital, Fuzhou, and penetrated the province of Zhejiang from the South. Only the forces of the third northern group, led by Zhang Zuo-lin, remained intact.

The upsurge of workers' struggles

With the advance of the armies of the Nationalist government, labor unions "sprang up like mushrooms after the rain." In January 1927, the newly created Provincial Federation of Unions from Hubei held a congress which brought together 580 delegates from 314 unions, representing 393,000 members. Around the same time the Provincial Federation of Unions from Hunan had about 400,000 members. In both cases these figures represented the modern proletariat as well as the artisans and coolies. These unions stood for the beginnings of true workers' power; there were well stocked treasuries, armed militias, intervention in the case of work conflicts, control of hiring, and punitive measures against those who were guilty of a lack of discipline or solidarity.

Strikes were numerous and well run in the regions liberated by the southern troops, particularly in the factories and other enterprises managed by foreigners. They were clearly anti-imperialist in spirit. But when strikes began in Chinese enterprises, the problems became more complex. The Nationalist government, which had moved from Canton to Wuhan in October, and which was controlled by the Communists and the left wing of the Guomindang, neither wanted to slow down the workers' movement nor upset the Chinese bourgeoisie. An attempt was made to set up a system of arbitration under the supervision of a mixed commission (management, the unions, the Guomindang, and the government). At first, this system received a relatively warm welcome. The right and the left put off their confrontation, since each hoped that the progress of the Beifa would work in its favor and strengthen its position.

In Canton, the principal center of the workers' struggle in the preceding phase, the victories of the Beifa had led to a settlement of the strike-boycott which had been going on since June of the previous year. Efforts were now concentrated on the Yangzi region, where the British government had agreed to give compensation in exchange for the lifting of the blockade.

The upsurge of the peasant movement

The peasant struggles that had begun in 1924 and 1925 had been encouraged by the line established by the Guomindang at the congress of January 1924. The peasant unions had grown in number in the territory controlled by the Canton government and even in the southern regions held by the militarists, such as Hunan, eastern Guangdong, where Peng Pai continued his work, and western Guangxi, in the zone populated by Zhuang minorities. These peasant unions waged an economic struggle against property owners in order to lower the rents on tenant farms, organized armed militias in order to combat the landowners' militias, and sometimes made direct attacks on the militarists. The Peasant Movement Training Institute, which was sponsored by the Guomindang and where Mao Tsetung was a teacher, helped to train many militants. In April 1926, the First National Congress of the Peasant Movement met at Canton, and the participating unions represented more than a million members, of which nearly two thirds were from Guangdong alone.

The peasant struggles also extended into the North, into the heartland of the warlords. In Henan and Shandong they were led by the old secret society the Red Spears, which was probably a branch of the White Lotus. Red Spears members, who practiced rites of initiation and relied upon amulets of invulnerability, organized village self-defense units against the soldiers of the warlords and bandits. They engaged in violent pitched battles against the troops of Wu Pei-fu. The militant Communists did their best to cooperate with them, in the hope of shaping them into peasant unions of a modern sort.

With the arrival of the revolutionary troops in Hunan and Hubei, the peasant unions continued to expand. In Hunan alone they had 1,300,000 members at the beginning of 1927. Their remarkable militancy was documented in a text that has become a classic, "Report on an Investigation of the Peasant Movement in Hunan," written by Mao Tsetung after several weeks of research in early 1927. This report, which announced that "in a very short time, in China's central, southern, and northern provinces, several hundred million peasants will rise like a mighty storm, like a hurricane, a force so swift and violent that no power, however great, will be able to hold it back," listed fourteen fundamental victories of the Hunan peasants: the organization of the peasant unions, the political and economic blows dealt the property owners, the liquidation of the traditional organs of local power and of the armed forces of the property owners, the overthrow of the authority of the district chief and of familial, religious, and marital authority,[2] the sharp prohibitions against luxury and vice, the elimination of abusive taxes

[2] See document 2.

and exactions, the cultural movement, the cooperative movement, and the repair of roads and earth banks.

In his report Mao took issue with those who were frightened by peasant militancy ("the revolution is not a dinner party . . . or doing embroidery") and those who spoke of "peasant excesses." In fact, this last phrase was very widely used, not only amid the right wing of the Guomindang (which was tied to the rural gentry) but among the Communists and even in the Comintern. The orders were to put a halt to these excesses. The line defended by Mao was marginal, very much in the minority during this period. The enormous potential force of the peasants was kept in the background of the revolutionary struggle, thus condemning it to defeat.

The support of the intellectuals

The momentum of the May Fourth Movement had brought left-wing intellectuals into the struggle along with the popular forces. Except for those who had entered the Communist Party, however, the intellectuals had somewhat withdrawn from public life since 1919. They devoted themselves to debates about ideas on literary creation, the possibility of imitating Western literary forms in China, scientism, and the comparative value of Eastern and Western philosophies. The revolutionary wave of 1925–1927 once again led the intellectuals into political activities.

The poet Guo Mo-ruo accompanied the Northern Expedition and told of it in his *Revolutionary Annals from the Spring and Fall (Geming chunqiu)*, the title being a parody of a Confucian classic. The essayist Lu Xun became deeply involved in supporting the revolution[3] and encouraged his students in Canton to do the same. The critic Mao Dun became the editor in chief of the Hankou daily newspaper, which was the organ of the Nationalist revolutionary movement. Dozens of other less illustrious intellectuals followed suit.

New upsurge of national struggles

From 1924 on, the Canton government, supported by the unions, the peasant movement, and the Communists, continued to call for the joint struggle against imperialism, militarism, the unequal treaties, and the old regime. The great anti-English strike in Canton-

[3] See document 3.

Hong Kong ended in October 1926, but in the regions of the Yangzi, which had been liberated by the southern army, the movement against foreign privileges and enterprises developed along with that of the trade unions and the peasant unions. The workers' strikes in the large foreign enterprises of Hubei (English and Japanese) were already strongly influenced by Nationalist ideas. In January 1927, the agitation suddenly increased in Hankou when it was learned that Guomindang militants had been arrested by the British police of Tientsin. The crowd swarmed into the British concession and forced the marines to evacuate. The Nationalist government declared that the concession had been returned to China. For the first time since the Opium Wars, the West had been forced to retreat in China. That same week, in the port of Jiujiang, an incident among the marines and a demonstration in support of strikers in a British factory led to the seizure of the English concession by the crowd. Throughout the middle Yangzi a new anti-English and anti-Japanese boycott developed. Several large Western factories were simply shut down, such as the English tobacco industry in Hankou.

The Break Between the Communists and the Guomindang

The bourgeoisie's new political problems

With the upsurge of popular struggles in the areas liberated by the Beifa army, the Chinese bourgeoisie found itself questioning the alliances it had formed in 1924. It was worried about the growing number of protest strikes in Chinese factories, the activities of the armed militias of the unions, the first attempts of the workers to take over the management of certain foreign enterprises, and the worsening economic crisis in Hubei (rising prices, unemployment, and the scarcity of essential goods). The bourgeoisie was also uneasy about the peasant unions and the actions taken against property owners. In fact, the bourgeoisie was often still tied to the property owners by numerous political and economic connections. Many capitalists, bourgeois intellectuals, and rich merchants held on to their country lands and drew income from tenant farms. Many officers of the Nationalist army were the sons of property owners and were directly threatened by the growth of the peasant unions.

At the beginning of 1927, the right wing of the Guomindang and its bourgeois base therefore envisaged a complete realignment of political forces in China. It had become necessary in their eyes to break with their popular allies, who up to that point had been so important to them in fighting the warlords and the unequal treaties, but who had now become a threat. Since the North had been weakened following the invasion of the Yangzi and many of its armies had defected to the South, this became increasingly possible. Wu Pei-fu's group had been completely eliminated and Sun Chuan-fang's was no longer an important factor. The one militarist force left was represented by the armies of the Northeast (Fengtian). Their leader, Zhang Zuo-lin, who controlled Peking, had reorganized his forces into an anguojun ("army of national pacification"). His power extended as far as Shanghai, which was held by his vassal Zhang Zong-chang (1881–1932), the *dujun* of Shangdong, who was a particularly brutal, rapacious, and violent militarist.

The influence of the powers

The tension in China following the May Thirtieth affair in Shanghai and the strike-boycott in Canton-Hong Kong continued to grow after the seizure of the English concessions in Hankou and Jiujiang. The Nationalist movement, following the line established in January 1924, openly attacked the whole political and economic system on which the domination of the powers in China was based. The Westerners and the Japanese retaliated by concentrating armed forces on the coasts and in the Chinese ports. There were several squadrons, numbering about 20,000 men. They made several attacks, for example at Wanxian (Sichuan), which was bombed in 1926 in reprisal for anti-English incidents, and at Nanking in March 1927, which was also bombed after the pillaging of foreign establishments by soldiers during the debacle in the North. Certain people, particularly in Comintern circles, felt that "imperialist intervention" was imminent and that an attempt would be made to crush the Chinese revolution from the outside just as there had been an attempt to crush the Soviet revolution in 1918 to 1920.

But the West tried to form alliances and divide its adversaries just as much as it sought to attack directly. The English formally acknowledged the return of its Hankou and Jiujiang concessions to the Nationalist government, which amounted to actual recognition of the government. The British authorities in Shanghai finally gave rich Chinese the right to enter the municipal council of the international concession, and promises for abolishing extraterritoriality were taken one step closer to implementation by the creation of study commissions. These overtures to the bourgeoisie encouraged the moderates in the Guomindang. For the right wing of the Nationalist movement, the rapprochement with the West made its plans for breaking with the left that much easier.

Wuhan against Hanchang

The Nationalist government was moved to Wuhan in October 1926. It was more and more dominated by the left, especially by the Christian jurist Xu Qian, Sun Yat-sen's widow, and his older son, Sun Fo. Borodin and his Soviet advisers were listened to carefully, and the Communists were very active, as were the mass organizations they influenced: the peasant unions, the student groups, and especially the General Pan-Chinese Union, which had three million members. The political line had not changed since 1924; it entailed an alliance between the Guomindang and the Communists, cooperation with the USSR, and support of the worker and peasant movements. There was certainly concern over the differences with the right wing, but, following the policy dictated by Moscow, the Communists tried to appease those still regarded as allies, even if they were already acting like enemies. The Communists continued to denounce "peasant excesses" and to trust Tchiang Kaï-chek.

Tchiang had set up headquarters in Nanchang, the capital of Jiangxi. He depended on the northern militarists who had come over to his side and, especially, on the bourgeoisie for support. He had maintained useful friendships in the financial circles of Shanghai, which he became familiar with around 1920 when he had been a small stockbroker. In February and March his plans for a break with the left took shape. In his speeches he attacked the "insolence and brutality" of the Communists. Some of the leaders of his entourage, such as Chen Guo-fu, started an "AB [anti-Bolshevik] League," which organized armed attacks against the southeastern unions in March. On March 11, the Wuhan left wing tried to fight back by stripping Tchiang of all the posts he still held in the government and the party, but without excluding him formally. They still hoped for a compromise.

The struggle for Shanghai

China's largest city was both the principal center of the workers' movement after 1919 and the principal base of Chinese financial groups and their Western friends. The left wing and right wing of the revolutionary movement both hoped that the taking of Shanghai would bring them decisive support. But, in several weeks, the balance would actually be tipped in favor of the right.

Twice, in November 1926 and February 1927, the Shanghai Communists and the workers' unions they influenced had attempted armed uprisings against the northern garrison in Shanghai. The first uprising had quickly miscarried. The second was helped by the advance of the Nationalist armies into the neighboring province of Zhejiang. Though the struggle against the militarists was to be combined with the defense of workers' interests,[4] the strike had been poorly planned, and its failure set off a wave of bloody repression. On March 18, 1927, the General Union of Shanghai, led by the Communists, unleashed an insurrection involving 800,000 workers. In four days the union militias succeeded in defeating and routing the northern troops of Zhang Zong-chang and taking control of the city. Tchiang Kaï-chek's troops did not arrive until March 23, when the fighting was over. This victory of the General Union of Shanghai precipitated the open crisis between the left and the right.

The break of April 12

The fighting had been very intense, and it gave the militants of the extreme left exceptional political authority. In liberated Shanghai the power was held by a provisional popular government, which included Communists, intellectuals, and members of the bourgeoisie. Political freedoms were re-established, and the unions grew in size, participating once again in legal activities and organizing strikes in many Chinese and foreign enterprises. But Tchiang's army held the city, and his influence counterbalanced that of the Communists. In this unstable situation, the Communists held to the conciliatory line they had established along with the Comintern. They agreed not to threaten the status of the international concession and the other local effects of the unequal treaties. They also agreed

[4] See document 4.

to keep labor activities within the narrow limits of economic action (agitation against low wages), and continued to treat Tchiang like a trustworthy revolutionary leader. If, in spite of the pressures, they refused to dissolve the armed militias of the unions, they nevertheless left the militias and the whole Shanghai labor force politically unprepared for a possible attack from Tchiang. They were taken by surprise when he attacked on the night of April 12.

Tchiang had been determined to strike once the last strategic operation for which the cooperation of the Communists and the unions was absolutely necessary to him had been successfully completed. He drew his support from the right wing of the Guomindang, which had based itself in Shanghai following the 1925 split in the party and the breakaway of the anti-Communist elements. He could count on the wealthy bourgeoisie of the city, the bankers, and the compradors, who solicited large sums of money on his behalf from the Westerners and attempted to assure him of the political good will of the powers and their advisers. He had his army tightly in hand and transferred units he suspected of leftist sympathies to other garrisons. He was also given help from the Shanghai underworld, the Green Band and the Red Band, whose leaders controlled the opium traffic and other dubious rackets in the large port, and who put men at his disposal who were ready to participate in the surprise attack against the unions.

At four o'clock on the morning of April 12, the gangsters attacked the buildings of the union militias and massacred the people inside. Some Communist leaders, such as Zhou En-lai, just managed to escape; others were killed. An attempt to organize a protest strike failed. Without arms, the workers' movement was no match in the fighting. The unions were dissolved or "reorganized," and the Communists were defeated. Tchiang Kaï-chek, his allies, and the forces he represented remained in control of Shanghai for a long time.

The wave of anti-Communism in the Southeast and the North

The repression of the unions and the Communists which began in March became widespread in April in all the provinces controlled by Tchiang Kaï-chek's army and the right wing of the Guomindang: Guangdong, Jiangxi, Fujian, Zhejiang, and Jiangsu. The unions were dissolved, strikes were banned, the peasant unions were liquidated, the Communists were hunted down, and militant workers were fired. A few weak attempts at retaliation were immediately crushed. A new chapter had begun.

In the areas of China held by the northerners, anti-Communist repression increased as well. Zhang Zuo-lin's police force no longer feared reprisals from the Nationalists. As early as April 6, the police searched the Soviet embassy at Peking and arrested thirty-five Communist militants who were found there—among them the important intellectual Li Da-zhao, who was immediately decapitated.

Wuhan: a reprieve for the revolution

The official Nationalist government, which had moved from Canton to Wuhan in October 1926, continued to hold the two provinces of Hubei and Hunan and to rely on the coalition between the Guomindang left wing and the Communists (who controlled the ministries of labor and agriculture). The Soviet advisers led by Borodin and General Galen had withdrawn to Wuhan. The peasant unions there remained strong and active (with nine million members in June), as did the workers' unions. On May 1, 1927, the labor unions held their Fourth National Workers Congress, which was attended by 300 delegates, representing three million union workers (the majority of whom, however, came from "white" zones, where union activity had already gone underground). In relation to the events of the preceding winter, the break of April 12 had clarified the situation: Tchiang Kaï-chek and his partisans had been officially expelled from the Guomindang. On April 18 in Nanking they had set up a "national government" of their own as a rival to the government in Wuhan and claimed to be the legitimate heirs of Sun Yat-sen's Guomindang.

Fundamental ambiguities remained. The strategy of supporting worker and peasant struggles conflicted with the desire to appease the Guomindang and to maintain the alliance at any price, both before and after the break with Nanking. That is why the Fifth Congress of the Communist Party, at a time when the party was apparently at the height of its power (with 58,000 members as opposed to 900 in 1925 at the Fourth Congress), decided after long discussions to push the agrarian revolution only moderately. The Wuhan government, with the help of the Communists who were part of it, continued to hold back workers' struggles and the union militias. When strikes arose, it imposed obligatory arbitration. The decisions it reached in May on the agrarian question were vague and amounted to a disavowal of the peasant unions. When a military unit from the Wuhan army mutinied in Changsha on May 21, for example, the leaders of the CCP did all they could to dissuade the peasant unions of the province from retaliating.

Except for a few resolute figures, such as Mme. Sun Yat-sen, the Wuhan government lacked true leaders. Its nominal head, Wang Jing-wei, was a hesitant intellectual. The social base of the Guomindang left wing was not essentially different from that of the party as a whole. Many influential members, tied to the rural gentry, were aghast at the idea of agrarian revolution. The left wing of the Guomindang, because of its weakness, was forced to rely on ambitious soldiers such as Tang Sheng-zhi, men who could not be counted on politically and who were no doubt already in contact with Nanking. During the three months of its existence, military revolts within its own army were numerous.

The climate of confusion and incoherence in the regions controlled by Wuhan was aggravated by economic difficulties and the military impasse. Large businesses were closed; the bourgeoisie had gone to Shanghai; there was unemployment, inflation, and prices continued to rise. In the military field, the offensive against Wu Pei-fu's northern troops continued (Kaifeng and Zhengzhou on the Yellow River were taken in June), but almost as a kind of competition with the Nanking armies, which also continued their drive toward the North. The four-sided military situation was further complicated by the presence in Henan of the armies of Feng Yu-xiang, who was still a nominal ally of the Guomindang left wing, but who was actually steering his own course.

Wuhan: the debacle

While anti-Communist incidents (officer purges, arrests) increased in the Wuhan armies in May and June, the leaders of the Guomindang were negotiating with Feng Yu-xiang, who met with Tchiang Kaï-chek. This rapprochement implied a break with the Communists. The break itself was precipitated when the Comintern representative at Wuhan, the Indian M. N. Roy, sent Wang Jing-wei a memorandum proposing draconian military measures. Frightened by this, Wang recalled Tang Sheng-zhi's army from the northern front, officially announced the expulsion of the Communists from the Guomindang on July 15, and made peace with Nanking. The Communists went underground and the Soviet advisers were expelled.

The defeat: objective causes

During the revolution of 1924–1927, the political struggle was centered in the cities. Mass struggles took place in Canton, Shanghai, and Wuhan. In these places were concentrated the social forces on which the alliance between the Communists and the Guomindang was based: the workers' movement and the bourgeoisie. The proletariat was a militant class, heavily concentrated in a small number of industrial centers and tied to strategically essential economic sectors. In spite of its political inexperience, it played an important role in Shanghai in June 1925 and March 1927. But its bourgeois allies were uncertain, hesitant, and still linked to the historical forces that the platform of January 1924 asked them to fight: feudalism (since many capitalists still practiced feudal exploitation) and imperialism (since the bourgeoisie was still connected to imperialism through the system of production and the market).

On the other hand, the large cities, which were the principal base of the revolutionary movement, were also the principal base of the system of the unequal treaties: the armed forces, finance, Chinese markets, and ideological influence through the press, the clubs, and the universities. Inasmuch as the struggle took place in the cities, therefore, it took place under unfavorable conditions. Allies could not be counted on there, and the adversaries were very powerful. What could have altered this balance of forces was the inclusion of the peasant masses, but Chinese strategy only gave them a secondary role and their "excesses" continued to be a cause for concern.

Finally, the Chinese revolution of 1924–1927 was the direct continuation of the republican revolution of 1911 and the May Fourth Movement, which were both centered in the cities. China's political structure in the 1920s clearly did not allow for the sudden abandonment of this privileged position of the cities.

The defeat: strategy and tactics

The strategy used by the Communists in 1924 to 1927 had been decided on in Moscow. Stalin certainly bears direct responsibility for the alliance with the Guomindang, the successive compromises that led to the defeat in 1927, and the denunciation of "peasant excesses." Stalin was all the more obstinate because at this time he was involved in his struggle against Trotsky, who strongly criticized him and demanded a break with the Guomindang. Trotsky, however, also saw the revolution as a fight centered in the cities and emphasized that it was to be waged by the proletariat alone. Chinese Communist historians pass over these Soviet mistakes in silence, accusing only Chen Du-xiu, the secretary-general of the CCP at the time, of "opportunistic" errors. Actually, he probably did no more than unwillingly execute the instructions of the Comintern.

Were there conflicting opinions on this subject within the Chinese Communist Party itself? Mao apparently had protested against a politics of appeasement in relation to the Guomindang right wing in 1926 and 1927. But Communist sources are very reticent about the matter; they avoid questioning the direction given by Moscow and thus refrain from evaluating Mao's eventual reservation about it. Rather than suggesting that the CCP should have broken with the Guomindang, they regret that the Communists within the United Front could not control the course of the struggle.

The congenital weaknesses of the Chinese bourgeoisie, both economical and political, suggest that it would not have been capable of promoting the joint struggle against the unequal treaties and the militarists, even to its own advantage. Once it had taken control in 1928, it made one compromise after another. The theory of "two revolutions" proposed by Chen Du-xiu at Borodin's suggestion (helping the bourgeois revolution to succeed and then grafting the Communist revolution onto it) did not correspond to the historical capabilities of the Chinese bourgeoisie. The Communist victory of 1949 was the result of another approach altogether.

Finally, on the tactical level, one is struck by the Communists' naive underestimation of the risk involved in Tchiang's complete change of policy, miscalculation which continued right up to April 12. The slogan of the international Communist movement was "Hands off China," which was intended to prevent the powers from trying to destroy the Chinese revolution as they had tried to destroy the revolution in the Soviet Union in 1918 to 1920. The militants were totally unprepared politically for the eventuality of attacks from within the revolutionary movement itself.

Lessons of the defeat

This painful experience of collaborating with the bourgeoisie permanently marked the Chinese Communists. In the future, when a new occasion presented itself for such a collaboration (as in the forties), they did so only according to their own political line ("New

Democracy"). Their mistrust of the ability of the national bourgeoisie in colonial and dependent countries to achieve political autonomy was one of the points of fundamental disagreement with the Soviet Union after 1960. The failure of 1924–1927 was also the failure of a revolution directed from Moscow by intermediaries. In 1927, the CCP began its long march toward national approaches to revolutionary struggle.

The failure of the revolution, deep and various though its roots, was centered around the balance of military strength. Tchiang and the right wing of the Guomindang had their own military forces, while the left wing and the popular movement did not. This lesson would be brooded over, as would that of limiting the struggle to the cities, where the peasantry could only play a minor role.

ADDITIONAL BIBLIOGRAPHY

Conrad Brandt, *Stalin's Failure in China, 1924–1927* (Cambridge, Mass., Harvard University Press, 1958).

P. Broué, *La question chinoise dans l'internationale communiste* (Paris, 1965).

Harold R. Isaacs, *Tragedy of the Chinese Revolution* (Stanford, Calif., Stanford University Press, 1961).

L. Wieger, *La Chine moderne*, volume V, *Nationalisme* (Hien-hien, 1924), vol. VI, *Le feu aux poudres* (1925), vol. VII, *Boum* (1927).

China Year Book (Peking and Tientsin, years 1925–1928).

Benjamin I. Schwartz, *Chinese Communism and the Rise of Mao* (Cambridge, Mass., Harvard University Press, 1951).

DOCUMENTS

1. THE WOMEN'S MOVEMENT: PROCLAMATION OF THE WIVES AND DAUGHTERS OF TIENTSIN, DECEMBER 25, 1924, TO URGE THE CALLING OF A NATIONAL CONVENTION

SOURCE: L. Wieger, *La Chine moderne,* vol. VI (Hien-hien, 1925), pp. 141–142.

We are still almost a kind of merchandise, we are still slaves. We are not yet human beings. We must still, as in 1915,* call for equal rights for the two sexes, and for suffrage and employment for women . . .

After the historic days of May 1919, we have also demanded free marriage, independent ownership, the freedom to earn our living by

---

* Anti-monarchist movement against Yuan Shi-kai.

engaging in a profession, and particularly the right to make a career of teaching. We are fully awakened now and we know what we want. But our China has fallen into such a state of disrepair that the fulfillment of our just demands has been greatly delayed. Our sisters, ardent and brave, are demonstrating more and more often. But what will a crumbling government be able to grant us? Nothing, it seems. . . . Moreover, we no longer even have a government. Wu Pei-fu has fallen, Cao Kun is in prison, the former emperor, Xuan-tong, has been done away with.* What can we hope for, from now on, if Mr. Sun Yat-sen does not succeed in calling together a national convention to give leadership to our country? It alone is capable of creating a new organism from the present disorder. Let us therefore join the men who are working and suffering to give us a legitimate and capable government. We proclaim this to all of you, wives and daughters of China. . . . Support Mr. Sun Yat-sen's project for a national convention. This convention will realize what it has to do. Yet without wanting to impose upon it, we are taking the liberty of indicating the following points. We should . . .

1. For the good of all the people. —Abolish all unequal treaties, take back control of customs, repeal the unfair laws favoring, for example, the police or discriminating against strikers. The military governors should be removed and the armies disbanded, a small militia should be created, whose members would be assured of a decent life. All taxes added arbitrarily should be abolished. Let the wealth of Cao Kun and of others responsible for our misfortunes be confiscated and contributed to the relief fund for the poor. Let the public schools be endowed with untouchable funds to keep them safe from want. Let the workers' lives be improved; let the work day be a maximum of eight hours. Let all the former members of parliament be removed. Let the constitution of Cao Kun be made null and void.

2. For the good of women in particular. —Let their legal, financial, and "educational" situation be equal to that of men. They must have dignity and equal rights. From the lowest through the highest grades of elementary school, let boys and girls receive the same instruction and let the special classes "for girls" be eliminated. Let all careers be open to girls, for them to choose. Let daughters inherit as well as sons. Let the old educational system which produced "good wives and tender mothers" (Confucius) be abolished and one created which turns girls into real human beings. Let very severe penalties be imposed upon those who drown little girls, who mistreat their wives or daughters-in-law, who bind their daughters' feet or pierce their ears. Provision will be made in workshops and in the teaching profession for the necessary rest period for women who are carrying children, without loss of salary or with special financial aid. Let the enslavement of girls, concubinage, the practice of raising a fiancée along with her future husband, and prostitution be abolished. Let the patriarchal

* When Feng Yu-xiang occupied the "Forbidden City" in 1924.

family system be replaced by that of the "small family," each married couple constituting a separate household. Let the ridiculous honors formerly given to chaste women—including commemorative arches, etc.—be abolished. Let a man who is contemplating marriage with a young woman or with a widow first be able to enter into a social relationship with her which will allow him to get to know her. Let the right to divorce be granted to women who are unhappy in their marriages. Let the freedom of young women who do not want to marry be respected.

2. THE STRUGGLE OF HUNAN PEASANTS AGAINST SOCIAL AND RELIGIOUS TRADITIONS IN 1926

SOURCE: Mao Tsetung, "Report on the Peasant Movement in Hunan," translated by Stuart Schram in *Mao Tse-tung* (New York, Praeger, 1972), pp. 257–259.

A man in China is usually subjected to the domination of three systems of authority: (1) the system of the state (political authority), ranging from the national, provincial, and *xian* government to the *xiang* government; (2) the system of the clan (clan authority), ranging from the central and branch ancestral temples to the head of the household; and (3) the system of gods and spirits (religious authority), including the system of the nether world ranging from the King of Hell to the city gods and local deities, and that of supernatural beings ranging from the Emperor of Heaven to all kinds of gods and spirits. As to women, apart from being dominated by these three systems, they are further dominated by men (the authority of the husband). These four types of authority—political authority, clan authority, religious authority, and the authority of the husband—represent the ideology and institution of feudalism and patriarchy; they are the four bonds that have bound the Chinese people, particularly the peasants. We have already seen how the peasants overthrow the political authority of the landlords in the countryside. The political authority of the landlords is the backbone of all other systems of authority. Once this has been overthrown, so clan authority, religious authority, and the authority of the husband all begin to totter. Where the peasant association is powerful, the clan elders and administrators of temple funds no longer dare oppress the younger members of the clan or embezzle the funds. The evil clan elders and administrators have been overthrown, along with the local bullies and evil gentry . . .

Religious authority begins to totter everywhere as the peasant movement develops. In many places the peasant associations have taken over the temples of gods as their offices. Everywhere they advocate the appropriation of temple properties to maintain peasant schools and to defray association expenses, calling it "public revenue from superstition." Forbidding superstition and smashing idols has become quite the vogue in Liling. . . . In the Lungfeng Nunnery in the North Third

District, the peasants and school teachers chopped up the wooden
idols to cook meat. . . . *Everywhere, by the nature of things,* only the
older peasants and women still believe in gods, while the young and
middle-aged peasants no longer do so. Since it is the young and
middle-aged peasants who are in control of the peasant association,
the movement to overthrow religious authority and eradicate superstition is gathering momentum everywhere. As to the authority of the
husband, it has always been comparatively weak among the poor
peasants, because the poor peasant women, for financial reasons compelled to engage more in manual work than women of the wealthier
classes, have obtained greater rights to speak and more power to make
decisions in family affairs. *They also enjoy considerable sexual freedom.*
Among the poor peasantry, triangular and multilateral relationships
are almost universal. In recent years, the rural economy has become
even more bankrupt, and the basic condition for men's domination
over women has already been undermined. Lately, with the rise of
the peasant movement, women have begun to organize rural women's
associations in many places; they have been given the opportunity to
lift up their heads, and the authority of the husband is tottering more
and more with every passing day. In short, all feudal and patriarchal
ideologies and institutions are tottering with the rise of the power of
the peasants. . . . At present, however, such attacks have just "begun,"
and there can be no complete overthrow of the three until the economic struggle of the peasants is completely victorious. Hence, our
task at present is to guide the peasants to wage political struggles with
their utmost strength so that the authority of the landlords will be
thoroughly uprooted. An economic struggle should also be started
immediately, so that the economic problems of the poor peasants can
be completely solved.

3. THE INTELLECTUALS' INVOLVEMENT IN THE REVOLUTION: LU XUN IN
1927

SOURCE: French translation: Mme. Loi. Lu Xun has just reported on the
repression raging in Peking in spring 1927.*

It is the same in nature: the sparrow hawk falls upon the sparrow,
the discreet and silent sparrow hawk upon the cheeping, peeping
sparrow; the cat falls upon the mouse, the discreet and silent cat
upon the squeaking, squealing mouse. The ones who open their
beaks and mouths are the ones devoured by those who keep their
beaks and mouths closed. . . . I am afraid that certain writers in
revolutionary circles, those who like talking about the powerful relationship between literature and revolution, about the possibility of using

---

* Lu Xun was in Shanghai at this time; his criticism is aimed at the rightist
bourgeoisie of the Guomindang, who were influential in Jiangsu and Zhejiang
(the native province of Tchiang Kaï-chek) and who paid only lip service to the
revolution.

the press to spread, kindle, quicken, carry out revolution, produce, I think, nothing but useless articles, because good works of art are not made to order. They have nothing to do with the hope of making money or with the fear of loss, and spring quite naturally from the heart. If one begins by assigning the subject for an article, it is not surprising if one falls into a stereotyped style which is not only without literary value, but naturally incapable of arousing the reader. The fact is that in order to portray the revolution, one must be a revolutionary.

As for revolutionary literature, it is not urgent that we think about it. When revolutionaries begin to produce literature, it will be revolutionary literature. I do believe, of course, that there are ties between literature and revolution. The literature of revolutionary periods is different from that of ordinary periods. Once the revolution has come to pass, it is true that literature changes color. But, while great revolutions can change the color of literature, it is not the same for small ones, for it is not just any revolution that can change the color of language. How many times have I heard the word "revolution"! In Jiangsu, in Zhejiang, they talk about revolution. People who hear the word are frightened. People who say it are in great danger. However, the revolution is not such a strange thing. It is through revolution that society corrects itself, that mankind progresses, evolving from the worms that men once were into human beings, moving from barbarism to culture, so that there is no moment in time that does not belong to revolution.

4. AUTONOMOUS POLITICAL INITIATIVES BY THE WORKING CLASS: PLATFORM FOR THE GENERAL STRIKE OF FEBRUARY 19, 1927, IN SHANGHAI

SOURCE: Jean Chesneaux, *Les syndicats chinois, 1919–1927* (Paris, Mouton, 1965), pp. 267–271.

Since the May Thirtieth Movement (1925), the revolutionary national government has been constantly expanding. The militarist Sun Chuan-fang, who governed the provinces of the Southeast, has already been defeated . . . Even though Shanghai should belong to the citizens of Shanghai, we, the citizens of Shanghai, have suffered from the oppression of the militarists for dozens of years. The imperialist Powers have used Shanghai as a base for invading China, and today they seek even more strenuously to use military force to threaten the national movement.* We, the citizens of Shanghai, wish to overthrow the obscurantist regime of the militarists and to resist the advance of the imperialists. We, the workers of Shanghai, have vigorously moved to the vanguard since May 30, we have fought for the freedom and the emancipation of the nation. . . . Our working class is now the vanguard of the protest movement. The revolutionary masses must

---

* Large military contingents from the West and Japan had been concentrated in Shanghai since the beginning of the year. By March 1927 their numbers had grown to 33,000 men.

act with ardor, eliminate the militarist forces, and help the "Northern Expedition" army to victory. Our General Union* makes a special appeal to the workers of Shanghai. On this day we proclaim a general strike. The 17 articles that follow constitute the most basic demands of the Shanghai workers:

1. A movement of ongoing resistance against imperialism.

2. Suppression of the political power of the obscurantist militarist forces.

3. Liquidation of all reactionary forces.

4. Establishment of a government to protect the true interests of the workers.

5. Let the people enjoy the freedoms of assembly, association, speech, press, and the freedom to strike.

6. Recognition of the right of the unions to represent the workers.

7. Limitation of the rise in prices and protection of the workers' standard of living.

8. The right to an eight-hour work day.

9. Increases in workers' salaries, the establishment of a minimum wage.

10. Double pay for working on Sundays and holidays.

11. Work for the unemployed; the bosses may no longer close factories under the pretext of a strike and boycott certain workers.

12. No arbitrary firing of workers; the agreement of the Union must be obtained before any worker is discharged.

13. It is forbidden to strike or abuse the workers, or to take money from their salaries in the form of fines.

14. Establishment of indemnities for deaths and injuries that occur at work.

15. In case of illness, the bosses must pay the workers' medical costs and continue to pay at least half their salary.

16. Let men and women receive the same salary for the same work, working women receive better treatment, women be given six weeks' leave during pregnancy with regular salary, and children not be forced to do heavy labor.

17. Let conditions within the factories be improved, for example by enlarging doors and windows, skylights, toilets, etc.

Each one of these points is for us, the workers of Shanghai, a cause for immediate action. During the struggle to annihilate the remaining militarist forces, we wish to struggle in common with the masses from all social groups. We desire a new government which will accept the demands of the workers. Consider this proclamation with respect!

---

* Established during the May Thirtieth Movement and led by the Communists.

Chapter Seven

China Under the Guomindang from 1927 to 1934[1]

In the twenty-two years following 1927, the course of Chinese politics was divided into two main currents. The Communist movement no longer defined itself only as an opposition to the established order, but as a movement which could operate in a territorially autonomous way, in "red bases," "soviet bases," "revolutionary bases," or "liberated regions." The history of these bases was distinct from that of the government of China and would remain so until the liberation of 1949. The China of the established order and the China of rebellion will be discussed separately, since the latter had already succeeded in establishing a revolutionary order with its own dynamism.

Bases of the Guomindang Regime

Formation of the central government and the end of the warlords

When the leftist government of Wuhan collapsed in July 1927, the power of the militarists remained intact in North China. The

---

[1] The Guomindang campaigns against the Communist zones will be studied in the following chapter.

Fengtian clique was in solid possession not only of the Northeast but also of Peking and all of the region up to the Yellow River. The Nationalist offensive against it did not take place right away. Relations between Tchiang Kaï-chek and the other political and military forces of the Nationalist camp—the warlords who had come over to the Nationalist side (Yan Xi-shan of Shanxi, Feng Yu-xiang) and the provincial armies of the South (particularly that of Guangxi) —were not good. The formal reunification of the Guomindang in September, which benefitted both the former leftist opponents from Wuhan and the dissident rightist group called "the Western Hills Group" (which had broken away in 1925), had not settled anything. Tchiang even resigned for a time, a maneuver which allowed him to resume control of the army, the party, and the government with increased authority in January.

The second Northern Expedition (Beifa) got under way in February 1928. Three armies, those of Tchiang, Feng, and Yan, converged near Peking and attacked the northerners. In May, when they crossed Shandong, Japan intervened by occupying the provincial capital, Jinan, "to protect Japanese citizens." Tchiang withdrew for a while. But Japan had ceased to have confidence in Zhang Zuo-lin, for the past twenty years its main political representative in China. When Zhang was defeated and evacuated Peking at the beginning of June, his train set off a mine that was probably planted by Japanese spies. He was killed, and his son joined the Guomindang. The Guomindang seemed to be in complete control of China. Peking ("capital of the North") was renamed Beiping ("peace of the North"), and the government of Nanking was established as the central government. The national holiday on October 10, 1928 (the anniversary of the 1911 uprising), was celebrated as the end of the era of civil wars and warlords, and as the victory of a national revolution which had been able to defeat both its rightist and leftist enemies.

The government and the party

The political theory handed down to Tchiang Kaï-chek and his group by Sun Yat-sen included one valuable formulation: the principle of tutelage. Between the period of insurrection led by the vanguard and the period of democracy open to the masses, Sun Yat-sen had envisaged an intermediary period, during which the party would exercise a benevolent guardianship over the people and would gradually teach them to govern themselves. From 1927 on, the authoritarian regime of the Guomindang was based on this theory of guardianship.

The party was no longer what it had been during the revolutionary years. The "movement for the purification of the party," begun by Tchiang in 1927, had expelled all those who were suspected of having Communist sympathies or who were simply moderates. The party's submissiveness to Tchiang was assured by the new statutes adopted at the Third Congress of the Guomindang in 1929. They strengthened both the power of the center and the power of the Control Committees (which were made up of the oldest and most conservative members). The Guomindang had 266,000 civilian members in 1929, of which 21 percent were officials worried about their careers, 30 percent intellectuals and students, and 10 percent "agriculturists" (actually landowners).

The cliques and those who benefitted from patronage were allied by their ambitions and had great influence on the Guomindang leadership. They included such groups as the former students of the Whampoa Military Academy (which Tchiang had been in charge of at Canton during the revolution), the "CC" group of the brothers Chen Li-fu and Chen Guo-fu, who were open admirers of Mussolini, and a group from Zhejiang (the province that Tchiang came from), which was particularly influential. One of the most powerful members of this group was Dai Li (1895–1946), the head of the secret services (*tewu*) and one of the leaders of the pro-Fascist organization, the Blue Shirts.

According to the constitution drawn up in 1931, the government of Nanking was officially organized into the "five powers" which Sun Yat-sen had defined. Five supreme government branches (*yuan,* "courts") were responsible for making the laws, executing them, administering justice, supervising state functions, and choosing officials. But their members were appointed, and the executive *yuan* was the only one which had any real function, since it was composed of the various ministries. In contrast to the formality with which these five organs functioned, the real centers of power lay elsewhere, in Tchiang's entourage.

The army and the police

The Guomindang regime was based on military force. There were 2,000,000 armed men in 1929, and 2,600,000 in 1930. These high figures reflected the authoritarian character of the regime. The counter-revolutionary order had to maintain itself against the popular movements which had been defeated in 1927, but which were showing new strength in the "red bases" (see next chapter). In 1929, more than half the members of the Guomindang were soldiers (280,000). These huge armies also reflected the fact that Tchiang governed by compromising with the regional political and military forces, each of which was remaining on its guard. China was in a permanent state of virtual civil war, and flare-ups were frequent. The scourge of militarism and the warlords had not disappeared in 1926 to 1928 with the success of the Beifa as the official propaganda claimed.

These armies were very expensive to maintain; the costs amounted to 78 percent of the resources left to the state after payment of the foreign debt. In January 1929, a conference on the disbanding of troops called for reducing the armies to one million men (41 percent of the budget); but the military leaders who participated in the conference did not carry out its decisions.

The army of the Guomindang was aided by the West; it had French tanks, Italian airplanes, English artillery, and a seventy-man German military mission, directed by Generals von Seeckt and von Falkenhausen. This mission was attached to Tchiang's personal troops, which from 1931 became increasingly superior to the armies of his provincial rivals.

The police force was also indispensable to the regime. Dai Li, "Tchiang's Himmler," and his department organized political assassinations (for example, the assassination of the manager of a large liberal newspaper in Shanghai), engaged in spying, and practiced terrorism. There were no clear demarcations between the official police, the special services, and the Shanghai gangs, which had already been used in 1927 against the Communists. These gangs (the Green Band and the Red Band) controlled the traffic in opium, women, and weapons. This traffic was tolerated (the "pact with the devil," said the French consul general in Shanghai) in exchange for the political help of these gangs, especially for their terrorist attacks on workers and the unions.

The Guomindang ideology

The ideology of the Guomindang aimed at consolidating its authoritarian power. Just as its power was founded on the coalition of

CHINA IN 1935
ADMINISTRATIVE DIVISIONS
- - - national boundaries
.... provincial boundaries
○ provincial capitals

U.S.S.R.

MONGOLIA

HEILONGJIANG

○Tsitsihar

○Harbin
JILIN
○**Jilin**

CHAHAR

Changchun○

JEHOL

○**Shenyang**

Chengde

LIAONING

○Niuzhuang

NINGXIA

SUIYAN **Guisui**○

Kalgan○

Baotou

Tangshan

Dalian (Dairen)
Lushun (Pt. Arthur)

PEKING○

Tientsin

Ningxia○

Taiyuan○

HEBEI

Zhifu Weihaiwei

KOREA

XINGHAI

Xining○

SHANXI

Yanan

Xingtai

Jinan○
Qingdao

○**Lanzhou**

GANSU

Huanghe

Kaifeng○

SHANDONG

Sian○
SHENXI

HENAN

JIANGSU

Nanking○

Suzhou○

SICHUAN

HUBEI

ANHUI

Wuhu○

Shanghai

○**Chengdu**

Hankou

Yichang Shashi

Wuchang○

Anqing○

Hangzhou○

Chongqing○

Yangziliang

Jiujiang

ZHEJIANG

Changde○

Nanchang○

Wenzhou○

HUNAN

Changsha○

JIANGXI

○**Guiyang**

GUIZHOU

Fuzhou○

FUJIAN

Kunming○
YUNNAN

Guilin○

Taibei○

GUANGXI

GUANGDONG

Xiamen (Amoy)○

TAIWAN

Nanning

Xijiang

Canton○

Shantou○

TONGKING

Pakhoi○

Macao○Hong Kong

Guangzhouwan○

500 km

Qiongzhou○

HAINAN

the conservative managerial classes (the military and the land-owners) and the pro-Western business classes, its ideology combined elements of Chinese tradition and modernist borrowings from abroad, without undue concern about coherence.

Tchiang proclaimed that he was restoring traditional Confucian virtues (that is, respect for the established order). Confucius' birthday was made a national holiday. Zeng Guo-fan, who had put down the peasant insurrections of the nineteenth century (Nian and Taiping) and had restored orthodoxy and order, was particularly exalted. His writings were integrated into the doctrinal writings of the Guomindang. The basis of Guomindang doctrine continued to be the work of Sun Yat-sen, who was also canonized by the Nanking regime. His will was recited from memory, and he was called *Guofu* ("father of the country"). But his theories of the three people's principles and the five powers were only referred to in a formal way, while what made them original and vital at the time of the alliance with the Communists was ignored. The other part of the Guomindang ideology was taken from less ambiguous sources: Fascist Italy and, after 1933, Nazi Germany. Kemalist Turkey was included as an example of the authoritarian modernization of an Asiatic country. Obedience to the "supreme chief" was called for, democracy (which had been so praised by Sun Yat-sen) was criticized, and the slogan "Nation-army-production" became dominant.

Bourgeois acceptance and capitalist stabilization

The modern bourgeoisie upheld the regime both for political (the "great fear" of 1926–1927) and economic reasons. The effects of the 1921–1923 economic crisis, which had pushed it into the alliance with the Communists, had disappeared. The market recovered its stability. The modern Chinese capitalists put their confidence in the Guomindang, which in their eyes would be able to ensure the progress of business. The Shanghai industrialists and financiers in Mao Dun's novel *Midnight*[2] were as concerned about the Chinese national interest, which was identified for them with the Nanking government, as they were eager for economic expansion. But, in fact, the capitalist stabilization of this period was much more profitable for banking and transportation than for industry, and agriculture hardly profited at all.

[2] See document 1 at the end of the chapter.

Four large banks (the Central Bank, the Bank of China, the Communications Bank, and the Farmers' Bank) cooperated with one another and in effect played the role of state bank. They were connected with the regime and controlled by the two financial magnates of the Guomindang, T. V. Soong and H. H. Kung (they liked to write their names American style), both brothers-in-law of Tchiang Kaï-chek. These banks ensured the stability of the Chinese silver dollar and guaranteed a balanced budget by their backing of the bonds issued by the state. The wealthy, anxious for political stability but wishing to avoid economic risks, preferred to buy these bonds rather than to invest in industry. Fifty percent of the capital funds in Shanghai was invested in state bonds. Thus the apparent prosperity of Nanking China was based on economic stagnation. The actual "deinvestment" between 1931 and 1936 has been estimated to have been 1¾ million dollars.

Progress in transportation reinforced the political and military unity of China and widened the scope of the market economy in the countryside. The railroad network was increased from 11,000 to 16,000 kilometers, and almost 100,000 kilometers of new roads were built. Industry, however, lagged behind. Even if it continued to grow steadily, it was still handicapped as in the past. There was an imbalance between light and heavy industry, and control of certain important sectors remained in the hands of foreign capital. In 1932, matches, tobacco, textiles, and flour accounted for 45 percent of the industrial production, while the production of machines accounted for only 1 percent. The progress made by the cotton industry, which had been considered a pilot sector since the beginning of the twentieth century, did not alter the ratio between national and foreign capitalism (57 percent–43 percent).

1928	2,060,000 Chinese spindles	1,550,000 foreign spindles
1934	2,800,000 Chinese spindles	2,130,000 foreign spindles

The political and financial leaders of the Chinese capitalist forces continued, therefore, to prefer speculative investments, to look for easier profits in light industry, and to accept the partial control of the Chinese economy by foreign industrial and banking groups.

Their cooperation with the powers was paradoxically reinforced by the worldwide economic crisis of 1929–1931. Chinese currency was based on the silver standard. But the price of silver fell during the crisis, as did the other world prices. China was thus placed ipso facto in a deflationary position and withstood the crisis rather well, as far as the sale of its raw materials on the international market was concerned.

The Guomindang and labor

The vast union structure built between 1924 and 1927 by the Communists quickly collapsed under the Guomindang's repression; the "red" unions went underground and continued to exist only in a few small pockets. In 1930, the government noted that there were more than half a million union members (in 741 unions), but these were "yellow" or "black" unions. The union law of 1929 put the control of these unions and the arbitration of work conflicts in the hands of the Offices of Social Affairs of the Guomindang.

The yellow unions had been in existence for a long time. Their strategy was reformist, and their methods were moderate. They had a real mass base, including commercial press workers, the workers at the British and American Tobacco Co. in Shanghai, the mechanics in Canton, the post office workers, and the sailors. But they collaborated with the Guomindang to avoid the risk of being outlawed. The black unions were created by the Guomindang police and the special services. They used terrorism in businesses and were in direct contact with gangsters and the secret societies that controlled the hiring of workers and ran rackets, particularly in Shanghai.

Strikes were comparatively numerous because of the miserable conditions of the workers. But they were spontaneous strikes and were almost never followed up. There were 120 strikes in Shanghai in 1928, 111 in 1929, 82 in 1930, and, according to another source, 145 strikes in all of China in 1931, 104 in 1932, 79 in 1933. Labor conditions continued to be characterized by low salaries, unstable employment, oppression by overseers and gangsters, long work days, and miserable housing. The Guomindang belonged to the International Bureau of Labor in Geneva and set up a branch of that organization in Shanghai. But this was only to gain prestige and had no real effect.

The Guomindang in the countryside

The revolutionary upsurge in 1926 to 1927 had been strong in the rural areas as well as in the cities. The power of the Guomindang was based on the great fear of the landowners as well as that of the urban bourgeoisie. The rural gentry went over to the side of the Guomindang, either joining it formally themselves or else having a close relative or reliable member of their entourage join. In 1930, Sun Fo, the son of Sun Yat-sen, denounced the "yamenization" of the rural sections of the party—the fact that the local organizations of the Guomindang increasingly resembled the old *yamen* hated by the peasants. In 1905 to 1910 and in 1924 Sun Yat-sen had outlined a radical agrarian program, though in vague terms. He had spoken of equalizing rights to the land and of supporting the peasant movement. But these aspects of his thought, even though they became part of the official doctrine of Nanking, were completely forgotten. The Guomindang became the party of rural conservatism and of feudal order. Supported by the landowners, it fought against the agrarian revolution led by the Communists in South China in 1928 to 1934. The repressive structure in the villages was built up by bolstering the old traditional system of the *baojia*; at the local level, families were grouped in units (*bao, jia*) which were held jointly responsible when incidents occurred.

The deterioration of the rural economy and the worsening of peasant conditions continued, following the trend that had begun in the second and third decades of the century. The price of land rose and land rent increased, usury became more widespread, cash rent and preliminary deposits for tenant farmers were increased, and landholdings were concentrated in the hands of a few owners. The growth of finance capitalism in the cities increased the need for new money by the landowners who lived there and who were tempted by easy speculation, particularly in state bonds. They therefore were compelled to put more and more pressure on their peasants, as in the Russia of Turgenev and Tolstoy. Agrarian exploitation increased because of capitalism, instead of being eliminated by it as the Chinese and foreign Trotskyites had imagined it would be. Feudal profit and capitalist profit were clearly interdependent even at the level of production in the regions where the landowners controlled both the cultivation and the marketing of export products like oilseeds, tobacco, and cotton. In essence, they played the role of rural compradors.

In addition to the increased suffering caused by the economic system, the peasants were victimized by many forms of political and social oppression. The tax collectors and the stewards collecting rent, who were the public and private representatives of the power of the rural gentry that was now behind the Guomindang, were guilty of excesses and abuses. The peasants were subjected to pillaging and requisitions by the troops of the central government and its provincial allies, as well as to raids by bandits and brigands. To deal with all these problems, the peasants sometimes organized modern revolutionary movements. These were known as the "Chinese soviets" (see next chapter). But quite often, in remote regions where the name of the Communist Party was not even known, their revolt took the more traditional forms of village self-defense units, of *jacqueries* or secret societies. In 1928, the Red Spears controlled whole villages in Shandong, the Big Knife was organizing an insurrection against bandits and tax collectors in the Northeast, and the Sacred Soldiers of the Buddhist Way attacked the warlord Yang Sen and killed 800 of his soldiers in Sichuan.

A certain number of intellectuals and agricultural experts (primarily Protestants) connected with the Nanking regime attempted reform measures. Among them were the activities of the International Commission of the Struggle Against Famine; the Movement for Rural Reconstruction, inspired by one of the great names of the May Fourth Movement, the philosopher and sociologist Liang Shu-ming (born in 1893); the movement for the improvement of seeds and of silkworm breeds; and the Movement for Education of the Masses, started by Peking teachers. All these efforts were aimed at improving agricultural techniques, setting up hydraulic works, making the peasants literate and instructing them in the principles of hygiene, and developing rural credit. They were carried out by devoted activists who were unfamiliar with the villagers, and the villagers had scarcely any confidence in them. These undertakings lacked financial support. They attacked only the technical and financial aspects of the agrarian crisis, not its social and political roots. They therefore remained local and largely ineffective. Their most lasting result was perhaps the massive sociological research they gave rise to; these very rich materials have provided a deeper knowledge of Chinese peasants, for both the Communist revolutionaries and the Western Sinologists.

The Guomindang and the intellectuals

The great majority of intellectuals, teachers, engineers, doctors, journalists, and lawyers backed the Guomindang as a symbol of and an instrument for the modernization of China. For this modernization conferred on them a privileged status quite different from the ancient Confucian intellectual privileges, but just as advantageous; they became the indispensable intermediaries between China and the West. The Guomindang valued its good image in the West, and the West had an interest in consolidating a regime which acknowledged its influence. In libraries, hospitals, universities, the press, and scientific institutes, the tone was set by intellectuals who had been trained either in the West or in China by Western teachers or by teachers themselves trained in the West. Institutions such as the Academia Sinica, the Geological Survey of China, the National Library of Peking, the Peking Union Medical College (Rockefeller), Yenching University of Peking (American), Aurora University of Shanghai (Jesuit), and many others were better known by their foreign than by their Chinese name. Their members lived and dressed in the Western style and preferred to socialize with their foreign colleagues rather than with their own people. The great majority of doctors with modern training were concentrated in the few cities where they could find a Westernized practice.

The Western cultural model was therefore predominant, usually in its Protestant form. The directors of the YMCA and of the NCC (National Christian Council) were very influential. The people in power set the example. The wives of Tchiang Kaï-chek and the financier H. H. Kung (Kong Xiang-xi), their sister Song Qing-ling, who was the widow of Sun Yat-sen, and their brother T. V. Soong (Song Zi-wen), the other big financier of the regime, were all four the children of a Bible salesman who worked for the English missions, "Charlie" Song.

Some of these Westernized intellectuals were cynical opportunists. Others (such as the YMCA people) were more hesitant and continued to have faith in "reforms." Only a few refused to go along and took refuge in isolation or joined the struggle. Guo Mo-ruo left for Japan. The leftist leaders Mao Dun and Lu Xun only influenced small minority groups.

Western aid

The Nanking regime claimed to be the heir of the Nationalist revolution led by Sun Yat-sen in which anti-imperialism had been an essential element. Public opinion obliged it to carry on with the revision of the unequal treaties. The powers, for their part, had felt the same "great fear" as the Chinese ruling classes in 1926 to 1927. They favored compromises, such as Great Britain's compromise in spring 1927 when it acknowledged the loss of its Hankou and Jiujiang concessions, which had been taken over by the Nationalists with Communist support.

The situation, nevertheless, was considerably different from that of the preceding period. The Nanking government abandoned mass struggle in favor of negotiation. The person mainly responsible for this diplomatic motion was Wang Zheng-ting (1882–1961), a former leader of the YMCA who had been educated at Yale in the United States and was a typical representative of the new intelligentsia of Nanking. He achieved some genuine, though incomplete, successes. Twenty out of thirty-three concessions were returned to China, but these did not include the largest ones (like those in Shanghai). England also gave up its "leased territory," Weihaiwei. A certain number of secondary powers (such as Denmark and Belgium) gave up the privilege of extraterritoriality; but France, England, and the United States declared that they would wait until a "modern" reform of the Chinese codes was effected. With this in mind, Nanking formed commissions of experts and published a whole series of new codes directly inspired by Western law. When the war broke out, the question was still unresolved.

Where customs was concerned, China recovered its full autonomy in 1933. The Nationalists took over full management of the customs departments, the salt-tax administration, and the postal services, which had been managed by foreigners for a long time.

The powers also ended the embargo on arms to China, an embargo that had been put into effect in 1919 so as not to encourage civil wars among the militarists. The aim of this measure was as much to give material support to the Nanking government, which was threatened by Communist insurrection, as it was to respect its sovereign rights.

During this period, the West supported the Nanking government in many other ways: with military supplies, by sending legal and financial experts (to draw up the new codes, for example, and to prepare the monetary reform of 1935), and by giving technical assistance. The League of Nations intervened actively, particularly after 1931, partly to make up for its passive reaction to Japanese aggression in 1931. A mission of "intellectual cooperation" was sponsored, in which the great scholar Langevin took part, and which seriously discussed projects for educational reform by the Nanking government.

The system of Chinese dependence on the West, the system of

the unequal treaties, remained largely intact, however. The only changes made were those which enhanced the prestige of Tchiang Kaï-chek, and these did not seriously threaten Western domination of China. Financial subordination ("the debt") still existed, as did Western control over a part of the mines, the railroads, the factories, and urban services. The powers (except the United States, which had given up its share) even continued to insist that payment of the installments of the 1901 Boxer indemnity be made in gold francs, despite the sharp devaluation of European currencies (the franc in 1925, the pound in 1931). Chinese foreign trade, too, continued to have the same colonial character, and there remained a quantitative and, even more, qualitative imbalance between imports and exports. France, England, and Japan continued to benefit from such state privileges in China as extraterritoriality, concessions, and military rights.

New relations were formed during this period based on a highly Westernized managerial class[3] that collaborated much more closely with the West than the old Confucian managerial class had in the period before 1911. Even as the compradors were disappearing as an institution in commercial establishments because of the greater familiarity between foreign agents and their Chinese clients, relationships of the comprador type became widespread in the fields of finance, politics, and culture. As these new types of dependent relationships were consolidated, the United States found itself in a privileged situation compared to its old rivals (France, England, and Japan). The United States had only played a minor role in the classical period of the unequal treaties, but now it acquired a certain prestige and greater freedom of action, because it did not have to defend the traditional interests (railways, mines, and concessions). It could adapt itself more easily to the new and advantageous form of control initiated in the Nanking period, and this underlay the special relationship between Washington and the Guomindang during and after the Second World War.

Appraisal of the Nanking regime

Some people have spoken almost lyrically about the "ten years of Nanking": "The most modern government China has ever known" (John K. Fairbank); "Its deficiencies were less terrifying than the

[3] See document 2.

problems it confronted . . . it imposed something that resembled order where chaos had reigned . . . it represented for a time a positive step in the evolution of modern China" (Lucien Bianco).

Instead of judging the Guomindang in terms of such notions as "order," "modernity," and "positive steps," which are charged with an implicit ideology, it would probably be better to try to comprehend its essential workings and to suggest a provisional definition of it on the basis of this understanding. For example, the power of the Guomindang of Nanking was built on a coalition between conservative social groups from the countryside and the modern business-oriented bourgeoisie from the cities, which were defending their interests against the popular forces whose militancy had become apparent in 1926 to 1927 and whose struggle continued in the red bases of Jiangxi. These interests essentially coincided with those of the powers, hoping to maintain their influence in China and therefore collaborating with a new, "modernized" political class. The "unification" brought about by Nanking was limited by its necessary compromise with provincial militarists, who went along with the general policy of the central government, but only on condition that their own local power remained intact. While it still had a certain prestige as the heir of Sun Yat-sen, the Nanking government made no provision for the popular masses in the decision-making process, which was under its total control, and it did not serve their economic interests.

The Nanking economy is a good example of the regime's fundamental character and presents an accurate picture of the workings of the government. There were no income taxes, which was advantageous to the property owners in the cities. The *lijin* (internal customs) were eliminated, which also helped the business community. Twenty-five percent of the state revenues came from loans on the Chinese financial market, and the handling of these bonds absorbed a third of the budget. An enormous class of speculators came into being which grew rich because of the state and therefore supported it. Half of the state's revenues came from customs, and from China's participation in the world economic market through the intermediary of the powers which traded with it. Indirect taxes on such items as flour, salt, tobacco, and oil accounted for the rest of the essential resources, which meant that the government's prosperity depended on prices, and ultimately on the people. Finally, Nanking left the land tax to the local military powers—a compromise with military neofeudalism which weighed upon the poor peasantry, since the rural gentry, as local political supporters of the regime, were scarcely taxed at all.

Tchiang Kaï-chek's character is another useful key to understanding the system of forces on which the Nanking government was based. Tchiang, who was born in 1887, had been a broker on the Shanghai Stock Exchange and had made contacts with the Western financial community in the city. His connections with business circles were strengthened by his marriage; his two brothers-in-law were foremost in Chinese finance. He was also a military man, in control of what was really the principal political force of the country. At the same time, his power had more traditional foundations. He was a member of the secret society of the Green Band and was tied to the powerful gangsters of Shanghai. He had his own entourage, derived from provincal (Zhejiang) and family loyalties. Finally, his stay in Russia (where he had been sent by Sun Yat-sen) and his collaboration with the Communists made him familiar with a certain vocabulary, a certain system of political reference which he knew how to use, while at the same time he was closely tied to the classical Chinese tradition in which he had been steeped.

Just as the revolutionary base of Canton during the time of Sun Yat-sen was the precursor and prototype of a number of regimes (Sukarno, Nkrumah, Sihanouk) which tried to find a "third way" between capitalism and socialism in the 1960s, the Nanking regime was the precursor and prototype of a certain system of relations between the West and the countries of the Third World which became general in the 1960s and the 1970s. According to the economist Samir Amin, this neocolonialism was above all based on the appearance of a new political class that was much more tied to the West and its life style than to the old feudal or tribal ruling classes.

Political Crises of the Nanking Regime

The regional political and military powers

The choice of Nanking as the capital has been depicted as a break with the China of the warlords, a return to the democratic and national tradition of 1911. Actually, the Guomindang could scarcely go elsewhere. The rest of China was controlled by military groups which supported Tchiang only on condition that he allow them freedom of action in their local areas. These were the new warlords. Some of them *were* newcomers, who had risen to power during the campaigns against the North in 1926 and 1927. Li Zong-ren and Bai Chong-xi controlled not only their native Guangxi but also Guizhou, Hubei, and Hunan. Li Ji-shen controlled Canton. But in the North, Feng Yu-xiang and Yan Xi-shan, who shared this region and were old militarists, went over to Nanking in 1927. The same was true of Yang Sen in Sichuan, and many others. The head of Manchuria was Zhang Xue-liang—the heir to the power of his father, Zhang Zuo-lin—who also threw in with Tchiang, in 1928.

In 1928 to 1930, these regional political and military forces were given an official institutional status. The "regional political coun-cils" established in Wuhan, Canton, Kaifeng, Taiyuan, and Mouk-den legalized the authority of Bai and Li, Li Ji-shen, Feng, Yan, and Zhang.

Unification, which was the slogan of the regime, was therefore little more than an empty word. China was in a state of latent civil war, and war did in fact break out on several occasions among these rivals. The increase in the number of splinter groups in China following the death of Yuan Shi-kai was not offset by the centraliz-ing measures taken by Nanking in the peripheral zones where it was clearly in control. All of Inner Mongolia, which had previously been left to tribal authorities under the distant control of Peking, was divided into provinces (Jehol, Chahar, Suiyuan, Ningxia), as was Northern Tibet (Xigang). These new administrative structures offered careers, sinecures, and profits to the supporters of the regime.

The conflicts of 1929, 1930, and 1931

Tchiang Kaï-chek not only had to contend with the regional military leaders but also with his adversaries within the Guomin-dang, particularly Hu Han-min on the right and Wang Jing-wei, who belonged to the "reorganization" group. On several occasions, he was almost defeated by coalitions among them.

In April 1929, after the failure of the conference on the disband-ing of regional troops, the Guangxi group seceded, but this threat was quickly overcome. During the summer, tension mounted be-tween Nanking and the armies of Feng Yu-xiang, which were forced to yield in November, after a short war. In May 1930, a triple alliance against Nanking was formed, consisting of Feng,

Yan, and the Guangxi group. Bloody fighting took place in Hunan and Henan. In September, the confederates formed a dissident government in Peking, which was joined by Wang Jing-wei. It was beaten, primarily because of the defection of Feng's chief lieutenant, who was bought off by Tchiang. Feng retired from political life. Yan withdrew to his "model province" of Shanxi. Wang left for Canton, where he got together with the partisans of Hu Han-min, formerly his adversary, whom Tchiang had just arrested in Nanking. Another dissident government was formed in Canton in May 1931, supported by such prestigious names as Sun Fo and Eugene Chen, former revolutionary minister of foreign affairs in 1926, as well as by the armies of the Guangxi group. These southerners were supported by the "third party," which had been recently formed by leftist dissidents of the Guomindang, such as Deng Yan-da, and former Communists who had been opposed to armed struggle.

In September, Japanese aggression against Manchuria further confused the crisis. The southerners agreed to a compromise that had been worked out at a "Conference for Peace and Unification." The fickle Wang Jing-wei went over to the government's side and became president of the executive *yuan* (that is, prime minister). But Deng Yan-da, a man of principle, was arrested and executed.

Tchiang had played a difficult seesaw game. It was partly based on his agreement with Zhang Xue-liang, the "young marshal" of Manchuria; this agreement allowed him to outflank his northern adversaries in 1929 and 1930. He also brought about a setback for Japan in an area that was particularly important to Japan. In autumn 1929, Tchiang persuaded Zhang himself to confront the Soviet Union and occupy the East China Railway (the Trans-Manchurian), which had come under Soviet control in 1924 after having been a tsarist enclave in Manchuria for many years. But the Soviet division led by General Blücher (Tchiang's former military adviser in Canton) routed Zhang Xue-liang's armies, and the railroad was returned to Soviet control.

The Xinjiang crises

The Soviet government, which had been dominated by Stalin after Trotsky's elimination, defended the positions acquired earlier by Russia in Manchuria and remained interested in Xinjiang. In 1931, an agreement was signed with Jin Shu-ren, the governor of the province, which was under the control of Nanking in name only. Soviet trade missions were set up in one of the province's cities, and telecommunications became jointly controlled by the Soviets and the provincial government.

The political situation in Xinjiang at that time was very confused. Jin's authoritarian methods had provoked a rebellion of the Ouighour Moslem tribes, which went so far as to proclaim a "Republic of Eastern Turkestan." Also, in 1931, and again in 1933, Ma Zhong-ying, an adventurer of Doungan origin (the Doungan were Chinese Moslems from Gansu), tried to set up an autonomous principality there. Nanking was not able to re-establish its sovereignty, and although order was restored in 1934, a new warlord, Sheng Shi-cai, who was practically independent of Nanking and supported the Soviet Union, benefitted in the process.

Local conflicts in Sichuan

The Nanking regime, preoccupied by its struggles against the major military factions (the Guangxi group, Yan, and Feng) was powerless against the small local militarists whose ambitions were confined to their own provinces. These condottieri, who were particularly strong in remote and mountainous regions, ignored the political and military games of Nanking, and in turn Nanking did not intervene in their affairs and intrigues. This was the case with the minor warloads of the Fujian war, of Shandong, and of Guizhou. It was the case in Yunnan, where Long Yun, former gang leader of the Society of Brothers and Elders, became governor of the province. It was also true of the militarists in Sichuan, a province enclosed by its mountains and beyond reach of Nanking's intervention. Three minor military leaders were fighting over the northern part of the province. In the south, Liu Xiang and his uncle Liu Wen-hui came into conflict, since each wanted the high-paying post of provincial governor. Yang Sen, the strong man of Sichuan in 1927, who had gone over to the Guomindang at that time and had later been ousted, also maintained an army and therefore still had some influence. More than 200,000 men, lured by intrigues and financial offers, changed their allegiance from one army to another. Open war between these rival cliques broke out several times— in 1929, 1932, and 1935. Nanking attempted to maintain a nominal sovereignty by appointing Liu Xiang commissioner for the suppression of banditry (that is, communism) in 1933, but the province really eluded its control, and continued to do so until 1938, when the central government was driven back to Chongqing.

Japanese aggression in 1931:
the political repercussions

In its 1927 Tanaka Plan, Japan had openly revealed its expansionist schemes for Eastern Asia. In September 1931, the Japanese army attacked Moukden. With Nanking's agreement, Zhang Xueliang decided not to resist. Tchiang Kaï-chek did not even declare war on Japan and preferred to take his case to the League of Nations in Geneva. The Japanese army occupied the whole of the Northeast and in 1932 restored Pu Yi, the last Chinese emperor, who had been dethroned in 1912, as emperor of Manzhouguo. All Geneva did was to issue verbal protests and set up an investigative commission (headed by Lord Lytton) whose long report in 1933 advised a compromise with Japan.

The Chinese people violently resented the passivity of the League of Nations, the West, and the Nanking government. The only troops which fought at all, against orders, were some troops on the northern border (Heilongjiang), and in Shanghai the Nineteenth Army of General Cai Ting-kai (1892–1968), whose forces were attacked by the Japanese in January 1932. In the tradition of the May Fourth Movement, students demonstrated, went on strike, and collected funds for the resistance. Initially showing complete confidence in Nanking, begging that it resist Japan, the students gradually turned against the government. Student riots against the regime and its conciliatory policy broke out in Shanghai, Nanking, and Peking. In Shanghai, the resistance of the Nineteenth Army was supported by the population. In Peking, workers organized an "Association to Resist Japan and Save China." An anti-Japanese boycott was launched at the beginning of 1932 and was supported by the chambers of commerce, the industrial groups, and the large bourgeois newspapers, such as *Shenbao* of Shanghai. But none of these movements was strong enough to influence the Guomindang in any real way. And the Communist Party did not actively participate in these demonstrations, which were basically run by the middle classes. The same would not be true in 1935.

New progress by Japan and Fujian dissidence

The catastrophic floods which ravaged the Yangzi region and claimed millions of lives in 1931 further demonstrated the incapacity of the central government to deal with crises and scarcely rein-

forced the authority of Nanking.[4] Japanese aggression had suspended internal conflicts only temporarily. Tchiang's position remained uncertain. Once, at the end of 1931, he even withdrew
from power in exchange for the backing of the dissident Canton
government, only to return almost immediately and participate in
a triumvirate with Hun Han-min and Wang Jing-wei. In fact, however, this triumvirate never really functioned, and power returned
once again to Tchiang. The Guomindang regime continued to be
based on subtle shifts and complicated intrigues.

The South remained a source of potential dissidence. In 1933,
when Japan occupied Jehol, penetrated into Chahar, and intrigued
with the princes of Inner Mongolia to woo them away from Nanking and ally them with Manzhouguo, Tchiang conceded once
again and in May signed the Truce of Tanggu, which was a recognition of Japan's *fait accompli*. Once again, as in 1931, the nation
protested, particularly the South. In November 1933, a rebel government was formed in Fujian, a province that was particularly
vulnerable to Japanese attack because of its position across from
the Japanese colony of Taiwan. This government was headed by
General Cai Ting-kai, who had become popular in 1932 when he
resisted the Japanese at Shanghai and forced them to evacuate the
city. Cai was supported by military leaders from the South such as
General Li Ji-shen, and by opposition politicians such as Eugene
Chen, who became minister of foreign affairs of the rebel government. But this government remained isolated. Later, the Communist
Party would severely criticize itself for its "leftist" attitude at this
time and its refusal to support the Fujian dissidents. These dissidents were liquidated by Tchiang in January 1934.

"Suppression of the bandits" and "reconstruction"

From 1928 on, Tchiang Kaï-chek had to contend with the Communist guerrillas in South China. He justified his delays and conciliatory policies against Japanese aggression by saying that it was
necessary to give priority to the fight against the "Communist
threat," which he summed up in the slogan "First reunification,
then resistance." In fact, all the political and military energy of
the Nanking government was devoted to the "suppression of bandits" (the official term for the campaign against the Communists).
Between 1931 and 1933, four campaigns of encirclement failed,

[4] See document 3.

but a fifth succeeded in 1934, more because of the political difficulties of the Communists than because of a sudden recovery of
military effectiveness by the Guomindang. Because of their internal
divisions and their hesitations, the Communists were no longer capable of mobilizing popular forces against a militarily superior enemy,
as they would be in 1937–1945 and again in 1947–1949. They
were forced to evacuate the "soviet bases" as they began the Long
March.

In 1934, Tchiang tried to complete his military victory by launching a political and ideological offensive. As his wife, Song Mei-ling,
declared in the preface to an English work of propaganda in favor
of the "generalissimo," it was a question "of giving the people something to identify with, of raising them to the full understanding of
their duties toward the village, toward the family, and toward the
nation." Here again, as in military matters, Tchiang's model was
Zeng Guo-fan, who had defeated the Taiping in the same areas
seventy years earlier and who had promoted a "Confucian restoration" that had succeeded in recapturing the rebel villages on an
ideological level.

In order to achieve this, Tchiang proposed to bring about a
"rural reconstruction" by creating a "New Life Movement." A
"New Life" manifesto was published by Tchiang in 1934 at Nanchang, the capital of Jiangxi, the province where the Communists'
work had been most effective. All the characteristic elements of the
composite Guomindang ideology were made use of in the New
Life. Neo-Confucianism was emphasized, as Tchiang called for
the re-establishment of the ancient virtues of *li* (proprieties), *yi*
(justice), *lian* (honesty), *chi* (honor, self-respect). Christianity,
and particularly Protestant puritanism, was manifest in a campaign
against short hair and short dresses for women; the networks of
YMCA activists, several of whom became national leaders of the
New Life, were depended on. But fascism was present too: the
need to militarize the country and obey leaders was stressed; children paraded through the streets in uniform, mass meetings were
held in imitation of Hitler's Nuremberg rallies, and most of the
cadres of the New Life Movement were recruited from among Dai
Li's Blue Shirts. Tchiang stated that work and discipline had been
the secret of the success of the Chi and Chu dynasties in ancient
times, and of Fascist Italy and Nazi Germany in modern times.
Finally, on the practical level, the New Life Movement was heavily
infused with modernist American-style empiricism. Ninety-six rules
were promulgated relating to the observation of traffic regulations,

to daily hygiene (washing one's hands), and the like. Luxury and idleness were criticized.

The beginnings of the Manzhouguo

In the northeastern provinces, which had officially been independent of China since 1931, Chinese tradition was also evoked. In order to establish the power of the new emperor Pu Yi, who was formally enthroned in 1934, an appeal was made to the old Confucian idea of the "Royal Way" (*Wang dao*) of the benevolent monarchy. Pu Yi's prime minister was Zheng Xiao-xu, a poet and calligrapher who was a mandarin of the old school, but the real power belonged to the Japanese "advisers" to the new state.

Beginning in 1931, popular resistance took form in the three northeastern provinces. Sometimes encouraged by militant Communists, it was sometimes supported by the secret society of the Honghuzi (Red Beards), whose outlaw groups had been brigands in the northern mountains since the end of the nineteenth century.

ADDITIONAL BIBLIOGRAPHY

Lloyd Eastman, "Fascism in Kuomintang China: the Blue Shirts," *China Quarterly*, January 1972.
M. Lachin, *La Chine capitaliste* (Paris, 1938).
Han Su-yin, *A Mortal Flower* (New York, Putnam, 1966).
Olga Lang, *La Vie en Chine* (Paris, 1952). Original in English: *Chinese Family and Society*.
James C. Thomson, Jr., *While China Faced West: American Reformers in Nationalist China* (Cambridge, Mass., Harvard University Press, 1969).
L. Wieger, *La Chine moderne*, vol. VIII, *Chaos* (Hien-hien, 1931).
P. Kramer, *Ma vie, par Pou Yi, dernier empereur de Chine* (Paris, 1968).
Tien Hung Mao, *Government and Politics in Kuo-min-tang China, 1927–1937* (Stanford, Calif., Stanford University Press, 1972).
Lloyd Eastman, *The Abortive Revolution, China Under Nationalist Rule, 1927–1937* (Cambridge, Mass., Harvard University Press, 1974).

DOCUMENTS

1. PROJECTS FOR FINANCIAL SPECULATION AND INDUSTRIAL EXPANSION AMONG SHANGHAI CAPITALISTS: WU SUN-FU AND HIS ASSOCIATES

SOURCE: Mao Dun, *Midnight* (Peking, 1962), pp. 113–116. In this excerpt, the industrialist Wu Sun-fu and other businessmen discuss a project for an industrial bank that would be able to assist industrialists in trouble and help promote new Chinese factories. In the introduction to his novel Mao Dun explicitly stated that his aim was to demonstrate the incapacity of the Chinese national bourgeoisie to solve its economic problems. The action takes place around 1930, at the beginning of the economic crisis.

"Won't the group be too small?" worried Tang Yun-shan, who burst out laughing for no apparent reason.

Wu Sun-fu smiled but did not answer. He knew that Tang Yun-shan was impatient and that he dreamed of nothing else but gathering together all the industrialists, big and small, into a group with political aims; but he also knew that he was a complete novice to the difficult and heated struggles of the industrial world. Wu Sun-fu, who was acquainted with Europe and the United States, was not one of those men of the old style—the merchants who were incapable of being anything but merchants. But, after all, he was still an industrialist, and even though he kept an eye on politics, he never lost sight of his business interests . . .

Tang opened his briefcase and took out a large envelope. The project had been reduced to a single piece of paper on which were written only a few lines dealing with the essential points:

One: capital of five million, one third in cash.

Two: projects for several new businesses, including textile factories, long-distance buses, mines, and industrial chemicals.

Three: financial support of several existing factories (raw silk, cloth mills), navigation companies, etc. In fact, the notes dealt with what had been decided on at the last meeting, which had been put into a written report by Sun Qi-ren.

Wu Sun-fu picked up the paper and looked at it. The words brought forth images of all sorts of gigantic accomplishments: forests of towering chimneys spewing out black smoke, steamboats cutting through waves in a favorable wind, buses streaking across the plains! He could not help smiling at this dream as he thought how possible it was to fulfill it! He had learned from experience that in starting a business it was always better to be small at first, but that you must always have a glorious destiny in mind!

Three or four years earlier, while he was enthusiastically developing his native region, he had already put this principle into practice. At that time he had started with a power station and had gone on to establish his "Zhuangqiao Kingdom," the group of factories he had set up in his birthplace. He had been fairly successful in this enterprise, but a market town of one hundred thousand people was not big enough for his ambitious plans, and now, compared to the current project, all that seemed like child's play. Tang Yun-shan suddenly interrupted.

"Didn't you say before that you wouldn't include Zhu Yin-qiu and the others? But now, looking at the plans for helping businesses in trouble, I see that their three factories are mentioned. Isn't this a contradiction? . . . Of course, I don't have much experience in all this, but if an idea occurs to me, I always like to ask about it!"

Tang Yun-shan had spoken softly, but with a cunning air that seemed to imply that he sensed something but had not quite grasped its secret.

Wu Sun-fu and Wang He-fu looked at each other and began to laugh. Then they looked at Tang Yun-shan—whose face seemed to combine both malice and honesty—and he burst out laughing too. He was not sure of getting an answer, he thought, and now he tried to guide the conversation toward another subject. He picked up the paper from the table and scanned it for some points to discuss.

But Wu Sun-fu took the paper out of his hands.

"Yun-shan," he said, "your question is very interesting. You are not a stranger, any way, and whether we set up a bank or something else, we want very much for you to be the director of it. It is important for you to know the ins and outs of this whole business. We had decided against including Zhu Yin-qiu and the others because they did not have any real capital; their participation would have been nominal only and would not have contributed to the development of our enterprise. Nevertheless, their factories are a part of Chinese industry, and they are no longer in a position to save them. The closing of these factories is almost inevitable, and this would be a loss for national industry. If they are given over to foreigners, the power of foreigners in China would be still further reinforced, and this would still further weaken our industry. It is thus in thinking of the future of our industry that we want to help them. We have acted on this principle in deciding which businesses we think should be helped."

He stopped speaking. His face was enlivened by an expression of "supreme justice." With the index finger of his left hand he struck the corner of the table. His words had been earnest and clear, and Tang Yun-shan felt that his suspicions of a few moments ago had lacked nobility. Wang He-fu, who so often had a smile on his lips, suddenly became serious also. He sincerely approved of the way in which Wu Sun-fu had spoken, and he could not restrain himself from expressing a few patriotic ideas.

"Mr. Wu, you are right to take the interests of the country to heart. Chinese industry has been in existence for fifty or sixty years, not counting the industry of the Qing dynasty, with Li Hong-chang, Zhang Zhi-tong,* and others. There are also quite a few private businesses, but what has been happening? They have failed because of poor management. The majority of these businesses have fallen into the hands of foreigners! . . . You must know, Mr. Tang, that a business in the hands of an incompetent is truly a lamentable and regrettable thing, both for the individual and the country. In the end, there is no advantage to be gained from it, and in the final analysis the only ones who profit are the foreign industrialists. We must therefore be very firm on this point: even if they are our relatives or good friends, we must advise them not to look for difficulties and to give their businesses over to more capable people!"

---

* For more on these statesmen from the nineteenth century who gave their patronage to the first Chinese industries, see vol. 1, *China from the Opium Wars to the 1911 Revolution.*

2. The American contribution to the formation of the new leading class: Leighton Stuart and the Yenching University

Source: Han Su-yin, *A Mortal Flower* (New York, Putnam, 1966), pp. 265–268.

John Leighton Stuart was born in 1876, of a missionary family already two generations in China . . . He was at once the product of such an investment in the Christianization of China, and an instrument for its accomplishment. Through education and missionary work, ineluctably linked, the promotion of a policy which had begun in the 1850s was pursued with far-sighted tenacity. Leighton Stuart realized that this Americanization could be achieved through the co-operation of nuclei of Christian Chinese intellectuals, who would continue, of their own volition, the process of turning China into a client state of America.

The outcome of this idea was Yenching University. It was as the founder of Yenching University that Leighton Stuart emerged from the level of the average missionary, deeply sunk in theological squabbles. In 1918 he began to campaign for a *Christian* Chinese University, whose academic standards would be as good as anywhere else in the world and which would rival the atheistic, left-wing, and brilliant focus of intellectuals represented by Peking University. In other words, it was in the field of the mind that the battle for America and Christ would be waged in China. . . . He believed in creating an elite, which would stand up against "dangerous and extreme" currents. It took him almost ten years before he could collect the cash necessary for the University.

Most of the foundation money came from American private individuals, none from the American government. The grounds of Yenching University and some of the buildings, altogether five hundred acres, were donated by a Chinese ex-governor of the province.

Thus, due to the generosity of the American people, and also to many contributions from Chinese, the most beautiful university campus in the world, Yenching, was created.

By 1937 Yenching University endowment had reached the sum of $2,500,000 in American currency. Two other Americans whose efforts in this respect must be recorded are Harry Luce and his son Henry W. Luce, now owner of *Time* and *Life*. A pavilion erected to the memory of Mr. Luce Senior stood in Yenching campus, and was a picnicking spot for the students.

Yenching's name came from the ancient name, some 2,500 years ago, of a state of which today's Peking was the chief city. "Yen" means swallow, the city thus named because of the millions of swallows winging over it in autumn. "Freedom through Truth for Service" was the motto of Yenching.

Writing about the students of Yenching in his autobiography, Leighton Stuart interjects a sad note: "Some of them have been disappointing—most of them perhaps in some respects." The present government of China counts among some of its younger leaders, its diplomats abroad, its professionals at home, students of Yenching University. Perhaps this is what Dr. Stuart found disappointing. . . .

Leighton Stuart felt that an educated, American-Christian Chinese elite, self-propelled and self-supporting, would play a role of great benefit. That it would primarily be shaped to preserve America's best interests and markets in China may not have occurred to him. Perhaps he really believed that such an "enlightened" elite would bring prosperity to China's millions without a revolution, and especially without getting rid of the financial thraldom imposed upon China by the West —including America. This was an illusion; no such elite is going to serve *any* interests but those of its own class, and its interests are irremediably tied to the interests of its mentors and financial backers, and *not* to those of its own people. And since these backers would be foreign rulers, intent on returns for their investments, this elite would become an ideal servant one, keeping its own countrymen in tutelage, turning its own country into a state, dependent upon America's bounty . . . Never in a thousand years could such an elite accomplish, in spite of the most pious expressions and flamboyant announcements, the reforms that it would proclaim itself ready to accomplish. It would be pie-in-the-sky for ever. Many in the world are still fooling themselves today, as perhaps Leighton Stuart fooled himself then.

"I have observed," wrote Stuart, "an unpleasant phenomenon of Chinese student life . . . organized outbreaks of patriotic demonstrations . . ." He was aware that even the most Christian of educational trees, Yenching University, might one day bear strange fruit.

3. MME. SUN YAT-SEN DENOUNCES THE TREASON OF THE GUOMINDANG (1931)

SOURCE: Song Qing-ling, *The Struggle for New China* (Peking, Foreign Languages Press, 1952), pp. 27–31.

In the Central Government, Party members strove for the highest and most lucrative posts, forming personal cliques to fortify their positions, while in their local districts they likewise exploited the masses to satisfy their personal greed. By allying themselves with one militarist after another, they have been able to jump to high positions in the Party and Government. But faithful and true revolutionaries have been deliberately tortured to death in many cruel ways, the latest example being the murder of Deng Yan-da.

Recently came the split between the Nanking and Canton factions, forming two conflicting forces. Each accused the other and boasted of its own virtues. Hypocritical catch-phrases, such as "open politics," "democratic rule," and "revolutionary diplomacy," have been used as weapons to deceive the Chinese masses. But in reality, both Canton and Nanking are dependent upon militarists, both are pleading for the favor of their imperialist masters, and both are betraying and slaughtering the Chinese masses.

Since Japan has openly invaded Manchuria, both the Canton and Nanking cliques, facing the national crisis and public criticism, have been forced temporarily to cease fighting openly, and have held a so-called "Peace and Unification Conference." Three months were spent in intrigues, the debates centering on the division of spoils in the Central Party Committee and the Government. Of the abject misery and desperate needs of peasants and workers, who form the overwhelming majority of the nation, not one word was uttered in this conference. Self-interest has completely blinded these rival cliques to the fact that personal dictatorship, demoralization of the Party, and partition of the country by foreign imperialists have all resulted from the gulf created by themselves between the Guomindang and the masses.

Only a party that is built on the basis of a worker and peasant policy can establish a foundation for Socialism, break the power of militarism and throw off the yoke of foreign imperialism. If "peace" and "unification" go smoothly, enabling each clique to get all it wants, "peace" will mean nothing but a peaceful division of the spoils, and "unity" nothing but a united looting of the masses. It is utterly unthinkable that the masses of China should have any interest in such a "peace," or the nation should desire such a "unity."

We are now witnessing the first fruits of this unification in Nankin. Only three days ago, by the order of the imperialist ministers, the "United Government" tried to suppress the patriotic student movement. In less than 12 hours soldiers and gangsters surrounded the students, brutally beating and bayoneting them, and driving them out of the city like beasts. Many students were injured and killed; a great number are reported missing.

Chapter Eight

The Communist Movement from 1927 to 1934

In its special meeting on August 7, 1927, the Central Committee of the CCP abandoned its policy of a United Front with the Guomindang, thus calling into question the strategy it had pursued since 1923. Chen Du-xiu, who had been secretary-general since the party's founding, was discharged, and the leadership was entrusted to a series of leftist teams, which remained in a dominant position until the Long March of 1934. Through many changes in personnel and despite many failures, these leaders of the CCP primarily sought their support from among the working class of the big cities. The year 1927 also marked the beginning of a very different and quite new approach that originated with Mao Tsetung's "Report on the Peasant Movement in Hunan" (January 1927). This approach emphasized the essential role of the peasantry in the Chinese revolution.

From 1927 to 1934, the development of the Communist movement reflected the contradictory relations between these two tendencies. A series of abortive revolutionary attempts during the second half of 1927 marked the transition from the great urban movements of 1924–1927 to the peasant uprisings of the following period.

The Nanchang insurrection

Control of this important provincial capital, which was situated midway between Wuhan and the lower Yangzi region, would have allowed the Communists to reverse the situation and to regroup the revolutionary forces scattered all over the country. On August 1, Zhou En-lai led an uprising there, with the support of He Long, Ye Ting, and Zhu De, the leaders of the local Nationalist armies. A Revolutionary Committee consisting of Zhou En-lai and the military and leftist members of the Guomindang was formed that same day. Its program called for a struggle against imperialism and the warlords, defense of the rights of workers and peasants, and the institution of agrarian reform. As early as August 5, however, the insurgents were forced to evacuate the city because of pressure from the Nationalist armies. They went on to occupy the port of Swatow for a while at the end of September, then withdrew to the interior. Some of the insurgents joined Peng Pai's soviet in east Guangdong. Zhu De, a former warlord (born in 1886) turned Communist, and another group of insurgents remained in Hunan for a time before rejoining Mao Tsetung's troops the following year.

The aim of the insurrection was to assume power in a large city with the support of workers' strikes, the local peasant movement, and divisions in the Nationalist army. But the Communists' strategy failed to take into account the fact that they were so badly outnumbered. The abortive uprising at Nanchang nevertheless led to a regrouping of revolutionary military cadres hostile to the Guomindang's new orientation and prepared to cooperate with the Communists. In the People's Republic of China today, the anniversary of this insurrection is celebrated as the beginning of the People's Liberation Army.

The Autumn Harvest Uprising

The leaders of the CCP decided to stir up the Hunan peasants to revolt, and they put Mao Tsetung, who had carried out his famous investigation among the peasant unions there the year before, in charge of the insurrection. The tradition of revolutionary peasant movements was strong in the area around Changsha. Nevertheless, the first attempt to mobilize the peasants there around a revolutionary army led by the CCP was a failure. The Nationalists reacted violently; the revolutionary troops were routed and retreated to the mountains inland. Some of them retired to the Jinggangshan Mountains with Mao; others continued to agitate locally from time to time, in very isolated and almost impregnable regions.

The only Communist effort that succeeded in creating a relatively stable base was that of Peng Pai in the Haifeng and Lufeng districts in east Guangdong. Active peasant unions had been established there as early as 1925 to 1926. In 1927, they transformed themselves into a "soviet government" and held out until February 1928, when they were massacred by the Guomindang during an extremely bloody wave of repression.

In spite of the mixed results, these first attempts at Communist infiltration in rural areas led to the formation of young cadres who, after many reverses and difficulties, participated in the founding of "red bases" during the years that followed.

The Canton commune

At the end of 1927, the leaders of the CCP prepared for a third insurrection. Canton was chosen because of the strong Communist influence among the workers there and the perceptible dissension among the region's Nationalist authorities, as well as the help anticipated from the neighboring peasant soviets of Haifeng-Lufeng. Qu Qiu-bai, the new secretary-general of the CCP, had lived in Moscow for some time, and he was encouraged in his plans by the Comintern. Stalin's conflict with Trotsky was becoming acute; he had been severely reproached for the Chinese defeat in spring 1927 and was impatient for a substantial victory in Canton with which to answer his critics. The Comintern delegates in China pushed for the insurrection.

On December 11, the Communists occupied the city and proclaimed a soviet government. Property was confiscated and nationalized; all debts were canceled. But the Nationalist generals, whose troops were five times larger than those of the revolutionaries, reacted immediately. They were supported by the city's merchants and by the "yellow" unions that the Guomindang had organized in Canton. The insurgents could not defend themselves, and a wave of brutal repression swept through the city. There were 600 deaths during the three days of the uprising, but 5,700 people were killed by the Guomindang in the days that followed.

With the crushing of the Canton commune the Chinese proletariat temporarily withdrew as an effective revolutionary force.

The First Red Bases

The Jinggangshan base

Jinggangshan, at the border of Hunan and Jiangxi, was an isolated region of hills covered with forests; its climate was mild and
humid, and vegetation and crops grew well there. The territory
where the revolutionaries established themselves (250 kilometers
in circumference) was almost unpopulated. It included only five
villages, where 2,500 people lived far away from any urban influence, and where social relations were still based on the clan system. This isolated region was also a refuge for highway bandits,
deserters from the Nationalist armies, and peasants who had been
dispossessed of their lands.

When Mao Tsetung's small army of workers, peasants, and soldiers who had participated in the Autumn Harvest Uprising arrived
in the Jinggangshan, it was still quite an ill-assorted group. Its survival depended in part on the help of bands of local outlaws. The
base (really two small, separate bases) was run by a provisional
organization, the Front Committee, which was outside the official
hierarchy of the CCP. The tactic chosen by Mao Tsetung and Zhu
De, who joined him somewhat later in Jinggangshan, was to "establish a soviet zone of six *xian* [districts], to stabilize and gradually
consolidate Communist power in these frontier districts of Hunan,
Jiangxi, and Guangdong, and using this base, to extend our operations to larger territories."

New principles

In the beginning, the base was scarcely more than an expedient.
The important thing was to survive after so many setbacks, to per-
mit revolutionary forces to fall back in order to summon new
strength. Its empirical nature was clear from the terminology used.
"Red bases," "revolutionary bases," "border regions," and "liberated
zones" were terms that were used only later. In the beginning, the
Communists were content to speak of zones of "dissidence" (*gequ*).
They began theorizing only gradually, for example in 1929, with
Mao's essay "Why Is It That Red Political Power Can Exist in
China?" But Jinggangshan was the prototype of a long series of

revolutionary bases that little by little extended through South China until 1934 and then in North China after the Long March, during the war against Japan. The success of this strategy of red bases would ultimately permit the Chinese Communists to assume power over the whole country in 1949.

This strategy was based on new principles. First, the revolutionary struggle was an *armed* struggle. The revolutionaries were beaten in 1924 to 1927 because they did not have their own armed forces. Their strength had to be built up until it was equal to that of the enemy, which included the troops of the Guomindang as well as the troops of the warlords who had gone over to the Guomindang side.

Second, this armed struggle depended on the *peasantry* for its *principal strength,* since it took place in remote rural areas least accessible to regular armies. Because of this, agrarian reform became an important element in the general strategy of the Communists. The peasants had to be helped both to liberate themselves from the feudal system and to integrate themselves into the larger revolutionary struggle. The tradition of the old *jacqueries* and secret societies was followed, but carried one step further. The peasants were no longer stirred to action by old slogans and the simple egalitarianism of the old secret societies, but by men, ideas, and organized structures from the cities: professional revolutionaries, militant intellectuals, survivors of the anti-labor repression, and Marxist ideology and the Communist Party.

Third, the struggle for power took place on a local level. Red bases were called soviet districts in order to affirm a solidarity with Moscow, but the method was very different; power was exercised only locally, without any immediate hope of extending it to the entire country. The first red bases were located in the South, in the provinces where the Beifa had awakened the political consciousness of the masses in 1926. More precisely, they were often located within the borders of two or three provinces, in regions that were almost inaccessible. As a result, for a long time, the large industrial centers and the working class would no longer be the principal revolutionary center. The struggle's center of gravity shifted toward the backward economic zones.

Finally, this struggle was one *of long duration,* whereas in 1927, everything had been decided in a matter of days. For this long-term struggle, rural areas offered the most favorable conditions. One could survive there in a natural environment. In the cities, the problems of wages and the market could not be ignored for very long.

Armed struggle, a peasant base, local seizure of power, and a long-term struggle were therefore four closely related themes.

Soviets and agrarian reform in the soviet zones

In every district, there were soviets—if only embryonic ones—of workers, peasants, and soldiers, since traditional relationships and the influence of peasant families, which generally remained patriarchal, still dominated social relations.

Agrarian reform was accomplished at the village level. All the land was confiscated and then redistributed according to the type of land: good, average, and poor. The division was to be as equitable as possible, according to the work force available in each family. The landowners (*dizhu*), if they had not been executed already, were not given a share. Rents were abolished. The only tax was fixed at a rate of 15 to 20 percent of the harvests. These changes did not take place without difficulties and many arguments among the Communists. The Front Committee initially adopted a policy of "total confiscation and redistribution" of lands, but in a region that had not been touched by the great movements of the past few years, this policy was bound to encounter some resistance, particularly from the rich peasants and the upper level of the middle peasants. Primarily because of this opposition to measures that were too radical for the situation, agrarian reform progressed very slowly in the territory of Jinggangshan. In some cases, it had not even been completed when the revolutionaries were forced to depart from the first red base.

Organization of the army

After leaving for Jinggangshan, the revolutionary army was reorganized within the framework of what was called the "First Division of Workers and Peasants." It actually included some working class cadres who had survived the repression, some young miners and railwaymen from the area, and some local peasants. But other social elements were also important, including professional soldiers, who were often from the Beifa armies, and outcasts (local bandits, outlaws, members of secret societies). In 1929, when Mao criticized the mentality of the outlaw and the military commando ("Erroneous Conceptions in the Party"), he confirmed the political importance as well as the large size of these groups. In addition to these elements, there were units that had deserted from the Guomindang, often in whole regiments, and which were made up of the same kinds of men as the revolutionary army.

The army had hardly been established when it successfully withstood several Nationalist attacks. In spring 1928, when Mao's troops were reinforced by those of Zhu De, Lin Biao, and Chen Yi, a more thoroughgoing military and political reorganization took place. Mao became "delegate of the party," and Zhu "commander in chief." Their troops, which Edgar Snow estimated to include 50,000 men, formed the Fourth Army of Workers and Peasants. Their sphere of influence was enlarged, and their political awareness was strengthened. They were supported by a peasant militia which provided information, provisions, and evacuation for the wounded. Through this militia, the army maintained a relationship between the regular troops and the civilian population. This was a completely new situation in China, where soldiers had always been mercenaries. They had traditionally been accustomed to profiting as much from local pillaging as from wages, and the villagers had unanimously despised and detested them.

Differences on military issues within the CCP

There were differences between the party members who had established the base and the official authorities of the CCP in Hunan, and these differences extended beyond simple problems of organization. The Provincial Committee, on whose "territory" Jinggangshan was located, wanted to be directly in charge and to push the more flexible Front Committee organized by Mao and his friends into the background. There were even sharper disagreements over the fundamental problem of political organization within the army. Leaders of the CCP on the provincial and national levels were in favor of an autonomous political organization (basic units of the actual party) within the army. Mao and his friends in the red base defended a less cumbersome system, which entrusted the role of political vanguard to the army itself and to the local soviets. A system of political commissars would ensure the liaison between the military groups and the base's mass organizations. The Maoists supported their views by pointing to the lack of political cadres and the political weakness of the new recruits, who were either local peasants or deserters from the enemy's armies.

Shortly after the troops of Zhu De had joined the original core in Jinggangshan, the forces of the red base scored an important victory over Nationalist troops. Thanks to this victory, the First Congress of Delegates from the CCP was held at Maoping in the red base. A transitional plan was adopted that involved the formation of a "Special Committee," of which Mao was the secretary and which was under the jurisdiction of the Provincial Committee. Nevertheless, differences soon arose again between the Special Committee and the Provincial Committee, as well as between the red base and the party hierarchy established in the cities.

The disagreement was over the radical policy proposed by the Provincial Committee, "burn and kill if necessary," an approach that the committee in the base area considered "ultra-leftist." There were also two opposing attitudes toward military strategy. Those in Mao's group believed that it was necessary to strengthen the base, politically and militarily; the others wanted to extend the Red Army's sphere of influence as far as possible and to attack the Nationalist armies. The latter group prevailed for a time. Mao Tse-tung was even relieved of his post as secretary of the Front's Special Committee. In effect, the base's defenses were rapidly depleted once the troops advanced toward the South. This tactic was soon shown to be dangerous, since it permitted the troops of the Guomindang to launch a second campaign in July 1928, even though they had been defeated a month earlier. The attack failed in the end, however, and after having threatened the revolutionary troops, the Nationalist regiments were forced to retire following disagreements among their leaders. Tchiang Kaï-chek became absorbed in his struggle against the warlords again. During these campaigns the tactic of "retreat in order to advance,"[1] widely developed later on, was used for the first time.

At the end of 1928, the red base was strengthened by the desertion of a large Nationalist unit whose leader, Peng De-huai, would later become one of the principal leaders of the Red Army. With a letup in fighting that lasted several months, the internal problems of the CCP became prominent again. At the second Maoping conference, a Front Committee with an intermediate status between the ordinary party hierarchy and the political leadership of the army was established, and Mao became its secretary. At the same time, a general assembly of the Red Army refused to abolish the

---

[1] See document 4 at the end of the chapter.

soldiers' soviets in order to establish the political commissariats as a separate structure. Mao supported this position, which he repeatedly justified by referring to the acute scarcity of political workers. He claimed that there were only enough of these workers to be distributed among the soviets of the soldiers.

Differences on agrarian reform

Conflicts over agrarian reform had broken out immediately after the region was occupied. One sector of the Front Committee did not approve of the radicalism of the policy supported by the Provincial Committee. The Provincial Committee favored confiscation of all land and its subsequent redistribution. The positions that Mao Tsetung advanced at the time of the second Maoping Conference were opposed to the policy of complete confiscation of land. He only favored the confiscation of land belonging to the landlords. On the other hand, Mao believed that the process of redistribution should permit the middle peasant to sell his land. Rather than simply receiving a lot which would remain collective property, each peasant would be the owner of the land he personally cultivated. If one failed to recognize—as the Provincial Committee had, for the past year—that the peasants had been fighting for the right to cultivate their own land, Mao argued, the relationship between agrarian revolution and the redistribution of land could not be understood. One would be underestimating how important agrarian reform and the mobilization of the peasants were to China's bourgeois democratic revolution.

From Jinggangshan to Jiangxi

At the end of the winter of 1928–1929, the revolutionaries decided to leave Jinggangshan. In a region that was already extremely poor, the blockade by the Guomindang armies had created increasingly difficult problems of food supply. In January 1929, the troops began to leave under the leadership of Mao Tsetung and Zhu De, with Peng De-huai and his soldiers acting as rear guard.

After retiring from Jinggangshan, the revolutionaries settled close to Guangdong on the border of Jiangxi and Fujian. Like Jinggangshan, it was a region of hills and mountains less than 2,000 meters high. It covered about 30,000 square kilometers and was inhabited by five to six million people. The climate there was humid and hot with abundant summer monsoon rains, but the winters were quite severe. Though very mountainous, the area was less wild than Jinggangshan; its principal products were rice, tea, and tung oil. Several market towns were scattered across the region—Ruijin, Ningdu, Jiangshou, Dingshou—but it was generally poor, and communications were difficult.

The geographical and climatic characteristics were not very different from those of Jinggangshan and presented the same strategic advantages: a sphere extending through several provinces which was difficult to penetrate and isolated economically from the influence of the large industrial urban centers.

Other small bases in Central China

Besides the Jiangxi region, which was to become the birthplace of the first Chinese Soviet Republic, there were other small soviet zones in Central China. These were also situated in mountainous regions on the borders of several provinces, and their establishment and development benefitted from the numerous conflicts that broke out between Tchiang Kaï-chek and the warlords in 1929 and 1930. In the summer of 1930, there were about fifteen bases. In 1928, Fang Zhi-min, a militant Communist, had established a red base in northeast Jiangxi, close to the borders of Zhejiang and Fujian. The Tenth Army was organized there in 1930. Under the leadership of Zhang Guo-tao and Xu Xiang-qian, a group of revolutionaries who had participated in the Autumn Harvest Uprising formed the Fourth Group of Armies on the Henan-Hubei-Anhui border. This base would survive until 1933. The Second Army was mustered and created on the northeast border of Hunan by one of the former insurgents from the Nanchang uprising.

All these red bases resembled those of Jinggangshan. Adapted to the needs of a strategy based on long-term armed struggle, they were primarily committed to the poor peasantry.[2] Located in remote regions that covered two or more provinces, they were far away from the large industrial centers and from the zones of financial and military influence of the great powers. Once the revolutionary struggles were taken into the rural areas, the great powers could no longer intervene against them as easily as they had in Shanghai in 1927.

[2] See document 1.

The Struggle in the Cities

The Sixth Congress of the CCP

There were two general feelings among the delegates to the Sixth Congress of the CCP held from July to September 1928 in Moscow for security reasons. Despite the failures of the armed insurrections of 1927, the leftists predicted a new revolutionary uprising in the very near future. The rightists despaired of seeing the revolutionary tide reappear in China. The former group included Li Li-san, the future secretary of the CCP, Zhou En-lai, and Qu Qiu-bai. The later was represented by Zhang Guo-tao, Cai He-sen and Xiang Ying. Pavel Mif, the Comintern representative, tried to strike a balance between these two groups.

While criticizing the previous orientation of the party, the political resolutions that were adopted stressed reorganization of the party in the cities. The guerrilla units were expected to turn into a national army capable of attacking the cities. Priority was still given, therefore, to the revolutionary struggle and the organization of the revolution in the large industrial centers. The CCP was defined as the vanguard of the working class, the only class that was considered capable of conducting the revolution and of leading the peasant struggle against the landlords. The conference reiterated the idea that the national bourgeoisie in China was too weak to free the peasants from the feudal regime. The peasantry continued therefore to be considered only as a reserve force, and the rural guerrillas only as a supplementary force for tactical use.

The former sailor Xiang Zhong-fa, who represented a centrist position between the two tendencies at the congress, was elected secretary-general. Except for him, the ones elected to the politburo were partisans of a policy that aimed at a short-term revolutionary uprising in China. Li Li-san became chief of the propaganda department, and Zhou En-lai was designated head of the organization bureau. Neither Mao Tsetung, who was then head of the Front Committee of the Jinggangshan base, nor any of the party members from the first red base participated in the Sixth Congress. In a text that was not published until 1945, Mao criticized the erroneous predictions of the participants in the Sixth Congress concerning the imminence of the Chinese revolution and the rising revolutionary feeling. Where the analysis of Chinese society and the drafting of a revolutionary strategy were concerned, the texts of the Sixth Congress followed the positions defined at the Sixth Congress of the Comintern (June–September 1928). According to these positions, the Social Democrats were considered to be the worst enemies of the working class and its party and to be traitors to their class. Consequently, the Communist parties of the different countries that were members of the International were obliged to adopt very radical positions and to break completely with any united-front policy.

As we have already seen in regard to the implementation of agrarian reform, Mao had a very different point of view. The fundamental criticism that he raised against party members present at the Sixth Congress was that they did not analyze the instability of the "intermediary strata," China's national bourgeoisie and rich peasants. He felt that full advantage should be taken of the contradictions within the reactionary camp. This divergence between the CCP leadership and the representatives of the liberated zones continued to grow during this period.

The condition of the working class after 1927

After the terror of 1927–1928 inflicted by the Guomindang on the Communists and the revolutionary union cadres had literally decimated their ranks, the revolutionary movement's campaigns were comparatively weak for a whole year.

Despite the fact that the union movement had made progress and spread through China since the beginning of the decade, it was still too young in years and in politics to resist such a wave of repression. Most of the workers were young and had just arrived in the city. They had been forced to leave the surrounding rural areas because of lack of work. As a result, factory work was still very unstable. Workers returned to their villages at harvest time and absenteeism was very high. Ideologically, traditional peasant influences remained very strong among the workers. Regional characteristics remained quite marked, and the workers tended to gather in groups according to their native districts. The diversity of dialects also hampered the development of a centralized organization. The labor movement had originally grown and organized mass struggles on a larger and larger scale at a time when unions were still legal, from 1924 to 1927, and it had great difficulty in adopting clandestine forms of struggle.

Finally, the political stand that the CCP took in regard to the working class, particularly that of Li Li-san, forbade revolutionary workers to join the "yellow" unions that were founded by the Guomindang after 1927. These unions were formed at the time of the wave of repression that hit the revolutionaries, and for the Guomindang they represented an important union apparatus which would cooperate with the Chinese bourgeoisie in defending Nationalist and reformist positions. The great strike movements were primarily directed at the foreign enterprises. By means of this union apparatus, which grew very slowly, in spite of the pressures put on the workers through bribery and threats, the Guomindang intended to develop a system of police control over the working class. The workers joined the yellow unions out of fear of repression.

In opposition to the formation and growth of such unions, the Communists tried to create revolutionary, "red" unions. The violence of the repression made attracting members and extending these unions' influence extremely difficult. The extremist attitude of the revolutionaries prevented them from regaining lost ground; their activities, particularly in Shanghai, consisted mainly of engaging in brawls with members of the secret societies and members of the gangs connected with the Guomindang. In 1929, however, the resumption of strikes marked a renewal of Communist labor activity.[3] This renewal began at the time of the Fifth Pan-Chinese Labor Congress, which was again held in Moscow and at which the delegates from the clandestine red unions were present.

Labor struggles

Despite the new and very difficult conditions in which the labor movement developed after 1927, strikes were continually breaking out between 1928 and 1930. They were for the most part spontaneous and were always provoked by economic demands. This was particularly true after 1930, when there was an unprecedented rise in prices and a new increase in unemployment caused by the 1929 world crisis. There were sometimes demands for improved working conditions, but there were scarcely any political strikes.

This wave of strikes, which sometimes affected Shanghai's large factories—such as the B.A.T. match factory (English)—gave some substance to the policy of urban uprisings that had been decided on by Li Li-san and the CCP leadership in the summer of 1930.

[3] See document 2.

After the failure of this policy and Li Li-san's loss of influence, the Central Committee withdrew to Jiangxi. The organized labor movement faded. Labor was more and more closely controlled by the gangs connected with the Guomindang, which intimidated and terrorized the workers.

Conflict between Li Li-san and Mao Tsetung

When the armed forces of Jinggangshan moved to Hunan-Jiangxi in 1929, Li Li-san dominated the Central Committee as he had done since the Sixth Congress. A native of Hunan like Mao, he was a veteran of the labor movement and had led the unions in 1925 to 1927.

Contact between the Maoist Front Committee and the Shanghai leaders of the party was resumed through an exchange of letters. In these letters, Li Li-san revealed a very definite pessimism, to which Mao replied with a essay known as "A Single Spark Can Start a Prairie Fire."

In answer to Li's general pessimism, Mao retorted that in a semicolonized country where prolonged struggles were taking place within a divided ruling class, it was possible to construct a base where the democratic power of workers and peasants could be exercised. Mao also said there was no basis for Li Li-san's fear that the ascendancy of the peasantry would threaten the hegemony of the proletariat.

During the long wait for the revolution, Li Li-san wanted to protect the army from the enemy by dispersing it into small guerrilla groups. Considering that small armed units were easier for the enemy to annihilate, Mao was completely opposed to this suggestion. At a stage where there was such great ideological disparity among them, Mao argued that it was the concentration of troops which maintained the soldiers' morale and fighting spirit. Mao opposed "the spirit of guerrilla warfare." In a text written in December 1929, he argued against encouraging a "military" attitude within the Red Army and stressed the importance of building up political power. Only through such power could agrarian reform and the development of the armed forces be intensified.

Extension of the conflict; preparation for the 1930 insurrection

In various documents written in 1930, Li Li-san and the Central Committee emphasized the sharpening of international contradictions, particularly because of the crisis of 1929, and the ripening of the revolutionary situation in China. A letter to the Front Committee (Mao, Zhu De) gave the Red Army immediate targets. These targets were the large cities of Central China, specifically Wuhan, Changsha, and Nanchang. A conference of delegates from the red bases met in Shanghai to prepare the military insurrection in these cities. A resolution of June 11 ("The New Revolutionary Wave and the Preliminary Victory in One or Several Provinces") reiterated the same themes. "The great struggle of the proletariat is the decisive force for preliminary successes in one or several provinces. . . . It is a completely erroneous idea not to attach special importance to urban work and to count on the villages to encircle the cities." The attitudes expressed here were in complete disagreement with those of the party leaders in the red bases. Their tactics of training peasant guerrillas in the less industrial areas and of preparing for a long-term encirclement of the cities by the countryside were in opposition to the resolution of the Central Committee, which called for an immediate armed uprising in the cities, supported by the Red Army.

The renewal of the union movement in the cities, the extension of soviet zones throughout Central China, the persistent disagreement between Tchiang Kaï-chek and Wang Jing-wei in 1929 to 1930, and the continuing conflicts between Tchiang and the warlords all led Li Li-san and the Central Committee members to believe that the time had come to launch a Communist offensive.

But they were not taking into account the absence of political organization in the labor movements; nor were they considering the technological weakness and the small numbers of the Red Army compared with the Nationalist armies, which were supported by the great powers. Finally, they forgot that quarrels between reactionary generals could quickly be set aside when it came to fighting against revolutionaries.

The 1930 uprising and its failure

The object of the 1930 offensive was to take the three large cities of Central China: Changsha, Wuhan, and Nanchang. The Third Group of Armies under the leadership of Peng De-huai was to take the first of these three cities. The attack on Nanchang was assigned to the troops of the Red Army of Jiangxi, under the leadership of Mao Tsetung and Zhu De. Finally, the attack on Wuhan was to be launched by the armies of He Long, which were located in western Hubei and Hunan.

Strikes were simultaneously to break out and be transformed into insurrection in all the large cities of the Yangzi valley, in Canton, and even in Manchuria. As it turned out, only Changsha was occupied, when Peng De-huai's troops entered it on July 27. Ten days later they were dislodged and had to retire to the region of Liuyang. Ferocious repression followed, which destroyed the party's clandestine organization in Changsha.

After the retreat of the revolutionary troops from Changsha, the troops led by Mao Tsetung and Zhu De, who disapproved of the general plan of the offensive, decided not to pursue the attack on Nanchang. They headed for Liuyang to reinforce the Third Army. The combined troops formed the First Army of the Front, of which Zhu De became the commander in chief and Mao the political commissar. Later, Zhu De would say to the journalist Agnes Smedley, "For the first time we had openly disobeyed the orders of the Central Committee."

In the other cities, the disturbances, doomed from the beginning, were quickly repressed, and the terror that inevitably ensued practically destroyed the ranks of militant Communists and union members.

The so-called Lilisanist policy was totally defeated, and Li Li-san was removed from the party's leadership at the meeting of the third plenum of the Central Committee in September 1930. Qu Qiu-bai, the Comintern representative, and Zhou En-lai, who had recently returned from Moscow, presented a report recognizing that the CCP leadership had overestimated "the unequal development of the revolutionary movement in different regions, and that if a revolutionary situation was developing in China, it did not yet objectively exist in July 1930." The Central Committee had underestimated the role of the areas controlled by the soviet bases and the report affirmed the necessity of developing and reinforcing them by creating a central soviet government and a strong Red Army.

The criticism of Lilisanism was intensified in January 1931 at the fourth session of the Central Committee established by the Sixth Congress. Whereas Li Li-san had represented a leftist line that was more or less independent of the Comintern and Moscow, now representatives of Moscow took over the leadership of the party. Twenty-eight "Bolsheviks" arrived fresh from the Chinese Revolutionary University of Moscow with their professor Pavel Mif. Among them were Wang Ming, Po Ku, and other young theoreticians who criticized the "adventurism" of Li Li-san. But like him and like all of the Comintern at that time, they were convinced that the cities and the working class, and not the peasantry, would dominate the revolutionary movement. The "mountain communism" of the Maoists only aroused distrust and incomprehension. This attitude never fundamentally changed, even when the twenty-eight Bolsheviks, forced to abandon Shanghai in 1931 to 1932 in order to escape the Guomindang police, retired to the soviet districts along with all of the leadership of the CCP.

The leftist intellectual movement

In the large cities like Shanghai, the CCP's influence was greater among leftist intellectuals than among the working class. The intellectuals were very much aware of the authoritarian degradation of the Nanking regime and had more means of expression at their disposal. In 1930, the League of Leftist Writers was founded. Politically, it strongly criticized the Guomindang government and called for a literature that was related to the people. The Communist organizer Zhou Yang was its secretary-general, and Qu Qiu-bai, the former secretary-general of the CCP, was one of its principal supporters. A large number of independent writers were involved, including Mao Dun (pseudonym of Shen Yan-bing, born in 1896), who was well known for political novels like *Midnight*,[4] and Lu Xun (pseudonym of Zhou Shu-ren, 1881–1936). One of the prominent figures among literary radicals since the May Fourth Movement, Lu Xun abandoned literary work in 1930 in order to write pamphlets and political essays. He had considerable influence among the student population. Watched by the police, he led a semiclandestine life. Within the framework of the League, he did not view the fight against the Guomindang as any different from his condemnation of the old China, which in his view represented passivity and weakness. This was the meaning of "A Q," one of his best-known stories.

The impact of the CCP could also be seen in the increased influence of Marxism on historians and archeologists. In 1930 to 1931, a very lively controversy developed over the "Asian mode of production" and the Marxist definition of ancient Chinese society.

---

[4] From which an excerpt is reproduced on pages 206–8 (Chapter 7, document 1).

The Soviet Republic of Jiangxi

The fact that the "Bolshevik" Central Committee joined the Maoists in Jiangxi did not make it any easier to merge these two hostile tendencies in Chinese communism. As their differences became more pronounced, their conflict and, shortly thereafter, their common defeat was precipitated.

The First Congress of Chinese Soviets (November 7, 1931)

The name and date of this congress are significant. The twenty-eight Bolsheviks wanted to emphasize their allegiance to the October Revolution while the Maoists sought to reassure Moscow by toning down the profoundly original parts of their line. The congress included 610 delegates from all the red bases (the local soviets, the army, the unions). Four years of mass struggle among the peasantry had resulted in the passing of an agrarian law and the proclaiming of a popular political power comprising all the red bases (a "central" government). This new power was codified in a "constitution," however, that was much more influenced by the Soviet model than by Chinese experience. The bylaws on national minorities, for example, were closely modeled on the Soviet constitution of 1924. The same formalism was to be found in the electoral regulations: One hundred peasants, fifty soldiers, and only twenty-five workers were necessary to elect a delegate, and this was in districts where there was no industry at all. The congress also adopted a "work law," which meticulously regulated the length of the factory work day and working conditions for women and children.

The congress therefore represented a compromise, a balance between the popular momentum gained by the red bases between 1927 and 1931 and the priority that the "Bolsheviks" gave to structures and institutions. This precarious balance existed in the top echelons, where Mao was President of the Soviet Republic of Jiangxi while the two vice-presidents were Xiang Ying, a cotton worker who had ties with the Central Committee, and Zhang Guo-tao, an intellectual who had worked in the labor movement. In the lower echelons, the local soviets were not always prepared to accept the instructions of the party representatives.

The agrarian policy of the soviet districts

The agrarian policy was based on the classifications which Mao Tsetung made in his investigation in Hunan and elaborated in a document written in 1933 (*How to Differentiate the Classes in the Rural Areas*); those listed were landlords, rich peasants, middle peasants, and poor peasants. The landlords lived by exploiting other people and by engaging in usury. Among them were the "local tyrants" (*tuhao*) and "evil gentry" (*lieshen*), both enemies of the revolution. The rich peasants worked part of their land and rented another part. Few subjects evoked such strong disagreements among the revolutionaries as the handling of these rich peasants; most of the time, the rich peasants were neutralized without being attacked. The middle peasants, who either owned or rented their land, did not profit from the labor of others. Because their goal was to increase their income and their property, the middle peasants were often hostile to all forms of cooperative enterprise. Finally, the poor peasants—farmers or agricultural workers who sold their labor— were the declared vanguard of the party's agrarian policy.[5]

Although agrarian reform had been hard on the rich peasants in the early Jinggangshan period, the agrarian law that was approved by the First Congress of Chinese Soviets in November 1931 provided only for the confiscation of the lands belonging to the landlords. Allowance was made for the middle peasants who hoped to enlarge their holdings, and for rich peasants who wanted to buy back confiscated lands. Only after all the middle peasants had accepted agrarian reform was it to be implemented.

Carrying out agrarian reform; mobilizing the masses

In the mass mobilization for implementing agrarian reform in all the villages of the Soviet Republic, the largest role was played by the poor peasants, the unions of agricultural workers, and the other mass organizations. These groups worked with the government personnel from the local soviets and with the administrative cadres from the base. Once confiscated, the lands were arranged into categories and then distributed. The inventory was public. The implementation of the reform was controlled by inspection teams.

---

[5] See document 3.

Yakhontoff, a White Russian journalist in Shanghai, noted the radical change in peasant conditions in the soviet districts in a published letter: "I.O.U.'s, mortgages, property titles, have all been burned . . . rent collectors have been eliminated . . . each peasant now receives enough water to irrigate his fields, and there are no more quarrels over water . . . some soviets have founded rural banks or credit associations, and the peasants can borrow without being robbed by usurers . . ."

Moreover, because they were encircled by the Guomindang troops, the struggle for production was as important for the mass movement as the division of lands. In August 1933, a conference on economic development urged the semi-independent production of clothing, tools, and paper, and the exportation of mountain and forest products (camphor, tungsten, oils) to outside regions.

Not all the peasants had a clear awareness of the changes that were taking place. Some joined the party or the army. Others, following the tradition of village cults and secret societies, confused the names of the new leaders and revered a "Zhu-Mao" or "Zhu Mao-peng." But the benefits of the new power for the great majority of the peasants were clear to everyone.

The army

The revolutionary armies in the soviet zones were organized into divisions and regiments, down to the basic unit of ten men. Soldiers were recruited primarily from among the young peasants (*shaonian-fengdui*), while the villagers between the ages of eighteen and forty usually became Red Guards (*chiweidu*). The local troops were responsible for provisioning, transportation, hygiene, and rear-guard safety. They secured information on enemy movements and went in advance of the regular troops as scouts. All of these paramilitary activities on the part of the local population were very important for the morale of the troops. The local and auxiliary troops fought as equals alongside the regular army, and included the Red Guards and the young vanguard units.[6]

Political organization extended to all levels of the Red Army. There was a political department for the large units and a political commissar for the smallest units down to the company. Their

[6] See document 4.

role was not only to supervise political training and to strengthen the consciousness of the soldiers, but also to arrange for political work with the local population and to act as liaison between the soldiers and the villagers. In the newly liberated regions, the political department of the army set up the new provisional administrations. In all the newly formed units, there was a "Lenin Hall," which was the center of all local political activity. At all levels, the role of the political commissar and his authority were of considerable importance.

Red army discipline was condensed into "three rules" and "eight points" that were tirelessly taught and explained in an effort to combat the usual carelessness of soldiers and their customary scorn for the civilian population.

The three rules were:

Obey orders.

Take nothing from the people, not even a needle and thread.

Return "confiscated goods" to the authorities.

And the eight points were:

Speak with courtesy.

Be fair in your purchases.

Return everything that you borrow.

Compensate for the damages that you have caused.

Do not strike or insult the people.

Do not damage the harvests.

Do not bother the women.

Do not mistreat prisoners.

This discipline, then, was based on the political awareness of the soldiers: "The Red Army does not make war for the sake of war, but for the people—to organize the people, to arm the people, to help the people to establish revolutionary power."

Distribution of soviet bases

With three million inhabitants, Jiangxi-Fujian, which was near the city of Ruijin, was the largest of the bases. There were about ten others, including one near Hubei-Henan, to the north of the Yangzi, one in western Hunan, one on the island of Hainan, and one in the Northwest, in which the survivors of the Long March were

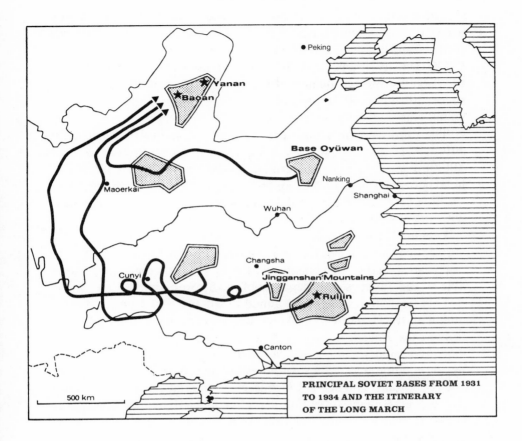

PRINCIPAL SOVIET BASES FROM 1931
TO 1934 AND THE ITINERARY
OF THE LONG MARCH

to take refuge in 1935. These bases were in precarious communication with the central soviet government. They practiced the same agrarian policy. The places in which they were located had the same geopolitical conditions: they were far away from the industrial centers and arteries of modern communication, in remote regions on the borders of several provinces.

The first four extermination campaigns of the Guomindang

After extricating himself from the 1930 provincial rebellions, Tchiang Kaï-chek ordered the "extermination of the Communist bandits."

The first campaign, which took place at the end of 1930, was very short. Zhu De's 40,000 men managed to isolate and rout the 100,000 Nationalists who were headed for Ruijin.

The second campaign, which took place in May 1931, lasted only a month. The Communists drove back more than 200,000 enemy soldiers and inflicted large losses on them. The Communist tactic ("if the enemy attacks, retreat; if the enemy retreats, pursue him; if the enemy stops, harass him; if the enemy regroups, disperse") was successful. The civilian population actively supported the Red Army, which was a "fish in water."

The third campaign was in fact a continuation of the second. In July 1931, Tchiang himself took over the operations. He had 300,000 men and many German military advisers. Nevertheless, he experienced heavy losses and was quickly forced to retreat when the Japanese attack on Moukden in September obliged him to deal with other priorities.

Tchiang Kaï-chek postponed his assaults on the Communists only long enough to work out a compromise with the Japanese. As soon as he had signed an agreement on May 1, 1932, that was very favorable to the Japanese, he began his fourth campaign.

This time, the attack was aimed at all the soviet zones, beginning with the Henan-Hubei-Anhui base, where the Nationalists confronted the Fourth Group of Armies of the Front. Because it was more accessible to attacking armies, this region had to be abandoned by the Communists. They withdrew to the West, to the Sichuan-Shenxi border. The Second Group of Armies also had to abandon its base at Hunan-Hubei for a region located on the borders of Hubei-Hunan-Sichuan. The Communists were therefore forced to abandon the rich and populous regions of the middle Yangzi for positions further to the west. Nevertheless, the operations which were undertaken against the Jiangxi zone from January 1932 to February 1933 were no more successful than the preceding ones.

Worsening of the crisis within the CCP

The conflict between the "Bolsheviks" of the Central Committee and the Maoists, the disparity between the rigid directives of the Comintern and the experience accumulated since the days in Jinggangshan, continued to grow. There were conflicts over the rich peasants, whom the "twenty-eight" wanted to deal with more harshly. There were conflicts over strategy as the party leadership refused to follow the Maoists' suggestion that the Communists withdraw, despite the increasing imbalance of forces. And there was sharp disagreement concerning methods of political activity. The

Central Committee preferred the established machinery and the party hierarchy, and the others favored work at the base among the peasants. In January 1934, the Bolsheviks excluded Mao from the political leadership of the soviet districts and he was left with only the honorary title of President of the Republic of Soviets. Many of Mao's friends were ousted, but Zhou En-lai cooperated with the twenty-eight.

This conflict left such deep scars that in republican China and at Yanan, all references to the soviets of Jiangxi, to the soviet districts, and to the soviet constitution of 1931 completely disappeared. This term, adopted from the Russian (*Suweiai*, for example, was the name of the principal press organ of the red base), was too closely related to the memory of the period when the Maoist faction had been defeated by a group whose disastrous authority was based on the support of Moscow, the Comintern, and Stalin. In later years, this group would be called the "third leftist deviation." The first involved the brief dominance of the CCP by the writer Qu Qiu-bai in 1927 to 1928, and the second referred to the period between 1928 and 1931, which was dominated by Li Li-san.

In 1934, the Communists were handicapped by their internal problems. Their relations with the peasants of the red bases deteriorated. On the other hand, the authority of the Guomindang was no longer undermined by the provincial divisions which had worked to the Communists' advantage during the campaigns of 1930–1931. The 1934 rebellion in Fujian had failed. The Communists had not intervened and were later critical of themselves for this wait-and-see policy. The Guomindang also had much greater resources in 1934. They had hundreds of thousands of men who were well trained by the German military mission and well equipped with Italian, French, and English materiel. Their next military offensive was much more solidly based, politically and economically. Commercial exchanges with the red zones were tightly blockaded. Local militias recruited from the entourage of the feudal landowners backed up the regular army of the Nationalists,[7] and the police system of the *baojia* enforced the collective responsibility of the villagers, who became hesitant to support the Communists openly.

---

[7] In the same regions almost a century earlier, the private militias of the landowners had contributed decisively to the defeat of the Taiping. (See Volume 1, *China from the Opium Wars to the 1911 Revolution.*)

The fifth extermination campaign;
the end of the Republic of Soviets

The fifth campaign began at the end of 1933. The term "campaign of encirclement" used in the official Communist history was an accurate description. The encirclement succeeded, but the extermination promised by the Guomindang did not take place. Month by month, the Nationalists gained ground and completely blockaded the red base of Jiangxi-Fujian. Several attempts at diversion failed. In August 1934, the situation became untenable, and the base was abandoned. The Communists forced their way through the blockade and began the Long March.

ADDITIONAL BIBLIOGRAPHY

Chen Po Ta, *Notes on Ten Years of Civil War, 1927–1936* (Peking, Foreign Languages Press, 1954).

Fundamental Laws of the Chinese Soviet Republic (London, 1934).

Charles B. MacLane, *Soviet Policy and the Chinese Communists, 1931–1946* (New York, Columbia University Press, 1958).

Miao Min, *Fang Chih-Min, Revolutionary Fighter* (Peking, Foreign Languages Press, 1962).

John E. Rue, *Mao Tse-tung in Opposition, 1927–1935* (Stanford, Calif., Stanford University Press, 1966).

Agnes Smedley, *The Great Road: The Life and Times of Chu Teh* (New York, Monthly Review Press, 1956).

Shanti Swarup, *A Study of the Chinese Communist Movement* (Oxford, Oxford University Press, 1966).

Richard C. Thornton, *The Comintern and the Chinese Communists, 1928–1931* (Seattle, University of Washington Press, 1969).

Victor A. Yakhontov, *The Chinese Soviets* (New York, Coward-McCann, 1934).

DOCUMENTS

1. COMMUNIST CADRE WANG CHENG* RECOUNTS THE BEGINNING OF THE SOVIET MOVEMENT IN A HUNAN VILLAGE

SOURCE: Helen Foster Snow (Nym Wales, pseud.), *Red Dust: Autobiographies of Chinese Communists as told to Nym Wales* (Stanford, Calif., Stanford University Press, 1952), pp. 96–97.

* The author was born in 1909 and was the son of a peasant who died fighting while part of a Communist band of guerrillas. Wang Cheng was a railway employee and was active in the trade-union movement around 1925 to 1927. Founder of the union in the district of Liuyang in Hunan, he returned there in 1929 after the failure of the revolution in the cities.

As soon as I arrived, I went out into the villages and organized secret Red Peasants' and Workers' unions and local branches of the C.P. In the winter of 1929 the C.P. was well organized in the villages near by, and in the north suburb of Liuyang *xian* city I organized a very good peasants' union.

One day a peasant told me that a local landlord in Xiajiasan had four guns in his house. The C.P. branch decided to send him a letter demanding that he surrender these guns to us. It was signed in the name of the Communist Party! We went to his home that very night and took the four guns. He "gave" us five thousand dollars at the same time, but we did not confiscate anything else and did no harm to the landlord himself. At that time the C.P. had the slogan of confiscating the landlords' property, but we hadn't begun to realize it then. Our political program for the moment was merely to arm ourselves—the confiscation of land would come later. We had several thousand peasants armed with agricultural implements but only our four guns.

At the time of the old-style Chinese New Year, when debts and taxes had to be paid, the C.P. branch led the peasants to oppose the collection of taxes, always unbearably oppressive. At the same time the tailors and carpenters got only one dollar for ten days' work. The workers' union demanded one dollar for five days' labor, and the peasants and workers united for action. The workers' union had four or five thousand members and the C.P. had several hundred. That New Year the *tuhao** and the other landlords dared not collect any taxes, and the workers' wages were increased thirty percent. It was the happiest New Year the people had ever had! The party expanded rapidly, and out of these original economic demands new political consciousness arose.

At that time Peng De-huai† was active in Hunan. His work had been phenomenally successful. By the beginning of 1930 the countryside was full of revolutionary agitation. In all the near-by *xian* C.P. branches were established and interconnections made. We still had only four guns—but our political influence was enormous. I was secretary of the Communist party of the district.

In the spring of 1930 we organized our own armed Red Vanguards of twenty or thirty partisans in this way: Four thousand peasants and workers attacked the estate of a big landlord in the north suburb of Liuyang city. His name was Po Sheng-chen. This landlord had about two hundred *min tuan‡* organized, with one hundred twenty guns. We brandished our four guns at the head of the big column when we went to the attack. The landlord imagined that we were well armed, and so didn't put up much resistance. We defeated the *min tuan* and

* Feudal landowner.
† Born in 1898, he was a Nationalist army officer who went over to the Communists in 1928. Later he became one of the main leaders of the Red Army. He resigned as chief of staff in 1959 following disagreements over the "great leap forward."
‡ Private militia of landowners.

captured many of them, together with twenty precious guns. None of the *min tuan* were killed and only one of our peasants died. I had led the C.P. work of the uprising, and the open leader was Xu Hing, a paper worker.

In the spring all peasants are very poor and hungry because the crops have not been planted, and so they are in desperate need. Part of our reason for attacking Po Sheng-chen's estate was to get salt and grain to distribute to the people—as well as guns for the partisans—as he had many rich granaries. Everyone jubilantly carried a sackful of food home to his starving children after our foray on this landlord. Our Red Vanguards then increased to fifty or sixty.

2. ATTEMPTS BY THE COMMUNIST PARTY TO RE-ESTABLISH AN ORGANIZATION OF LABOR UNIONS IN SHANGHAI IN 1929

SOURCE: Alain Roux, "Le mouvement ouvrier à Shanghai de 1928 à 1930," supplementary documents. Typed thesis, troisième cycle (Paris, 1970).

Having re-established an organization, the leaders of the Red labor unions are devoting themselves to an intense education and propaganda drive, for they lack cadres and they have lost contact with the factories. The question of education was raised at the 2nd Plenum of the Central Committee in February 1929. It was suggested that a manual of 1,000 characters be published for illiterate workers; its 96 chapters could be mastered in 4 months. Another manual is planned which, in 4 more months, would enable a worker to write a letter, take notes, keep a diary. . . . Manuals for "practical knowledge for the worker" are planned in physiology, hygiene, mathematics (for studying wages). A manual for technical English is envisaged. This program, which serves to remind us of the problem of the considerable number of illiterate workers, will be completed by the publication of a song book "to stimulate class consciousness and a feeling of unity" and various booklets (on contemporary history, the history of the workers' movement, economics, the history of the cooperative associations, labor unions and clubs . . .). We are even thinking of publishing working-class novels. The general policy has been established: "remain firmly within class subjects, while taking circumstances into account and watching for a chance to be published legally"; "start with the situation of the Shanghai worker, his daily life, his psychology, his habits . . ."; use 1,000 characters, avoiding European words, technical terms, literary allusions, "but let the writing be alive and animated, rich in interest without its strength turning sour." This program, astonishing when one thinks of our terrible clandestine conditions, has been put into practice. . . .

The results are undeniable. Two kinds of schools have been created, under the direction of a "school committee" of 5 members helped by union leaders; manuals have been published and put to use in 52 reading and writing classes with 400 students; there are, moreover, a few dozen higher-level schools, each having approximately twenty students. Elsewhere, a central school for the training of cadres has been opened; inaugurated by a three-week term attended by 14 railway workers and sailors, it will continue with 70 militants of which the majority are Shanghai union leaders (railway workers and metalworkers).

As for the propaganda drive, we have concentrated on the press. Between November 1928 and October 1929 the general management of labor unions published 326,500 copies of newspapers, booklets, and tracts.

3. LAW ON AGRARIAN REFORM, 1931

SOURCE: *Fundamental Laws of the Chinese Soviet Republic*

Article 1

All lands of feudal landowners and other lords, militarists, *tuhao*, and other large landowners will be subject to confiscation without compensation, whether they work the land themselves or rent out the land to tenant farmers. The soviets will distribute the confiscated lands to poor and middle peasants. The former landowners of confiscated lands will have no right to redistributed lands. The agricultural workers, coolies, and peasant workers will have equal right to receive land, whatever their sex. The independent workers who live in the villages and who have lost their work have an equal right to pieces of land, with the agreement of the peasant masses. Aged people, orphans, and widows who are incapable of working and who cannot be put under anyone's care must receive assistance from the soviet government if lands to which they have a right are not being worked by someone else for their profit.

Article 2

The Red Army is fighting vigilantly for the defense of the soviet government and for the overthrow of imperialism. Each soldier from the Red Army must therefore receive a plot of land, and the soviet government must make sure that his land is properly cultivated, whether he comes from a district under the control of the soviet government or from a zone in which there is still a counter-revolutionary power.

Article 3

One of the peculiar characteristics of the Chinese *tuhao* is that he is both a landowner and a usurer; his land must therefore be confiscated. If, after the confiscation of his land, a *tuhao* does not participate in any counter-revolutionary action and agrees to work his land by the sweat of his own brow, he may be given a parcel of land, but it will not be of the best quality and its size will depend on the amount of work he is capable of doing.

Article 4

All the goods and lands of the counter-revolutionaries and the military organizations of the white army, as well as those of active counter-revolutionaries, will be confiscated. However, exceptions can be made for poor and middle peasants recognized by the local soviet. But the leaders, without exception, must be dealt with according to the new law.

Article 5

The First Congress of Soviets recognizes the principle that an equitable distribution of all lands is the best method for destroying the entire system of agrarian feudalism and the bases of private property and lands held by the landowners. However, the local soviet governments must in no case apply these measures by force, even on orders coming from higher authorities, but rather, by explaining the principle in all its aspects to the peasants. The measures for confiscation and redistribution cannot be taken except with the direct support of large masses of the peasantry, and they must proceed according to their wishes. Thus, if the majority of peasants desires it, they can be exempted from the principle of equal distribution.

Article 6

All lands belonging to religious institutions, temples, and to other public groups or organizations, will be without exception given over to the peasants by the soviet government. However, in distributing these lands, it is essential that the voluntary agreement of the peasants be obtained, so that their religious beliefs are not offended.

4. ZHU DE'S TROOPS CONDUCT THE REVOLUTIONARY WAR IN SOUTH FUKIEN [FUJIAN]

SOURCE: Agnes Smedley, *The Great Road: The Life and Times of Chu Teh* (New York, Monthly Review Press, 1956), pp. 248–251.

Reaching the foot of the mountain, small groups of the swiftest marchers made off in the direction opposite to the main forces and made feints at large towns to draw the enemy after them, then faded away in the villages and appeared suddenly before other towns. All the while Zhu and Mao were after the landlord Min-tuan in villages far away, arousing and arming the people and leaving cadres behind to continue what had been begun.

After a time the enemy was baying across all south Jiangxi, hunting for the elusive Reds who, guided by the peasants, made surprise attacks on them at night, pinched off their supply columns in swift, fierce raids, and disappeared only to appear again miles away shortly afterwards.

Then came the windfall of Tingzhou, a turning point in revolutionary development. The Reds had not planned to take it. Following a twenty-hour march to evade numerically superior forces gathered against them, the army bivouacked on the mountain range that runs north-south along the Jiangxi-Fujian border but a short distance north of the walled city of Tingzhou in south Fujian Province.

Tingzhou was held by the ex-bandit chieftain, Guo Fang-ming, who by successful banditry had become a great landlord and Guomindang general. Guo's troops, most of them professional bandits and opium smokers who had been incorporated into the Guomindang armies, could be defeated if enticed out from behind the walls of Tingzhou, but this would be impossible unless they believed their enemy was small and poorly armed.

They could come by one route only, and this was along a footpath that led from Tingzhou northward through a narrow valley through which a swift and deep river ran. The Red Army was bivouacked on the mountain range overlooking this valley.

The Red troops sent their peasant guides into Tingzhou to spread the news that the "Red bandits" were encamped just a stone's throw from the city, that their weapons were few and their ammunition none; then they pillowed their heads on their guns and waited for the morning to come.

Before noon next day two regiments of enemy troops came marching single file along the footpath through the valley. When runners reported that the enemy commander was riding in a sedan chair borne by four carriers, General Zhu smiled, saying: "It may be General Guo himself seeking merit." When the enemy was where Zhu and Mao wanted them, Red outposts fired a few random shots and then ran noisily up the mountainside as if in fear. "Our outposts have fired and will draw them into the mountains," guessed General Zhu. The enemy troops immediately took up the chase, climbing higher and higher, panting and sweating, and growing bolder as they met no resistance. The Red troops finally erupted from their concealed positions and the enemy turned and tumbled in terror down the mountainside with the Reds on top of them. There was some fighting on the footpath but the enemy remnants were soon pinned against the river and totally disarmed. . . .

By nightfall the Red Army had taken Tingzhou, disarmed the enemy troops within its walls, and by daybreak next morning had established its power over the walled towns and surrounding territory within a radius of fifty miles. And, as was the practice, Mao Tsetung set to work without rest to revive the people's organizations and organize Councils of People's Delegates, or Soviets, exactly as had been done since the agrarian revolution began. Tingzhou was the center for the entire region. Some landlords were captured, others fled to the great walled city of Shanghang to the south. Soon the land was being divided by village and town committees. . . .

The Red Guards, a people's militia, were attached to agricultural production and armed chiefly with spears. These spears were often more effective than rifles in hand-to-hand contests in forested mountains. The regular peasant partisans were able-bodied young men, all of them better armed than the Red Guards. They formed a reservoir for the regular Red Army, but they fought only as auxiliaries, not as front-line fighters. Operating in the enemy rear, they waylaid enemy messengers and patrols, destroyed enemy camps and communications, sniped in the forests and carried on their own propaganda war by shouting to White soldiers:

"Brothers! Don't be dust for the landlords and generals! Shoot your officers who beat and curse you. Poor men should not fight poor men. Come over to us!"

Chapter Nine

The Long March:
The Political Turning Point of 1935–1937

When the Long March began, Tchiang Kaï-chek appeared to be in control of China. The hard battle which the Chinese Communists fought across the whole country from Jiangxi to Shenxi began as nothing more than a headlong flight. However, the very rigor of this experience led the CCP fundamentally to reorient its political and military strategy at the crucial Zunyi Conference in 1935. After a difficult struggle against both natural obstacles in one of the most hostile regions in the world and armed adversaries, the Red Army produced one of the most remarkable feats in all of military history.

Though it began as a defensive move, the Long March had taken the offensive by the time it was over. By 1937, the Japanese threat had become paramount and the Shenxi Communists were in a better strategic position to fight Japan than were the dispersed and vulnerable forces of the Guomindang. Armed struggle with Japan was imminent. In 1937, Tchiang, who had been forced to change his position after he was kidnapped at Xian, had no choice but to accept the United Front proposed by the Communists.

New Political Balance Between the Guomindang and the CCP

In 1935, relative peace reigned in China. Though they had not completely destroyed the Communist forces, the Nationalists had eliminated the red bases from South China. The central government had tightened its control over the warlords. The government's only response to the Japanese threat, which had been growing since the attack against Manchuria, was a wait-and-see policy.

Stabilization of the Guomindang (1934–1937)

During the brief period of stability, some reforms were attempted. Agrarian reform yielded few results. Some aid went to poor peasants, but the power of the landlord-usurers who formed the social basis of the regime in the countryside was never challenged. This limited reform was largely a political propaganda move in the zones evacuated by the Red Army.

Financial reform at this time was undertaken for two basic reasons: 1) the desire to control domestic assets, especially the finances in zones still held by the warlords; and 2) the desire to keep Chinese money safe from the fluctuations provoked by the worldwide economic crisis. The national currency, the yuan, was more strictly defined. The power and responsibility of the four state banks were increased. In 1935, they received more than half of the deposits and two fifths of the capital and reserves of the Chinese capitalist sector. However, this reform did not stabilize or simplify Chinese finance; rather, it served to increase speculation. The state banks, controlled by private groups close to Tchiang (the "four great families"), financed governmental credit by paying interest rates of 20 percent to 40 percent to their bond holders. The owners of these bonds were none other than the ministers themselves, who were privileged in every way. The government spoke of a "controlled economy" (tongzhi jingji); actually, the administration of public funds was monopolized by the bureaucratic bourgeoisie tied to the party and to the government. On the other hand, this reform increased the financial supremacy of the central government in the provinces, and funneled larger sums of money to Nanking. But it did not put any life into the economy.

The survival of separatism in the provinces

The warlords remained most active in the provinces of the Northwest, the West, and the Southwest, far from the central government, which proved unable to establish new financial power over them. Among these warlords were Liu Xiang in Sichuan, Yang

Hu-cheng (the son of a poor and illiterate peasant) in Shenxi, and Zhang Xue-liang, who had retreated to the Northwest after the defeat of his Manchurian armies by Japan. The case of Sheng Shi-cai in Xinjiang was noteworthy. His separatism was founded not only on the local potentates' traditional independence from the central government, but also on a national demagogic appeal which drew on anti-Japanese feeling and led him to form closer ties with the Communists.

As Tchiang Kaï-chek's protégé, Sheng Shi-cai had been one of Nanking's military personnel before becoming chief of staff for Jin Shu-ren, the local governor of Xinjiang. Following a series of Moslem rebellions, he finally took control of all of Xinjiang in 1934 and proclaimed the "Eight Great Declarations" and the "Six Great Principles," which included anti-imperialism and friendship with the USSR. In this way an alliance with the USSR was formed which was to last until 1942, in spite of a temporary rapprochement with Tchiang Kaï-chek. In May 1935, an agreement was signed in which Moscow gave Sheng loans and technical aid; in 1937, he received military aid to fight a Moslem rebellion. The war against Japan also strengthened ties; during a trip to the USSR, Sheng Shi-cai became a member of the Communist Party, and upon his return, he appointed some officers of the Chinese Communist Party to positions in his provincial government.

Manzhouguo under Pu Yi

After the invasion of Manchuria by the Japanese and their victory over Zhang Xue-liang's army, a puppet government run by the Japanese was created. Pu Yi, the last emperor of the Qing, became chief executive of Manzhouguo on March 1, 1932, but, like the old Manchurian ministers of the State Council, he was unable to exert any real power. All the power belonged to the council of minister-delegates, who were all Japanese who politically defended the interests of the "Guandong Bureau of General Affairs" (the center of Japanese power). Neither the continuation of traditional Chinese ceremonies (such as the coronation of Pu Yi on March 1, 1934, as emperor of Manzhouguo) nor the arrival of an international control mission under the aegis of the League of Nations (whose conclusions were rejected by Japan) challenged in any way the power of the occupation army. The Japanese had both an economic and strategic interest in Manchuria. Economically, the region was an incomparable reservoir of energy sources—particularly coal, which could be used in Japanese industry. Strategically, Manchuria was a springboard allowing the Japanese army to infiltrate and then to launch an attack on Chinese territory.

The Long March: the departure

After the fifth campaign of encirclement, the revolutionary troops had to abandon the Soviet Republic of Jiangxi, but they did not move out in a single stage. The original plan was to make a breach in the blockade line in order to join the troops led by He Long in western Hunan. During the summer of 1934, many vanguard detachments took this way out. Some succeeded but others were wiped out while attempting diversionary maneuvers to lure the enemy away from the main lines of combat.

The first army to move was that of Fang Zhi-min. It took the name of "Vanguard Corps of the Northern Expedition of Resistance Against Japan." A second movement began in August 1934, led by Xiao Ke, who directed the Sixth Group of Armies. Having joined the troops of He Long, they then formed the Army of the Second Front and created the base of Hunan-Hubei-Sichuan. Finally, a third group left from the Hunan-Anhui border and went to Shenxi, where a new soviet was created.

The maneuvers of these three detachments upset the plans of the opposition and alleviated the pressure on, the central base. This allowed the main body of the Red Army (First Army of the Front) to finish its preparations for departure in less difficult conditions.

At first, the Long March was much more a headlong flight (and this attitude was later criticized at the Zunyi Conference) than a new form of battle. The morale of the troops, which were poorly prepared militarily and politically, was not good. The date of departure, which was announced on October 1, 1934, left the 120,000 to 130,000 soldiers only a week to prepare themselves.

By the middle of October, the army began to march and broke through four lines of enemy outposts.[1] Originally, the objective had been to join the Second Army of the Front in western Hubei-Hunan. The retreating army reached Hunan, but only after difficult battles and heavy losses. A political debate then began. One section of the troops, along with the Maoists, opposed the tactic of retreating in

[1] See document 1 at the end of the chapter.

a straight line, a tactic that had been followed since the beginning of the Long March because of a decision by the Central Committee. They succeeded in abandoning this tactic in favor of following a route situated more to the west, in the direction of Guizhou. At the same time, there was a new general political orientation, whose aim was to give priority to the resistance against Japan and therefore to allow the army to participate in this resistance in the best geopolitical conditions possible, namely, in the Northwest, where it could retrench.

The Zunyi Conference: military and political turning point

The turning point came at the end of 1934, at the Communists' conference in Liping on the Hunan-Guizhou border. A decision was made to change not only the geographical direction of the march, but also the straight-line tactic, in favor of a zigzag march in which the army would keep turning back. The troops abandoned a great deal of their equipment in order to be more mobile and to be better prepared for forced marches. The advantage of these changes became evident in January: the Red Army occupied the town of Zunyi in the province of Guizhou. The CCP held a conference there at which it further developed the discussion of the new orientation as sketched at Liping.

After very intense debates between the Central Committee and the advocates of the new line (Mao Tsetung, Zhu De, Peng Dehuai, and the "one-eyed general," Liu Bo-cheng), the conference drafted a strong criticism of the "leftist deviationist" leadership and its positions. The manner in which the battle against the fifth campaign of encirclement had been fought was singled out for attack. The leaders had preferred positional to mobile warfare. Toward the end of the campaign, they had resisted inch by inch without trying to launch an offensive against the rear guard of the enemy, and without trying to lure the enemy away from the interior of the base, in order to decimate it. This passive military strategy could only end in flight.

The organization of the Long March was also criticized. It had not been conceived as a "strategic retreat" but rather as a "headlong flight," in the words of Mao Tsetung. And, during this particularly difficult phase, the leaders had neglected to keep the officers and soldiers of the Red Army and the Jiangxi peasants informed and to hold discussions with them. Moreover, the departure had been very hastily arranged, not allowing the soldiers, who had been engaged in difficult fighting for a whole year, enough time to rest and prepare for this new phase of the struggle.

During the breaking of camp and the crossing of the blockade lines, the speed of the troops' movement was considerably hampered by the encumbering weight of their equipment. The soldiers, who were already burdened with their supplies, finally had to get rid of the equipment. The army was actually a whole convoy, marching along narrow, steep paths, carrying machinery for making clothes, including sewing machines, and complete printing equipment. It had to move within a limited time, from one base to another, and wanted to carry along and keep all these goods. The horses, mules, and donkeys had also become a hindrance, particularly during the crossing of rivers. In the end, too many troops were occupied with taking care of the convoys. All this weight slowed the whole army down, held back the rear guard, caused engagement in operations that went on too long, and sometimes risked isolating groups of the army.

Such radical criticism called for a change in leadership. The "twenty-eight Bolsheviks" were eliminated. Zhou En-lai was the only member of the former politburo to join the new Maoist leadership. Actually, though Mao Tsetung had been President of the Chinese Soviet Republic since 1931, he had not had any political responsibilities in the CCP. At Zunyi, he re-entered a homogeneous politburo which had been won over to his ideas. However, at the international level there was still a double leadership heading the CCP. After 1935, the Comintern continued to count Wang Ming, the principal leader of the twenty-eight, among its vice-presidents, so that Moscow was in effect maintaining his precedence over the leaders newly appointed at Zunyi.

The Long March, from Zunyi to Shenxi

After the Zunyi Conference, there was a break with the preceding phase of operations. The army was crossing far more primitive regions. Its problem was not only to resist Nationalist pursuers but to survive. At the same time, its objective had changed; it wanted to reach the soviets which had already been set up in the Northwest, in order to be closer to the areas threatened by Japan.

Militarily, the Red Army now had the initiative. Despite very definite successes, however, it did not realize its goal of crossing the

Yangzi and was forced to turn back toward Sichuan before returning to Zunyi. In the process, the revolutionary troops for the first time came into contact with such large minority groups as the Miao.

Not until May 1, 1935, did the army cross the Yangzi. Dividing into three columns in order to fool the enemy, it then broke up into smaller groups most of the time. The troops traveled thousands of kilometers across the mountains of Guizhou, engaging in surprise maneuvers in the direction of Sichuan in the North and Yunnan in the South at such a rapid pace that they discouraged the enemy. In response to these feints, the enemy often devised elaborate but useless parries. Often the white troops found no adversary whatsoever where they expected one. Losses were frequently due, then, to fatigue, to illness, and to mistakes in itinerary rather than to the battles themselves. Soldiers who had been delayed formed small regiments or created small bases.

After crossing the river, the Red Army in its journey through Sichuan was incessantly harassed by Nationalist troops. When it penetrated into regions close to Tibet where the Lolo mountain people lived, its reception was extremely hostile. All the tribes had agreed to forget their own quarrels in order to attack the Red Army. All the diplomacy of the Communists was required to resolve the situation. Liu Bo-cheng, chief of staff of the army, concluded a ritual treaty with the chief of one tribe by drinking several drops of fresh blood from a chicken whose throat was cut for the occasion. Another large river, the Dadu, was crossed under very difficult circumstances—after a forced march of 120 kilometers in twenty-four hours by the Lin Biao vanguard. It forced its way across the famous suspension bridge of Luding under machine gun fire from the enemy. The high Tibetan valleys, where the altitude was very unhealthy, still had to be confronted.

In July, the main body of the Long March troops met up with the Fourth Army of the Front, which had come from the Oyuwan soviet in western Hubei and had gone through Sichuan as far as Gansu. Conflicts soon arose. Mao and the other leaders of the First Army did not want to entrench themselves in a base at Sichuan, which was so far from the anti-Japanese front. And even when this front was given priority, there were two opposing ideas. Mao's idea was to create an independent military-political power (which would continue to be called "soviet"). But Zhang Guo-tao, a veteran of the workers' movement of the 1920s whose troops had come from Oyuwan to join the Long March, wanted to compromise with Tchiang Kaï-chek and integrate the Communist troops into the Nationalist army. The conference held by the CCP at Maoergai on the Sichuan-Gansu border did not resolve these differences. One division of the army continued toward the North. Another, with Zhang Guo-tao, remained in Sichuan. Zhang soon broke completely with the Central Committee and shortly afterward joined the Guomindang.

In October 1935, the different units of the Red Army began to regroup at Shenxi, in the soviet base held since 1930 by the local Communist Liu Zhi-dan. Mao's troops were first joined by those of He Long (Second Army). Those of Zhu De, which had remained in Sichuan for a while because of the indecisive results of the Maoergai Conference, arrived in 1936.

The Baoan soviet

The Communists, having arrived and regrouped in the Northwest, were still at war with the Guomindang, and their objective was still to establish and defend a dissident political power. Their soviet districts in North and Central China had collapsed, but they had managed to withdraw their forces into a region where another small and more remote soviet district had existed since 1930, with its capital at Baoan (the capital would later be transferred to the better-known Yanan, the important village that would be the war capital of the Chinese Communists). Until then, the Baoan soviet had been run by local militant Communists, such as Liu Zhi-dan (who was also a member of the influential secret society of Brothers and Elders) and Gao Gang. Liu Zhi-dan was later killed by the Guomindang, but Gao Gang became one of the principal leaders of the liberated zones, later breaking with the Communist authorities in 1955 and committing suicide. The Baoan soviet was solid enough, in spite of its small size, to serve as a welcoming center for the leadership of the CCP and the Red Army after the Long March.

In principle, the military-political strategy from the Jiangxi period was adhered to. There was radical agrarian reform, affirmation of the legitimacy of soviet power as opposed to the Nanking dictatorship, and consolidation of the Red Army. However, during the winter of 1935–1936, the situation was difficult for the several thousand survivors who had come from South China and who were facing the rough Northwest climate for the first time.[2] Increasing Japanese pressure would force them out of their isolation and make them change their relations with the Guomindang and the entire Chinese political situation in a radical way.

The Movement for a United Front

Once the Communists had established themselves in the Northwest, they were in a better position to continue their anti-Japanese resistance. Of course, the Jiangxi soviets had declared war on Japan in 1932 as a protest against the invasion of Manchuria, but this was nothing more than a gesture for the sake of principle. On August 1, 1935, even before they had arrived at their new base, the leaders of the CCP and the soviet government had sent out an appeal to the whole country to join the Communists in fighting against Japan. Despite the friction that had existed between the CCP and Moscow since the expulsion of the Wang Ming group, the entire Communist International had decided at its Seventh Congress (the Dimitrov report) to give priority to the battle against Fascist powers. The Chinese United Front seemed to be a reply to the anti-Fascist united fronts in the West.

The Guomindang itself was being influenced by a growing movement of students, intellectuals, the middle classes, and the masses, particularly in the major cities of the East, against the threat from Japan. Japanese pressures intensified in 1935 and made Nanking's position more and more untenable. Nanking continued to give priority to the fight against Communism rather than the fight against Japan.

Renewal of the Japanese offensive

On January 1, 1933, the Japanese crossed the Shanhaiguan pass and penetrated into the whole of the North China plain. They occupied the province of Jehol, which was soon annexed to Manzhouguo. They forced Nanking to withdraw its troops from eastern Hebei in 1933 and from all of Chahar and Hebei in 1935. They also occupied Inner Mongolia. Their strategy was to present a *fait accompli* to the Chinese government, unilaterally proclaiming a territory to be under their control. They wanted to force Nanking

[2] See document 2.

into an alliance against their common enemies, the Soviet Union and communism. Using various infiltrating methods, the Japanese organized "spontaneous" movements for autonomy, such as Prince Dê's movement in Inner Mongolia and the eastern Hebei movement in November 1935. They also set up a systematic type of contraband activity. Because of the absurdly low customs tariffs set by the "autonomous governments," they were able to dump opium, sugar, synthetic silk, and cottons on all of China at unbeatable prices. Every incident became an occasion for them to threaten reprisal, and military pressure increased markedly after autumn 1935.

Nanking's policy; student unrest

Tchiang Kaï-chek, however, continued to maintain a moderate, patient position. He would step back, then give in to each new offensive, claiming "China's weakness." In reality, he was simply continuing to give priority to the anti-Communist struggle. Nanking's official watchword was "re-establish order at home, gain time abroad" (an nei, rang wai). Tchiang even announced a sixth and last campaign of encirclement against the red base in the Northwest, the only one left, and left for Xian to begin the campaign.

The strongest reaction came from the students. After the national upheaval which followed the invasion of Manchuria in 1931, the student movement, restrained by very tight police control of the universities, had become more sporadic. But the new Japanese offensive in North China provoked a mass student uprising, known today as the December Ninth Movement (1935). The largest demonstrations Peking had ever seen were held and the intelligentsia flocked to the side opposing Japanese aggression. As the mass political protest spread, a boycott movement against Japanese merchandise and personnel was launched by merchants and coolies in other towns. These different protest movements were aimed as much at Nanking's wait-and-see policy as at the Japanese threat.

Growth of the "frontist" movement

Agitation continued throughout 1936. The movement for a United Front, for cooperation between the CCP and the Guomindang, grew with the founding of the Pan-Chinese Federation of

Associations for National Salvation. These groups had some influence with intellectuals, merchants, and clerks. In the cities of the East, the federation cooperated with the Communists.

But the frontist movement also developed in Xian, because of the specific local conditions there. The army of the *dujun* Yang Hu-cheng, stationed in this major city of the interior, had been unfavorable to the left. This situation changed, however, when Zhang Xue-liang's troops took up positions in Xian. Zhang Xue-liang, son of the "old marshal," Zhang Zuo-lin, who had been assassinated by the Japanese in 1929, was already fully familiar with intrigue and rebellions when he succeeded his father at Moukden. Until now, he had always taken the side of Tchiang Kaï-chek against the other warlords. However, this was much less a matter of personal loyalty than a political choice. Zhang Xue-liang could not do without the aid of Nanking against the Japanese before 1931 and after. Yet, witnessing the total passivity of the Nationalist government first in 1932 and even more in 1935, he began to reconsider his political options. In Europe, where he underwent a detoxification cure, he became acquainted with the nationalism of Mussolini and Hitler. More and more disappointed by Tchiang, he readily responded to the call of frontism and favored a reconciliation between Nanking and the Communists against the common enemy. His officers, eager for revenge against the Japanese, were less than eager for the struggle announced by Nanking as the sixth campaign of encirclement, since the Red Army had beaten them many times in local combat. In 1936, a *modus vivendi* was established between the CCP and Xian's armies. No battles were fought. Zhou En-lai secretly met with Zhang Xue-liang and delegated one of his friends to be on Yang Hu-cheng's general staff. The two parties agreed to support the National Salvation movement. With the arrival of many students, become ardent nationalists, from the University of the Northeast, the movement gathered increasing momentum in Xian.

The "Xian Incident" (December 1936)

In early December, Tchiang Kaï-chek arrived in Xian to preside over the start of a new anti-Communist campaign conducted by the troops of Zhang Xue-liang and Yang Hu-cheng. At the same time, Prince Dê's Mongol troops, allied with the Japanese, invaded Suiyuan, the province adjacent to Shenxi. Zhang offered to lead his troops into battle against them, but Tchiang turned him down. This caused the final break between them.

During a demonstration on December 9, the police attacked and arrested some of the student demonstrators. Zhang Xue-liang sought to appease the students by asking them not to demonstrate further and to trust in him to resist the Japanese. But when he presented Tchiang Kaï-chek a memorandum to this effect, he was relieved of his post. In response Tchiang was arrested on the morning of December 11 by the troops of Zhang and Yang. They took control of the city, publishing a Manifesto for the Nation whose eight points reiterated the frontist program,[3] and announcing their intention to execute Tchiang.

Nanking, though it outlawed Xian's troops, was actually prepared to negotiate. Zhou En-lai immediately intervened and met with Mme. Tchiang Kaï-chek and her brother T. V. Soong. After two consecutive truces, Zhou En-lai persuaded the kidnappers to send Tchiang Kaï-chek back to Nanking. By such actions, the CCP tried to show the Chinese nation just how far it would go to maintain the priority of the fight against the Japanese. With its proposals for a united front having received firm, even spectacular, support, it was becoming impossible to ignore the CCP's demand for a united front any longer.

The United Front after Xian

At the beginning of 1937, a tacit agreement between Nanking and the Communists was established. Even in the official declaration it was clear that the political orientation of the central government was changing rapidly.

On February 19, 1937, the Central Executive Committee of the Guomindang officially called for the re-establishment of cooperation with the Soviet Union and the Communists. This was a response to a telegram from the CCP declaring that it was prepared to put an end to its policy of trying to overthrow the central government by armed revolt. The CCP announced its willingness to transform the "democratic (soviet) government of workers and peasants" into a "special region of the Republic of China," to introduce universal suffrage in the "special region," and to put an end to its policy of expropriating the holdings of landowners.

[3] See document 3.

In order to "save face," the central government had not responded to these proposals itself, but had asked the leadership of the Guomindang to do so in its place. In this way, the alliance against Japan came into being. On the day after the generalized Japanese aggression that began in July 1937, a final agreement was reached and made public in September. In order to ensure success in the fight against Japan, the central government promised to establish a democratic regime and to raise the standard of living of the masses. The Communists were to keep their own armed forces and to be included in the roster of the Nationalist general staff as the "Eighth Marching Army" (troops from the base at Shenxi) and the "New Fourth Army" (Communist contingents which had remained in the lower Yangzi area). For their part, the Communists gave up the idea of overthrowing the Guomindang by force, ended their radical agrarian policy, and declared that the soviet government of the Northwest had been dissolved.

ADDITIONAL BIBLIOGRAPHY

Lucien Bianco, *La Crise de Xian, décembre 1936*, supplementary documents. Typed thesis, troisième cycle (Paris, 1968).
Claude Hudelot, *La Longue Marche* (Paris, 1971).
John Israel, *Student Nationalism in China, 1927–1937* (Stanford, Calif., Stanford University Press, 1966).
Anna Wang, *J'ai combattu pour Mao* (Paris, Gallimard, 1967).

DOCUMENTS

1. THE LONG MARCH BEGINS

SOURCE: Claude Hudelot, *La Longue Marche* (Paris, 1971) pp. 190, 195–197.

On October 13, the six hundred men from the arsenal set out. The engineer, a native of Manchuria, who was in charge of the central arsenal, had come to watch them march by. Each man carried five pounds of rice. From the ends of his yoke (a pole acting as a balance bar) hung either two small boxes of munitions or hand grenades or two large gasoline cans containing the more important machine parts and tools. His pack held a blanket or a quilt, a quilted winter uniform, and three pairs of canvas shoes with thick cord soles, reinforced with iron at the tip and at the heel. The peasants had offered us all sorts of things, including dried vegetables and red peppers. For eating and drinking, each man had his pair of chopsticks and his mug tucked into his leg bands. Each carried thread and a needle stuck into the visor

of his cap. Each wore a large hat which protected him from both the
sun and the rain. It was made of two thin bamboo leaves separated
by oiled paper. Many had paper umbrellas sticking out of their packs.
Everyone had a gun. Those who left were all clothed and equipped
in the same manner.

We were in soviet territory and the people came out to say goodbye
to us, but we marched at night in anticipation of the moment when
we would be in enemy territory.

. . . In enemy territory we often marched at night to escape the
bombings. A night march is a marvelous thing when there is moon-
light and a gentle breeze is blowing. When we were far away from the
enemy, some of the companies would sing and others would answer
them. When it was a dark night, we would make torches from pine
branches or bamboo. Then what a grand sight was this long column
of light winding around the mountain like a fantastic dragon.

(After romanticism, realism):

We would march during the night. We would set out at nightfall.
When we reached safe areas, we lit torches of bamboo, of pine, or of
resinous wood. But we had to move without being seen by the enemy,
especially in the beginning. We floundered, single file, through the
yellow earth, the spongy mud composed of clayey loess. If a man fell
in the mud, he had to refrain from crying out or swearing. No one
said a word. We attached squares of white cloth to our packs so that
the comrades following behind could see the person marching in front
of them. To mark the way, the advance guard scattered pieces of rags
or white stones. We had to take care not to fall into a ditch from
exhaustion; no one would have noticed on a moonless night. The sick
and the wounded stuffed handkerchiefs into their mouths so as not to
cry out when the stretcher bearers stumbled and shook them. At dawn
we took cover in the villages, before the enemy planes began to prowl
over our heads. We had only one desire: to sleep.

(Drawn from real life):

To everyone's astonishment, a subsection bringing up the rear of
the column suddenly made an orderly dash toward a small forest
which stood alongside the road. "Faster!" "Attack!" "That one's mine!"
"Why waste wood, then?" "Maintain order!" we heard in the forest.
It was five-thirty in the evening. Seeing all that activity, one might
have thought enemy planes were coming.

Each man was trying to make the strongest stick possible. As a
matter of fact, it had rained the evening before and the road had
turned to a solid, slippery mire. The moon was in its third quarter.
And the soldiers knew from previous experience that a good stick
in one's hand was a great help in night marches.

After a ten-minute rest by the side of the road, we continued on our
way. After five *li* of marching, it was completely dark; a last bend in
the road and we joined forces with nearby units going in the same
direction. The road was narrow and slippery, the impenetrable darkness of the sky had descended upon our heads; we leaned on one

another as we marched, close together, pressed on all sides by comrades. "Go more to the right!" "More to the left!" "Get closer together!" we kept hearing in the darkness. . . .

We could barely make out a small village through our binoculars; it seemed that we were to stop there. . . . "Stop here with those next to you . . ." said the liaison soldier. And behind us the joyful cry was already ringing out: "We're here!" . . . "We're going to rest here!"

The fields ended and we entered the village. All the houses were already full to bursting. . . . Our stomachs were growling. We still had to find the head of the village. After discussing things with him, we decided to spend the night there, in cramped quarters, but with a roof over our heads. They assigned us our lodgings and, after having washed my feet, I stretched out on a wide bench. Someone could be heard shouting in the street: "Pick some vegetables, slice up some pork . . ." Another chopped wood, cut branches; still another did not feel like going to sleep. . . . Soon the faint light of the early dawn began to filter through the window panes.

2. "Snow," a poem written by Mao Tsetung in February 1936 after the ending of the Long March in the Northwest

Source: *Mao Tsetung, Poems* (Peking, Foreign Languages Press, 1976), pp. 23–24.

SNOW

—to the tune of *Chin Yuan Chun*

February 1936

North country scene:
A hundred leagues locked in ice,
A thousand leagues of whirling snow.
Both sides of the Great Wall
One single white immensity.
The Yellow River's swift current
Is stilled from end to end.
The mountains dance like silver snakes
And the highlands charge like wax-hued elephants,
Vying with heaven in stature.
On a fine day, the land,
Clad in white, adorned in red,
Grows more enchanting.

This land so rich in beauty
Has made countless heroes bow in homage.
But alas! Chin Shih-huang and Han Wu-ti
Were lacking in literary grace,
And Tang Tai-tsung and Sung Tai-tsu

Had little poetry in their souls;
And Genghis Khan,
Proud Son of Heaven for a day,
Knew only shooting eagles, bow outstretched.
All are past and gone!
For truly great men
Look to this age alone.

3. GENERAL ZHANG XUE-LIANG'S MANIFESTO TO THE CHINESE NATION, DECEMBER 1936

SOURCE: Lucien Bianco, *La Crise de Xian, décembre 1936*, supplementary documents. Typed thesis, troisième cycle (Paris, 1968).

To the Central Executive Committee of the national government, to President Lin Sen [president of the Nationalist government since 1932], to all the *yuan* [legislative, executive, and judiciary assemblies and assemblies for supervising examinations], ministries and councils, to all the provinces, to the associations for the National Salvation, to all the organizations, to all constituted bodies, to all the newspapers, to all the schools:

Since the loss of the northern provinces five years ago, attacks on the national sovereignty of China have continued to increase and our country's territory has been shrinking day by day. We have undergone many humiliations: first because of the Shanghai truce,* then at the time of the truce of Tanggu† and the He-Umetsu agreement.‡ There is not a single Chinese who does not suffer because of this state of affairs. Recently there have been considerable changes in the international situation: certain powers are plotting together and offering our country up for sacrifice. When fighting began in eastern Suiyuan, popular feeling was at its height and throughout China the soldiers expressed their indignation.

At so crucial a moment, the head of state should encourage the military and the civilians to organize the entire nation in a war of national defense. But, while the soldiers at the front endure death and carnage to defend our national territory, the diplomats are still seeking a compromise. . . .

. . . Surrounded by unworthy advisers, Generalissimo Tchiang Kaï-chek has lost the support of the masses. He is profoundly at fault for the harm this policy has done the country. I, Zhang Xue-liang, and the other signers of this appeal have begged him with tears in our eyes to change his policy; but each time our advice has been rejected and we ourselves have been reprimanded.

Quite recently, the students of Xian were demonstrating as part of their movement in favor of the National Salvation and General

* Accepted by Tchaing Kaï-chek in 1932, after the Japanese attack on Shanghai.
†‡ In these agreements—one of which was signed in 1933, the other in 1935—the Guomindang acknowledged the gradual penetration of Japan into China.

Tchiang sent the police to kill these patriotic young people. How is it possible that anyone with a conscience could do such a thing? We, who have been his fellow officers for a long time, could not stand by and witness this sight without doing anything.

This is why, while guaranteeing his safety,* we have given one last warning to Marshal Tchiang. We have acted this way in order to prod his conscience.

The military and the civilians of the Northwest unanimously present the following demands:

1. Reorganization of the Nanking government; let all political parties be part of the government and share the responsibility for ensuring the country's welfare.

2. Cessation of all forms of civil war.

3. Immediate release of the patriotic leaders arrested in Shanghai.†

4. Release of all political prisoners detained in China.

5. Freedom of action for the people's patriotic movements.

6. Guarantee of the people's political liberties (freedom to organize and to hold meetings).

7. True faithfulness to the will and testament of Dr. Sun Yat-sen.

8. Immediate convocation of a congress for the National Salvation.

. . . Signed by Zhang Xue-liang, Yang Hu-cheng, etc.

---

* Euphemism referring to Tchiang's capture by the Xian generals on December 11, 1936.
† Arrested in Shanghai at the time of the demonstrations in favor of the United Front against Japan.

Chapter Ten

The Guomindang War and the Japanese Occupation: *1937–1945*

The Japanese army occupied large sections of Chinese territory and all the major industrial centers after the beginning of its general aggression against China in July 1937 until its surrender in August 1945. The Guomindang forces took refuge in the Southwest and confined themselves to a defensive wait-and-see strategy. The true political, social, and military situation in "Free China" was very different from the picture of the heroic fighter that the warring Western democracies imagined. The actual contrast was not so much between this "Free China" and the Japanese zones, but rather between these two mutually tolerant adversaries and what they considered to be their principal enemy: the Communist guerrilla bases located behind the Japanese lines.

The Guomindang War

The war of movement (1937–1938)

As a Japanese official explained to an American journalist in 1937, this was a "special, undeclared war." Using a minor incident which had occurred in July 1937, at Lugouqiao, to the south of Peking (Marco Polo Bridge), Japan invaded all of China without declaring war. The initial successes of the Japanese were devastating. By August, they were in control of Peking, Tientsin, and the North. In Mongolia, they occupied Chahar and Suiyuan, and created an autonomous Federal Government of Mongolia with the support of the Mongolian feudal lords. They occupied the Shandong peninsula, taking over Qingdao in August and Jinan in December. Han Fu-ju, the governor, was a warlord who wanted above all to preserve his troops, which were the basis of his influence within the power structure of the Guomindang. Yan Xi-shan, the *dujun* of Shanxi, hardly put up any more resistance. His capital, Taiyuan, fell in November. Troops landed in the East, occupying Shanghai in November and Nanking, the nation's capital, in December. Others attacked in the South and took Canton in October.

At one point, the Chinese armies hoped to stand their ground at Wuhan, where the government had taken refuge. The incompetent Han Fu-ju was executed as an example and the more energetic Li Zong-ren severely beat the Japanese in March at Taierzhuang, in northern Yangzi. But this recovery was short-lived. Anhui and Jiangxi fell. Wuhan was abandoned in October. The Nationalist government finally fell back to Chongqing in Sichuan, where the front was to stabilize for six years, until the lightning Japanese offensive in 1944. "Free China" was reduced to a bastion in the Southwest (Sichuan, Yunnan, Guizhou, Guangxi), Shenxi, Gansu, and Xinjiang in the Northwest, and areas of the central and eastern provinces, in which the Japanese occupied only the large cities.

By evacuating the large centers of the East and the North, the government hoped to make sure that the industrial and intellectual potential of these areas would not be destroyed. Factory machines and laboratory equipment were dismantled and taken away under very difficult conditions. Industrial executives, technicians, students, and teachers left Peking, Tientsin, Shanghai, and Wuhan, reaching the Southwest after a dangerous journey over thousands of kilometers.

The suffering caused by Japanese brutality and the disasters resulting from the incompetence of the Guomindang were staggering. When Nanking fell, approximately 300,000 people were massacred. An irrational panic led the command at Changsha to set fire to the capital of Hunan, whose inhabitants had been swelled by the arrival of 800,000 refugees. Attempting to slow the Japanese advance, the Chinese authorities burst the dams of the Yellow

River, killing thousands. All along the roads of the middle Yangzi region, refugees were raked with machine gun fire by Japanese airplanes during the abortive resistance of Wuhan.

The Guomindang's strategic principles

According to the official propaganda of Chongqing, aimed largely at the United States, the Chinese were simply "trading space for time." Tchiang Kaï-chek was counting on Japan becoming engaged in conflicts with one or more of the major powers (the United States, England, and the Soviet Union), thus alleviating the pressure on China and eventually resulting in the defeat of the aggressor. Yet this did not prevent Tchiang from considering a compromise with Japan before all this happened. China did not declare war on Japan until 1941, after Pearl Harbor and the fall of Hong Kong and Singapore. During the entire war, political contacts between Chongqing and Tokyo were never broken. In December 1938, Wang Jing-wei, one of the leaders of the Guomindang, left for Hanoi and then Shanghai, apparently with the approval of Chongqing. Only during the course of negotiations with Japan in 1941 did Wang decide to break with Tchiang and become the head of a pro-Japanese Guomindang government in Nanking. Even after this break, contacts were maintained. The "front" was far from solid; an elaborate network of trafficking and complicity tied Chongqing to Shanghai. When Tchiang, during the course of his quarrels with the American general Joseph Stilwell, threatened to make a separate peace, he was not bluffing.

The countries of the West, whom Tchiang claimed to have relied upon since before 1941, followed the same ambiguous policies. They gave real aid to Chongqing between 1938 and 1940, even as they were seeking to appease Japan. In 1940, England closed the Burma Road, one of the few routes of communication which was still open to "Free China." This conciliatory gesture reinforced Chongqing's wait-and-see policy and its defeatist tendencies. In 1940, as secret Japanese-American diplomatic negotiations progressed, Japan made numerous peace offers to Chongqing. This "Far Eastern Munichism" (as the Chinese Communists put it) did not spare the Americans and the English the rude awakening of 1941: Pearl Harbor and the collapse of British power in the Far East.

The Guomindang's wait-and-see policy was based on a deliberate reluctance to challenge the political and social foundation of "Free China." To wage war in an energetic way would have required an attack on the entire corrupt and incompetent authoritarian system. And this Tchiang would not do.

The priority given to the defense of the system Tchiang relied on was identical with the long-term priority given to the confrontation with those who challenged this system: the Chinese Communists. Officially the policy was "unifying China so as to be able to fight better," but in reality, the best troops of the Guomindang were immobilized throughout the war in the Yanan blockade and in the guerrilla bases of the North. The compromise reached in 1937 between the Guomindang and the Communist Party soon fell apart.

Foreign aid to Chongqing (1937–1941)

The Soviet Union was the first to give substantial aid to China; it consisted of 250 million U.S. dollars, 1,000 airplanes, and 2,000 aviators. A large part of this aid came into China by the western routes, through Xinjiang, where the governor, Sheng Shi-cai, had established ties with Moscow in 1935. Their rapprochement became more solid, and a Soviet regiment was stationed at Hami. The 1940 mining agreement gave the Soviet Union the right to operate mines in Xinjiang. Soviet aid to Chongqing came to an end in April 1941, however, when the neutrality pact between Tokyo and Moscow was signed.

China also requested Western aid, but with indifferent results. The United States gave 170 million dollars in all, to which the American Treasury added purchases of silver in order to support Chinese currency; England and France gave much less. These purchasing credits were not completely used up, for communications remained extremely difficult. The railroad from Yunnan to Haiphong and the Burma Road could handle only lightweight traffic. Both were closed down in 1940, and England under Churchill adopted the same pro-Japanese position as Vichy.

The Guomindang army

The Guomindang army was a reflection of the regime. It was headed by Tchiang Kaï-chek, whose overwhelming incompetence, impulsiveness, and authoritarianism were denounced by Stilwell and other American advisers.[1] The distribution of commands among

[1] See document 1 at the end of the chapter.

the various groups of armies was much more a response to the balance of different political-military factions than to the requirements of strategy. The generals' rivalries and ambitions also resulted in an overlarge and unwieldy army; there were 350 divisions in 1941 against only 25 Japanese divisions. But many of these soldiers did not exist. The armed divisions, which were supposed to have 10,000 men, often had anywhere from 6,000 down to 2,000. On the basis of these inflated figures, money and rations were allocated, and the commanders profited, since the American advisers could hardly arrange for each soldier to be paid individually.

This army was recruited by force. As Stilwell said, "The draft hits the Chinese peasants in the same way as the floods and the famines, but it occurs more regularly, and it claims more victims." On the roads, one would see pitiful processions of conscripts, chained so that they would not run away; many of them died en route. Up to one third of the total manpower died or deserted before reaching the front.

The common soldier paid dearly for the general corruption. Supplies, equipment, and rations were resold on the black market; quinine was replaced by chalk. Malnutrition, malaria, tuberculosis, and dysentery ravaged the troops. The American soldier who slept under his mosquito net might make fun of the Chinese soldier, who was sleepy during the day, but the less fortunate Chinese had to stay awake all night beside an inadequate fire for lack of any other protection against the mosquitoes.

The management of the war (1938–1941)

There were few changes after the stabilization that occurred in autumn 1938. In 1939, the Japanese advanced as far as Nanning and Nanchang (the capitals of Guangxi and Jiangxi) and occupied Hainan. The Guomindang had to hold the Dongguan pass (along a loop of the Yellow River) and the upper Yangzi pass, the Changsha region (which often changed sides), and the eastern border of Yunnan. This geographically strategic disposition of troops worked to the advantage of the Japanese, who controlled the railways and whose troops could move from one area to another. The fronts held by the Guomindang were cut off from one another, and each one had to become self-sufficient. This further encouraged immobility, the feudalization of the regional military powers, and the tendency to swell the ranks of the armies.

The best Chinese troops were in the Northwest blockading Yanan and the Communist zones. In May 1941, 50,000 Japanese attacked and routed them south of Shanxi. The Chinese preferred to cross the Yellow River without fighting.

Because of such weaknesses, desertions were common. In 1942, about fifteen generals defected to the Japanese, taking with them approximately 500,000 men. Tchiang took few steps to stop them; he preferred to see his adversaries bear the burden of feeding the deserters. These "puppet" troops Tchiang considered as reserves, for the political confrontations that would come during the post-war period. Even before the capitulation of the Japanese, he had been preparing to start up the civil war again.

Relations between the Guomindang and the CCP (1937–1941)

The cooperation that had been arranged during the summer of 1937 worked fairly well within the framework of the official National Salvation policy until the fall of Wuhan. A Communist mission led by Zhou En-lai was set up near the seat of the National-ist government. The Communist press was tolerated. In Wuhan, Guo Mo-ruo, who was known for his Communist sympathies, was head of the propaganda services for the army. The Communists belonged to the National Political Council, which was established in 1938 and which, with their agreement, adopted a Program of Resistance and National Restoration. Some material aid was even sent to the Communist guerrilla zones.

With the stabilization that occurred in autumn 1938, two strategies for fighting against Japan—immobility and people's war —and two different concepts of China's future came into conflict. During the war, the Communist Party knew it would have to face 60 percent of the Japanese troops and 90 percent of the puppet troops, since for both of these the party was a more clearly defined adversary. Though well aware of the Guomindang's reasons for its wait-and-see policy, the CCP continued to defend the principle of a United Front as a way of emphasizing the priority of the struggle against Japan. Its criticism of that wait-and-see policy was strong, but conditional;[2] it did not want the contradictions between itself and Tchiang to become all-important.

[2] A whole series of Mao's writings expressed this criticism: "Fight the Spirit of National Capitulation" (1937); "On Protracted War" (1938); "Against the Spirit of Capitulation" (1939); "Surmount the Danger of Capitulation" (1940); and "Expose the Plot for a Far Eastern Munich" (1941).

The Communists reacted mildly to the anti-Communist measures taken by the Guomindang in 1938. Some of these measures were political: the banning of popular CCP-affiliated anti-Japanese groups, and the publication of secret circulars which outlined "limitations of the activity of dissident groups." Other measures were military. The Guomindang had underestimated the Communist guerrillas' vitality. When the Communist troops (the Eighth Army and the New Fourth Army) expanded their area of activity at the expense of the Japanese, instead of holding to the perimeters defined in 1937, the Nationalists accused them of "a lack of discipline." Again and again, Tchiang directly attacked his rivals. In spring 1939, his troops moved against the Communist troops at Pingxiang in Hunan, then in Hubei and in Hebei. In November they attacked in Henan and partially dismantled the southern part of the Yanan base.

A far more serious incident took place at the beginning of 1941 in Anhui. The Guomindang accused the New Fourth Army of violating its agreements and expanding its operations in the lower Yangzi. Though the Communist advance had hurt the Japanese, the Guomindang ordered the Fourth Army to make a dangerous retreat across the river toward the North. In January, the Communist headquarters was suddenly surrounded by Tchiang's troops, and many leaders were killed or captured, including the former trade unionist Xiang Ying and General Ye Ting.

The Communists responded to these "frictions" (they preferred this moderate term) by refusing to reciprocate in kind and appealing to a Chinese public opinion increasingly shocked by the immobility of the Nationalist troops and the pervasive corruption.

Chongqing within the American orbit

After the Japanese attack on the American base at Pearl Harbor, the Far Eastern conflict became international. Guomindang China sided with the British and finally declared war on Japan, as well as on Germany and Italy. The United States and Chongqing established special relations. On the military level, General Stilwell, commander in chief of the East Asian theater, became Tchiang's chief of staff. American contingents were sent to China; General Claire Lee Chennault's air force group was built up. Under lend-lease agreements, China received material aid worth 800 million U.S. dollars, which was sent primarily by way of the trans-Himalayan air route (the "Hump"). On the financial level, Washington extended 500 million U.S. dollars of credit to China in 1942. Finally, the United States sponsored "Free China" as the "fourth great power." At the Cairo Conference in 1943, attended by Roosevelt, Churchill, and Tchiang, the return of Manchuria, Formosa, and the Pescadores was promised. The United States and England had given up extraterritoriality and their concessions in 1942. The unequal treaties were rescinded a century after the aggression against Canton of Queen Victoria's "redcoats." Earlier, in 1937, China had stopped paying annuities on its debt and had done away with foreign control of customs.

Conflict between Stilwell and Tchiang Kaï-chek

For strictly military reasons, Stilwell was convinced that precedence had to be given to strengthening the Chinese territorial army. He criticized the inefficiency in management, command, and troop movement. He wanted to form modern, efficient units, directly under American control, and establish better control over the equipment sent to China under lend-lease. All these proposals met with fierce opposition from Tchiang. He was supported by Chennault, who was convinced that it was enough to establish a modern air force in the Southwest. Such an approach to fighting the war was quite acceptable to Tchiang, for it would avoid any challenge to the political and military structures of "Free China." Somewhat belatedly, and with great difficulty, Stilwell managed to get permission to modernize thirty Chinese divisions (the "Y" force) and to use some of them in Burma against the Japanese.

The Stilwell-Tchiang conflict soon became intertwined in the question of relations with the Chinese Communists. Stilwell wanted to give them material aid and, above all, to put an end to the Yanan blockade, which was immobilizing half a million of the best Chinese troops. When Yü Da-wei, one of Tchiang's close collaborators, suggested using lend-lease material against Yanan, which was part of the logic of Guomindang strategy, Stilwell firmly refused.

The conflict between these two general policies led to an impasse in 1942 and 1943. The Guomindang continued to insist upon its wait-and-see policy. In spring 1944, however, the Japanese took the offensive ("operation *Icho-go*"). In Henan, 50,000 Japanese defeated the 400,000 men under the command of the Guomindang general Tang En-bo (1899–1954) within a matter of weeks. In the

Southwest they swept across Hunan, Guizhou, and Guanxi, stopping just before the Sichuan bastion. This severe defeat destroyed most of the American air bases in the region, emphatically confirming Stilwell's position against that of Chenanult.

However, after much hesitation, Roosevelt decided for political reasons to replace Stilwell to appease Tchiang. At one time, FDR had taken a firm stand, refusing to loan Tchiang a billion dollars and demanding that Stilwell exercise real authority over the whole Chinese army. In the autumn, however, Patrick Hurley, the president's special envoy, replaced Ambassador Gaus and Wedemeyer replaced Stilwell. For the United States, postwar political problems were already taking priority over the military struggle against Japan.

The coming of the postwar period

Anxious to lay the foundations of its influence in China, the United States attempted once again to arrange a compromise between Yanan and Chongqing. In November, Hurley went to Yanan and signed an agreement acceptable to the Communists: the reunification of China would depend upon the formation of a democratic coalition government. But this move was hardly pleasing to Tchiang and he rejected the agreement, demanding that priority be given to "unification." Hurley supported him. However, the Communists, knowing how sensitive Chinese public opinion had become to the problems of civil peace, continued to negotiate until the Japanese capitulation. Zhou En-lai was in Chongqing again in January to February 1945.

For the United States, the most important thing was to strengthen the Guomindang. Lend-lease credits went from 49 million dollars in 1943, to 53 million in 1944, to 1,107 million in 1945. Aircraft equipment, which Stilwell had considered a misleading and palliative measure, was now given top priority. Tchiang could already foresee the possibility of reconquering by air attack all the large cities surrounded by the Communists at the moment Japan capitulated. Military and financial aid was supplemented by diplomatic support. In spring 1945, China was officially recognized in San Francisco as one of the great powers of the United Nations and given veto power in the Security Council.

However, the Yalta agreements limited Chinese sovereignty in a different direction. Stalin and the Soviet state re-established themselves in China, thus breaking with the Leninist tradition of opposing the unequal treaties. In February 1945 the Guomindang had to agree to let the Soviets use a naval base at Port Arthur (Dalien-Liuda) and to allow the Russians to regain control of the railways in the Northeast. For the Soviet Union, this was compensation for the defeat it had suffered at Xinjiang in 1942 when the governor Sheng Shi-cai had abruptly broken his agreements with Moscow, expelled the Soviet military advisers and civilians, massacred his Chinese Communist advisers (including Mao Tsetung's brother), and gone over to the Guomindang.

When the atomic bomb exploded in Hiroshima, the power struggle had already begun in China, and the United States was directly involved in it.

"Free China"

Political power structures

According to Stilwell, "The Chinese government was an edifice which rested on fear and favoritism, in the hands of an ignorant, arbitrary, and headstrong man. The whole government was interwoven with family and financial attachments and influences which, once removed, would lead to its total breakdown."[3]

Officially, the Nanking governmental structures had simply been transplanted to Wuhan, and then to Chongqing. The 1931 constitution remained in effect, with its five *yuan* (executive, legislative, judiciary, for control, and for examinations) and its State Council, to which a National Council of Defense and a National Council of the People were added. But it was merely an empty structure. The real power was exercised by a complex coalition of family interests, organized public forces, and private military-political cliques. Tchiang's role was that of an arbitrator, at the balancing point of the system.

At the top were the men from the "four great families": the Tchiang family (Tchiang Kaï-chek, his sons, and the members of his entourage, who often came from his native province, Zhejiang); the Soong family (headed by T. V. Soong, who was Tchiang Kaï-chek's brother-in-law); the Kung family (grouped around H. H. Kung, who claimed he was a direct descendant of Confucius and

[3] Joseph Stilwell, *Chinese Adventure*, p. 103.

who was considered to be the richest man in China; he too was Chiang's brother-in-law);[4] and the Chen family (the two brothers Chen Li-fu and Chen Guo-fu, nephews of a militant revolutionary who had helped Tchiang early in his career).

The principal cliques were: the pro-Fascist CC (Central Club) of the brothers Chen, paralleled by the secret society Fuxing (Renewal); the military-political group of the Whampoa Military Academy graduates who had followed Tchiang in his rise to power (such as Hu Zong-nan and Chen Cheng); the political science group, which was influential with businessmen and Westernized intellectuals; and finally the liberals, such as Sun Fo, the older son of Sun Yat-sen, who was relegated to the sinecure of president of the legislative *yuan*.

These family groups and cliques controlled the organized forces of power among themselves: everyone in the government, from Chen Li-fu in national education to the liberal geologist Weng Wen-hao (economy), and the brothers-in-law Kung (finances) and Soong (foreign affairs), the army, where politicians from the Whampoa group worked alongside military traditionalists, such as He Yin-qin (minister of war), and also with the regional military cliques (from Hunan, Yunnan, Henan, and the other provinces); the party, led by Tchiang himself along with Chen Li-fu, and including the Blue Shirts; finally, the police, controlled by the all-powerful Dai Li, who was in charge of political espionage in the Guomindang zone, the secret agents who infiltrated Yanan, and the emissaries sent into the Japanese zones.

Tchiang Kaï-chek, who was given the title *zongcai* (supreme leader) by the Extraordinary Congress of the Guomindang in 1938, accumulated a great number of positions and titles (eighty-two, according to an incomplete list), which were often honorary. He was the head of the party, of the government, and of the army. At the same time, he was the brother-in-law of Sun Yat-sen, a Christian, a former commander of the Whampoa Military Academy, and had been affiliated in his youth with the secret terrorist societies of Shanghai. He was a popular figure in the United States, thanks to a clever propaganda program, and stood in the center of the power coalition. Although his personal powers were considerable, he relied more on his ability to arbitrate among all his rivals in the higher

[4] The Soong sisters had married Sun Yat-sen, Tchiang Kaï-chek, and H. H. Kung. It was said of them that "Ai-ling, Mme. Kung, loved money; Mei-ling, Mme. Tchiang, loved power; and Qing-ling, Mme. Sun, loved the people."

interest of the established order and the privileged classes. As a dictator, he represented a solid social base.

Social and economic foundations of the regime

Through state organizations such as the Commission for National Resources, the leaders of the Guomindang controlled large areas of business and industry, particularly the mining industry. The industrial production index in "Free China" went from 133 in 1939 to 376 in 1943, and many of the new factories belonged to the Guomindang leaders, either directly or indirectly. This bureaucratic capitalism consolidated the position of the "four great families." Through the Central Agricultural Bank, they also controlled the network of village usurers. All this suggests the extent to which the social basis of the Guomindang had definitely changed since the Nanking period. The liberal business bourgeoisie in Shanghai was no longer an important factor while the Guomindang's ties with the landlords and the system of agrarian exploitation had been strengthened. Because of inflation a tax on grain was re-established in 1941. This grain tax was intended to pay the civil servants, but more importantly to facilitate the speculative operations of the privileged classes. If, in fact, the economic debacle of China under Chongqing, the rising prices, and the inflation weighed heavily on the people, they resulted in substantial profits for the stockholders and people protected by the government.[5]

	Paper money issued (in Chinese dollars)	Price index	Value, in Chinese dollars, of one U.S. dollar
1937	2,060,000,000	100	3
1938	2,740,000,000	176	6.5
1939	4,770,000,000	323	16
1940	8,440,000,000	724	20
1941	15,810,000,000	1,980	30
1942	35,100,000,000	6,620	50
1943	75,400,000,000	22,800	98
1944	189,500,000,000	75,500	680
1945	1,031,900,000,000	249,100	3,250

Source: A. Feuerwerker, *The Chinese Economy, 1912–1949*, p. 60.

[5] See document 2.

During the war, an arbitrary rate of exchange of twenty to one was maintained between the Chinese dollar and the American dollar. The Americans accepted this rate, thus obligating themselves to pay increasingly high prices in strong currency for all the goods that their bases and personnel bought in China with devalued money. In this way, an enormous hidden subsidy was added to such official forms of aid as lend-lease. The "great families" amassed huge reserves of American dollars in the United States. H. H. Kung really was "the richest man in China."

Several weak attempts were made to counter these growing speculative tendencies. The *induscos* (industrial cooperatives) movement was promoted, supported by liberal English, American, and Chinese groups. These workshops produced textiles, food products, and simple chemical products. There were 1,867 workshops in 1941 with 29,000 members. Later, their number declined. H. H. Kung and T. V. Soong supported them, aware of their prestige in England and America as a symbol of the Chinese war effort. But financial aid to them was always limited, and their democratic management left them open to accusations of having Communist sympathies.

Old and new privileged classes

The establishment of the central machinery of the Guomindang, with its political groups and entourage, in Sichuan irritated the conservative country gentry, whose way of life was abruptly disturbed and whose sources of profit were interfered with. There was strong competition between the old secret society Gelaohui (Society of Brothers and Elders), which had traditionally controlled dealing and trafficking (particularly in opium), and the profitable commercial monopolies run by Dai Li's secret services. The provincial troops of the warlords who had been in that region for decades, such as Long Yun in Yunnan and Liu Xiang and Liu Wen-hui in Sichuan, did not look kindly upon the arrival in their territory of military groups protected by the central government. Relations between traditionalist elements in the southwestern provinces and the Guomindang had deteriorated to such an extent in 1949 that the traditionalists defected without fighting and went over to the Communists.

Authoritarianism and its limits

Authoritarian tendencies, which had already surfaced during the Nanking period, came to the fore in the Guomindang during the Chongqing period. When the Guomindang wanted to give a reassuring picture of "Free China" to British and American journalists, T. V. Soong, Harvard graduate, H. H. Kung, former Protestant director of the YMCA, and Sun Fo, spiritual heir of his father, the great pro-Western democrat, were put in the limelight. The real behind-the-scenes powers were Dai Li, with his 600,000 Blue Shirts and his 100,000 secret agents; Hu Zong-nan and his elite armies immobilized in the Yanan blockade; and Chen Li-fu and Chen Guo-fu and their CC group. In ruling circles, the most widespread ideology continued to emphasize authority, the leader, and the nation. Pro-Hitler and pro-Mussolini sympathies survived the aggressions by Japan. The young officers in Tchiang's entourage considered it good form to have read *Mein Kampf*. Until 1941, military officers of the Guomindang continued to be sent to Nazi Germany for a period of instruction.

Tchiang Kaï-chek's book, *China's Destiny (Zhongguo zhi ming-yun)*, published in 1943, reflected his authoritarian orientation. Based on a narrow and archaic nationalism often bordering on chauvinism and racism, the book stressed the "uniqueness" of China and Chinese tradition. For Tchiang, China's welfare depended on an absolute submission to governmental authority, according to the Confucian tradition. The unequal treaties were denounced in the name of this conservative nationalism. Such popular movements as the Taiping and May Fourth Movement were derided or ignored. The book was edited by Tao Xi-sheng, a university professor who briefly followed Wang Jing-wei when he went over to the Japanese. No English translation of the book was authorized during the entire war, so that the liberal image of "Free China" would not be tarnished.

Chongqing freely admitted its involvement in "thought control." Such eminent university professors as Zhang Xi-ruo (political science) and Ma Yin-chu (economics) were suspended or arrested for their criticisms of bureaucratic capitalism and the theory of tutelage. When the famine of Henan broke out in 1943, the government did not attack the negligence of provincial authorities, but the newspaper *Dagongbao* (connected to the liberal political science group), which had denounced these authorities. Censorship became severe. Almost nothing was said about the Yanan blockade. The arrest of Ma Yin-chu was presented as a simple disciplinary measure of a member of the party. Only in 1946 did the Guomindang implement open and generalized political repression.

Despite the fact that there were few members of the working class in the Southwest, a region which had been belatedly and superficially industrialized after the withdrawal of 1938, there was very tight surveillance over them. In 1939, the official trade unions were reorganized. Severe provisional regulations on working class labor in time of war were passed in 1941 and 1942, and were complemented in 1942 by a National Mobilization Act, which sought to suppress any opposition rather than to stimulate the war effort.

The Guomindang was obliged to reckon with American public opinion, since it depended heavily on America for aid and credit. It attempted to win over the Americans by sending T. V. Soong and Mme. Tchiang Kaï-chek on public relations visits. But Roosevelt's image of the United States going to war to defend democracy was hardly compatible with the realities of Chongqing. American military men like Stilwell, and American journalists like Robert Payne, Theodore White, and Harrison Forman were extremely critical of the Guomindang, especially once they had witnessed the simple, brotherly society of Yanan. Chongqing's authoritarian tendencies were held in check by its reluctance to shock American public opinion. Journalistic criticism was growing, however. On May 1, 1944, the American magazine *Life* described "Free China" as a strange combination of the Spanish Inquisition and Tammany Hall.

Democratic opposition

The fear of American reaction provided some maneuvering room for the liberal Christian groups. Well-known members of the opposition, such as Mme. Sun Yat-sen and Feng Yu-xiang, were tolerated, although they were not given significant responsibilities.

In March 1939, a number of intellectuals and democratic politicians formed the Union of Comrades for Unity and National Reconstruction. Their union grew in 1941 into the League of Democratic Groups, and in 1944 into the Democratic League. The Democratic League had a loose structure and was hardly more than a confederation of small clubs (China Youth Party, Action Committee for the Liberation of the Chinese People, Union for National

Salvation, and the Society for Professional Training) which were influential among professors, writers, and journalists. They were in favor of Western democracy, individual liberties, and national reconstruction. Among their principal members were Zhang Lan, president of the league, a prominent figure in Sichuan and veteran of 1911; the poets Wen Yi-duo and Guo Mo-ruo; and the sociologist Liang Shu-ming, once secretary-general of the league and a pioneer of the rural reconstruction movement. Several of them were in touch with liberal leftist Americans, especially those with the magazine *Amerasia.* Their activities, tolerated by the police, were limited to a few meetings and some publications.

The condition of the people

One of the wartime slogans of the Chongqing government was: "Those who have money should give their money, those who have only their strength should give their strength." Only the second part of this statement corresponded to the actual situation. In "Free China," the workers' lot was as hard as in the China of Nanking, if not harder. The landowners' demands on the peasants were as great as before, and the peasants' situation was further aggravated by the double burden of the draft and the revival of the tax on grain. Working class wives suffered from the traditional harsh authority of their husbands and the superstitious fear of evil omens.[6] Like the workers in Tientsin and Shanghai, the factory workers who had been temporarily transferred to Sichuan or to Yunnan were subjected to the despotism of their foremen and the labor middlemen, to long working hours, job insecurity, no technical or medical protection, wretched lodgings, and low salaries. Runaway inflation further reduced their buying power.

Whenever a catastrophe occurred, such as the Henan famine of 1943, the situation became intolerable. The authorities seized upon such disasters as new occasions for adding to their own profits.[7] The peasants ate mud from the ponds, bark from the trees, and clay from the soil; they sold their goods, including their children, and attempted to flee to the west, falling dead on the roads. Yet local speculators hoarded grain, often with the complicity of the civilian and military authorities.

[6] See document 3.
[7] See document 4.

Tang En-bo, the principal commander of the Guomindang armies in Henan, did very little to fight the famine disaster. The peasants, who had suffered from his harshness and the pillaging of his troops, had a popular saying: "we are the victims of four plagues: floods, droughts, locusts, and Tang En-bo." When the Japanese attacked Henan in spring 1944, not only did the people allow Tang's army to be routed, but some rebelled openly. In 1940 to 1942, other rebellions had taken place on "Free China" territory, particularly in Sichuan and in the back country of Canton. These revolts did not in the least mean that the peasants were prepared to ally themselves with Japan, but the Guomindang's yoke seemed almost as intolerable. The 1947–1949 tidal wave which was to sweep away the Tchiang regime was already forming.

The Japanese Occupation and the Collaborators

The Chinese collaborating with Japan faced the same inextricable difficulties as those Frenchmen who sided with the Germans in Paris: they had to make themselves acceptable to the occupying forces and give in to their demands, while at the same time trying to maintain a minimum of public credibility.

The political apparatus and the ideology of the collaborators

The Japanese did not risk trying to bring about the political unification of the zones they controlled. They preferred to use a quadripartite system. Manzhouguo remained a separate entity, as did the United Mongolian Council in eastern Mongolia, which was run by Prince Dê, a descendent of Genghis Khan. In China proper, a "reformed" government was based in Peking, and a "provisional" government was based in Nanking in 1938. The Peking government lasted through the war, even when a pro-Japanese "central" government was proclaimed in Nanking in 1940.

Peking and Nanking presented two different political lines, and the Japanese preferred not to choose between them. The Peking collaborators, such as the banker Wang Ke-min, the diplomat Zhou Lu, and the generals Qi Xie-yuan and Wang Yi-tang, were ghosts from the twenties, former warlords or Anfu politicians. These old conservatives believed in the Wang dao (Royal Way) of Confucius and supported the values of established authority and filial obedience in opposition to the three peoples' principles demagogy of the Guomindang. In the occupied zone, they were supported by an official organization, the Society of the New People (Xinminhui).

The Nanking group claimed to be the legal Guomindang; it accused Tchiang Kaï-chek of having betrayed the tradition established by Sun Yat-sen, particularly Sun's ideals of pan-Asianism and friendship with Japan. A supposedly "pure" Guomindang existed at Nanking, with a central committee and a congress whose secretary-general was the former anarchist Chu Win-yi. The head of pro-Japanese collaboration in Nanking was Wang Jing-wei, Tchiang Kaï-chek's old adversary. Wang had left Chongqing in 1938 and was surrounded by friends like Zhou Fu-hai and Chen Gong-bo, both founding members of the CCP in 1921.

Whether Mongolian aristocrats, Anfu politicians, or leftist intellectuals, the collaborators all accepted Japanese domination. Wang Jing-wei signed a "basic treaty" in 1940 which placed China under Japanese economic and military control. Not until 1943 did Wang's government obtain a nominal sovereignty, when Japan gave back its former Chinese concessions to Nanking in exchange for a declaration of war against the Western powers. In order to glorify the "Sphere of Far Eastern Co-Prosperity," a spectacular conference was held in Tokyo in November 1943, bringing together all the collaborating heads of state. These were Wang Jing-wei, Prince Dê, the Burman Ba Maw, the Filipino José Laurel, the Indonesian Sukarno, Pu Yi, and the Indian Subas Chandra Bose. But defeat was already inevitable . . .

Social bases of the collaborators

The motives for collaboration in the Far East were not very different from what they had been in Nazi Europe: desire for power, hunger for profit, and fear of poverty. These collaborators were also sure that the occupying forces were going to win, and that one should therefore prepare for the future.

In the cities, the Japanese were supported by unemployed bureaucrats, who were offered advantageous positions by the collaborating governments. They were also supported by the business world, where the large Japanese companies were looking for those willing to play comprador-type roles. However, the main social base of the collaboration was probably in the countryside, among the landowners. These landlords had always sought support from the government (both the imperial and republican governments) against the peasants, who were being driven to the point of revolt by exploitation. The landlords needed governmental support now more than ever, because the vitality of the liberated zones was winning over the entire peasant population in the North. The landowners collaborated en masse, and the voluminous American accounts by Jack Belden and William Hinton, among others, provide many examples of this.

At the other end of the social scale, poverty and unemployment drove the poorest people, especially in the cities, to join the puppet armies of Nanking, which swelled to 900,000 men in 1944. Several important secret societies had gone over to the Japanese, particularly the Red Band from Shanghai, which was well established in the world of middle-sized businesses, and the Way of the Basic Unity (Yiguandao). An Institute of Ancient Classics sought to win over the conservative intellectuals, who were flattered that Confucian rules had been re-introduced into the schools. A United Moslem Association was active in the North and the Northwest. Workers' leagues promoted the idea of collaboration among the working class.

Economic pressure

Japan profited enormously from the occupation in North and Central China of both the large industrial centers and the more remote areas. Japanese economic policy aimed at controlling raw materials, organizing the local production for its own profit, and giving priority to the distribution of Japanese products in China. Two large holding companies were created with this end in mind: the Northern China Development Company and the Central China Development Company. Each one had numerous subsidiaries which were tied to huge Japanese trusts; each had monopolies in mining, navigation, buses, electricity, urban services, and railways. However, this cumbersome machinery did not function well. Capital and equipment were lacking. As a result, industrial production fell off in the occupied zones, and there were 600,000 unemployed workers in Shanghai by the end of the war. The economic stagnation which existed everywhere in the occupied zones was evident as well in inflation and rising prices. The cost of living index went from 100 to 410 between 1937 and 1940.

On the other hand, the small Japanese speculators were reaping large profits. There was free entry for them into China. From the port of Kobé alone in 1939, 220,000 Japanese embarked for China. The number of Japanese civilians in China increased tenfold from 1937 to 1944. They invaded the areas of film, construction, and opium and other drug traffic. Japanese authorities tolerated this traffic, which the Nanking government openly encouraged to increase its revenues. The former minister of the interior Wang Jing-wei spoke at the War Crimes Tribunal in the Far East of this incentive to grow opium.

Military repression

The Japanese army and the Nanking troops cooperated closely in the occupied zones to suppress potential sources of resistance. In the North, the arrest and "cleanup" methods of the Japanese were brutal. The policy was that of *sanko seisaku* (the three alls): kill all, burn all, destroy all, as an example to discourage the others.[8]

In Central China, Nanking's troops tried to carry out the repression more diplomatically. As the Guomindang had done before them in Jiangxi, they took advantage of the old system of *baojia* to establish collective responsibility at each level for public infractions. This movement of "rural pacification" was aimed at establishing "model zones of peace," but it worked successfully only in the immediate neighborhoods of large cities, particularly in the Nanking-Shanghai-Hangzhou triangle.

Wang Jing-wei's army participated in repressive activities everywhere. Wang was obliged to protect the railways in the occupied zone, and this became a burdensome duty for him. Sentinels had to be posted; an area where cultivation was not allowed had to be established along the railways; if necessary, parallel roads had to be built using forced peasant labor; and the peasants had to be made collectively responsible for any sabotage. In 1944, however, trains ran less and less efficiently in the Japanese zone.

There was not much active resistance in the centers held by the Japanese. The balance of forces was too unfavorable, and the active resistance fighters were concentrated in the liberated zones. The CCP still maintained its contacts and organized well-executed strikes, as for example in Hong Kong, where production fell by 25 percent. There were occasional attacks by the Guomindang com-

[8] See Chapter 11.

mandos. The collaborator Zhou Lu was killed in one in 1939. But beyond these isolated acts of resistance, the majority of the Chinese people deeply resented the occupation. Civilian and military collaborators, *hanjian* (traitors to China), and *weijun* (puppet soldiers) were equally unpopular.

The double game of Nanking-Chongqing

The Guomindang's wait-and-see policy had never required it to break its contacts completely with either Japan or Nanking. A secret radio link was maintained between Zhou Fu-hai, the real political head of the collaboration, and Dai Li, head of Tchiang's secret services. The Japanese entertained hopes all during the war that they would be able to win over more people, as they had won over Wang Jing-wei. They were especially interested in He Ying-qin, Tchiang's chief of staff, and other prestigious leaders of the southern armies, such as Xue Yue, Li Ji-shen, and Zhang Fa-kui.

The Americans were astonished by the existence of "roadless zones," where contraband ("one of the greatest traffics in history," stated Theodore White) overshadowed the sound of weapons and brought a return of 500 percent. Oil, clothing, and salt were sent out from the Japanese zone and traded for tires and medicine taken from the U.S. supplies, then traded in turn for rice, antimony, and tungsten from the southwestern mines. There was talk of one Shanghai entrepreneur who, having heard about the awarding of a contract, stole the construction agreement for a B 29 base in the Southwest, even though it had been classified as top secret. Mail and money orders were sent back and forth between Chongqing and Shanghai, across the front, without any problem.

The double game played by the Japanese, the Guomindang, and the collaborators was based on their common conviction that the "Communist threat" took precedence over everything else. This conviction grew as the vitality of the liberated zones increased and the end of the war approached. In 1945, when Chen Gong-bo replaced his friend Wang, who had died in Tokyo in 1944, the Chongqing secret services, in conjunction with Nanking, had even prepared to relieve the Japanese with puppet troops, in case of an unforeseen capitulation. But this agreement, which was arranged between Zhou Fu-hai and Dai Li, was not carried out, because in 1945 the United States supplied Chongqing with the necessary air transport. The heads of the collaboration, Chen Gong-bo and Zhou Fu-hai, were arrested and executed.

ADDITIONAL BIBLIOGRAPHY

John H. Boyle, *China and Japan at War, 1937–1945: The Politics of Collaboration* (Stanford, Calif., Stanford University Press, 1972).

Phillip Jaffe, ed., *Chiang Kai-shek, China's Destiny* (New York, Roy Publishers, 1947).

Graham Peck, *Two Kinds of Time* (Boston, Houghton Mifflin, 1950).

Lawrence K. Rosinger, *China's Wartime Politics: 1937–1944* (New York, 1945).

Joseph Stilwell, *Chinese Adventure* (New York, W. Sloane Assoc., 1948).

George E. Taylor, *The Struggle for North China* (New York, Institute for Pacific Relations, 1940).

Theodore A. White and Annalee Jacoby, *Thunder Out of China* (New York, William Morrow, 1946).

A. N. Young, *China and the Helping Hand, 1937–1945* (Cambridge, Mass., Harvard University Press, 1963).

DOCUMENTS

1. JOSEPH STILWELL, AMERICAN COMMANDER IN CHIEF, ASSESSES THE MILITARY QUALITIES OF TCHIANG KAÏ-CHEK

SOURCE: Joseph W. Stilwell, *The Chinese Adventure* (New York, 1948), pp. 329–345. These extracts from Stilwell's daily notes were written at the time of Japan's major offensive in Southwest China, in 1944.

SEPTEMBER 14, GUILIN   [Arrived] noon. Sent for Zhang Fa-gui* [Chinese commander of Guangxi defenses]. He came out; he says plan [is] to fight in Guilin due to orders of G-mo,† against his judgment. Three divisions in town, two of Thirty-sixth Army, one of Forty-sixth Army. Only two regiments left at Liouzhou, and one a student regiment; nothing else available except Ninety-third Army of two divisions now retiring [from north]. G-mo said [Chinese could hold] three months at Zhounxian actually three days.

Zhang says he can hold Guilin for two months, cannot protect airfield except with Ninety-third Army, which is not reliable. Remnants of Thirty-seventh Army presumably moving toward Guilin. Zhang cannot estimate strength or time of arrival; no Jap tanks yet. Zhang does not know location of Ninety-seventh Army.

SEPTEMBER 16 . . . (4:00 P.M.) Plain talk with T. V. Soong, all about the situation. He is appalled at gap between our conception of field commander and the G-mo's. I proposed Chen Cheng‡ for minister

---

* Former commander of "Ironsides," the best unit of the southern revolutionary army in 1926–1927.

† Generalissimo.

‡ Military chief who did not belong to the Guomindang leading group and had had ties, around 1938, with Deng Yan-da's third party.

of war, Bai Zhong-xi* as chief of staff. Gave T. V. the works in plain words. I do not want the God-awful job, but if I take it I must have full authority. Two-hour bellyache.

SEPTEMBER 17, THE MANURE PILE: LETTER TO MRS. STILWELL   We are in the midst of a battle with the Peanut,† and it is wearing us out. Crises are arising in quick succession here and there; there is disaster in Hunan and Guangxi. . . . In the so-called campaign for Changsha, Hengyiang and Guilin, the Peanut insisted on conducting operations by remote control and by intuition as usual, with catastrophic results.

SEPTEMBER 26   . . . Jap broadcast said I was plotting to oust Tchiang Kaï-shek and make myself czar of China. Clever. Just what would make Tchiang Kaï-shek suspicious. (Or was it manufactured in Chongqing to make his action plausible?) . . . [UNDATED]‡   Tchiang Kaï-shek is the head of a one-party government supported by a Gestapo and a party secret service. He is now organizing an S.S. of 100,000 members

[He] hates the so-called Communists. He intends to crush them by keeping any munitions furnished him and by occupying their territory as the Japs retire.

[He] will not make an effort to fight seriously. He wants to finish the war coasting, with a big supply of material, so as to perpetuate his regime. He has blocked us for three years and will continue to do so. He has failed to keep his agreements.

[He] has spoken contemptuously of American efforts and has never said one word to express gratitude for our help, except in one message to the President, in which he attacked me.

[He] is responsible for major disasters of the war. Nanking, Lanfang. Changsha and Hengyiang. Guilin and Liuzhou. Red blockade.

But [he] is the titular head of China and has marked me as *persona non grata.*

Therefore I cannot operate in the China theater while he is in power—unless it is made clear to him that I was not responsible for the September 19 note, and that the U.S. will pull out unless he will play ball.

Ignored, insulted, double-crossed, delayed, obstructed for three years. Orders to [my] subordinates during operations. False charges of disobedience and nonco-operation. Constant attempts to put the screw on U.S. Use our air force. Borrow our money. Refuse us men for the equipment we hauled. . . .

OCTOBER 19, THE AX FALLS   Radio from George Marshall. I am "recalled." Sultan in temporary command. Wedemeyer to command U.S. troops in China. CBI to split.

So F.D.R. has quit. Everybody is horrified about Washington.

---

* Since 1927 one of the leaders of the regional faction of Guangxi.
† Contemptuous nickname that Stilwell constantly uses in his notes to designate Tchiang Kaï-chek.
‡ Written when Stilwell thought his dismissal imminent.

2. Inflation and demoralization in the Guomindang zone

Source: Anna Wang, *J'ai combattu pour Mao* (Paris, Gallimard, 1967), pp. 272–274. The author, the Prussian aristocrat Anna von Kleist, wife of the Communist leader Wang Ping-nan, was in Chongqing with the Communist liaison mission during the war.

. . . One of the consequences of the rapid devaluation was to force wage earners to hoard and speculate too, naturally on a smaller scale. A Chinese friend told me that her amah was stockpiling aspirin tablets, for the use of other people, of course. The black market in foreign medicines was especially prosperous. These medicines, such as the sulfa drugs, came mostly from the reserves of charitable organizations; a Quaker told me that at least a third of all the medicines that their society received were stolen and sold on the black market.

Those who benefited most from smuggling were the generals. Their wives went to Shanghai or to other large cities occupied by the Japanese and bought luxury goods there which they then had transported very cheaply by the soldiers and resold to the nouveaux riches at a very high profit.

The officers hastened to emulate their superiors.

These widespread practices had such an effect on the army's morale that when the Japanese took the offensive again in 1944, they were able to invade and occupy vast territories without resistance.

The government itself no longer had confidence in its own currency; this was quite evident in 1940 when it issued a law stipulating that the peasants were henceforth to pay taxes in grain and not in cash.

. . . The consequences of inflation were even more catastrophic in the countryside than in the towns. The great majority of the peasants could not benefit from the increase in the price of rice, because once they had delivered what they owed the state, their landlord, and often the moneylender from whom they had borrowed, they had scarcely enough left to feed themselves. Thus no increase in their income made up for the constantly rising price of textiles, oil, salt, and farm tools, so that many farmers and even small and middle-income landowners were ruined during the war years. The proportion of middle-income peasants fell between 1939 and 1942 from 40 to 20 percent. Their land was bought by large landowners, war profiteers, and speculators, for landed property was considered a safe investment. These "operations" significantly increased the number of landowners who did not live on their land.

3. The maternity school in Chengtov (1940)

Source: Han Su-yin, *Birdless Summer* (New York, Putnam, 1968), pp. 163–165. The author worked as a doctor in this school during the war.

There was the countrywoman who came a long long way from Qingxian, eighty *li* or more, to be delivered of her tenth child, because all the others had been daughters; and a neighbour of hers had been to the hospital and had acquired a son; this woman thought she too could obtain a son by coming to be delivered at our hospital. She rode in a rickshaw all the way and this must have cost a good deal; and as she lay on the obstetric table in labour she told Miss Xu what had happened to her baby daughters: the first was alive, and also the third; but the second had been strangled at birth by the husband and so had the fifth and the sixth; the seventh had been born in a bad year, a year of famine when her belly skin stuck to her spine, and the husband had smashed her skull in with his axe; at the eighth female child the husband had been so angry that he had hurled it against a wall; the ninth was a year old and had been given away to a neighbour and now here was something in her belly . . . oh let it be a son, a male child.

As the pains came and went, Miss Xu, stethoscope upon the woman's belly, asked: "What happened to the fourth?"

We went through the whole list of infanticides again and again, and every time the woman missed one out—the fourth. As the pains became worse (and labour was not easy, for her flesh was exhausted; her belly muscles had parted so that the womb could almost be seen under the skin; and we were prepared for a haemorrhage [sic] which is usual after many births), the woman began to sob and told us how the fourth had been killed. She had been so frightened when it was born and it was a girl that she herself had pushed it in the big toilet jar, and there it had suffocated.

And now we hoped, we all hoped. All the midwives by now had heard the woman's story, and all the other patients, and some sat up in bed straining with the woman straining on the delivery table, turned in spirit towards it, waiting, waiting for the miracle, for the son which would truly consecrate the hospital as a miracle-working place. But this did not happen; the tenth was another girl.

"Such a beautiful little sister, look," said Miss Xu as the woman lay mute, her eyes fixed on the ceiling, in a frozen stare. "Look at her. She is so pretty."

"It is a girl, another girl." Perhaps she had not paid enough; she unwound the belt round her which she had pushed up under her breasts so as to free her belly for the work it had to do. And there was another twenty dollars in paper, and she said: "All, that is all I have, for a boy."

"But a girl is just as good as a boy," said Miss Xu to her; and for the next few days we all told her how good it was to be a woman, and how a woman now could do so many things, even become a doctor, or a midwife, and how pretty her baby was. After five days the woman went home, and she wanted to leave the baby behind, but this could not be. Miss Xu placed the baby, wrapped tight in its swaddling clothes in the approved Sichuan fashion, in its mother's arms and said, "Take care of her, she will bring you luck." Then she walked with her to the door, still trying to persuade her, while the hospital servant went to call a rickshaw. Many rickshaw or wheel-barrow men would not carry a woman that had given birth to a child only a week or ten days before. They would only take a mother if the baby was a full month old, thirty days, when all evil was reckoned purged away. Often Miss Xu would send out the servant to call a rickshaw, only to find the man pick up his shafts and go away when he realized that he was to carry a woman with a week-old baby. Then Miss Xu would get angry and cry out: "And where did you come from? Did not a woman bear you? Have you no mother?" to the back of the departing man. But in Little Heavenly Bamboo Street there were rickshaws who were used to carrying pregnant and new mothers, and laughed at the refusal of the others. So a rickshaw was obtained for the woman, an obliging smiling man, who also persuaded her to keep the baby, and told her: "These are new days, a woman child is also good, look at all those doctors here." Afterwards the porter told us that all the way home the woman was telling her story and that she did not dare to go back to her husband with yet another girl, and that on the way home she would find a convenient ditch, and throw the baby into it; but we never knew whether she did this or not, for neither the porter nor the rickshaw man would tell us.

4. The Hunan famine (1943): the inefficiency and corruption of the Guomindang according to American journalists in Chongqing

Source: Theodore A. White and Annalee Jacoby, *Thunder Out of China* (New York, William Morrow, 1946), pp. 172–174.

The Chinese government failed to foresee the famine; when it came, it failed to act until too late. As early as October, reports of the situation were arriving in Chongqing. In November two government inspectors visited Henan, traveled the main motor roads, and returned to say that the crisis was desperate and something must be done immediately. The Central Government dismissed the matter by appropriating $200,000,000—paper money—for famine relief and sending a mandate to provincial authorities to remit taxes. The banks in Chongqing loaded the bales of paper currency on trucks and sent a convoy northward bearing paper, not food, to the stricken. . . .

The relief money sent to Henan arrived gradually. By the time we got there in March only $80,000,000 out of the $200,000,000 appropriated had reached the provincial government. Even this money was badly managed. It was left to lie in provincial bank accounts, drawing interest, while government officials debated and bickered as to how it might best be used. In some places, when money was distributed to starving farmsteads, the amount of current taxes the peasants owed was deducted by local authorities from the sums they received; even the national banks took a cut of the relief funds as profit. The Central Government had sent relief money in denominations of $100 Chinese currency—small enough, since a pound of wheat was selling at $16.00 to $18.00. But the local hoarders refused to sell their grain for notes of large denomination; to buy grain the peasants had to change their money for five- and ten-dollar bills. And this they had to do through the national banks, which discounted their own currency by 17 per cent in changing large bills for small bills. What the people of Henan wanted was food. Up to March the government had provided some 10,000 sacks of rice and 20,000 sacks of mixed grain. This averaged almost a pound apiece for 10,000,000 people who had been starving since autumn.

Stupidity and inefficiency marked the relief effort. But the grisly tragedy was compounded even further by the actions of the constituted local authorities. The peasants, as we saw them, were dying. They were dying on the roads, in the mountains, by the railway stations, in their mud huts, in the fields. And as they died, the government continued to wring from them the last possible ounce of tax. The money tax the peasant had to pay on his land was a trivial matter; the basic tax exacted from him was the food tax, a percentage of all the grain he raised, and despite the fine-sounding resolution of remittance in Chongqing, the tax was being extorted from him by every device the army and provincial authorities could dream up. The government in county after county was demanding of the peasant more actual poundage of grain than he had raised on his acres. No excuses were allowed; peasants who were eating elm bark and dried leaves had to haul their last sack of seed grain to the tax collector's office. Peasants who were so weak they could barely walk had to collect fodder for the army's horses, fodder that was more nourishing than the filth they were cramming into their own mouths. Peasants who could not pay were forced to the wall; they sold their cattle, their furniture, and even their land to raise money to buy grain to meet the tax quotas. One of the most macabre touches of all was the flurry of land speculation. Merchants from Xian and Zhengzhou, small government officials, army officers, and rich landlords who still had food were engaged in purchasing the peasants' ancestral acres at criminally low figures. Concentration and dispossession were proceeding hand in hand, in direct proportion to the intensity of hunger.

Chapter Eleven

The Communist Movement from 1937 to 1945

Retrenched in the Yanan base since their arrival from the Long March, the Chinese Communists were favorably placed for active participation in the war of resistance against Japan. Within striking distance of the enemy bases in North China, they themselves were almost out of reach. For eight years the war against Japan entirely absorbed the forces of the CCP and, as a result, profoundly changed its internal workings and its relations with the other groups in Chinese politics. Though very much a minority after the Long March, after eight years of war the Communist Party had become a candidate for taking over the central power. Through its partisan struggles against Japan, the CCP had gradually constructed political and military power with a territorial base which by 1945 comprehended ninety-five million inhabitants distributed within the Yanan base and eighteen other liberated regions.

The strategy of the red bases, worked out in Jinggangshan, especially during the period of the soviets of South China, followed the same principles, but in a very different context. As in the earlier period, the liberated zones were founded on armed struggle, a socially dominant peasantry, exclusively local conquests of power, and a long-term policy. The geopolitical conditions were also the same: location of the bases on the borders of two or three provinces in poor regions almost inaccessible to the enemy and capable of surviving in semi-autarchy. But this strategy of the red bases was now geared to defeat Japan. The foreigner became the enemy, making it much easier to rally the masses and to obtain the support of certain privileged classes than when the enemy had been the Guomindang and the central government. In contrast with the Chinese soviets, therefore, the social base of the Communist strategy at Yanan had been greatly expanded.

At the same time, the struggle's center of gravity shifted from the South to the North. The democratic traditions of the South had favored the establishment of the Jiangxi soviets in 1930, but these traditions proved now much less important than the brutal fact of Japanese occupation of the North. The North, rather than the South, became the most politically advanced and active region up through the final phase of the liberation struggle in 1947–1948, a development that profoundly affected the beginnings of the People's Republic.

At Yanan, the Chinese Communists lived in caves dug out of Shenxi's thick loess, the legendary "yellow earth" from which their ancestors had drawn their living for thousands of years. This return to the Chinese earth, far from Westernized centers like Shanghai, was also a return to real China—the peasants and the people. The United Front strategy, bowing to the interest of "National Salvation," went along with a reorientation of the Communist movements in all areas, including ideology and culture. The militants had to give up their elitism (the rectification movement, *zhengfeng*) and writers their privileged culture (the Yanan "Forum"). Both groups had to learn to merge with the people and to be transformed in the process. Yanan was not only the nerve center which inspired exceptionally productive military struggles; it was a new social model, the prototype of new social and human relationships.

The Anti-Japanese Bases from 1937 to 1941

In an interview with the English journalist James Bertram (October 1937), Mao outlined the principles of the Communist strategy. China, and especially the CCP, was weak and isolated. Against a superior adversary which had concentrated all its forces against them, and no longer able to take advantage of the rivalries among the great powers, China would have to fight a long, protracted, and difficult war. This was especially true as long as the other powers were not drawn into the war.

The Guomindang also fought the war, but the CCP had no confidence in the Guomindang's capacities for struggle and absolutely intended to preserve its own armed forces and its means for military initiative. The Communists refused to be nothing more than a supplementary force, the Guomindang's left wing, as had been the case in 1924 to 1927. Yet this was the policy the Comintern and its Chinese allies wanted to continue. In 1938 at Wuhan, Wang Ming had attempted to adopt this rightist position, which the debacle of the Guomindang had rendered untenable. But Wang was defeated, and the CCP would therefore fight alone, even as it conscientiously adhered to the 1937 agreements and removed, for example, the red stars on its soldiers' helmets. While keeping an eye on the Guomindang's wait-and-see policy, prepared to respond to incidents and attempts to break the alliance, the CCP refused to allow its conflicts with the Guomindang to take precedence over the "principal contradiction," the war against Japan.

Establishment of the guerrilla bases

The Red Army had become the Eighth Route Army, formally attached to the Guomindang's Second Group of armies headed by Marshal Yan Xi-shan, the *dujun* of Shanxi. Under the general leadership of Zhu De and Peng De-huai, the Communist forces were organized into three divisions (the 115th, the 120th, and the 129th), which represented around 45,000 men. At the end of 1937, these troops engaged in harsh battles with the Japanese, but when the Guomindang evacuated Taiyuan, the capital of Shanxi, and the Japanese advanced along the railroads, the three Communist divisions remained behind enemy communication lines. They settled in the east, south, and north of Shanxi, at positions that were to become the core of three important Communist support bases. Other smaller Communist units established themselves in Shandong and elsewhere in North China. The New Fourth Army, which had been formed from other red units, set up guerrilla bases in the lower Yangzi, and still others were established in the South. In all, there were about fifteen of these bases in 1938 to 1939.

The Communists' decision to scatter their forces behind enemy lines was not the only way that these bases originated. Other fighting groups appeared spontaneously behind the Japanese lines: peasant self-defense groups, Guomindang dissidents, autonomous guerrillas, groups of patriotic students, and secret societies. The anti-Japanese guerrilla bases came into being out of the combined efforts and then the fusion, despite some difficulties, of these two sources, both equally founded on the popular will to resist Japan and opposition to the wait-and-see strategy of the Chongqing Guomindang.

The Shen-Gan-Ning base

The Shen-Gan-Ning base at the borders of Shenxi, Gansu, and Ningxia was the oldest in the country; the Communists had held it since 1931. A stopping place on the Long March, this base, with its flanking position, was also the only one that was not behind Japanese lines. The Central Committee of the CCP, the University of Resistance (Kangda), the central military leadership of the bases, and many other groups were settled at its center in Yanan. There the largest number of foreigners who had come over to the guerrillas were to be found, and it was there that Western journalists were received.

This zone was the first to be given representative institutions. As early as May 1937, there were elections for a people's congress and a regional government whose president was Lin Bo-qu, a veteran of the Long March and the Hunan teacher under whom Mao had studied. Politically, then, Yanan was a combination of a centralized organization (the organs of CCP leadership, on which the other bases depended) and a decentralized organization (all political power was local, as in the other bases). Until 1949, the Communists refused to set up a central political power that would rival that of the Guomindang, as they had prematurely attempted to do in 1931 with the Chinese soviets at Ruijin.

The Jin-Cha-Ji base

These three syllables represent the traditional names of the Shanxi, Chahar, and Hebei provinces. The main bastion of resistance was in the Wutaishan Mountains, where the 115th Division of Lin Biao and Nie Rong-zhen was stationeed. The Communists there joined other forces of armed resistance—the League for Sacrifice and the Taiyuan Students for National Salvation—collaborating with them politically and militarily. In 1938, an elected people's congress organized the base area's political power. Though it was geographically the closest to Peking, the base stood fast and grew

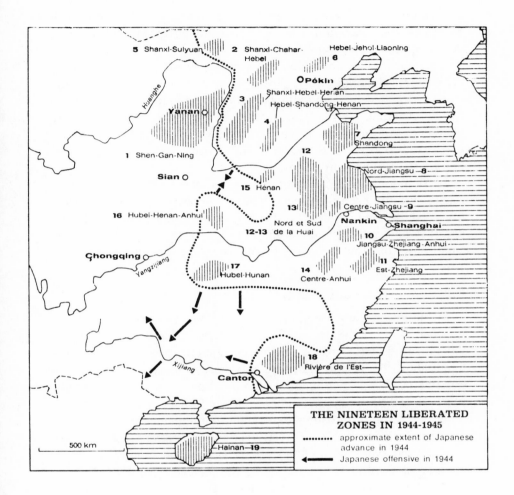

5 Shanxi-Suiyuan 2 Shanxi-Chahar-Hebel Hebel-Jehol-Liaoning 6

OPékin

3 Shanxi-Hebei-Henan

Hebel-Shandong-Henan

Yanan

4

1 Shen-Gan-Ning

12

7 Shandong

Sian

15 Henan

Nord-Jiangsu -8

16 Hubei-Henan-Anhui

13 Centre-Jiangsu -9

Nord et Sud 12-13 de la Huai

Nankin

Shanghai

10 Jiangsu-Zhejiang-Anhui

Chongqing

Yangzijiang

17 Hubei-Hunan

14 Centre-Anhui

11 Est-Zhejiang

Xijiang

Canton

18 Rivière de l'Est

500 km

Hainan—19

THE NINETEEN LIBERATED ZONES IN 1944-1945

·········· approximate extent of Japanese advance in 1944

◄—— Japanese offensive in 1944

in size despite the Japanese offensives. A good part of the base was in the plains. Deprived of mountain refuges, the resistance fighters dug immense tunnel networks between villages, as the peasant insurgents of this region had done in the past.

Other bases in North China

The Jin-Ji-Lu-Yu (Shanxi-Hebei-Shandong-Henan) base was formed around the Taihangshan Mountains, where the troops of

Liu Bo-cheng (the 129th Division) had been entrenched since 1937. The Nian had waged long-term resistance in the nineteenth century in this area, and secret societies like the Red Spears were still active and influential there. The Communists cooperated with them, as they also did with the spontaneously formed Peasant Associations for National Salvation.

The 120th Division of He Long was stationed in northern Shanxi (the Shanxi-Suiyuan base). There it encountered members of the League for Sacrifice and units of the Guomindang (New Army) which eventually joined up with it. This base developed more slowly, expanding to the edges of the desert. The scattered population lived poorly, and Japanese influence was well established among the neighboring tribes.

In Shandong, small Communist units entered into relations with local resistance groups, especially the Vanguard of National Liberation, led by Fan Shu-xin, a former Guomindang official. Secret societies and anti-Japanese student groups were numerous. Several small bases of resistance were gradually established in this area.

Bases in Central and South China

In the lower Yangzi region, the New Fourth Army consolidated its position in 1938 to 1939. The guerrilla base welcomed the village self-defense groups and secret societies that were very influential in the region. Because this base was close to large industrial centers like Shanghai, the working class had a certain place in it. The political commissar of the Fourth Army was Xiang Ying, a veteran of the Shanghai trade union movement.

Other smaller zones of resistance were scattered throughout Central and even South China. There were even some in the back country of Canton (the Column of the River of the East, for example, which had developed from the Hailufeng soviets founded by Peng Pai in 1928), and on the island of Hainan, where the Japanese landed in 1939.

The guerrilla war

Mao Tsetung gave a series of courses at the Yanan Military Academy in which he systematized the military experience gained by the Communists during the period of the Jiangxi soviets: "Problems of Strategy in China's Revolutionary War" (December 1936) and "Problems of Strategy in Guerrilla War Against Japan" (May 1938).

The chief lesson was the importance of transcending the conflicts of conventional warfare—between the army and civilians, between what is military and what is political, between defensive and offensive actions, and between modern and primitive weapons. A new attitude had become possible because the people themselves were waging the war. The sharp distinction between the military and civilians had therefore been eliminated. There was a whole range of military organizations—from the regular army to the regional militias and other auxiliary troops, down to the village self-defense groups and the peasants who occasionally participated in a military action without giving up their agricultural work. The support of the peasant population was therefore essential to the army. It not only provided the army with recruits, but also gave information and contributed transportation, provisions, and help during emergencies.

In much the same way, the distinction between the military and political spheres had been eliminated. The war was waged on the basis of a common political design: to defeat Japan by having confidence in the Communists. The army's ideological cohesion was very strong. The way in which a military secret could be kept by thousands of civilians was another sign of this political partnership. Only in very rare instances did the Japanese know the plans of their adversaries.

The tactics used by the Communists did away with the distinction between "offensive" and "defensive." The war was a mobile one in which the strategies of self-defense and attack were joined. These strategies included daily attrition, harassment, and the sudden dispersal and concentration of forces. To their advantage, the peasants were familiar with the terrain, while the Japanese army was not. Equipment consisted both of modern weapons taken from the Japanese (although the Communists could not do anything about their lack of tanks and planes) and of archaic weapons that were ingeniously constructed on the spot.

Japanese pressure in 1939–1941

Once the war-of-movement phase was over and the defensive wait-and-see attitude of Chongqing was adopted, Japanese pressure concentrated on the guerrilla bases. The situation did not change until the British and Americans entered the war against Japan in 1941. These were extremely hard years; it was necessary to hold on despite isolation, lack of equipment, and the growing risk of a break with the Guomindang. Mao's writings from this period repeatedly stress endurance and the importance of refusing to give in to the temptation of a compromise with Japan. The Anhui incident, in which the Communist general staff of the New Fourth Army was surrounded and massacred by the Guomindang, emphasized the precarious situation of the Communist bases at that time. The Guomindang blockade added to the burden of the Japanese blockade and caused very difficult economic conditions. Taxes had to be increased in the guerrilla bases, and a general appeal made for the acceptance of new sacrifices.

The Japanese increased their "raking" and "cleanup" campaigns, destroying harvests and homes. But the severity of the repression only hardened the peasants' resistance and increased the number of people who went to the Communist bases, their only refuge and recourse against the Japanese raids. Even during the hardest period, the Communist armies were still capable of making things difficult for the Japanese. They mounted offensives, such as the Hundred Regiments Offensive in August to December 1940 against the railways held by the Japanese. In Central China during the same period, the Fourth Army made a rapid advance into north Yangzi and expelled the Japanese from regions that the Guomindang had made little effort to contest. This advance was the excuse the Guomindang gave to justify its anti-Communist aggression in January 1941.

The Communists were not yet capable of seriously damaging the Japanese military power, but they had no trouble defeating the puppet troops of the collaborationist governments of Peking and Nanking. The Communists procured the arms and equipment they needed at their expense.

Yanan, a New Type of Chinese Society

Although spread out among fifteen or eighteen guerrilla bases, the social model that Yanan constituted, and the whole Yanan period, represented a complete break with the rest of China during the forties. War correspondents like Stuart Gelder, Harrison Forman, Gunther Stein, and Robert Payne felt a violent shock when they left Chongqing and arrived in Yanan. Their excellent reports on Yanan depict a radically different China.

Yanan, of course, came into being because of the unusual situation at the time: the war, terrible hardships, the blockade, and poverty. But no matter how contingent it may have been in the beginning, Yanan managed to create a coherent and innovative society that in time had considerable influence abroad (the guerrilla bases in Vietnam, Southeast Asia, black Africa). Even after the People's Republic had been founded Yanan continued to be referred to as an example, especially during the Great Leap Forward in 1958 and during the Cultural Revolution, which sometimes was described as a "Return to Yanan."

Yanan was much more than an expedient; it was a final step in the strategic and ideological quest that had led the Communists to Jinggangshan, Jiangxi, and on the Long March. The CCP returned to Peking after twenty-two years of absence from the large industrial centers, where it had been born and fought its first battles. In relation to Shanghai, Yanan was the other side of revolutionary history; Yanan was the peasant headquarters of the Chinese revolution.

The New Democracy

The short political treatise that Mao published in 1940, "On New Democracy," offered a definition of both the Chinese revolution and the new society it hoped to create. The Communists were concerned with waging a combined struggle against imperialism and feudalism—against Japan and against the landowners and the political groups that supported them. This struggle was to be led by the various social groups who had an interest in liberating the Chinese people from this double oppression: the working class, the poor and middle peasants, the petty bourgeoisie and the intellectuals, and finally the "national capitalists."[1] The revolutionary struggle was to be waged by these four classes under the leadership of the Communist Party. Mao insisted therefore that the New Democracy differed as much from Soviet democracy as it did from Western bourgeois democracy, since it was not founded on the dictatorship of the proletariat alone, but on the dictatorship of these four allied

---

[1] Unlike the compradors, National capitalists were hampered in their activities by the competition of state bureaucratic groups and large foreign interests.

classes. The flag of People's China (four small stars surrounding one large star) illustrates the idea of the four classes united around the CCP.

Establishing the New Democracy in the guerrilla bases

Western visitors to Yanan all emphasized the democratic life in the guerrilla bases and the sharp contrast with the fearful and authoritarian atmosphere of Chongqing. There were regularly organized elections at all levels—village, canton, district, and region (the "base"). Everyone over eighteen could participate in the secret-ballot elections of the members of the people's congress, the executive committees, and the local officials. But the candidates ran for office and their candidacies were classified according to the "three thirds" principle: One-third were to be Communists, one-third leftist independents, and one-third liberals and democrats (sometimes even Guomindang members). At Yanan in the Shen-Gan-Ning region, new elections were arranged in 1941 when those of May 1937 proved not to have enforced the "three thirds" principle rigorously enough. Even in the positions of greatest responsibility (such as the zone presidents or vice-presidents) one encountered intellectuals without party affiliation, liberal sympathizers of the Guomindang, persons known for their ties to the secret societies, rich merchants, and even landowners. Of the 10,926 members of the representative bodies in the Yanan zone, only 2,801 were Communists after the 1941 elections. There were 123 Communists among the 216 members of the regional congress. The consolidation of the United Front at the base became even more important to the Communist Party after it was threatened at the top following the Anhui incident of January 1941.

These scrupulous electoral practices, however, probably were not the most important aspect of the Yanan democracy. Popular participation was not limited to occasional elections in which a remote power structure was chosen. In the cooperatives and the *induscos* (industrial cooperatives), everyone participated in economic decisions; in the village self-defense militias, everyone participated in military decisions. This active cooperation was encouraged by the newspapers in the guerrilla zones, especially the leading paper, *Jiefang Ribao (Newspaper of the Liberation)*. People expressed their thoughts on current problems by writing a *dazibao* (a wall poster in large characters), a form of political discussion that amazed foreigners during the Cultural Revolution twenty-five years later.

This democracy had a purpose. Democratic rights were not meant to serve the individual; they were an expression of the exigencies of the common struggle against Japan and a prerequisite for engaging the vast majority in it more effectively. Almost the entire population of the support bases backed the new regime. Except for a few differences owing to immediate social conditions, the principles of "On New Democracy" were applied. Of the four revolutionary classes, the national capitalists and the industrial proletariat were present only in small, almost symbolic numbers. The representatives of the lower middle classes who came from the small market towns of each zone were more numerous, as were intellectuals from the large cities under Japanese control. But the peasantry constituted the primary social base of the guerrilla bases: poor and middle peasants, day workers and rural misfits, and even vagabonds and bandits. There were also rich peasants and even "enlightened landowners." This carefully chosen term (*kaiming dizhu*) emphasized the anti-Japanese political position taken by some landowners, and the precedence it had over pure economics and the landowner's part in the system of feudal exploitation. Li Ting-ming, the vice-president of the regional government of Shen-Gan-Ning, was a landlord and member of the Guomindang.

The power structures

Power was distributed among the state, the party, the mass organizations, and the army, and flexible relations, rather than a mechanical hierarchy, were established among them.

The state was in charge of the principal public services: finances, production, education, and general administration. Democratically managed, the state was decentralized throughout the various liberated regions. A specialized group of officials were either elected at the base or appointed. But these officials were unusual in that they were actively associated with production. A bureaucracy of passive consumers had given way to a community of part-time producers. The administrative cadres, as well as the political and military cadres, were expected to spend part of their time engaged in farming or crafts. Mao himself raised tomatoes and tobacco leaves near his cave between work sessions of the leadership organizations.

The Party's essential role was to unify the various efforts and coordinate the activities of the geographically and administratively separate liberated zones. It developed general policy and promoted the mass organizations indispensable for carrying out the military, political, and economic mobilization of the population. These organizations included the Workers' Organization, which later was turned into real unions when the industrial zones were re-integrated into the liberated regions; the Youth Association for National Salvation; the Association of Women; and peasant asso-ciations. There were about twenty of them, each with several hun-dred thousand members (except for the Workers' Organization).

The army also played a political role. Not only was it united by political ties that made it extremely cohesive, but it also helped to develop the political consciousness and political organization of the peasants in the villages it came to. The political commissars of the various army units were as concerned with civilians as they were with the military.

Within these four structures there was to be no hierarchical compartmentalization. The "mass line" was meant to simplify administrative relationships and to prevent the isolation of each organized structure. For example, there were no outward signs of hierarchy either for the military or for the civilians. The "movement for the simplification of administration" in 1941 attempted to re-duce the number of cadres and formal procedures, as did the "return to the village" campaign (*xia xiang*), which sent many intellectuals from the eastern cities to act as local cadres and teachers. The resulting atmosphere of frugality and brotherhood in Yanan impressed all foreign visitors.

The national and peasant struggles

Some observers, like Chalmers Johnson,[2] have argued that during the civil war, a radical agrarian policy had isolated the Com-munists and led to the defeat of 1934. During the anti-Japanese United Front, however, a moderate agrarian policy permitted them to win over "peasant nationalism" and to assume power. This argument is schematic and does not hold up.

The Communists' agrarian policy at Yanan was indeed moderate. The land confiscation policy enacted by the Chinese soviets was abandoned in favor of a more modest program that reduced land

[2] See the chapter bibliography.

rents by 25 percent and limited the usury rate. This policy helped the peasants and represented a serious setback for the landlords, who were burdened with heavy retroactive taxes while their debtors enjoyed a moratorium on debts.

But the political situation was more important than these partial economic measures, despite their real benefits. Yanan was a time of progress for the peasant movement, not of retreat. The peasant struggle for national salvation finally had a class as well as a patriotic base. By fighting the Japanese, the peasants discovered their military strength, and they discovered their political strength through active integration in the New Democracy of Yanan. Their horizons were enlarged as they discarded the traditional ideological frameworks (acceptance of feudal power or the egalitarian dreams of the secret societies) and began to think in terms of cadres (*ganbu*) and masses (*qunzhong*), national salvation (*jiu guo*) and collaborators who were traitors to China (*hanjian, weijun*). Traitors were often identified with the landowners as a class, for there were very few "enlightened" landowners. Most landlords had transferred their traditional allegiance to established authority to Japan.

The battle of production

With the liberated zones blockaded by Japanese, puppet, and Guomindang troops, production needs became an urgent priority. It was a question of survival.

Even though agricultural production was still largely confined to small private properties, efforts were made on the village level to encourage the development of mutual aid (common labor, rotation of equipment, for example). Political stimulation was important; examples were set and "work heroes" were honored.[3]

The Eighth Army was a case in point. In 1941, the 359th Brigade, an elite unit, was withdrawn from the front and sent to the wild and uninhabited district of Nanniwan in the Yanan region. The brigade proved that the people's army was capable of surviving "by its own efforts," without taking anything from the peasant population. "On our arrival," recounted a veteran, "the trees were so thick we couldn't even see the sky." Despite these extremely unfavorable conditions, the experiment was a great success; there was the clearing of land, textile crafts, the breeding of livestock, and

[3] See document 1 at the end of the chapter.

forest coal production. The exploits of the 359th Brigade were cited everywhere to promote the "battle of production" in the liberated zones.

In the area of crafts, efforts were made to develop the *induscos,* or industrial cooperatives. These had been introduced in Nationalist areas by liberal Protestants, but only flourished in the liberated zones. They produced their own agricultural equipment, textiles, paper, and medicines, among other things. This decentralized production demanded a great deal of ingenuity and cooperation. In an impoverished and defensive situation, a constructive social model paradoxically took shape, a model that would persist in the People's Republic.

This economic policy based on the "mass line" could not overcome such obstacles as inflation. In 1937, a bushel of millet cost 2.5 dollars (*renminbi*); in 1943, it cost from 150 to 2,000, depending on the region. But the policy was successful in that production was greatly increased. In the zone of Shen-Gan-Ning alone, the area under cultivation increased from 9 million mou in 1936 to 12½ million in 1942. In the same zone, cotton production rose from 7,370 bales in 1938 to 104,302 in 1943.

The women's movement

The mobilization of the people could not take place without the participation of the women. Appeals were made to women to help the army through reconnaissance missions, agricultural labor, work in the *induscos,* and particularly with home weaving. The women's associations that were formed in villages to organize this mobilization could not avoid specifically female problems such as forced marriage, subordination to parents-in-law and husband, and inferior political and moral status. These themes were important ones in the literature of the liberated zones, particularly in plays and short stories. A film made near the end of the war, called *The White-Haired Girl,* featured a young peasant woman who was terrorized by the local squire, sold, and, after hiding away in the mountains, was revered locally as a guardian spirit by the peasants. She joined an army group and returned to liberate the village. In many villages, the women's associations defended daughters-in-law against their mothers-in-law and broke up forced marriages.

Nevertheless the old habits were deeply ingrained. Only a minority of women, usually those from intellectual backgrounds, discussed the problem of complete equality between men and women. Despite encouragement from the authorities, only 8 percent of those elected to the local committees for political leadership were women. The political and military leadership of the liberated zones remained in the hands of men.

The *zhengfeng*

The social and political life of the liberated zones was so original that one is tempted to describe it as a unified whole. Nevertheless, in 1941, these zones approached a critical turning point. The Japanese blockade tightened. Japanese offensives became harsher as the demands of the distant campaigns against the English and Americans made the presence of enemy forces on their home front even more intolerable to the Japanese. The break with the Guomindang was almost complete. Even the advances made in the guerrilla bases since 1937 presented new difficulties. The old cadres from before the Zunyi Conference and the Long March remained influential, as well as their methods—militant elitism, dogmatism, and preference for ponderous organizational machinery. The structure of the Communist Party remained complicated. There was an intermingling of local hierarchies (from the village to the Central Committee) and specialized departments (youth, propaganda, organization, women). Many cadres had only just joined the CCP. Appeals had been made to the fighting peasants, who were without political education and therefore hesitant, and to the educated people, who still clung to their traditional privileges.

The rectification movement (*zhengfeng*, literally "to change the direction of the wind, to change one's style"), was launched in the Communist Party in 1941–1942. Its goal was full implementation of the mass line, the elimination of dogmatic and elitist tendencies, and the unification of the party with the peasant masses for the winning of the war. The method was that of "internal struggle." It was necessary to "take care of the sick," Mao said. "If a person who commits an error does not let the evil degenerate into an incurable state, if he honestly wants to be cured, if he wants to correct himself, we will welcome him as a good comrade." People must be changed rather than penalized in an authoritarian way. That required criticizing destructive behavior and those who practiced it.[4]

---

[4] Mao published several essays along these lines: "Oppose Stereotyped Party Writing" (January 1942), "Rectify the Party's Style of Work" (February 1942), "Some Questions Concerning Methods of Leadership" (June 1943).

Mao called for the elimination of scholastic stereotypes, the *bagu* ("essays in eight parts," which were typically found in old Confucian examinations). Even without challenging the influence of Stalin and the Comintern, the allusion was very clear. The "foreign *bagu*" (the Russians) were to be eliminated and there was to be a return "to the Chinese style, so simple and so agreeable to the people's ear." Other leaders participated in this campaign, particularly Liu Shao-qi, with his treatise "How to Become a Good Communist."

The *zhengfeng* was also a vast study movement in the Communist Party, which until then had been completely absorbed in immediate action. Unlike the brutal purge that had shaken Moscow several years earlier, the rectification campaign was a profound movement of collective reorganization that consolidated the Maoist mass line. No leaders were suddenly expelled except for Zhang Guo-tao, the former leader of the Fourth Army of the Front during the Long March, who defected and went over to the Guomindang in 1938. Past and future adversaries of Mao continued to occupy important posts: Liu Shao-qi, who was responsible for internal organization; Gao Gang, the secretary of the party for the Shen-Gan-Ning region; Wang Ming, president of the Women's University. This was either a temporary compromise or a real effort to achieve untiy.

Yanan as an international center

Seen from Yanan, the problematic relationship of Chinese communism to world communism took on a completely new perspective. Relations with Moscow were strained. In a practical sense, they had become much more difficult than they had been at the time when the Central Committee was based in Shanghai, in a large international port. They were particularly strained politically. "On New Democracy" was not translated into Russian, and Wang Ming, Mao's principal adversary, was kept in a leadership position in the Comintern even after his elimination at Zunyi. The CCP had essentially moved away from the political territory of the Comintern; it was acting according to a line and principles that were completely new. Instead of dissipating itself in polemics, as Trotsky had or as Tito would do later, the CCP kept its distance from Moscow by its very actions, by everything that was profoundly innovative in Yanan communism.

From Yanan's perspective, the dissolution of the Comintern in 1943 was of little importance. Mao's speech on May 26, 1943, in which he explained the meaning of this dissolution to the CCP cadres, has not been included in the official edition of his *Selected Works*. Nevertheless, the CCP was not isolated. There were many Communists at Yanan who had come individually from the West: the American doctor George Hatem, the Canadian surgeon Norman Bethune (who died of an infection in 1939), and some Spanish Communists. Most of all, there were Vietnamese Communists (Ho Chi Minh among them), Japanese Communists (such as Nosaka Sanzo, the reorganizer of the Japanese Communist Party after the war, who at that time set up a political re-education center for prisoners of the Japanese war), and Korean Communists. A new and predominantly Asian internationalism, based on the brotherhood of the battlefield, replaced the official internationalism of the central Communist organizations.

Cultural life

A large number of intellectuals, professors, students, writers, and artists from the cities settled in Yanan and the other liberated regions. Some of them, such as the great historian Fan Wen-lan, taught at Kangda ("anti-Japanese resistance") University. Many others went into the villages to participate in campaigns against illiteracy. But they often had difficulties in reconciling their political adherence to the anti-Japanese struggle and the New Democracy with their old habits as city intellectuals. In 1942, the CCP held a Forum of Writers and Artists in Yanan. Its participants were asked to renounce individualism, to live among the people and write for their sake, and to find literary and artistic inspiration from the conditions of the people. The Yanan writers, like Zhao Shu-li, published short stories and plays that reflected peasant life in very simple language. They described the struggle against Japan and agrarian reform, criticized old-style marriages and religious superstitions, and illustrated the authority of the cadres and the inventiveness of simple people. In the lengthy story "The Songs of Li Yu-cai," an old peasant defends his exploited neighbors, observes the mistakes of the Communist cadres who let themselves be fooled by the landlord, and sums up in a few improvised verses the objectives that the peasants should try to attain at each stage of the political conflicts in the village.[5]

The cultural life of Yanan was affected by these new works and

[5] See document 2.

this new orientation on the part of "professional" writers and artists. But it was fed just as much by the creativity of the people: peasant woodcuts, poems, pictures made with paper cutouts, and colored prints that represented the struggles and joys of the liberated zones. These modes of direct expression were especially important amid a peasant population that was still mostly illiterate. According to visitors' accounts, a striking expression of this new political and popular culture was a collective dance called the *yangge*, an immense celebration with many participants and group improvisation of themes that were often taken from current circumstances.

The Liberated Zones from 1942 to 1945

As the war in the Far East widened to include the British and Americans, pressure on the liberated zones increased. Japanese reprisals were intensified in a variety of ways. There were cleanup campaigns which aimed at eliminating the regular armed forces and the partisans' units of resistance by concentrating superior forces against them. Through mass incursions into the liberated zones, the "nibbling" missions attempted to break up potential for resistance. The objective of the raking campaigns was to terrorize the civilian population through police controls in the villages, searches, and mass arrests. In 1941 to 1943, the Japanese built enormous structures around their occupied zones and at the edge of the liberated zones. They made thousands of blockhouses, thousands of kilometers of trenches and stone walls, and hundreds of surveillance posts.

As the struggle grew more intense, these measures were systematized according to the formula of General Okamura, the Japanese commander in chief of North China: *sanko seisaku* ("kill all, burn all, destroy all"). A given area was surrounded, its inhabitants killed, its dwellings destroyed, and life made impossible. In August to October 1941, 10,000 Japanese soldiers were concentrated in the Beiyue district in the liberated zone of Jin-Cha-Ji, and 4,500 people were massacred, 150,000 houses burned, and 17,000 inhabitants deported to Manchuria.[6] The most brutal cleanup campaign was launched in the plain of central Hebei in May 1942. More than 50,000 people were either killed or arrested. Such offensives forced

---

[6] The figures are Chalmers Johnson's, based on Japanese military archives.

resistance to fall back. Mao indicated later that the liberated zones included no more than fifty million inhabitants at their lowest point, and that the regular army had gone down to 300,000 men in 1941 to 1942.

These Japanese offensives were supported by technically superior organization and logistics: aviation, heavy artillery, trucks, and telegraph lines. Nevertheless, the forces of the liberated zones managed to keep them in check. Their favorite tactic consisted of organizing counter-offensives outside the raking and cleanup areas. This was possible only because of their superior mobility, which was itself the result of support from the peasant population. These attacks on the rear lines forced the Japanese who had invaded the base at Jin-Cha-Ji in May 1942 to retreat. The same thing happened to a unit of 20,000 Japanese soldiers which had been sent against the Taiyue base in Shanxi. A group of high-ranking military observers that had been sent by the Japanese general staff to "draw lessons" from new anti-guerrilla methods fell into an ambush, and all its members were killed.

The peasant population was organized through self-defense units and the militia; by the end of the war, the militia had two and a half million members. The militia organized surveillance patrols and, relying on its knowledge of the terrain, carried out reprisal raids, infiltrated Japanese bases, and attacked collaborators and their properties. Primitive mines made with baked clay were spread throughout the zones where the Japanese passed. Their roads were cut by trenches. Their small forts were attacked through trench warfare and tunnel warfare, which was even deadlier.[7] All these clandestine activities depended on large-scale mobilization of peasant manpower; thousands of peasants were necessary to destroy railway lines and prevent the passage of enemy convoys.

The extension of liberated zones in 1944–1945

In 1944 and especially in 1945, the counter-offensive was expanded. The puppet troops came under the heaviest attack. Communist bases were enlarged in Shandong and Shanxi, as were those of the New Fourth Army in Jiangsu, to the north and the south of the mouths of the Yangzi. In the middle Yangzi region, at the borders of Hunan, Hubei, and Henan, resistance troops controlled

[7] See document 3.

territories of more than twelve million inhabitants. Their progress was equally striking in Guangdong. In 1944, according to the figures of the Communist general staff, resistance troops from North, Central, and South China engaged in 20,000 skirmishes and battles, captured 5,000 small forts, inflicted enemy losses of 260,000 killed or wounded, and took 60,000 prisoners. There were 30,000 puppet-troop soldiers who went over to the resistance forces, and 80,000 square kilometers, with nine million inhabitants, were recovered.

At the end of the war, the Japanese were practically surrounded in the large cities and their outlying districts. They only emerged when protected by heavy armored convoys, and land communications from one city to another became more and more precarious. Some cities, such as Baoding and Shijiazhuang, had even been occupied by the Eighth Army several times. These occupations were temporary but spectacular, and were undertaken for their propaganda value.

The Communists and those who engaged in the armed struggle with them controlled nineteen liberated zones by 1945. This represented a territory of 950,000 square kilometers, twice the size of France. The regular armies included 910,000 men, the militia 2,300,000 men, and the village self-defense units 10,000,000 men.

The seven oldest and most solid liberated zones were in North China near the large railway lines and the big cities. These were Shen-Gan-Ning, Jin-Cha-Ji, Jing-Ji-Yu, and those which were gradually consolidated on the borders of Hebei-Shandong-Henan, Shanxi-Suiyuan, Hebei-Jehol-Liaoning, and in the mountains in the interior of Shandong. Central China had ten bases in the peripheral regions of Zhejiang, Anhui, Jiangxi, Jiangsu, Hubei, and Hunan. This larger number merely meant that Communist infiltration was more recent, more superficial, and therefore more dispersed in the small units in Central China. The two bases in South China, east Guangdong and Hainan, were old and well established, although less extensive.

The Seventh Congress of the Communist Party

The Seventh Congress took place at Yanan in March 1945 at a time when the Japanese defeat was imminent. Fifty delegates and 208 deputies participated, representing 1,210,000 members.

The congress, the highest organized body of the Communist Party, had not met for seventeen years, and the Sixth Congress had been held in Moscow during a period of underground retreat. During this long interval the CCP's "sinuous line" (Mao) had faced many difficulties. There had been divergences between the Maoists and the leftist deviationists, the Jiangxi soviets had been undone, the Long March had taken place, and the guerrilla bases had been established after many hardships. The unity and cohesion of the CCP had only been re-established with the *zhengfeng* of 1941–1942. This unity was based on the new situation in China rather than on skillful political manipulation. The CCP had come to have considerable influence in Chinese affairs. Its strength came from eight years of struggle against Japan, from its armed forces and its liberated zones. This situation called for a total re-examination of its relations with the Guomindang.

At the Seventh Congress, Mao recalled the foolhardy decisions of the Sixth Congress. In 1928, the imminent renewal of the urban revolutionary struggle had been announced, even though the CCP had just been driven out of the cities. According to Mao, conditions were now ripe for seeing the adventurist illusion of 1928 as a possibility.

The major question was the organization of political power in China once the war was over. A coalition government was proposed by the CCP, and the question of coalition dominated the Seventh Congress. For more than a year, it was discussed in negotiations between Yanan and Chongqing, with the American ambassador to China, Patrick Hurley, participating in the talks. The lifting of the Nationalist blockade against the liberated zones was discussed at great length; so were the new political and military relations to be established between the Nationalists and the Communists. During the winter of 1944–1945, the Communists continued to have discussions with Chongqing, and various official missions were sent and received by both sides. But in March 1945, Tchiang Kaï-chek suddenly convened the national assembly of the Nationalist government. Such a unilateral measure eliminated much of the practical value of the Yanan-Chongqing negotiations for a Chinese central government. The Communists broke off discussions and preferred to use the occasion of the Seventh Congress for a systematic presentation of their proposals to the Chinese public.

Mao presented a very long report on the question of coalition government to the congress, based on an analysis of the two "lines" of current and future opposition. The Guomindang line was violently attacked for its "dictatorial" policy and the wait-and-see attitude on which this policy was founded. The other line was that of the people's war led by the Communists. Faced with these two lines, civil war had to be avoided and thus it was essential to form a coalition central government. The military command was to be unified, the freedom of democratic parties guaranteed, all authoritarian measures abolished, bureaucratic monopolies controlled, and farm rents reduced. All of these measures were similar to the ideas in "On New Democracy" (1940), but the coalition program also contained numerous references to Sun Yat-sen and to the "three people's principles." The Communist Party wanted to present itself as the heir to the Chinese democratic traditions that had survived in the Guomindang, to join forces with this aspect of the Guomindang, while bypassing the authoritarian leadership in Chongqing. But Mao's report on coalition government insisted that the liberated zones should remain intact during the transition period. The Communist Party should preserve its own forces in order to play the vanguard role it felt ready to take on.

Zhu De, commander of all the armed forces in the liberated zones, gave a military report to the congress on the experience of war in the liberated zones which stressed the political principles of people's war as Mao had defined them in his essays of 1937 and 1938.

Liu Shao-qi presented the congress's third in-depth report, "On the Party." This political and organizational evaluation included the proposal that the statutes of the CCP be reorganized, and involved a number of practical measures designed to combat elitism and bring the party and the popular masses closer together. This report called for a chairmanship of the CCP, above the position of secretary-general, and Mao Tsetung was elected to it. The new political orientation adopted at Zunyi and gradually consolidated in the liberated zones during the war against Japan had now been institutionalized.

The Northeast

The three northeastern provinces—Liaoning, Jilin, and Heilongjiang—were occupied by the Japanese and their auxiliaries from Manzhouguo in 1931. Resistance there was very weak in the beginning, confined to a few islands of Communists, several Guomindang groups, and most importantly, popular units made up of outlaws from the old secret societies, the Honghuzi (Red Beards).

This armed resistance had gradually become more widespread, and in September 1933 the Northeastern People's Revolutionary Army (Dongbei renmin gemingjun), consisting of six armed units, was founded. By 1936, this force had adopted the name of Dongbei kangri lianjun (Northeastern United Army of Anti-Japanese Resistance), following the general line of the Communist Party, and its numbers continued to grow, reaching eleven armed units at the beginning of the war. It included Communists, outlaws, and various other patriotic anti-Japanese groups. A large number of Koreans were active (there was a Korean minority of one million people in Northeast China), among them Communist cadres which had been driven out of their country by Japanese police repression. Many of these Korean Communists were superior officers and included the future leaders of the People's Republic of North Korea: Kim Il-sung, President Choe Yong-kin, Vice-President Kim Il.

During the first years of the war, the United Army was spectacularly successful, crushing entire units of the Japanese army, sometimes in pitched battles. Yet beginning in 1941, Japanese repression became much more severe. The units of the United Army deliberately struck in very small guerrilla groups and were only sporadically active. On the other hand, the liberated zones began spreading beyond the Great Wall in 1943 and 1944. The one farthest north, established at the borders of Hebei and Jehol, took on the zone name of Hebei-Jehol-Liaoning and extended far into southwestern Manchuria.

In 1945, these different resistance forces were just beginning to be important, when the Soviet army entered Manchuria on August 8 in accordance with the Yalta agreements. Its armored columns were very successful, but the atomic bomb forced Japan to surrender on August 14. The Northeast, to which the Communists returned in great numbers at the end of the war—and the northern part of which the Soviets had occupied—would play an important role in the 1946–1949 civil war.

ADDITIONAL BIBLIOGRAPHY

Jack Belden, *China Shakes the World* (New York, Monthly Review Press, 1970).

Chao Shu-li, *Le Printemps des villageois* (Paris, 1960).

―――, *Les rythmes de Li Yu-tsai* (Peking, 1966).

Chu Teh, *On the Battlefront of the Liberated Areas* (Peking, Foreign Languages Press, 1952).

Boyd Compton, ed. and trans., *Mao's China. Party Reform Documents 1942–1944* (Seattle, Washington University Press, 1966).

Harrison Forman, *Report from Red China* (New York, Holt, 1945).

George Stuart Gelder, *The Chinese Communists* (London, Gollancz, 1946).

Chalmers A. Johnson, *Peasant Nationalism and Communist Power: The Emergence of Revolutionary China, 1937–1945* (Stanford, Calif., Stanford University Press, 1962).

Récits de la guerre de résistance contre le Japon (Peking, Foreign Languages Press, 1961).

Mark Selden, *The Yenan Way in Revolutionary China* (Cambridge, Mass., Harvard University Press, 1971).

————, "The Yanan Legacy, the Mass Line," in A. Doak Barnett, *Chinese Communist Politics in Action* (Seattle, University of Washington Press, 1969).

Guenther Stein, *The Challenge of Red China* (New York, McGraw-Hill, 1945).

Lyman P. Van Slyke, *Enemies and Friends: the United Front in Chinese Communist History* (Stanford, Calif., Stanford University Press, 1967).

DOCUMENTS

1. WU MAN-YU, A LABOR HERO OF THE BORDER REGION

SOURCE: Harrison Forman, *Report from Red China* (New York, Henry Holt, 1945), pp. 63–64.

The first to start a labor exchange brigade, and prove its worth, was Wu Man-yu. When, back in 1939, he and a group of his neighbors demonstrated that collective effort was more efficient than the old system, hitherto hesitant peasants throughout the Border Region quickly took up the idea. The slogan of the labor exchangers today is: "Keep Pace with Wu Man-yu." Today Wu Man-yu is the Border Region's Labor Hero Number One. There are 180 such Labor Heroes in agricultural, industrial, army, cultural, and transportation fields. Wu Man-yu was the first to achieve this honor, which the Border Region Government conferred upon him in 1942. His portrait is hung prominently in galleries, homes, and public places alongside those of Mao Tsetung, Zhu De, and other high political and military figures.

Wu is sixtyish, strong-bodied, red-faced, with merry eyes and a friendly smile, a wispy white mustache, and a shiny bald head. He can neither read nor write, but he has an extraordinary knowledge of farming methods, together with a great ability to improvise and adapt. They made him a Labor Hero because he was able to cultivate three times as much land and raise three times as many crops as an average farmer. As a Labor Hero, Wu Man-yu, and others like him, are not only held in high esteem by the people but are invited to attend all public and state functions, at which they occupy seats of honor along with the highest government and military officials.

"Mao Tsetung himself came and called upon me several times and invited me to his home for dinner," he said proudly; "and actually shook my hand," he added, showing me his calloused palm. Not so many years ago, before the coming of the Red Army, Wu Man-yu came to Yanan as a destitute refugee from a famine-stricken area.

"I had to sell my three-year-old daughter for six pounds of corn to feed the rest of my family until I was able to cut enough firewood in the hills to buy more food and farm tools to till the acre of poor land that I rented," he continued. When the landlord had him thrown into jail for failure to pay his rent, his wife starved to death. The Communists came shortly afterward and divided up the landlord's land and Wu Man-yu got "one hill" as his portion. (The Border Region, by the way, today subsidizes refugees with land, farm implements, and food until they are able to become self-supporting.)

With this modest start Wu Man-yu in the past eight years has built up a farm of over sixty-five acres, all of which he has reclaimed from uncultivated wasteland. Moreover, he has a flock of forty sheep and goats, four oxen, one horse, four beehives, and "I don't know how many chickens," he concluded. He has invested thousands of dollars of his savings in a farmers' retail co-operative. Frequently the army, in its self-subsistence campaign, calls upon him to teach the soldiers his techniques.

2. A VILLAGE SONGWRITER ENCOURAGES THE PEASANT UNIONS AND MOCKS
A FALLEN FEUDALIST*

SOURCE: Zhao Shu-li, *Nouvelles choisies* (Peking, 1957).

> Form your union,
> Peasants, to be victorious;
> We will multiply our strength
> All of us united against the oppressor.
> Let us call Heng-yuan to account
> Without giving him any mercy:
> No more mortgages on our fields,
> Mortgages repaid like our money.
> Let us demand the reduction
> Of the rent on our houses, on our farms.
> And then the removal
> Of the bad cadres from the village.
> We will no longer let ourselves be duped
> Nor always burdened with forced labor.

* Zhao Shu-li's short story "The songs of Li Yu-cai" tells of the struggle for agrarian reform in the village of Yanjiashan. The feudal lord Heng-yuan succeeds for a while in deceiving the Communist cadres and getting one of his confederates elected mayor of the village. The peasants expose him, helped mainly by the songs that old Li Yu-cai improvises to give shape to the villagers' aspirations and to harass their enemy.

Let us greatly rejoice
Over these coming changes.
Then quickly form
The peasants' union.
A great event
In Yanjiashan:
The meeting is held,
Victory ensured.
Our old Heng-yuan
Has turned in his accounts,
Freed the land
And paid for his thefts!
As for Liu Guang-qiu,
He has been brought
Before the tribunal
For his misuse of public funds.
An end of suffering
From these injustices.
All the people of the village
Dance with joy because of it;
From the heart of the village
To its furthermost reaches
All the villagers
Sing of it with joy.

3. UNDERGROUND WARFARE: THE TUNNELS OF HEBEI

SOURCE: Harrison Forman, *Report from Red China* (New York, Holt, 1945), pp. 138–141.

From the very beginning their job had been to develop and co-ordinate the peasants' individual efforts in the People's War. Trained by the Balujun*—which had picked leader-types in every community for this work—they in turn organized Self-Defense Corps units in the villages surrounding their own homes. The people, long used to handling explosives in the making of firecrackers, were making crude mines of earthenware jugs, teapots, bottles, and tin cans packed with black powder and detonated by a simple fuse. Wang and Chao and scores of others trained by the Balujun taught them how to improve their mines by using heavy metal containers made from melted temple bells. The villagers were shown improved methods for planting and camouflaging mines as well as precautionary methods very necessary in the handling of these improved weapons. . . .

In some districts mine warfare has been developed to a fine art. Mine fields are laid at strategic points along the highway. From each

---

* Eighth Army of the Road. Name taken by the Red Army since the 1937 agreements with the Guomindang.

mine in the field a string runs through an underground system of brick tubes to a primitive "switchboard" in a farmhouse or other observation post near by. As an enemy column moves into the mine field the operator calmly pulls this or that string on the "switchboard." The mines explode like lights in a pinball machine as the bewildered enemy dashes back and forth in an effort to extricate himself from the field.

Innumerable booby traps litter the countryside: leaping mines, delayed mines, upside-down mines. . . .

In the early days of the war the villagers dug cellars under their houses, in which to hide from the enemy. . . .

So there exists in Central Hebei today an amazing system of tunnels linking hundreds of villages for miles and miles around, built on a scale that makes New York's subway system seem a child's toy railway by comparison. . . .

When the Japs discovered that the tunnels ran in straight lines from one village to the next, they dug deep lateral trenches in the fields so as to cut through and expose these tunnels. Thus they were able to isolate one village from its neighbors. . . .

Undaunted, the Central Hebei villagers devised new tunnel designs. Tunnels were built zigzag, and up and down; they connected, through emergency entrances, with wholly independent subsidiary tunnel systems at different levels going off in all directions. All the entrances were furnished with simple antigas devices, and provision was made to wall up and section off any portion of a tunnel system entered or exposed by the enemy.

Chapter Twelve

The Fall of
the Guomindang:
1945–1949

When Japan surrendered, the balance of forces between the Communists and the Guomindang seemed to weigh heavily in the Guomindang's favor. The Guomindang controlled the major portion of Chinese territory and had held its ground for eight years. Recognized as one of the five great powers, Nationalist China was supported by the most powerful countries in the world. Yet in less than four years the Nanking regime collapsed like the decadent "kings of perdition" whose reign had brought the dynasties to an end.

The civil war did not begin again, however, until spring 1946, after the failure of long and difficult negotiations for the forming of a coalition government with the Guomindang, the Communists, and the small groups from the center. For a little while, the Guomindang took the offensive. Militarily, this led to the capture of Yanan (March 1947) and, politically, to the convening of a national assembly in Nanking (March 1948), which was an attempt to reassure the good democratic conscience of the Americans. But the regime was undermined from within and was incapable of offsetting the growing strength of the liberated zones. The People's Republic of China was proclaimed on October 1, 1949, and the Guomindang was forced to take refuge in Taiwan.

Toward a Coalition Government?

With the exception of the extreme rightists in the Guomindang, few people felt that civil war was inevitable in 1945. The overwhelming mood of the people was for internal peace and the reconstruction of the country—two slogans which had found a large following since the Communists first used them on August 25, 1945. These aspirations and hopes were shared by a large proportion of the army and the central government. The Americans thought it possible to support these desires, at least temporarily, and then come to terms with the Communists. For their part, the Communists sought for as long as possible to reach a political agreement with the Guomindang. They did not go to war again until fifteen months later, when the people understood that all possibilities for agreement had been exhausted.

The surrender of Japan

The war did not formally end until August 14. As early as August 10, 1945, however, Zhu De ordered the Communist troops to advance, to accept the surrender of the Japanese, seize their military supplies, and occupy the villages—on the strength of the rights that had been acquired through eight years of struggle. But at the same time the Guomindang ordered the Japanese to surrender only to its own troops. Until the Nationalist troops arrived, Chongqing gave the Japanese the job of "keeping order." The same mission was assigned to the puppet troops of the Nanking pro-Japanese government. The Americans supported this intransigence. MacArthur, commander in chief of the Far East, gave Tchiang Kaï-chek the mission of receiving the Japanese surrender. The American army put at his disposal the necessary planes for the massive transportation of his troops to the North and Northeast, where the Japanese were encircled by the Communists.

Immediately following the war, then, two strategies and two claims to legitimacy came into conflict.

The Chinese Communists' position

The Communists drew their strength from the nineteen liberated zones that extended from the Siberian borders to the tropical island of Hainan, from their three million armed men (regulars and local militia); and from the moral authority they had achieved after eight years of struggle. On August 15, Mao publicly denounced Tchiang as a Fascist, accused him of wanting civil war, and denied him the right to speak in the name of the Chinese people. But the Communists also knew that the people wanted peace; therefore, it was necessary to make concessions, "concessions judged as necessary, which will not infringe upon the fundamental right of the Chinese people," Mao said on August 26, when political negotiations were begun between Yanan and Chongqing. "Without these concessions, we will not be able to shatter the Guomindang's plot for civil war, nor take the political initiative, nor gain the sympathy of the rest of the world as well as the sympathy of the centrist elements in our own country, nor obtain legal status for our party and a condition of peace. But these concessions have limits, the principal limit being that they must not violate the fundamental interests of the people." Until July 1946 the Chinese Communists strove to establish a coalition government, which they had proposed as early as March 1945, during their Seventh Congress. Militarily, their approach was the same as it had been during the war: counterattack energetically, but only when the Guomindang's forces attacked first.

The Chinese Communists had very little international backing for this line. The Soviet Union occupied Manchuria on August 9, according to the Potsdam agreement. On August 14, however, it signed a friendship treaty with the Guomindang. The Chinese Communists later declared that they "had not understood" Stalin's Chinese policy during that period.

The Guomindang's position: American support

Tchiang Kaï-chek still had some backing among the people. "Free China's" eight years of resistance had gained prestige for him, in China and abroad. But the fundamental authoritarianism and corruption of the Chongqing regime became even more widespread after the war. Governmental monopolies of the "four great families" and small smugglers quickly moved into the zones the Japanese had surrendered: the villages of the Northeast, the North and East, and Taiwan. They bought up everything, from big factories to the rags of imprisoned soldiers. In the zones where they resettled, American surplus gave them further opportunities to ac-

cumulate goods and speculate, as did the material provided by the
UNRRA, the United Nations Relief and Rehabilitation Agency.
"It is," said an American consul, "one of the biggest carpetbagging
operations in history."

American power was behind the Guomindang. The United States
gave it logistic aid (540,000 men brought back to the former
Japanese zones), financial aid (the lend-lease agreements were extended for the benefit of Guomindang China), and material aid
(military supplies and stock). Added to this was all that the
1,200,000 Japanese had left behind in China. In 1945, the Guomindang had an enormous war machine, which was reinforced by the
56,000 American marines who had landed at the northern ports
and by the "advisers" of the American Military Advisory Group,
which was formed in Nanking at the beginning of 1946.

As during the war, the basic American policy called for support
of the central government—to aid it in re-establishing power and
in putting an end to Chinese Communism—but without entering
immediately into civil war and without direct military intervention,
which neither international nor American opinion would tolerate.
The frictions between the Americans and Tchiang were as frequent
after the war as before. Wedemeyer and George Marshall criticized
the "generalissimo" as severely as Stilwell had. The Americans were
ready to make concessions where the Communists were concerned,
and the Communists themselves were aware of these contradictions
and were willing to play along. In August 1945, Mao arrived in
Chongqing in the airplane of the American ambassador, Patrick
Hurley. Zhou En-lai agreed to participate with Marshall and a general of the Guomindang in a three-party commission assigned to
enforce the January 1946 ceasefire agreement.

The Chongqing negotiations (October 1945)

On October 11, after several difficult weeks of negotiations, Mao
and Tchiang signed an agreement which provided for the withdrawal of the Communists from eight liberated zones (in the South),
the reduction of the Communist armies to twenty divisions (a tenth
of their forces), and a meeting of a Political Consultative Conference, which would be open to the Communists and to the center.
The Communists made substantial concessions, but they did not
want to relinquish all their liberated zones and armies unless the

central power became democratic. The Guomindang's priorities were the reverse.

During autumn 1945, the Chongqing agreement worked poorly. The Political Consultative Conference project was at an impasse. Tchiang reissued copies of his 1933 *Manual on the Suppression of Communist Bandits* for his military cadres and launched offensives against the Communist bases of Suiyuan, Shanxi, and Kalgan. Political repression was severe. On December 15, secret agents attacked a meeting of liberal students at Kunming, the incident resulting in four deaths and many wounded. Such examples were becoming increasingly common.

Spectacular trials were held against Japanese collaborators, and several scapegoats were executed, including Chen Gong-bo. But the puppet troops, the official collaborators, and even the Japanese were left untouched in the formerly occupied territories. "I don't understand anything," said American Consul John Melby in December. "Officially the Japanese are disarmed, but in Shanghai fifteen thousand of them patrol the streets fully armed, and in the North tens of thousands guard the railways and help to fight the Communists."

At Chongqing, the Communists signed an agreement at the "summit meeting," but at the same time they were looking for support from the base. This was the Gao Zho-Xiun Movement (named after a general of the Guomindang who went over to the Communist side in October with his men).

The Marshall mission

General Marshall, the former chief of staff of the U.S. army, arrived in China as President Truman's special envoy in December. According to Dean Acheson, then under-secretary of state, his mission consisted of "trying to stave off civil war through a compromise between the two parties, and helping the Nationalists to establish their authority over as large a portion of China as possible." In effect, these two objectives were incompatible, and the second quickly took precedence over the first.

In January, a ceasefire agreement between the Communists and the Nationalists was signed. The two sides also agreed to stop all troop movements. Supervision of the agreement was put in the hands of a tripartite military organization set up in Peking (Communists, Nationalists, and Americans). That same month, the Political Consultative Conference met in Peking with delegates from the CCP, the Guomindang, and the Democratic League. As the majority of the Democratic League became more and more sharply opposed to the Guomindang, its moderate elements (the Young China Party) broke away in October 1945 to join Tchiang.

Under the pressure of public opinion, the conference adopted five resolutions which amounted to a step backward for the Guomindang: reorganization of the central government with democratic participation of parties, national reconstruction, extensive modification of the Nationalist military system (which could pave the way for a fusion with the Communist troops), the convening of a national assembly, and finally a democratic constitution granting a large degree of provincial autonomy.

The Guomindang did not truly accept this surrender. In March its Central Committee disavowed the Consultative Conference and Marshall let it happen. Signs of a tightening of policy in the Guomindang were increasing: a secret service attack against a meeting in Chongqing celebrating the Consultative Conference; police raids against the Democratic League; refusal to free political prisoners; and the destruction of the Communist newspaper offices. The Communists denounced these violations, but without retaliating at the time. The Americans did no more than characterize them as vaguely troubling.

The Manchurian crisis

The Northeast, formely Manzhouguo, had been occupied by the Soviets since the Japanese surrender. They had taken advantage of the situation by dismantling the heavy installations, especially electric works, as "war booty"—which the Guomindang had exploited to develop anti-Communist propaganda in the interior. The departure of the Soviets, delayed many times, was finally scheduled for the end of the winter of 1946. The Guomindang was impatient to set itself up in their place, and the Communists protested against this as a violation of the ceasefire agreement forbidding all movement of troops. The Americans admitted the validity of such objections and Wedemeyer and Marshall worried that Tchiang, in occupying the Northeast, risked stretching dangerously his lines of communication. Nevertheless, they furnished him with the necessary air transport. Thus the Guomindang was able to occupy Moukden in March, immediately after the departure of the Soviets.

The Communists then decided to counter. They took the key position at Sipingkai, in north Moukden, and defended it for a month. This was the first major battle of the civil war. The two sides each had 100,000 men. The advance of the Nationalist troops was blocked long enough for the Communists to entrench themselves in the back-country. In this region, which had been cut off from the rest of China since the formation of Manzhouguo in 1931, the Communist guerrillas had had little effect until this time. When the Communists evacuated Sipingkai in May, Tchiang's troops were reduced to occupying only the large cities of the Northeast: Moukden, Changchun, Jilin, and Anshan. They were already encircled here, and these were the first cities to fall in 1948. Immediately after the departure of the Soviets, the Communists occupied Harbin and all of the northern regions of the country.

Peasant struggles in the liberated zones (1945–1946)

The political line adopted during the war in the liberated zones gave absolute priority to the struggle against Japan. Yet the more fundamental struggle of the peasants against their feudal exploiters had not been abandoned. The connection between the patriotic and agrarian struggles of the peasants was based on the support that the vast majority of the *dizhu* had given Japan. Immediately following the Japanese surrender, the transition to the antifeudal struggle was accomplished on the same foundation, and the leaders of the liberated zones launched a "movement against the traitors." The collaborationist landlords were denounced in village assemblies, their goods confiscated, and their accounts and debts owed them liquidated.

From there, a direct agrarian defense policy of the poor and middle peasants was developed. In 1946, on the basis of the November 7 (1945) Directive, a mass movement was launched for the reduction of rents and interest rates in all liberated zones. In May 1946, a new and more radical directive revived the slogan "The land belongs to the tiller." The land belonging to the landowners was "bought back," but paid for with vouchers distributed by local authorities. The reduction of rent was declared retroactive, forcing landlords to pay considerable sums to the peasants. Extremely heavy taxes also hit the *dizhu*. With the decisive battles between the CCP and the Guomindang approaching, the Communists opened the way for agrarian revolution and prepared for the mobilization of the peasant masses against the Nanking property owners.

Toward civil war

Of the two initial aims of General Marshall's mission—searching for a compromise and supporting the Nationalists—the second had a clear priority in spring 1946. The Guomindang government, which had moved to Nanking in April, was given 51 million dollars in long-term credit by a vote of the American congress in June.

Fighting continued in the Northeast, and the number of the Nationalists' offensives against the Communist troops increased in June. A truce was signed for fifteen days, on June 7, but this only resulted in an ultimatum from Tchiang passed on to Zhou En-lai by Marshall. The Communists refused to evacuate their principal positions in the North and Northeast, as their enemies demanded. Nor was the Guomindang willing to offer a single reciprocal concession. The truce ended and the Communists no longer hesitated to engage wholeheartedly in the civil war.

They knew that in the eyes of the people they had given proof of their good will and patience, and that the Guomindang bore much of the responsibility for the failure of the attempts to reach a reconciliation—from the agreements of October 1945, which were never put into effect, to the ultimatum-truce of June 1946. Militarily, the CCP had responded only locally to the numerous incidents provoked by Tchiang's troops, which had openly sabotaged the January ceasefire agreements. Politically, the defeat of projects unanimously adopted at the January Consultative Conference was due to the bad will of the Guomindang. Thus, public opinion was ready to accept what had been unthinkable fifteen months earlier: the taking up of arms to settle the conflict between the Nationalists and the Communists.

These fifteen months had not only been a test of the behavior of the CCP and the Guomindang, but also of the Nationalist government's ability to manage China's affairs. The government was assured of the services of the Japanese and their detested collaborators, but it was soon discredited by its speculations, corruption, and negligence. Inflation and rising prices had continued in the Nationalist zones,[1] at a time when the austere integrity of the liberated zones brought prestige and fame to the Communists. The Mandate of Heaven was once again in the process of changing hands.

---

[1] The amount of paper money in circulation increased from 189 billion Chinese dollars at the end of 1944 to 1 trillion at the end of 1945 and 3.7 trillion at the end of 1946. The price index (100 in 1937) rose from 75,500 at the end of 1944 to 627,210 at the end of 1946.

Guomindang Offensives and Their Defeat: *July 1946–1947*

Military offensives

The size and scope of the military offensives undertaken in the summer of 1946 by the Nationalist forces confirmed how long they had been wanting to go to war. For the ultra-conservative civilian and military elements of Nanking, this seemed to present an opportunity to finish the business that had been begun in Shanghai on the night of April 11, 1927, and continued in South China between 1934 and 1935: to settle their score with the Chinese Communists once and for all, by liquidating them militarily.

In June 1946, close to two million men attacked the large Communist bases in North and Central China. They pushed back the Communist forces from the central plain and the lower Yangzi. In August, they seized Chengde, the capital of the liberated zone of Jehol; in October, Kalgan, the capital of the liberated region of Shanxi-Chahar-Hebei; in January 1947, Linyi, the center of the liberated zone of southern Shandong; in March 1947, Yanan, which had been the heart and symbol of the Chinese Communist movement since the Long March.

The Communists did not try to defend these territories and cities, but rather to disengage their forces while harassing their adversaries. This strategy of mobile defense and the return to guerrilla warfare proved fruitful. The military strength of the Communists remained essentially intact, and a series of surprise attacks in the area of the Longhai railway, in southern Shandong and Shanxi, and in the lower Yangzi allowed their troops to weaken the Nationalist forces, whose lines of communication had been stretched dangerously thin during their offensives. From June 1946 to February 1947, the Communists announced that they had put 710,000 men out of action. The loss of Yanan was more symbolic than significant since at the same time the Communists had regained control of the vast and rich regions of neighboring Shanxi. As Marshal Yan Xi-shan—governor of Shanxi and ally of his old adversary, Tchiang Kaï-chek—remarked, not without malice, the Guomindang, in the final analysis, had done little more than trade a well-fattened cow for an emaciated horse.

Political offensives

On June 4, 1946, the State Council, hoping to crush the Communist revolution and open the way to peaceful reconstruction, declared that China was in a state of national mobilization. The mobilization order signed by Tchiang provided for military conscription, the revival of the tax on grain, as in wartime, and the strengthening of political surveillance.

General Marshall undoubtedly did not consider his mission as mediator completed. In August, Zhou En-lai, who had remained in Nanking despite the deteriorating situation, agreed once again to consider a proposal by the Guomindang to establish a "Committee of Five"—one American, two members of the Guomindang, and two Communists—who would be responsible for drawing up a plan to reorganize the State Council. This proposal was accompanied by a repetition of the June ultimatum (unconditional evacuation by the Communists from the vast liberated zones). Zhou refused and made it known that before participating in the Committee of Five, the Communists demanded that an immediate ceasefire be put into effect as well as a guarantee that the State Council not be set up in such a way that the Guomindang would control a majority and block decisions. The discussions dragged on into the autumn, but it was clear that the Guomindang was determined to impose its own political solutions, to abandon the line laid out in Chongqing in January by the Consultative Conference, and to establish new political institutions in opposition to the Communists.

In October, encouraged by the capture of Kalgan (the largest town held by the Communists), the Guomindang unilaterally convened the National Assembly at Nanking, such as it had existed before the war, setting aside only a few seats for the CCP and the Democratic League, both of which refused to attend. Only two small groups of the right center—the Young China Party and the Social Democrat Party—agreed to participate in the National Assembly, hoping to exert some liberal influence on the Guomindang. In December, the assembly adopted an authoritarian constitution which put extensive power in the hands of the President of the Republic, Tchiang Kaï-chek.

From this time on, a politically negotiated settlement between the Guomindang and the Communists became impossible. Marshall returned to the United States. In February 1947, the Communist Central Committee called for the overthrow of the Nationalist government. The remaining Communist missions in Chongqing, Nanking, Shanghai, and Peking were closed in March; Zhou En-lai had returned to Yanan in November, in protest against the convening of the National Assembly. In March, the Nanking government (the *yuan* executive branch) was expanded for form's sake to include the participation of politicians from the right center who had gone over to Tchiang's side in November. In July, the government abolished the last political body which had supported the Consultative Conference and kept alive the hopes for national reconciliation the conference had inspired. In autumn, in accordance with the new constitution, elections were held. The candidates of the extreme right of the Guomindang (the Central Club) won an enormous victory. Nanking was no longer even able to give seats to independent candidates, whose participation would have helped keep up a certain appearance of democracy it found useful for maintaining the good opinion of America.

Reinforcement of American support to Nanking

In August 1946, the United States handed over considerable supplies to the Guomindang which had been taken from the Pacific islands at the end of the war. These supplies, which were valued at 900 million dollars, were declared "civilian," whatever military use they might have (trucks, for example), and were leased for 175 million dollars at very easy credit terms. Military materiel was given directly on several occasions. American pilots took charge of the Chinese airline company, which became associated with CAT (China Air Transport, which was run directly by the Americans).

This help, however, led to tighter and tighter American control over the activities of the Nationalist authorities. MAG (Military Advisory Group) had considerable power over the Chinese army, just as SACO (Sino-American Cooperation Organization) had considerable power over the police, although theoretically they were only supposed to be advisers. In November and December 1947, the Sino-American Assistance Pact and the Naval Pact further strengthened the influence of the United States over the Nationalist army, the navy, finance, and the economy. In his report of July 1947, General Wedemeyer, President Truman's special envoy in charge of a fact-finding mission, recommended giving the Chinese substantial aid for five years. At the same time, he also proposed establishing American control over Manchuria through a United

Nations trusteeship and bringing American "advisers" into all the important operations of the Nationalist government.

In the area of economics and finance, direct aid (in dollars) and indirect aid (by accepting nominal exchange rates) were also given. American technicians in the fields of agriculture, irrigation, and industry arrived in large numbers, recruited by the U.S. government through agencies of the United Nations. But the same dependent relationship was established. The November 1946 Sino-American Treaty of Commerce and Navigation, under the guise of a reciprocity, opened China to American products, especially war surplus items that could not be sold in the United States. By 1946, the United States occupied a preponderant place in China's foreign commerce: 51 percent of all imports (as opposed to 22 percent in 1936) and 57 percent of all exports (compared to 19 percent in 1936).

America's economic inroads, especially the 1946 treaty, blocked the expansion projects of the Chinese bourgeoisie, except for the compradors and others who directly benefitted from American aid. In 1948, therefore, a large portion of this bourgeoisie was pushed toward political collaboration with the Communists.

The economic and social crisis in the Guomindang zones

Having seized upon the Japanese industrial goods and equipment of China in 1945, and controlling financial and banking relations with America, the leading groups of the Guomindang (the "bureaucratic capitalists") dominated Chinese economic life. They controlled 70 to 80 percent of industrial production (37 percent of the spinning mills, 38 percent of the coal, 60 percent of the cloth works, 84 percent of electricity, 90 percent of the steel). Through the large state banks and speculation on the difference between the official rate and the "free" rate of the American dollar, they made profits which led to further economic deterioration.

In spite of their almost legendary financial talent, such people as T. V. Soong and H. H. Kung were incapable of stabilizing the state finances. Scarcely 25 percent of the budget was provided by fiscal resources, because neither the landowners nor the "four great families" paid any taxes. Ten percent of the budget came from reserves of hard cash which had accumulated during the war. The remainder was supplied by inflation: 3.7 trillion paper dollars were in circulation at the end of 1946 and 33 trillion by the end of 1947.

The price index (100 in 1937) increased to 627,210 by the end of 1947. The summer floods in 1946, which ravaged large regions of North China, provided new proof of the incompetence and negligence of the government.

In June 1947, the American consul at Moukden delivered a report to the American ambassador which showed little optimism concerning the Guomindang's future: the military situation was deteriorating, personal quarrels were splitting the command, the vitality of the Communists was disorganizing and upsetting the balance of the government forces, the economic situation was crumbling, the morale of the population was at its lowest point, and the local population was ready to welcome any change. The report painted a graphic picture of the corruption, inefficiency, and disarray of a government on the brink of disaster.[2]

The opposition movement in the Guomindang zones

The popular discontent which swelled in the diverse regions and among various groups reflected the decline of the Guomindang's authority. This discontent was sometimes led by underground Communist cadres, but more often than not it was expressed in spontaneous outbursts which undermined the Guomindang from within, wore away what remained of its legitimacy, and prepared the way for a radical change in the system.

The student movement, which had fully awakened, demonstrated all these characteristics. At the end of 1946, the rape of a Peking student by an American soldier incited the universities and high schools to go on strike and organize demonstrations which involved approximately 500,000 young people. In May 1947, a "New May Fourth Movement" was proclaimed. Shanghai students demonstrated against the civil war, rising prices, and financial speculation. This led to student movements in Peking, Nanking, Moukden, and other cities. On May 20, police lashed out in Tientsin and Nanking. They wounded many people and made mass arrests, which led to more student disturbances in May and June. Repression increased; there were 13,000 arrests in two months. In autumn 1947, after the murder of a Hangzhou student by a secret service agent, a new wave of student strikes was touched off; it became known as "the movement for the protection of civil rights."

[2] U.S. Relations with China (Blue Book), p, 242.

After a long period of inactivity, the workers' movement started up again in the large cities. In May 1947, riots and strikes broke out in Shanghai protesting the high cost of living and the hunger it was causing. A police station was attacked. At the same time, "rice riots," triggered by rising prices, broke out in the cities of the lower Yangzi. In December 1946, 5,000 Shanghai shop owners demonstrated against police repression and restrictive regulations and mobbed a police station.

In the areas of the countryside held by the Guomindang, even far from the Communist military forces, peasant agitation started up again in its traditional forms: demonstrations, riots, refusals to pay taxes and rent, and attacks on the rent collectors. These traditional manifestations of the "withdrawal of the Heavenly Mandate" coincided this time with the agrarian revolution, which was being led by the Communists in the liberated zones.

Regional dissidence in Taiwan and Xinjiang, which was not led by the Communists either, weakened the Guomindang and expressed the same popular impatience with a detested and unbearable regime. In Taiwan, which was reoccupied in 1945, the new administration of the Guomindang was so unpopular that riots broke out in February 1947. They were brutally quelled by troops sent from the continent which killed approximately 10,000 people.[3]

Xinjiang had been nominally under Guomindang control after Sheng Shi-cai's break with Moscow. But this restoration did not benefit anyone except the army officers, the Nanking officials, and the profiteers who returned with them. In 1944, the Ouighour autonomist forces, supported by the widespread disenchantment among the people, created an autonomist Republic of Eastern Turkey. In 1946, Nanking tried to negotiate a compromise and make room for the autonomists, who were led by Saifudin (1914–   ), in the provincial government of Urumchi. In 1947, the Ouighour autonomists broke with Nanking once again and formed a dissident government in the Yili Valley which the Guomindang was unable to defeat.

As had been the case with the student movements, brutal repression only increased resistance and pushed the non-Communist opponents to a more radical position. The poet Wen Yi-duo, an intellectual associated with the Democratic League, was murdered in the streets of Kunming in broad daylight in the summer of 1946

[3] See document 1 at the end of the chapter.

by the local military authorities, who did little to cover up their actions. The liberals, who were deeply shocked, sought a rapprochement with the Communists, especially after the league was banned in October 1947. In May 1947, "provisional measures for the maintainance of order" outlawed strikes, demonstrations, and even petitions of more than ten people. The "third way," which had been sought for a long time by many people and which the United States (particularly Marshall) was holding as a trump card, was closed to the centrist elements, the business bourgeoisie that was not tied to the United States, and the intellectuals; they went into exile in Hong Kong or even went into the liberated zones.

In Hong Kong, the exiles from the league joined forces with the dissidents from the Guomindang: Mme. Sun Yat-sen, the widow of Liao Zhong-kai, the Christian marshal Feng Yu-xiang, Marshal Li Ji-shen, and Cai Ting-kai, leader of the 1934 revolt in Fujian. In January 1948, they created a Guomindang Revolutionary Committee, which in its first statement declared that they were prepared to fight with the Communists to overthrow the Guomindang and resist American intrusion into China.

Political strengthening of the liberated zones

Harshly attacked at the end of 1946 and the beginning of 1947, the liberated zones were still able to hold together. The solid bonds established between the peasants and the cadres during the war against Japan were a major factor. The peasants gave information and provisions to the retreating guerrillas, hid the cadres, and cleared out areas as the Nanking troops approached. In exchange, their demands increased, and they were no longer satisfied with the moderate objectives (reduction of rent and interest rates) of the period between 1937 and 1945. The peasants were no longer at war against the Japanese, but against the Guomindang and the hated landowners. The upsurge of agrarian radicalism in 1947 coincided with the political goals of the Communists, who wanted to deprive the Guomindang of all political support in the countryside and cut it off from the rear. This was why the October 1947 Agrarian Reform Law called for the confiscation of the lands and other goods of the landowners without indemnity. The rich peasants, who were the natural allies of the landowners, lost only those lands which exceeded their basic needs. This reform was put into effect on October 10, the date of the official Nationalist holiday, and the date on which, in 1946, Nanking had convened a National Assembly, which it hoped would remain submissive. Within several months, throughout the liberated zones controlled by the Communists, a hundred million peasants had been affected by the reform and had received land.

These measures were not carried out simply by administrative decisions from above. In the villages, the peasants' anger, which had already begun to rise in 1946, was unleashed. There were public meetings for accusations and the "airing of bitterness"; landowners, as well as their friends and family, were tried and often punished physically. There were searches for hidden goods; titles of ownership, rent accounts, and usury lists were destroyed. This tidal wave became known in the West, particularly through the reports and investigations of the British and American authors who were in China at the time: David and Isabel Crook, Jack Belden, and, above all, William Hinton. As agrarian reform progressed, the rift between the rich and poor peasants became more noticeable. The "Committees of Poor Peasants" were in sole charge of carrying out an agrarian struggle that gave them a chance to throw off their centuries-old yoke, to denounce the sexual terrorism of the gentry, forced marriage, the despotism of in-laws, and domestic slavery.[4]

One of the key words of the 1947 agrarian reform was *fanshen*, "turning one's skin inside out" to create a new man through struggle (one is reminded of Saint Paul's "casting off of the old man"). Often the Communist cadres lagged behind this movement, paradoxically clung to their power, preferred to engage in a personal kind of politics, and looked for profits and advantages.[5] The Communist Party, Mao recalled in December 1947, had grown in ten years from twenty or thirty thousand members to 2,700,000, and this growth posed certain problems. In the liberated zones in 1947 to 1948, the crisis was serious enough for the authorities to organize, as they had done in 1941 to 1942, a rectification campaign. The local party organizations were reorganized; party members had to "pass through the door," a process which required them to appear in front of the peasants' assemblies, which had the right to criticize them harshly before readmitting them or disciplining them.

The liberated zones were in full flower in 1947. Their vitality, their frugal and fraternal atmosphere, and their democratic prac-

---

[4] See document 2.
[5] See document 3.

tices contrasted sharply with the political and moral decomposition of the Guomindang zones. The experience accumulated during the eight years of war against Japan in popular politics, in the struggle for economic autonomy, mass culture, and ideological development was now put to work in the struggle against the Guomindang and the landowners. On the other hand, the liberated zones were isolated internationally. The European Communist parties clung to the line dictated by Stalin, who was less and less able to understand the dynamism of Chinese communism. The Chinese mistrusted them and did not hide the fact that they were putting up with a compromise which allowed a vast area of American influence to remain in Central and South China. Responding to this state of isolation, Mao, in his August 1946 interview with Anna Louise Strong, launched the slogan: "Imperialism is a paper tiger" which should not be appeased.

The Communists' military counter-offensive (late 1947)

In June 1946, the Communists were only able to set a little more than a million men against the Guomindang's four million men, who were supported by aircraft and heavy artillery. But the Guomindang troops were severely handicapped by the length of their supply lines (from Yunnan to Siberia); by the heaviness and costliness of American materiel (which often could not be used against the guerrillas); by the tension between Tchiang's personal troops and the other Nationalist armies; and by the internal rivalries within the high command. High-ranking generals like Xue Yue, who had defended Hunan against the Japanese, Tang En-bo, leader of Henan, and Tou Yu-ming, were fired during the summer of 1945, under the pretext of incompetence.

The Communist strategy, inspired by the experience acquired during the war against Japan, exploited the differences and weaknesses within the Guomindang and depended, above all, on the political support of the people. Even when the peasants were left without the presence of the Red Army, the people did not lose confidence. The CCP's first task was to wipe out the enemy forces without trying to occupy or defend territories. As a September 1946 Communist directive explained, it was essential to "concentrate superior forces in order to annihilate enemy forces one by one." In this way, the Communists hoped to compensate on the local level for their numerical inferiority on the national level.

Behind this Communist strategy was the conviction that the generals and the Guomindang troops were not fighting for a cause and therefore would be gradually defeated.

In 1947, the Communist offensive not only allowed Lin Biao's troops to defeat numerous enemy forces, but to complete the occupation of the Northeast and encircle the three large cities of the region: Changchun, Jilin, and Moukden. At the same time, a counter-offensive was launched in the central plain. The troops of Communist generals Liu Bo-cheng and Chen Yi, coming from Shanxi and Shandong respectively, crossed the Yellow River and the Longhai railway in the summer of 1947. By the end of the year, Communists controlled the greater part of the provinces Hebei, Shandong, and Shanxi, and had occupied Shijiazhuang, the first major city captured by the Guomindang since the beginning of the civil war. According to the Communists' estimates, in the period following July 1946 they had defeated 56 brigades in February 1947, 90 brigades in May 1947, and 97 brigades in September. This amounted to nearly a million men, a quarter of the Nationalist troops. Their own forces had grown from one to two million men.

Nationalist Collapse and the Coming to Power of the People's Republic of China: *1948–1949*

The growth of anti-Americanism and the political collapse of the Guomindang

The last American ambassador to China, John Leighton Stuart, former president of the American Missionary University of Peking, gave up all hope of a mediated settlement after Marshall's departure. Washington's policy was to support the Guomindang in its struggle against Chinese and international communism, if not "to take virtual control of the economic, military, and governmental administration of China."[6] The China Aid Act of April 1948 provided the Guomindang with 400 million dollars, bringing the total given them since 1945 to more than three billion dollars. In 1948, American control of China became less and less discreet; there were military advisers, bank dealings, and economic experts, and the

---

[6] *U.S. Relations with China (Blue Book)*, p. 382.

Americans even began to control Chinese foreign relations. Washington urged Nanking to consider a reconciliation with MacArthur's Japan against the common Communist enemy and to accept Japan's remilitarization. The student movement, which had started up again in February and March in the large universities of the Nationalist zone, swelled in May and June and became an anti-American protest movement against the project to remilitarize Japan. There were hundreds and thousands of demonstrators throughout the entire country. Stuart, a former professor, only aggravated the tension when he reproached the students for neglecting their work, for letting themselves be influenced by agitators, and for being ungrateful toward the United States.

In a country that had just emerged from an eight-year period of mobilization for "national salvation," the less and less disguised collusion between Nanking and Washington further weakened the Nationalist government. A very popular cartoon compared Tchiang to Wu San-gui, a general of the Ming dynasty who in the seventeenth century had roused the Manchus against the revolting peasants and thereby surrendered China to a foreign power.

In April 1948, a meeting in Nanking of the recently elected National Assembly provided an opportunity for an enormous propaganda campaign. This democratic facade was extremely fragile. Tchiang was unanimously elected "constitutional" president, but his power remained intact. Clan rivalry grew worse within the Guomindang and Li Zong-ren, head of the Guangxi clique, was elected vice-president against Sun Fo, the official candidate. But this final attempt to transplant parliamentary government onto Chinese soil came too late and was not sincere in any case. Tchiang raised neither his own prestige nor that of the assembly by declaring before it that "the economic situation is constantly improving."

Economic collapse

In 1948, the Nationalist zones were paralyzed. The price index (100 before the war) rose to 10,300,000 at the end of 1947, and to 287,000,000 by the end of 1948. Between January and July the value of the U.S. dollar on the Shanghai black market increased forty-five fold. Civil servants and teachers were paid with rice. Everyone tried to get rid of the cumbersome paper money (to save face the government refused to print any notes worth more than

10,000 yuan), which was devalued by the evening of the very day
it was printed. Shopkeepers and administrators spent their time
readjusting prices and wage scales. Production in the major cities,
which the rural areas depended on, came to a halt for lack of basic
materials. Supplies became scarce. The ruling classes panicked, and
the rising prices caused terrible hardships among the people. In
Shanghai, there were 300,000 unemployed workers, and 6,000
refugees arrived each day. Violent strikes became widespread, even
though the yellow unions of the Guomindang prided themselves on
having recruited 500,000 of the 800,000 workers in the city.

The American agencies of the Economic Cooperation Administration, which had been set up by the China Aid Act, spent all their
time trying to provide essential goods to the thirteen million people
living in the seven largest cities. Tchiang's son, Jiang Jing-guo, was
ineffectual when given extensive powers to re-establish economic
stability in Shanghai. He announced severe measures against speculators, but took action only against several minor figures, not daring
to attack the big smugglers who supported the government. He
resigned after several months. In August 1948, Nanking made another effort to improve the situation: the paper yuan was replaced
by the "gold yuan," at an exchange rate of 3,000,000 to 1. But
after only a few weeks, inflation and prices were again rising at the
same rate.

Old and new liberated zones

In June 1948, before the Communists' great military offensives,
the population of the liberated zones was greater than what it had
been in 1946: there were 168 million inhabitants and 3 million men
in arms. The liberated zones had thus considerably overflowed the
traditional peasant bastions of Communist resistance during the
war against Japan. These new liberated zones were different from
the old ones geographically, sociologically, and politically. They
were situated in flat, open country which was more extensive and
less remote; they included major cities, had industrial potential, and
comprised members of the middle classes and the bourgeoisie; and
their experience in mass revolutionary struggle was much less com-
prehensive. The administrative problems that the CCP faced in
these new liberated zones were much more complex and became
even more so as the moment for taking control of the entire country

approached. A report presented to the Central Committee of the Communist Party by Mao Tsetung in December 1947 ("The Present Situation and Our Tasks") elaborated on the CCP's major political and military strategies during the last period of the civil war: the change from the defensive to the offensive, from guerrilla warfare to a tactical war and increased offensives against the big cities; elimination of leftist errors committed during the course of the 1947 agrarian reform and union with the middle peasants; "rectification" of the party cadres; and cooperation with the middle classes and national capitalists in the cities.

In setting up agrarian reform, many leftist errors had in fact been committed by the Committees of Poor Peasants, which too often rushed into attacking the middle peasants rather than the rich peasants and landowners. These excesses were dealt with in 1948. In the new liberated zones an even more flexible policy was adopted. The "February and May directives" recommended acting in stages, beginning with a policy of reducing rents, without suddenly trying to enforce the radical measures that had been decided upon in 1947 in a much tenser political atmosphere.

In the new liberated zones, the Communists' most important task was to reassure the middle classes and the bourgeoisie, to gain their political confidence, and to make it possible to revive industrial production and the urban economy. The Communists hoped to achieve this goal by capitalizing on the antagonism which existed between the well-to-do urban classes and the leading groups of the Guomindang, which were responsible for the economic depression in the Nationalist zone. In April 1948, when the Communist troops re-entered Luoyang, the historic capital of the Tang dynasty, Mao sent them a telegram, advising them to be prudent and suggesting that they temporarily leave the officials alone. He recommended that it would be unwise to rush quickly into organizing movements for salary increases or democratic reforms, and forbade the peasants to go into the cities to settle their scores with their landowners.

The CCP thus re-entered the major cities again in 1948, renewing a tradition that had been interrupted twenty-one years earlier. That same year, the Sixth National Congress of Chinese Labor Unions was symbolically held at Harbin, the first since May 1927 in Wuhan.

During this period of transition the army played an essential political role. "Turn the army into a work force," recommended Mao in February 1949. The army was supposed to be economically self-sufficient and, instead of being a burden on the liberated cities, was to provide them with experienced cadres. The same was true for the Communist Party, which had expanded enormously since 1945, to a membership of approximately three million in 1948. Directives were issued frequently in order to strengthen the party's internal organization and improve the cadres' education, work methods, and above all their contact with the base. The objective was to promote a collective leadership by committee on all levels.

In 1948, the prestige of the old and new liberated zones was considerable. Intellectuals, students, and young people left the big cities, which were isolated and under siege, to join what many of them already considered to be the "New China" (Xinhua).

Progress of the United Front

The term New China implied a much greater emphasis on the tasks of national reconstruction and broad popular unity than on the civil war and the victory of one side over the other. As the balance of power leaned decisively toward them, the Chinese Communists became very attentive to the problems of the United Front. The Guomindang group became more and more isolated and was only able to survive due to American support.

As in the early forties, political control in the liberated zones was in the hands of the various organizations of the New Democracy, which provided a large place for the independents and democrats, including the "enlightened gentry."

But it was particularly with the centrist groups that the Communists sought a rapprochement in order to isolate the Nanking Nationalists; they appealed to the Guomindang dissidents who had gone to Hong Kong, to liberal intellectuals, and to businessmen hostile to Tchiang. On May 1, 1948, the Central Committee called for a new Political Consultative Conference, which would bear the same name as the group that had met unsuccessfully in 1946, only this time it would exclude reactionaries. Its purpose would be to discuss the formation of a coalition government. Preliminary negotiations had been going on for several months. On May 5, favorable responses arrived from the Democratic League, the Revolutionary Committee of the Guomindang (the dissidents from Hong Kong), and numerous other groups, including the League for the Autonomy of Taiwan and the Zhigongdang. This last organization was influential with Chinese abroad, and was the direct heir of the ancient

Triad, or Society of the Sky and Earth, a large anti-Manchurian organization of imperial times.

In Xinjiang, the Nanking government made a last-ditch attempt to preserve what power it still had by giving the governorship to the Ouighour autonomist James Burhan (1894–   ). But Burhan allowed the Xinjiang League to remain active. This league, an organization for the protection of peace and democracy led by Saifudin and the group from the Yili Valley, was one the Communists were eager to have on their side. In 1949, Burhan, Saifudin, and their friends immediately gave their support to the Communists after the proclamation of the People's Republic of China.

In November 1948, the centrist parties signed an agreement with the CCP concerning a new Consultative Conference; a preparatory committee was set up and met in June 1949 in the recently liberated Peking. In July, for the CCP's twenty-eighth anniversary, Mao Tsetung wrote one of his basic works, "On the People's Democratic Dictatorship," which was addressed to the Communists' allies and sympathizers. Mao insisted that the Communist Party must play the leading role in the country's affairs, with the agreement of all the groups and classes hostile to the Guomindang and imperialism (an idea which had already been set forth in 1940 in "On New Democracy"). And he presented the Communists' actions as a continuation of the hopes and struggles of the Chinese people—those of Sun Yat-sen, the Taiping, and even those which in ancient times were symbolized by the Confucian utopia of *datong* ("the great peace"), which communism had finally realized.

The military turning point of 1948–1949

In spring 1948, the Communist armies occupied Luoyang and Kaifeng, the major cities along the Yellow River. They reoccupied Yanan, the center of their war operations which had been abandoned in 1947. In September, they defeated the Nationalist forces of Shandong and took the provincial capital, Jinan. These successes led to three great battles which sealed the fate of the Guomindang.

The battle of Manchuria, which was fought between September and November 1948, led to the fall of such major cities as Moukden, Jilin, and Changchun. The whole Northeast came under Communist control. Several Guomindang armies, particularly the troops that were belatedly sent from Yunnan, surrendered without fighting.

The battle of Huai-hai, which lasted from November 1948 to January 1949, represented the Guomindang's last serious military effort. Half a million men on each side fought in the region of Huai and the Longhai railway. The Nationalist troops were entirely encircled and destroyed by the troops led by Chen Yi and Liu Bo-cheng; their generals were killed or captured. Finally, the battle of North China, in December and January, allowed the Communists to defeat the troops defending Kalgan, which fell in December, and Tientsin, which fell on January 15. On January 31, the Nationalist commanding officer at Peking, Fu Zuo-yi, negotiated his surrender and went over to the Communist side.

In 1946, Mao Tsetung had estimated that it would take five years to defeat the Guomindang. In November 1948, he reduced his estimate to approximately one year.

Failure of the Nanking peace offensive

In January, following these severe defeats, Tchiang offered the Communists a negotiated peace, but one which would maintain, as before, the power of Nanking (its army, constitution, and other structures). Mao responded by proposing an eight-point program that would include the replacement of the Nanking government by a democratic power, agrarian reform, confiscation of the goods of bureaucratic capitalism, and punishment of war criminals, beginning with Tchiang himself. On January 21, Tchiang resigned and handed over his power to Vice-President Li Zong-ren, who continued to negotiate with Peking in March and April. But Li did not really control the army and the administration; he continued to consult with Tchiang and to base his policy on the alliance with America. He even suggested to Washington that it place the finances and the Nanking administration under the direct control of American advisers. In January, the Nationalists were no doubt hoping to use their peace offensive to regroup their forces in the South and sustain themselves there with increased American aid. But the United States hesitated. The Peking negotiations led nowhere, and the Communists had no reason to give in at such a late date to what they had unsuccessfully tried to make Nanking accept before the civil war had broken out again. Tchiang himself had no illusions. Since the spring he had been arranging for his departure to Taiwan with the government's gold reserves and his best troops. In April, the Communist troops crossed the Yangzi for their final attack.

Military collapse of the Guomindang; founding
of the People's Republic of China

In a few months the Communists completed their occupation of the large cities of the North and East, which they had been threatening to take for a long time, and their troops spread out toward the West, the South, Central China, and the Southwest, all regions where until then the rear lines of the Guomindang had been relatively inactive. Entire provinces fell in a matter of weeks. Repeatedly, civilian and military authorities of the Guomindang went over to the Communists, as Fu Zuo-yi had done in Peking in January. This was the case in Sichuan, Hunan, Yunnan, and Xigang, provinces in which the Communist guerrillas had not been very active in the preceding period but where the provincial authorities were not on good terms with the Guomindang central government. It also happened in Xinjiang, whose last governor, Burhan, had been won over by a liberated Peking.

Nanking was taken in April; Hangzhou, Shanghai, Xian, Nanchang, Wuhan, and Shanxi in May; Shandong in June; all the Northwest up to Xinjiang and Inner Mongolia during the summer; Hunan, Hubei, and Fujian in August; Canton and the South in October; Sichuan and Guizhou in November; and Nanning in December. From July to December 1949, the Communists defeated nearly two million of the Guomindang's men and took control of more than half the territory of China (5 million square kilometers) with a population of 180 million people. The Nationalist central government—which had announced as a final propaganda gesture in the spring that it was abandoning Nanking to carry on the resistance at Canton, then had moved its capital once again (with great symbolism) to Chongqing, then to Chengdu—finally withdrew permanently to Taiwan in December under American protection.

The way was open for the creation of new state structures, which until then the Communists had purposely delayed setting up. The administration committees of the liberated zones had only local and provisional administrative powers. A new central government was to be created after complete military victory had been achieved and broad political alliances had been formed. These two conditions were realized in the summer of 1949. The Nationalist downfall came during the preparatory work for the Political Consultative Conference decided on in November 1948. The preparatory committee met several times during the summer and formally on September 21, 1949, in Peking. The distribution of delegates perfectly reflected the complex processes by which the Communists had finally isolated and defeated the Guomindang: armed struggle, liberated zones, United Front political alliances with centrist groups, mass political work among different social groups, and the winning over of enemy leaders. There were:

142 delegates from political groups: 16 from the CCP, 5 to 6 from each of the thirteen small parties of the center (mainly the Democratic League and the Guomindang Revolutionary Committee)
102 delegates from liberated zones
60 delegates from the liberation armies
206 delegates from popular organizations (such as women's groups, labor unions, youth organizations, and intellectual groups)
75 specially invited people, including Mme. Sun Yat-sen, a long-standing friend, and the Guomindang leaders who had just recently been won over to the Communist side

In a few days, the Political Consultative Conference proclaimed a new state power: the People's Republic of China. It adopted a "common program" of government and an "organic law" for the provisional organization of the state. A popular central government was elected, presided over by Mao Tsetung with the help of Zhu De, Liu Shao-qi, Song Qing-ling (Mme. Sun Yat-sen), and Li Ji-shen and Zhang Lan, who were the presidents, respectively, of the Guomindang Revolutionary Committee and the Democratic League.

On October 1, before an immense crowd, in the Square of Heavenly Peace (Tienanmen) in Peking, Mao Tsetung announced the new people's government: "Never again will the Chinese people be enslaved!"

ADDITIONAL BIBLIOGRAPHY

A. Doak Barnett, *China on the Eve of Communist Takeover* (New York, Praeger, 1963).

Derk Bodde, *Peking Diary: a Year of Revolution* (New York, Fawcett, 1967).

L. Chassin, *La conquête de la Chine par Mao Tse-toung, 1945–1949* (Paris, 1952).

David and Isabel Crook, *Revolution in a Chinese Village, Ten Mile Inn* (London, Routledge, 1959).

William Hinton, *Fanshen: A Documentary of Revolution in a Chinese Village* (New York, Vintage, 1968).

Liao Kai-lung, *From Yenan to Peking, the Chinese War of Liberation* (Peking, Foreign Languages Press, 1954).

Pichon P. Y. Loh, *The Kuomintang Debacle of 1949, Conquest or Collapse* (Boston, Heath, 1965).

John F. Melby, *The Mandate of Heaven: Record of a Civil War, China 1945–1949* (Toronto, University of Toronto Press, 1968).

United States Relations with China with special reference to the period 1944–1949 (Blue Book), preface by Dean Acheson (Washington, State Department, 1949).

DOCUMENTS

1. THE BLOODY REPRESSION OF TAIWAN DISORDERS BY THE GUOMINDANG, MARCH 1947

SOURCE: Memorandum of American Ambassador Leighton Stuart to the Chinese Government. White paper, *U.S. Relations With China* (Stanford, Calif., Stanford University Press, 1967), p. 931. In February 1947 an insurrection had broken out in Taiwan protesting the methods used by the Guomindang administration since the departure of the Japanese.

After dark ships docked and discharged the troops for which the Governor apparently had been waiting. Fairly reliable sources estimate that about 2,000 police were landed, followed by about 8,000 troops with light equipment including U. S. Army jeeps. Men and equipment were rushed to Taibei. It is reported that about 3,000 men were landed at Takao simultaneously. Troops were reportedly continuing to arrive on March 17.

Beginning March 9, there was widespread and indiscriminate killing. Soldiers were seen bayonetting coolies without apparent provocation in front of a Consulate staff residence. Soldiers were seen to rob passersby. An old man protesting the removal of a woman from his house was seen cut down by two soldiers. The Canadian nurse in charge of an adjacent Mission Hospital was observed bravely to make seven trips under fire into the crowded area across the avenue to treat persons shot down or bayonetted, and once as she supervised the movement of a wounded man into the hospital the bearers with her were fired upon. Some of the patients brought in had been shot and hacked to pieces. Young Formosan men were observed tied together, being prodded at bayonet point toward the city limits. A Formosan woman primary school teacher attempting to reach her home was shot in the back and robbed near the Mission compound. A British business man attempting to rescue an American woman whose house was being riddled with machine gun fire from a nearby emplacement was fired upon and narrowly escaped, one bullet cutting through his clothing and another being deflected from the steering gear of his jeep. Another foreigner saw a youth forced to dismount from his cycle before a military policeman, who thereupon lacerated the man's hands so badly with his bayonet that the man could not pick up his machine.

Anyone thought to be trying to hide or run was shot down. Looting began wherever the soldiers saw something desirable. In the Manka area, near the Consulate, a general sacking by soldiers took place on March 10; many shopkeepers are believed to have been shot.

On March 11 it was reported that a systematic search for middle school students had begun during the night. School enrollment lists were used. A broadcast earlier had ordered all youths who had been members of the Security Patrol or the Youth League* to turn in their weapons. Concurrently, all middle school students were ordered to remain at home. If a student was caught on the street while trying to obey the first order he was killed; if the searchers found a weapon in his house, he met a like fate. If a student was not at home his brother or his father was seized as hostage. A reliable estimate was made that about 700 students had been seized in Taibei by March 13. Two hundred are said to have been seized in Keelung. Fifty are reported to have been killed at Matsuyama and thirty at Kokuto (suburbs of Taibei) on the night of March 9.

From March 8 the Government instituted searches for all members of the Settlement Committee† and for all editors, lawyers and many prominent businessmen who had in any way been identified with the activities of the Committee between March 1 and 8. Wang Tian-deng, Chairman of the Settlement Committee, was seized and is alleged to have been executed about March 13. Tan Gim, a leading banker, was taken from his sick bed; Lim Mo-sei, editor of the *Min Pao*, was seized in the night and taken without clothing. Gan Kin-en, head of a large private mining interest, was arrested.

2. A MEETING OF WOMEN IN A VILLAGE OF A LIBERATED REGION (1947)

SOURCE: Jack Belden, *China Shakes the World* (New York, Monthly Review Press, 1970), pp. 289–293.

[Gold Flower has been forced to marry a rich peasant and to part from her fiancé; her father-in-law mistreats her.] Gold Flower questioned them with infinite caution, trying to find out what their strange views of this newly promised life might be. She made up her mind, after rallying the other two on their temerity, that they had confidence in being able to obtain equality for the women in the village. Suddenly she blurted out to the two girls everything she had suffered. Once the words were out she had to use all her self-control. The speaking

---

* Groups formed the day after the insurrection of February 27.
† Originally "Committee for Settlement of Incidents Provoked by the Illegal Tax on Cigarettes" (this tax had given rise to the insurrection). The committee became the provisional organ of the insurgents and was supported by the local bourgeoisie.

aloud of what had been going round and round in her mind for so long brought a rush of feeling such as she had not experienced since the days she had known Libao. She bit her lips to keep back tears and sobs. Then she was glad to hear her friends promising to do what they could to alleviate her sorry life. There was some difficulty about it, apparently, she was not curious to understand. The girls advised her to stay quietly at home and wait developments.

Within a few days, four women called on Gold Flower's father-in-law.

"Our investigation department has found out that you are treating your daughter-in-law badly," said Dark Jade.

The old man's jaws dropped open. He could not believe what he had heard. Recovering from his first astonishment, he burst out angrily, "Don't interfere with my family. I can do what I want with my daughter-in-law." . . .

One girl went away. The others fell into silence. In a moment the girl came back with fifteen more women. They were all carrying clubs and ropes. The old man was startled.

"Won't you really change your mind?" asked Dark Jade.

The old man raised his fists. "Nothing! Get out!"

"Bind him up!" shouted Dark Jade.

The old man's arm was just rising up when four women reached for it. The next moment he was caught like a fish in a net, both his arms bound with ropes. Gold Flower looked on amazed. This terror of her life had been overcome with miraculous ease. But when she saw her father-in-law being led through the gate, she experienced a momentary twinge of fear. "I have not suffered," she called. "Don't hurt my dear father." . . .

Gold Flower's father-in-law was held a prisoner for two days in a room in the building of the Women's Association. On the third day a general meeting of all the women in the village was called to decide what to do with him. . . .

Forty or fifty women were crowded into the room and on the steps of the courtyard outside. Up front, behind a table, was a smaller group of women, among them a girl whom Gold Flower had never seen before. Dark Jade went up to the front of the room and called for silence . . .

The woman whom Gold Flower did not know stood up. From the very first words of her speech the others all came under the spell of her eloquence. She spoke of the feudalism of China, which was making the women slaves of men, of the common interests of brides and maidens, of the necessity to struggle against in-laws who oppressed daughters-in-law, of the need to fight parents who opposed freedom of marriage, of the aims of the 8th Route Army and the Communist party, which were carrying on a struggle against the old black society for the equality of women. . . .

After the cadre finished speaking, Dark Jade, as chairman of the meeting, stood up. Her talk was burdened with clumsy, involved phrases, for she had never made a speech before. But the women listened to her with a great deal of sympathy as she was from their own village and was one of them. Rarely did someone interrupt, and her words found a vivid response.

Suddenly she paused, and Gold Flower felt herself grow weak as Dark Jade looked directly at her and spoke in an intimate way.

"Now," she said, "the time is come to talk of the case of our dearest sister, Gold Flower. Her sufferings are the sufferings of all women. If she is not freed, we cannot be free ourselves. . . ."

The meeting finally decided to call in the old man.

Dark Jade threw open the door at Gold Flower's back and her father-in-law, his arms bound to his sides, was led in, guarded by two women. His face was pale. . . .

"Old man! Be frank. Tell your bad treatment," said Dark Jade, and the rest of the women echoed her shouting: "Be frank!"

"I have done nothing." The father-in-law spoke with deliberate roughness. "If you don't believe me, you can ask my daughter-in-law." His eyes looked over the heads of the other women and fell on Gold Flower with a look that expressed his hostility, and seemed to say: "Be careful."

Looking at him from afar, Gold Flower felt a shiver of apprehension. She saw all eyes were on her. Pressing her fists against her chest, she ran on her toes to the front of the room. Then feeling it was now or never, she summoned all her determination.

"I married into your family—yes!" she hissed into his face. "But there's been no millet for me to eat. No clothes in the winter. Are these not facts? Do you remember how badly you have treated me in these past five years? Have you forgotten the time my mother was sick and you made me kneel in the courtyard for half a day? In the past I suffered from you. But I shall never suffer again. I must turn over now. I have all my sisters in back of me and I have the 8th Route Army."

She shouted these words. His face grew dark and red.

"Is it right for you to treat me like this? There is much that I could say. If I should speak, all these women would beat you to death."

As she said this, a wave of agitation ran through the meeting and a loud shout arose. "Speak!" Then as the roar of the voices sank, a thin girlish shriek pierced the growing quiet:

"Down with those who treat daughters-in-law badly! Long live our Women's Association!"

The crowd groaned. In the heavy swelling voices, the sound of shuffling feet could be heard. Gold Flower felt herself being pushed aside. A fat girl was at her elbow and others were crowding close. "Let us spit in his face," said the fat girl. She drew back her lips over her gums and spat between the old man's eyes. Other darted in, spat in his face, and darted away again. The roar of voices grew louder. The old man remained standing with his face red and his beard matted with saliva. His knees were trembling and he looked such a poor object that the women laughed and their grumbling and groaning grew quieter. Then Dark Jade, pushing the others back, cried:

"Are you ready to reform yourself?"

"I will change." The old man's voice was low and subdued.

"Will you torture your daughter any more?"

"No."

"All women unite," the same girlish voice that had cried from the crowd before shouted out in another slogan.

"Women unite," echoed the crowd.

3. THE LOCAL REVOLUTIONARY CADRES FALL BACK INTO OLD HABITS

SOURCE: William Hinton, *Fanshen: A Documentary of Revolution in a Chinese Village* (New York, Vintage, 1968), pp. 224–227.

Without realizing what was actually happening, many leading cadres in Long Bow began to issue orders instead of educating and persuading people, and because most people obeyed these orders— some because they too thought the redundant attacks necessary, some because they always followed orders, and some because they dared not do otherwise—the leaders did not realize how much support they had lost. Those peasants who did not obey they condemned as backward. Some of these were arrested, beaten, and punished with extra work for soldiers' families, or extra terms of rear service such as stretcher bearing or transporting supplies to the front. Some were even sent off to join the army, but since they went unwillingly the army wisely rejected them. . . .

The militia, on whom the main burden of each campaign fell, were quick to slide into certain habits well known to traditional upholders of "law and order." They developed among themselves a battlefront psychology that served as justification for everything they were tempted to do. . . . Among them were some who also thought it unfair to be judged by ordinary standards of morality. As heroes of the hour, these began in small ways to help themselves. When some article among the hundreds confiscated from the gentry caught their fancy, they took it when nobody was looking. If some comely woman aroused their passion, they seduced her if she was willing. If she were a "struggle object,"* they took her whether she was willing or not. When asked to do their share of labor service, these men began by thinking up all kinds of excuses and ended up with outright refusals. They even shirked work for soldiers' families and prevailed upon their neighbors to go in their stead.

Perhaps the most notorious practitioner of this type of abuse was Wang Man-xi, the rank-and-file militiaman and Communist Party member who was known as "The King of the Devils" for his readiness to beat up the people's enemies. He had played a very important part in the Anti-Traitor Movement† and the campaign against the

---

* That is, people or goods belonging to landowners who had collaborated with the Japanese.

† Peasant mobilization movement against the collaborators.

gentry. Now, like the cop in the city market place who helps himself to the fruit in the stalls, Man-xi took it for granted that the people owed him a few extras. The nighttime check-ups of the campaign against counter-revolution gave him ample opportunity to tip the scales in his own favor. Since the homes which he entered were almost all homes of "struggle objects," he had no qualms about carrying off whatever suited him. He took two catties of hemp seed from Li Bao-jin's house. From a widow's garden he helped himself to garlic and chives. He liked the fruit on Yuxian's trees so well that he came back several times for more. In Shao Lao-zhang's yard he not only picked ripe plums, but broke off a whole branch and carried it with him on his rounds. From Guo Fugui, ex-puppet police chief, he took a beautiful dry gourd because "it was so pretty." From another ex-puppet he took a ripe watermelon. When the man protested, he shut him overnight in the village lockup. . . .

From being the scourge of the gentry it was an easy transition for Man-xi to become the scourge of the average man. By rapid stages he developed many of the habits of the traditional village bully. When Li Pan-ming, the peasant in charge of public affairs, asked him to do rear service, Man-xi swore at him, claimed that his ox was sick and sent him to see the poor peasant Laocun instead. When Laocun, for his part, also refused to transport grain, Man-xi beat him up as a shirker. Another time, when asked to transport grain, Man-xi went grudgingly, took the straw and beans another man had set aside for the trip and, by depriving the other man's animal of feed, caused it to founder on the road. On that same trip he beat an honest poor peasant and threw his quilt on the floor because the fellow had the nerve to take for himself the only empty spot on an otherwise crowded k'ang* in the only inn in the village.

Man-xi refused to do his own share of work for soldiers' families, but became very angry when others were slack in this respect. He beat them and brought them to the village office for questioning. . . .

Later, as conditions deteriorated even more, the regional leaders of the CCP required the cadres to "go through the door," that is, to confront the poor peasants' accusations before they could be reintegrated into the party.

---

* Large bench made of baked clay which was heated from underneath and where everyone spent the night.

Conclusion

In 1919, few people outside of China heard of the May Fourth Movement; the few press dispatches about it were hardly noticed and quickly forgotten. In 1921, the founding of the CCP was completely ignored. But October 1, 1949, was considered a major international event everywhere. The difference between these dates indicates the special significance of the Chinese Communist revolution in Chinese history during these thirty years, a significance which this book has deliberately tried to demonstrate.* This does not mean that the other political and social forces, such as the warlords, the feudal landowners, or the Guomindang modernists, had become unimportant; whole chapters of this book are devoted to them. But in the end, their role was defined by the fact that they were ousted in 1949. As Marc Bloch once said, the historian must know "how to run the film backward."

From this point of view, the events of 1949 put in the background a question long considered central by Westerners and by those Chinese who went along with them: the question of modernization. A whole generation of politicians and intellectuals—and not only within the Guomindang—was influenced by Japan's decision to modernize half a century earlier and was convinced that China's future also depended on its ability to "modernize," to model itself on the West, which meant adopting free capitalist enterprise, parliamentary democracy, and intellectual liberalism. From 1921 to 1949, this "Western path" proved to be impracticable. Sun Yat-sen experienced this bitter truth in 1923–1924, as did many others after him. This explains why such huge numbers of people joined

---

* There are very basic reasons for this, the same reasons which explain the fact that most specialized works, particularly in the United States, are devoted to the Communist movement. People are seeking the source of the 1949 upheaval, which was such a severe shock to the American public ("the loss of Asia," it was termed at the time, rather naively).

the Communists and why the Guomindang became more and more isolated. Seen from this perspective, China was not a special case. The Western model in economics, politics, and culture has been increasingly questioned by the new African and Asian states that came into being during the decolonization after World War Two, and the men and women who questioned it very often admired the West as much as Sun Yat-sen had.

In the People's Republic today, the experiences of the period from 1921 to 1949 are frequently referred to for the light the problems and solutions of that time can throw on the present and the questions which still exist.

Is history written from the top or from the bottom? On the one hand, there are the organized political machinery and the prominent figures; on the other hand, there are the popular masses. To what extent is each capable of influencing the changes taking place and of determining the final direction of history? There is no doubt that men like Mao Tsetung and Tchiang Kaï-chek played considerable personal parts, each on their own side, and that the institutions of the CCP and the Guomindang constituted very important frameworks for decision-making and action. Yet this whole period of complex and tumultuous political conflicts was also marked by the direct intervention of the popular masses through the typically Chinese phenomenon of the *yun-dong* ("movement"). The May Fourth Movement, the May Thirtieth (1925) Movement, the December Ninth (1935) Movement, the Movement for National Salvation during the war against the Japanese, and the protest movements against the Guomindang in 1946 to 1948, though often provoked by minor incidents, eventually involved immense numbers of people that brought about a change in the balance of political forces in the course of events.

More generally, the success of Chinese communism should not be defined in terms of political apparatus, discipline, or "line," as a certain school of Americans is prone to do; this attitude is manifested in the lists of members of governing organizations or works written by them, which are meticulously studied by experts trained in the secrets of "Kremlinology." What really counts, in the end, is that the CCP was able to adapt its own political aims and organized actions to the movements with which it joined forces, but which had come into being outside the CCP and had their own historical roots; primarily the peasant movement, then the national movement, the workers' movement, and the student movement.

Even if the millions of members of the Chinese industrial proletariat were a relatively small minority (most of them had recently emigrated to the city and were concentrated in a few large centers in the outlying areas, particularly in Shanghai), they formed an active and dynamic sector of society, one capable of carrying out economic, and eventually political, struggles by itself. They demonstrated this most notably in 1919, 1924–1927, and 1948.

Even more than the workers' movement, the peasant movement turned out to be a vigorous social and political force with very deep historical roots. The peasants' profound hostility to landlords, usurers, rent collectors, and all civilian and military forms of authority had been expressed for hundreds of years in the *jacqueries*, the agitation of secret societies, and peasant wars like that of the Taiping. The agrarian crisis from 1930 to 1940, the aggravation of the peasants' miserable condition, and the Japanese occupation aroused this powerful force once again, and the CCP provided it with new political perspectives, cadres, and a revolutionary ideology.

As in many African and Asian countries, the intellectuals and students of China formed an active and influential sector of society. They were in a strong position because of the prestige traditionally given to the scholar. Deeply concerned about the national interest, they were very sensitive to everything that threatened it from within and without. Unlike the workers and peasants, however, they were not united by common economic imperatives, by their condition as workers. In Shanghai during the twenties and thirties, and even more in Yanan, the left-wing intelligentsia drew closer and closer to communism and defined itself as revolutionary, while the right wing clung to its intellectual and social privileges, defended liberal values, and drew closer to the Guomindang. The Chinese intellectuals never succeeded in forming a "third party."

In the end, the Communist revolution formed its closest ties with the peasant movement. The Chinese Communists established themselves in the countryside in 1927 and remained there for twenty-two years. The cities and the urban proletariat no longer played more than a subsidiary role. This was perhaps the essential contribution of Maoism, which baffled and irritated the Comintern leaders and the Chinese who advocated a strategy favoring the cities, from Chen Du-xiu and Li Li-san to Wang Ming. The profound originality of this strategy, which was based on protracted armed struggle and peasant revolutionary bases, helps one appreciate that the differences between Peking and Moscow had existed long before their break in 1960.

From 1921 to 1949, Chinese political life was even more distinctly characterized than in the previous period by profound regional differences. The 1924–1927 revolution was an act of the South against the North, which was dominated by warlords, and it resulted in the establishment of the Chinese soviets in 1927 to 1934. The Long March represented a major turning point. The center of gravity of the revolutionary struggles shifted toward the North as popular resistance developed first against Japan and later against the Guomindang. Geopolitics was not a rigid imperative, but the concrete expression of a fluid political situation.

During these years, China ceased to define itself as the splendidly isolated "Middle Kingdom." It was struggling against the system of unequal treaties established by large foreign interests, and later against the threat from Japan. This was the basis of the national movement, which was one of the vital forces of Chinese politics, both before and after 1937. The formula "save the country" (*jiu guo*), created by the May Fourth Movement, continued to inspire anti-Japanese resistance. In the end, the popular verdict would be in favor of the Communists and against the Guomindang, largely because of the fact that during a critical period the Communists proved to be the better defenders of the national interest.

Throughout this book the emphasis has been on short-term political changes and their social foundations. It was necessary to analyze as closely as possible the changes which led to the situation in 1949. During this entire period, however, the old Chinese heritage remained singularly alive. Only a very small social stratum of Shanghai's privileged citizens preferred to quote Shakespeare rather than the "Three Kingdoms," and to send their sons to Harvard or put initials in front of their family names. The overwhelming majority of the population continued to live by the rhythm of the lunar calendar, to count with an abacus, and to visit acupuncturists. This vitality of the old Chinese customs was not an ethnographic curiosity but a major political factor which worked in favor of those who were close to the peasant masses.

The 1949 "liberation" was not a Communist revolution in the conventional sense of the term. The Chinese saw it as the outcome of the entire national movement, as the victory of peasant struggles, and also as the restoration of unity in a country which for so many years had been torn apart by conflicting forces.

Glossary of Chinese Terms and Names
for Chapters 1–3

A aiguo huo 愛國貨

Aiguoxueshe 愛國学社

Anfu 安福

ansha tuan 暗殺团

B bagu 八股

bai lang 白狼

baihua 白話

Bailong 白龙

bang 帮

bao jing an min 保境安民

baoan 保安

baogong 包工

Baoguohui 保国会

Baohuanghui 保皇会

Baolutongzhihui 保路同志会

Beida 北大

Beijing daxue 北京大学

Beitang 北堂

Beiyang 北洋

Ben-ming 本明

bianfa 变法

Bianshanxian 遍山線

bianshi 变事

C Cai E 蔡锷

Cao Fu-tian 曹福田

Cao Ru-lin 曹汝霖

Changxindian 長辛店

Chaoyang 朝阳

Chen bao 晨报

Chen Chi 陈炽

Chen Ji-tong 陈季同

Chen Qiu 陈虬

Cheng De-quan 程德全

Chouanhui 筹安会

Chu ren zhi Chu 楚人治楚

Chu Wang-tai 楚望台

D da dui 大队

Da Qing 大清

Danzhou 儋州

datong 大同

Datong shu 大同书

Dazu 大足

Deng Xiao-ke 邓孝可

Ding Wen-jiang 丁文江

Dongfang zazhi 东方杂誌

dongnan hubao 东南互保

dudu	都督	He Qi (Ho Kai) 何启
dujun	督軍	Hongbang 紅帮
dujuntuan	督軍团	Hongkou 虹口
F fan Qing fu Ming	反清復明	houdun 后盾
Fang Wei	方維	hu fa 护法
fu Qing mie yang	扶清灭洋	hu guo 护国
G Gelaohui	哥老会	Hu Li-yuan 胡礼垣
gong	工	Hu Ying 胡瑛
Gong Bao-quan	龚宝銓	Huanghuagang 黄花崗
Gong-yang	公羊	Huasheng 华盛
Gong Zi-zhen	龚自珍	Huaxinghui 华兴会
Gongchandang	共产党	Hubu 户部
Gonghedang	共和党	Huguang 湖广
Gonghe jianshe taolunhui	共和建设讨论会	hui dang 会党
Gonghe tongyidang	共和統一党	Huizhou 惠州
Gongjinhui	共进会	**J** Jiang Yi-wu 蒋翊武
guan ban	官办	Jianghong (Xieng Hong) 江洪
guan du shang ban	官督商办	Jiangnan 江南
guan shang heban	官商合办	Jianshe 建设
Guangxuehui	广学会	Jiao Da-feng 焦达峰
Guanxian	冠县	jiao men 教門
Gui jiao gai si	鬼教該死	Jiefang yu gaizao 解放与改造
Guomindang	国民党	Jilong 基隆
Guowen bao	国闻报	Jinbudang 进步党
Gutian	古田	jindai 近代
H Han	汉	Jindan dao 金丹道
Hanyeping	汉冶萍	Jindehui 进德会

jingshi	經世		Long-hai	陇海	
jingtian	井田		Long Ming-jian	龙鳴剣	
jiu guo	救国		Longshuizhen	龙水镇	
Jiulong	九龙		Longzhou	龙州	
junjichu	军机处		Lu Run-xiang	陆润庠	
K *Kong-zi gai zhi kao*	孔子改制考		Lu Zong-yu	陆宗與	
L *Laodong jie*	劳动界		*lujun*	陆军	
laodong shensheng	劳动神聖		Luo Lun	罗綸	
Laoxikai	老西开		Luo Pei-jin	罗佩金	
Leping	乐平		Lutai	芦台	
Li Lie-jun	李烈钧		*Lüying*	綠營	
Li Shi-zeng	李石曾		**M** Ma Fu-yi	馬福益	
Li Zhong	李中		Manhao	蛮耗	
Liang-bi	良弼		Mao Ze-dong	毛泽东	
Liang Shu-ming	梁漱溟		*Meizhou pinglun*	每周评论	
Liangguang	兩广		*Min bao*	民报	
Lianghu	兩湖		Ming	明	
Liangjiang	兩江		*Minzhudang*	民主党	
liansheng zizhi	联省自治		Mohe	漠河	
Liao Zhong-kai	廖仲凱		Mu Ou-chu	穆藕初	
lijin	厘金		**N** Nandao	南道	
Lin Sen	林森		Nantong	南通	
Liu Gong	刘公		Nanyang	南洋	
Liu Si-fu	刘思復		*Nei chu guozei*	内除国賊	
Liu Xiang	刘湘		*neige*	内阁	
liushou	留守		Ni Si-chong	倪嗣冲	

P	Pingdu	平度
	Pu Dian-jun	蒲殿俊
	Pudong	浦东
Q	*Qiangxuehui*	強学会
	qianzhuang	钱莊
	Qing	清
	Qing yi bao	清议报
	Qingbang	青帮
	qingliu	清流
	Qingxi	青溪
	Qiu Feng-jia	丘逢甲
	Quan xue pian	劝学篇
	quanguo	全国
R	*Ren xue*	仁学
	Rihua	日华
	Rong-lu	榮祿
	Rui-cheng	瑞澂
S	*Sanminzhuyi*	三民主义
	Shen bao	申报
	Sheng shi weiyan	盛世危言
	shenshang	紳商
	shenshi	紳士
	Shi Zhao-ji (A. Sze)	施肇基
	Shiwu bao	時务报
	Shiwu xuetang	時务学堂
	shuyuan	书院
	Simao	思茅

	Su bao	苏报
	Sujing	苏經
	Sulun	苏绵
	Sun Jia-nai	孫家鼐
	Sun Wu	孫武
	Sun Yu-wen	孫毓汶
	Sun Yuan-fang	孫圓方
T	*taiping*	太平
	Taiyushan	太嶼山
	tan	坛
	Tan Yan-kai	谭延闿
	Tang Hua-long	湯化龙
	Tang Jing-song	唐景崧
	Tang Shao-yi	唐紹仪
	Tang Zhen	湯震
	Tao Cheng-zhang	陶成章
	Tianyi bao	天义报
	Tieshan	铁山
	Tong wen guan	同文馆
	Tongmenghui	同盟会
	Tongyidang	統一党
	Tongzhihui	同志会
	tuan	团
	Tucaozi	土槽子
	tufei	土匪
W	*Wai zheng guoquan*	外争国权
	waiwubu	外务部

	Wan guo gong bao	万国公报		Xiong Ke-wu	熊克武
	Wang Mang	王莽		Xiong Xi-ling	熊希龄
	Wang Zhan-yuan	王占元		Xu Shu-zheng	徐树铮
	Wang Zhi-xiang	王芝祥		Xu Xiang	徐骧
	Wangsanshi	王三石		Xuantong	宣統
	Wen Ting-shi	文廷式		Xujiahuai (Zikawei)	徐家滙
	Wenxuehui	文学会	**Y**	Yadong	亞东
	wenyan	文言		*yamen*	衙門
	Wu Lu-zhen	吴禄贞		Yang Du	揚度
	Wu Zhao-lin	吴兆麟		Yang Zong-lian	揚宗濂
X	*xian*	县		Yangshupu	揚树浦
	xiandai	现代		*yangwu*	洋务
	Xiang jiang pinglun	湘江评论		Yeqin	业勤
	Xiangxue xin bao	湘学新报		Yichang	宜昌
	Xiaoshadu	小沙渡		Yihequan	义和拳
	xiaozu	小组		Yihetuan	义和团
	Xin chao	新潮		Yimintuan	义民团
	Xin min cong bao	新民丛报		Yiyan	易言
	Xin qingnian	新青年		Yizhou	沂州
	Xin Shandong	新山东		*yong*	勇
	Xin she	新社		Yu Dong-chen	余栋臣
	Xin shiji	新世紀		Yu Qia-qing	虞洽卿
	Xin xue wei jing kao	新学伪经考		Yubeilixiangonghui	预備立宪公会
	Xingzhonghui	兴中会		*Yue ren zhi Yue*	粤人治粤
	Xinminxuehui	新民学会	**Z**	Zai-feng	載澧
	Xinyang	信阳		Zai-ze	載泽
	Xinzhu	新竹		*Zaili*	在理

Zeng Guo-quan	曾国荃	Zhongguo tongshang yinhang	中国通商银行
Zhang Bai-xi	張百熙	Zhonghua	中华
Zhang Biao	張彪	Zhonghuagemingdang	中华革命党
Zhang De-cheng	張德成	zhongxue wei ti xixue wei yong	
Zhang Ji	張継		中学为体西学为用
Zhang Jing-yao	張敬堯	Zhou Han	周汉
Zhang Ming-qi	張鳴岐	Zhu Bao-san	朱葆三
Zhang Ru-mei	張如梅	Zhu Cheng-gui	祝承桂
Zhang Shao-zeng	張紹曾	Zhu Rui	朱瑞
Zhang Zhen-wu	張振武	Zhu Zhi-xin	朱執信
Zhang Zong-xiang	章宗祥	Zi yi ju	谘议局
Zhao Er-feng	赵尔丰	Zi zheng yuan	谘政院
Zhengwenshe	政闻社	Zichuan	淄川
Zhennanguan	镇南关	zongli geguo shiwu yamen	
Zhili	直隶		总理各国事务衙門
Zhongguo	中国		

Glossary of Chinese Terms and Names
for Chapters 4–11

Anfu	安福	Dalian	大连
Anguojun	安国军	datong	大同
annei rangwai	安内攘外	dazibao	大字报
Anyuan	安源	Di-er zhengfu	第二政府
bagu	八股	dizhu	地主
balu	八路	Dongbei kangri lianjun	
bao	保		东北抗日联军
Baoan	保安	Dongbei renmin gemingjun	
Baoerhan	鲍尔汉		东北人民革命军
baogong	包工	dujun	督军
baojia	保甲	E-yü-wan	鄂豫皖
Beifa	北阀	fabi	法币
Beiping	北平	Fang Zhi-min	方志敏
Cai He-sen	蔡和森	fanshen	翻身
Cai Ting-kai	蔡廷锴	Funü zhou bao	妇女周报
changxindian	长辛店	fuxing	复兴
chi	耻	ganbu	干部
chiweidui	赤卫队	Gelaohui	哥老会
Chu Min-yi	褚民谊	Geming Chunqiu	革命春秋
Dagongbao	大公报	gequ	革区

Gongshangxue lianhehui	工商学联合会
Guandong	关东
Guo Feng-ming	郭凤鸣
Guofu	国父
guohuo	国货
Guomindang	国民党
Guominjun	国民军
guoquan	国权
Guoshi huiyi	国事会议
Haifeng	海丰
Hanjian	汉奸
He ying-qin	何应钦
Honghuzi	红胡子
Huai-Hai	淮海
jia	甲
Jiefang Ribao	解放日报
Jing-Han	京汉
Jin-cha-ji	晋察冀
Jinggangshan	井冈山
Jin-ji-lu-yu	晋冀鲁豫
Jin Shu-ren	金树仁
jiuguo	救国
Julebu	俱乐部
kaiming dizhu	开明地主
kang	坑
Kangda	抗大
li	礼

lian	廉
lieshen	劣绅
Li ji-shen	李济琛
Lincheng	临城
Lin Sen	林森
Linyi	临沂
Liping	黎平
Liu Wen-hui	刘文辉
Liu Xiang	刘湘
Liuyang	浏阳
Long-hai	陇海
Luding	泸定
Lufeng	陆丰
Lugouqiao	芦沟桥
lülin	绿林
Maoergai	毛儿盖
Maoping	茅坪
Ma Zhong-ying	馬仲英
Minbao	民报
mintuan	民团
Nanyang	南洋
Nian	捻
Ningdu	宁都
qingbang	青帮
qunzhong	群众
renminbi	人民币
Saifudin	赛福鼎
Shamian	沙面

Shanghang	上杭	Xinhua	新华
Shaonianfengdui	少年锋队	Xinminhui	新民会
Shenbao	申报	Xinqingnian	新青年
Shen-gan-ning	陕甘宁	Xuan Tong	宣统
Shen Yan-bing	沈雁冰	Xue Yue	薛岳
Shunde	顺德	Xu Qian	徐谦
Siping	四平	Xu Shu-zheng	徐树铮
Suweiai	苏维埃	yamen	衙门
Taierzhuang	台兕莊	yangge	秧歌
taiping	太平	yanjing	燕京
Tang En-bo	湯恩伯	Yang Sen	揚森
Tanggu	滄沽	yi	义
Tan Yan-kai	潭延闓	Yiguandao	一貫道
tewu	特务	Yili	伊犁
Tiananmen	天安门	yuan	院
tongzhi jingji	统治经济	Yu Da-wei	俞大维
tuhao	土豪	Zhang Fa-kui	張发奎
wangdao	王道	Zhang Jing-yao	張敬堯
Wang Ke-min	王克敏	Zhang Lan	張瀾
Wang Yi-tang	王揖堂	Zhang Zong-chang	張宗昌
weijun	伪军	zhengfeng	整风
weiqi	围棋	Zhigongdang	职工党
Wu San-gui	吳三桂	Zhongguo zhi mingyun	
Xiangdao	响导		中国之命运
Xiang Zhong-fa	向中发		
Xiao Ke	萧克	Zhou Lu	鄒魯
xiaxiang	下乡	zongcai	总裁

Index

About the Authors

Françoise Le Barbier studied Chinese language and civilization at the School for Oriental Languages in Paris and was a foreign research fellow at the Contemporary China Institute, University of London, before she began collaborating with Jean Chesneaux.

Marie-Claire Bergère is Professor of Chinese History at the Institut National des Langues et Civilisations Orientales. She is the author of *La Bourgeoisie chinoise et la révolution de 1911* and *Une Crise financière à Shanghai à la fin de l'Ancien régime.*

Jean Chesneaux is a professor at the Sorbonne. He is the author of numerous works, including *The Chinese Labor Movement 1919–1927, Peasant Revolts in China, 1840–1949,* and *Secret Societies in China.*